Sources of World Societies

VOLUME 2: SINCE 1450

SECOND EDITION

Walter D. Ward

UNIVERSITY OF ALABAMA AT BIRMINGHAM

Denis Gainty

GEORGIA STATE UNIVERSITY

BEDFORD/ST. MARTIN'S   BOSTON ◆ NEW YORK

For Bedford/St. Martin's

Publisher for History: Mary V. Dougherty
Executive Editor for History: Traci M. Crowell
Director of Development for History: Jane Knetzger
Developmental Editor: Lynn Sternberger
Production Supervisor: Dennis J. Conroy
Senior Executive Marketing Manager: Jenna Bookin Barry
Project Management: Books By Design, Inc.
Permissions Manager: Kalina K. Ingham
Cover Designer: Billy Boardman
Cover Art: Facing the Mirror, by Ito Shinsui, 1916. © Christie's Images/Corbis
Composition: Books By Design, Inc.
Printing and Binding: Haddon Craftsmen, Inc., an RR Donnelley & Sons Company

President: Joan E. Feinberg
Editorial Director: Denise B. Wydra
Director of Marketing: Karen R. Soeltz
Director of Production: Susan W. Brown
Associate Director, Editorial Production: Elise S. Kaiser
Manager, Publishing Services: Andrea Cava

Library of Congress Control Number: 2011935168

Manufactured in the United States of America.

7 6 5 4
f e

For information, write: Bedford/St. Martin's, 75 Arlington Street, Boston, MA 02116 (617-399-4000)

ISBN: 978-0-312-56972-3

Acknowledgments

PREFACE

The primary sources comprising *Sources of World Societies* span pre-history to the present, capturing the voices of individuals within the context of their times and ways of life, while enriching the cross-cultural fabric of history as a whole. Now with visual sources and 50 percent more documents, *Sources* draws from the records of rulers and subjects alike, men and women, philosophers, revolutionaries, economists, laborers, and artists, among others, to present a textured view of the past. With a parallel chapter structure and documents hand-picked to extend the textbook, this reader is designed to complement *A History of World Societies*, Ninth Edition. *Sources of World Societies* animates the past for students, providing resonant accounts of the people and events that changed the face of world history, from myths of creation to accounts of hardship and conflict, from a local to a global scale.

With input from the textbook authors, as well as from current instructors of the world history survey course, we have compiled these documents with one goal foremost in mind: to make history's most compelling voices accessible to students, from the most well-known thinkers and documentarians of their times to the galvanized or introspective commoner. While students have access to formative documents of each era, lesser-heard voices reveal life as the great majority of people lived it. In Chapter 30, for example, popular folk song lyrics, a speech before a National Socialist association, letters to the editor debating abortion in Russia, and the Nuremberg Laws illustrate the social effects of the Depression, the radicalization of fascist movements, and the social and political developments that helped fuel the Second World War from multiple citizen and government perspectives. Students can juxtapose President Truman's press release on the bombing of Hiroshima with the firsthand account of a Japanese survivor of the atomic bomb drop.

We have stepped back from drawing conclusions and instead provide just enough background to enable students' own analysis of the sources at hand. Chapter-opening paragraphs briefly review the major events of the time and place the documents that follow within the framework of the corresponding textbook chapter. A concise headnote for each document provides context about the author and the circumstances surrounding the document's creation, while gloss notes supply clarification to aid comprehension of unfamiliar terms and references. Each document is followed by Reading and Discussion Questions that spur student analysis of the material, while chapter-concluding Comparative Questions encourage students to contemplate the relationships among the sources within and, when called for, between the chapters. All of the questions in *Sources* aim to form a dynamic connection for students that bridges the events of the past with their own evolving understandings of power and its abuses, of the ripple effects of human agency, and of the material conditions of life. The excerpts range in length to allow for a variety of class assignments.

New to This Edition

The second edition of *Sources* offers new pedagogical tools and provides instructors with greater flexibility in the development of their syllabi. Now expanded to an average of six sources per chapter with over half new sources overall, this edition offers a greater variety of topics to explore and further illuminates the themes of the textbook.

Each chapter now features two or three "Viewpoints" selections that allow students to compare and contrast differing accounts of one topic or event. In Chapter 7, for example, students can debate the origin and practice of Buddhism in China after analyzing a sixth-century image of a preaching Buddha, studying Zhu Seng Du's biographical defense of Buddhism, and reading Emperor Wuzong's ninth-century edict suppressing the religion. In Chapter 19, a "Viewpoints" feature on the African slave trade juxtaposes free British citizen Anna Maria Falconbridge's account of her voyage aboard a ship transporting slaves with Olaudah Equiano's controversial tale of his own enslavement and eventual freedom.

The addition of visual documents gives students the opportunity to practice the analysis of art and photographs. Volume 1 includes images ranging from a Neolithic burial to the high art of ancient Greece, from Islamic and African architecture to a Song Dynasty landscape painting. Volume 2 pairs an excerpt from the Islamic tale *The Conference of the Birds* with an original illustration of the story and presents photographs documenting people and their conditions of life in an increasingly global world, such as early twentieth-century Jews in Munich and the present-day residents of Venezuelan slums.

ACKNOWLEDGMENTS

Thanks to the instructors whose insightful comments and thorough reviews of the first edition helped shape the second edition: Cynthia Bisson, Belmont University; David Bovee, Fort Hays State University; Rick Gianni, Westwood College; Nicole Howard, Eastern Oregon University; Robert Kunath, Illinois College; Elaine MacKinnon, University of West Georgia; Erik Maiershofer, Pacific Christian College; Larry Marvin, Berry College; Anne Parrella, Tidewater Community College; Chris Rasmussen, Fairleigh Dickinson University; Kenneth Straus, North Shore Community College; Teresa Thomas, Fitchburg State College; and Amos Tubb, Centre College.

Thanks to Lynn Sternberger for her tireless encouragement, her warm support, and her good ideas, all of which made this experience a real pleasure; to Jan Fitter for her insightful comments and prudent edits; and to Jane Knetzger and Laura Arcari for their guidance throughout. Andrea Cava of Bedford/St. Martin's and Nancy Benjamin of Books By Design produced this book with remarkable finesse. Thanks also for the support of the wonderful student assistants in the Department of History at Georgia State University, whose help made this book possible. Thanks to John van Sant, Brian Steele, Forrest Sweeney, Brandon Wicks, and Yorke Rowan for loaning materials and making suggestions about source selections; and to Melissa Anderson, Agatha Anderson, and Nico Ward for their love and support.

CONTENTS

INTRODUCTION: ANALYZING PRIMARY SOURCES

Historians credit the ancient Greek writer Herodotus (fifth century B.C.E.) with inventing the study of history, which today is defined as the rational study of the past of the human species. Although many peoples kept records prior to the Greeks, only a few groups attempted to interpret the past and form a cohesive narrative for understanding their place in the world. For example, the ancient Hebrews recorded events from their past, and their works still survive in the form of the Hebrew Bible and the Old Testament of the Christians. The Hebrews, however, believed that their history was dictated by divine providence and that it was affected by the will of their God. Herodotus, and many later Greek and Roman writers, excluded the divine and supernatural from their histories and sought the causes of events in the actions of humans.

The Greek word *historia*, the origin of our word *history*, was used in the sense of "inquiry" and indicated an active seeking of information. Historians, therefore, practice an inquiry about the past. They ask questions about the past to produce an interpretation of events. In doing so, they look for change and continuity; they want to determine cause and effect. Historians also seek to make history relevant to today's society, which means that our understanding of the past changes as our culture transforms. Not only does history itself change as we perceive it, but historians are not always in agreement. One historian's inquiry into the past may very well lead him or her to draw a different conclusion than another historian. To determine cause and effect, and to shape those dynamics into a fuller picture, historians must carefully examine the available sources, which provide the evidence for their interpretations.

HISTORY AND PREHISTORY

Historians are most accustomed to working with written and visual documents. For more modern periods, recorded documents abound: newspapers, archives, magazines, law codes, merchant records, novels, religious works, and almost everything else that is written, not to mention photographs and films. The farther back one looks, the less written material remains. For example, very few records exist of the day-to-day running of the Roman or Han Empires compared to the more plentiful records of the early modern British Empire. To compensate for missing written records, but also to provide more material for analysis, historians often examine artifacts from the period they are studying. From early Egypt, for example, scholars investigate pharaohs' tombs, mummies, paintings, and royal architecture, in addition to everyday artifacts like plates and drinking cups. Religious sculpture and images can be of vital use for historians seeking to understand belief systems, just as coins can indicate chronological periods and state propaganda.

Historians are traditionally so indebted to written evidence for developing historical narratives that they designate any place and period that lacks writing as "prehistoric." This just means that because of the lack of a written record it is virtually impossible to understand specific events and their causes in these societies. Writing began around 3000 B.C.E. in Mesopotamia and Egypt, and later elsewhere. The earliest writing in China is thought to have been developed sometime before 1200 B.C.E., while in Mesoamerica, it first appeared around 900 B.C.E. Thus, prehistory extends longer in some places than in others. The fact that writing did not exist in these places does not mean people were not keeping oral records of their past or of how they understood the world. For historians, working with oral histories can be problematic because of the possibility that they have changed over time, but they remain one of the few ways, along with artifacts, of understanding the past and exploring the beliefs of prehistoric societies.

PRIMARY AND SECONDARY SOURCES

Documents and artifacts used by historians can be divided into two categories: primary sources and secondary sources. Primary sources are those sources that are captured as close to the events they record as possible. In today's world, primary sources could be diaries, home movies, census records, or other items that tell how life was at the time a document or artifact was created. Secondary sources, in contrast, use primary sources to build a particular narrative. These include textbooks, documentaries, and most works of scholarship. In other words, secondary sources are histories. They attempt to make sense of the past, often by examining the order of events and the cause and effect of human actions.

To take a simple example from modern life: in a traffic accident, the eyewitness statements would be primary sources, but the police officer's report, which is an interpretation of several eyewitness accounts, would be a secondary source. The officer attempts to determine how the accident occurred by analyzing the eyewitness accounts. The officer's report is a history of the accident.

The older the source, the more difficult it is to differentiate between primary and secondary sources. Many secondary sources can also be considered primary sources about their own time. For example, in his first book on the history of Rome, Livy (59 B.C.E.–17 C.E.) described events that he believed took place over seven hundred years prior to his lifetime. Livy's history could therefore be considered a secondary source: He clearly used accounts by other Roman writers and oral histories to compose his narrative of the history of Rome. However, we can also think of Livy's work as a primary source because the author reflects what Romans of his day thought about their past, and in many ways his work reveals more about Livy's own time than about the Roman past.

DOING HISTORY: CONTEXT AND INTERPRETATION

Just because a document was written close in time to the event or person it describes, that alone does not make it trustworthy. Everyone sees the world through his or her own lens of life experiences. A wealthy elite may have a very different idea about manual labor than a woman who has worked her entire life. Members of social groups constructed around occupation, wealth, gender, ethnicity, religion, or any combination of characteristics might view other people and their beliefs with suspicion, tolerance, or maybe curiosity. Frequently, people are not conscious of the agendas or biases that inform their assumptions about what they perceive and influence the way they record and interpret events.

To return to our traffic accident, for example, each eyewitness has a different viewpoint. The drivers who were involved in the accident might remember things differently than someone who was not involved. The drivers even have an incentive to describe the accident in a way that minimizes their responsibility. The officer who listens to these accounts must therefore critically examine the statements and the intentions of the witnesses to determine what most likely happened.

To study history properly, you need to learn how to interpret primary sources. To interpret any primary source, it is necessary to ask the following five questions about it:

- Who wrote the document or created the artifact?
- Where and when was it made?
- What kind of document or artifact is it?
- Why was it written or created?
- What was the audience for the source?

The point of asking these questions is simple: you need to determine whether the source is trustworthy and what the source's bias might be. For example, an outsider's writings about a culture will surely be much different from the writings of a member of that culture. With the answers to the basic questions in mind, you can address the deeper questions: What does this source tell us about the events, the society, or the individuals involved? Each of the sources in this book is followed by a set of questions that asks you to delve deeply.

To understand the documents in this book, it will be important to understand the context of the source. In literature, this would be called "the setting." To begin to understand the complexities of each document, you need to know something about the culture and society of the time; these will not be explained by the source. Therefore, pay close attention to the headnotes that introduce each of the documents; they will often highlight issues that might affect your interpretation of the source. The headnotes explain the specific historical context of the sources and give you a brief introduction to the life of the author. Your other course work and your textbook will provide the broader historical context for the period.

The sources in this book have been selected to allow you, the student, to accomplish two goals. First, these documents provide tangible examples of human life and expression in world history. Second, they give you a way to practice being a historian. By reading and analyzing these documents and artifacts, you will learn what a historian does, and along the way you will develop critical reading skills.

To help you understand how this analysis works, we will begin by looking at a document and an artifact from the period covered in Chapter 16 of the textbook, "The Acceleration of Global Contact, 1450–1600." These sources are presented in the format used throughout this book. Let's begin with the following document.

CAH OF TAHNAB

Petition to the Viceroy of Mexico

1605

Columbus arrived at the Yucatan Peninsula in modern Mexico in 1502 and encountered a native people who spoke a dialect of the Mayan language. By 1562, smallpox had ravaged the indigenous Maya population, and Spanish

---

Matthew Restall, *Maya Conquistador* (Boston: Beacon Press, 1998), 173–175.

forces easily conquered the area. In addition to imposing Christianity, the Spanish quickly set up institutions to exploit the remaining natives, often requiring tribute in the form of both goods and unpaid labor. The following petition from the cah, *a self-governing village of indigenous Maya in Tahnab, was an attempt to lessen the villagers' burden. Written by the village council, it is addressed to the Spanish viceroy (governor) of Mexico.*

For the Viceroy, who is in the great *cah* of Mexico. I who am don Alonso Puc, the governor, along with Simón Piste and Francisco Antonio Canul, the *alcaldes*,[1] Juan Ucan, Gonzalo Poot, Gaspar Ku and Pedro Dzul, the *regidores*,[2] we the *cabildo*[3] have assembled ourselves in the name of God Almighty and also in the name of our redeemer, Jesus Christ. We now lower our heads before you, kneeling in great adoration in your presence, in honor of God, beneath your feet and your hands, you our great lord the king [i.e. the Viceroy], supreme ruler, in order that you hear our statement of petition, so that you will hear, our lord, what it is that we recount and explain in our said petition. O lord, we reside here in the heart of the road to the *cah* of San Francisco Campeche. O lord, here is the poverty that is upon us, that we are going through. Here at the heart of the road, O lord, day and night, we carry burdens, take horses, carry letters, and also take turns in serving in the guest house and at the well. Here at the road's heart, O lord, it is really many leagues to the *cah* of Campeche. Our porters, letter carriers, and horse takers go ten leagues as far as our *cah*, day and night. Nor are our people very great in number. The tribute that we give, O lord, is sixty cotton blankets. The tally of our tribute adds up to sixty, O lord, because they add us, the *alcaldes*, and all the widows too. That is why we are relating our miseries for you to hear, O lord. Here is our misery. When the lord governor marshall came he gave us very many forced labor rotations, seventeen of them, though our labor rotations had been abolished by our lord the *oidor*[4] Doctor Palacio because of the excessive misery we experience here on the road. Our misery is also known by our lords the past governors, and our lords the padres also know it, O lord. Every day there are not enough of us to do so much work, and being few, neither can we manage our fields nor sustain our children. In particular we are unable to manage the tribute burden that is upon us. Within each year we give

---

[1] *alcaldes*: Members of the Maya nobility.
[2] *regidores*: Village councilors.
[3] *cabildo*: The village council.
[4] *oidor*: A judge and member of the high court in Mexico City.

a tribute of two *mantas*, two measures of maize, one turkey and one hen. This is what we give, O lord, and we really cannot manage it, because of the great work load that we have. Thus our people run away into the forest. The number of our people who have fled, O lord, who have left their homes, is fifty, because we are burdened with so much work. O lord, this is why we humbly place ourselves before you, our great lord ruler, the King, in honor of our redeemer Jesus Christ, we kiss your feet and hands, we the worst of your children. We want there to be an end to the labor obligations under which we serve, with which we are burdened. Because our fathers, many of them principal men, along with our porters, letter-carriers and horse-takers, serve day and night. We want to look after you, our lord, and greatly wish that you will be compassionate and turn your attention to us. We have neither fathers nor mothers. We are really poor here in our *cah* in the heart of the road, O lord; nobody helps us. Three times we have carried our petition before you, our lord the *señor* governor, but you did not hear our words, O lord. Nor do we have any money in order that we may petition before you; our *cah* is poor. Here, O lord, is the reason why our people flee, because it is known that in the forest, through the use [sale] of beeswax, one is given money on credit by our lord Francisco de Magaña. It really is the governor's money that is given to people. This is our petition in your presence, lord, our great ruler, the king, made here in the *cah* of Tahnab, today the ninth day of the month of July in the year 1605. Truly we give our names at the end.

> Don Alonso Puc, governor; Pedro Ku, notary; Francisco Antonio Canul, *alcalde*; Simón Piste, *alcalde*; Juan Ucan, Gonzalo Poot, *regidoresob*; Gaspar Ku, *regidor*.

READING AND DISCUSSION QUESTIONS

1. What is the power relationship between the Spanish and the Maya?

2. How does the *cah* attempt to reduce the level of the villagers' tribute?

3. How did the Spanish treat the conquered Maya?

Before answering the specific Reading and Discussion Questions, begin your analysis by revisiting the basic questions listed earlier. Who wrote the document? Where and when was it made? What kind of document is it? Why was it written? What was the audience for the source? After answering these questions, you can proceed to the Reading and Discussion

Questions, which help reveal what the source tells us about the place, time, and people.

After reading this document, we understand that the petition was written by the village council of the *cah* of Tahnab. The headnote makes clear that it was written about forty years after the Spanish conquest. The petition asks for a reduction in the amount of labor that the Maya people have to perform for the Spanish rulers, and it was addressed to the senior member of the Spanish administration in Mexico.

1.   What is the power relationship between the Spanish and the Maya?

The *cah* is undoubtedly the inferior in this relationship, and the petition-ers feel obligated to employ flattery, as shown by the way they address the viceroy as "great lord" and "supreme ruler." They humble themselves before the viceroy, stating that they kiss his feet and hands and calling themselves the worst of his children. They lower their heads and kneel "in great adoration" before him.

The reason for the supplications is not clear from the document itself, and this is where historical background and a close reading of the head-note are helpful. The headnote introduces the document by stating that it had been a generation since the Spanish conquered these people, which explains the power dynamic at play here. In the document, the petitioners mention that the *cah* has repeatedly requested similar benefits from the viceroy, but its requests have gone unheeded. This happened even though a Spanish governmental official, the *oidor* Doctor Palacio, had previously abolished the labor requirement of the village. Therefore, we can assume that in the established administrative structure, the viceroy has supreme power and the *cah* is unable to stand up for itself, even with the occasional support of other Spanish officials.

2.   How does the *cah* attempt to reduce the level of the villagers' tribute?

The petitioners attempt to obtain redress for the *cah*'s concerns through a few methods. The first is the expression of subservience to the viceroy. They also present evidence of the *cah*'s poverty and oppression. They claim to be unable to provide the assessed tribute because of the time they spend laboring on behalf of the Spanish. Because of the forced labor and their inability to pay the tribute, many of the *cah*'s people have run away, making it even harder for the remaining villagers to pay their due. Third, the petitioners stress the *cah's* Christian faith, opening the document by invoking "God Almighty" and "our Redeemer, Jesus Christ." This reflects one of the most lasting policies of Spanish occupation: the forced conversion of the native inhabitants to Christianity. By proclaiming their faith, the councilors emphasize the *cah's* obedience to the Spanish and the common ground between the Spanish and the Maya people.

3. How did the Spanish treat the conquered Maya?

Through this document, we can also examine how the Spanish treated the conquered people. As we read here, the Spanish imposed both tribute on the sixty people of the village (two cotton blankets, two measures of maize, one turkey, and one hen) and forced labor. The petition states that this tribute is excessive and has damaged the village, but we have no way of knowing if this is true. On the other hand, this document indicates that some Spanish officials have attempted to protect the villagers. The *oidor* Doctor Palacio abolished the requirement of forced labor. The *cah* seems to be able to use the Spanish legal system fairly well, and the councilors demonstrate that they know how to present an argument to the viceroy. So this document tells us how conquered peoples were subjugated, but it also indicates that the relationship between the authorities and conquered peoples was one based on negotiation, showing that the natives did have an ability to try to better their lives within the Spanish system, if only with limited success.

Now we move on to a visual source: an image from an anonymous woodcutter, probably from Augsburg, Germany.

The Peoples of the Islands Recently Discovered
1505

Following Columbus's first expedition to islands in the Caribbean, he and later explorers reached additional New World lands, such as Brazil, where the Portuguese explorer Pedro Álvares Cabral (ca. 1467–1520) arrived in 1500. These new lands came to be known as America because of the writings of Amerigo Vespucci (1454–1512), who published a series of descriptions of the European explorations. The following woodcut image, carved in 1505 by an unknown artist in Germany, was based on the description of Brazilian natives found in Vespucci's works. From this model, thousands of cheap paper copies of the image were printed, allowing Europeans of all social classes to possess a copy.

The New York Library/Art Resource, N.Y.

READING AND DISCUSSION QUESTIONS

1. How are the natives depicted in this image?
2. What might Europeans have thought about the natives in this image?

Once again, you should first address the five guiding questions. Who created the artifact? Where and when was it made? What kind of artifact is it? Why was it created? What was the audience for the source? The image was made by a woodcutter in Germany, and it was used as a model for many printed copies, but the name of the artist is unknown. It was carved in 1505, only five years after Cabral reached Brazil, and was created for a European audience to publicize the encounter with the natives of Brazil.

1. How are the natives depicted in this image?

Looking at the entire image, we see that the artist has depicted a group of about ten people. The men and women wear a bare minimum of clothing.

Both sexes wear loincloths, anklets, necklaces, and headbands made of feathers, leaving the women's breasts exposed. One woman is nursing a completely naked baby, while two almost naked children stand nearby. Under the canopy of branches lashed together, a couple engages in an amorous scene in public. The impression is that the people in the newly discovered islands lack European ideas of sexual modesty. No Europeans would engage in such behavior in the open, nor would they wear such scanty clothing.

If we examine the woodcut a little closer, we see that most of the male figures are armed with bows. A torso is hanging from a tree and looks like it is roasting on a fire. In the top-left corner of the woodcut, it appears that a figure is eating a severed arm. There is a definite suggestion that the people depicted in this drawing are warlike cannibals.

2.   What might Europeans have thought about the natives in this image?

When interpreting the impact of this woodcut, or any of the artifacts in this book, you will have to rely on what you know about the period and culture based on the other documents in the chapter, your class work, and the textbook. In this woodcut, it is very clear that the people depicted are alien to Europeans. They lack clothing, perform intimate acts in public, and eat human flesh. Depending on how you interpret this image, you may think that the Europeans would view the islanders as savages because of their practice of cannibalism. Or perhaps the Europeans would see the islanders as innocent because they are not shamed by love, nudity, or breastfeeding. Maybe the Europeans would see them as fresh minds ready to accept Christianity, as indicated by the crosses on the European ship in the background. All of these interpretations involve some knowledge of European culture at the time, and all are valid based on what we know.

While reading the documents and examining the images and artifacts in this source reader, you will find that most sources can invite different interpretations. Differing interpretations can be considered valid until more extensive study of the relevant period and place suggests otherwise. In fact, new and different interpretations of primary source material constitute one of the ways that new historical discoveries are made. Newly found sources and new interpretations of older ones keep the study of history relevant and moving forward. If you use the five questions given here as a guide for analysis, you will produce revealing interpretations of the sources in this book. Good luck!

CHAPTER 16

The Acceleration of Global Contact

1450–1600

Although long-standing trade routes meant that many of the world's civilizations were in contact with one another before 1500, this interaction accelerated drastically in the sixteenth century when Europe became a much larger player in world trade. Europe began establishing trade routes to the newly discovered Americas and sent Christian missionaries to all corners of the globe. The sources in this chapter examine the impact of Europe's entrance into the global community and address the continued importance of the civilizations that had established earlier trade routes in the Indian Ocean.

DOCUMENT 16-1

ZHENG HE

Stele Inscription

1431

Before the Europeans crossed the Atlantic and began exploring the New World, the Indian Ocean was the center of the world's sea trading routes and China dominated much of the trading activity. Zheng He (1371–1433) was an admiral during the Ming Dynasty who led seven naval expeditions to locations such as the Arabian peninsula, East Africa, India, and Southeast Asia. Compared to the three ships that made up Columbus's initial expedition, Zheng He's earlier fleet was massive, somewhere between 200 and 300 ships carrying around 28,000 men. Zheng He's inscription is a stele, or large rock monument, that describes his expeditions.

Teobaldo Filesi, *China and Africa in the Middle Ages,* trans. David Morison (London: Frank Cass, 1972), 57–61.

Record of the miraculous answer (to prayer) of the goddess the Celestial Spouse.[1]

The Imperial Ming Dynasty unifying seas and continents, surpassing the three dynasties even goes beyond the Han and Tang dynasties. The countries beyond the horizon and from the ends of the earth have all become subjects and to the most western of the western or the most northern of the northern countries, however far they may be, the distance and the routes may be calculated. Thus the barbarians from beyond the seas, though their countries are truly distant, "with double translation" have come to audience bearing precious objects and presents.

The Emperor, approving of their loyalty and sincerity, has ordered us (Zheng) He and others at the head of several tens of thousands of officers and flag-troops to ascend more than one hundred large ships to go and confer presents on them in order to make manifest the transforming power of the (imperial) virtue and to treat distant people with kindness. From the third year of Yongle[2] (1405) till now we have seven times received the commission of ambassadors to countries of the western ocean. The barbarian countries which we have visited are: by way of Zhancheng, Zhaowa, Sanfoqi, and Xianlo crossing straight over to Xilanshan in South India, Guli, and Kezhi, we have gone to the western regions Hulumosi, Adan, Mugudushu, altogether more than thirty countries large and small.[3] We have traversed more than one hundred thousand li[4] of immense water spaces and have beheld in the ocean huge waves like mountains rising sky-high, and we have set eyes on barbarian regions far away hidden in a blue transparency of light vapors, while our sails loftily unfurled like clouds day and night continued their course (rapid like that) of a star, traversing those savage waves as if we were treading a public thoroughfare. Truly this was due to the majesty and the good fortune of the Court and moreover we owe it to the protecting virtue of the divine Celestial Spouse.

The power of the goddess having indeed been manifested in previous times has been abundantly revealed in the present generation. In the

---

[1] **the goddess the Celestial Spouse**: While in human form during the Song Dynasty, the goddess Tian Fei, or Mazu, was believed to have miraculously saved her merchant brothers during a storm at sea. As such, she was a natural choice for the explorer Zheng He to direct his prayers.

[2] **Yongle**: He was Emperor during most of Zheng He's expeditions.

[3] **by way of Zhancheng . . . small**: The journey that Zheng He describes routes around present-day Indonesia, south below India, and into the eastern coast of Africa.

[4] **one hundred thousand li**: One li is roughly a third of a mile, so they have sailed over 33,000 miles.

midst of the rushing waters it happened that, when there was a hurricane, suddenly there was a divine lantern shining in the mast, and as soon as this miraculous light appeared the danger was appeased, so that even in the danger of capsizing one felt reassured that there was no cause for fear. When we arrived in the distant countries we captured alive those of the native kings who were not respectful and exterminated those barbarian robbers who were engaged in piracy, so that consequently the sea route was cleansed and pacified and the natives put their trust in it. All this is due to the favors of the goddess.

It is not easy to enumerate completely all the cases where the goddess has answered (prayers). Previously in a memorial to the Court we have requested that her virtue be registered in the Court of Sacrificial Worship and a temple be built at Nanking on the bank of the dragon river where regular sacrifices should be transmitted for ever. We have respectfully received an Imperial commemorative composition exalting the miraculous favors, which is the highest recompense and praise indeed. However, the miraculous power of the goddess resides wherever one goes. As for the temporary palace on the southern mountain at Changle, I have, at the head of the fleet, frequently resided there awaiting the [favorable] wind to set sail for the ocean.

We, Zheng He and others, on the one hand have received the high favor of a gracious commission of our Sacred Lord, and on the other hand carry to the distant barbarians the benefits of respect and good faith (on their part). Commanding the multitudes on the fleet and (being responsible for) a quantity of money and valuables in the face of the violence of the winds and the nights our one fear is not to be able to succeed; how should we then dare not to serve our dynasty with exertion of all our loyalty and the gods with the utmost sincerity? How would it be possible not to realize what is the source of the tranquillity of the fleet and the troops and the salvation on the voyage both going and returning? Therefore we have made manifest the virtue of the goddess on stone and have moreover recorded the years and months of the voyages to the barbarian countries and the return in order to leave (the memory) for ever.

I. In the third year of Yongle (1405) commanding the fleet we went to Guli and other countries. At that time the pirate Chen Zuyi had gathered his followers in the country of Sanfoqi, where he plundered the native merchants. When he also advanced to resist our fleet, supernatural soldiers secretly came to the rescue so that after one beating of the drum he was annihilated. In the fifth year (1407) we returned.

II. In the fifth year of Yongle (1407) commanding the fleet we went to Zhaowa, Guli, Kezhi, and Xianle. The kings of these countries all sent as tribute precious objects, precious birds and rare animals. In the seventh year (1409) we returned.

III. In the seventh year of Yongle (1409) commanding the fleet we went to the countries (visited) before and took our route by the country of Xilanshan. Its king Yaliekunaier [King of Sri Lanka] was guilty of a gross lack of respect and plotted against the fleet. Owing to the manifest answer to prayer of the goddess (the plot) was discovered and thereupon that king was captured alive. In the ninth year (1411) on our return the king was presented (to the throne) (as a prisoner); subsequently he received the Imperial favor of returning to his own country.

IV. In the eleventh year of Yongle (1413) commanding the fleet we went to Hulumosi [Ormuz] and other countries. In the country of Sumendala [Samudra] there was a false king Suganla[5] who was marauding and invading his country. Its king Cainu-liabiding had sent an envoy to the Palace Gates in order to lodge a complaint. We went thither with the official troups [troops] under our command and exterminated some and arrested (other rebels), and owing to the silent aid of the goddess we captured the false king alive. In the thirteenth year (1415) on our return he was presented (to the Emperor as a prisoner). In that year the king of the country of Manlajia [Malacca] came in person with his wife and son to present tribute.

V. In the fifteenth year of Yongle (1417) commanding the fleet we visited the western regions. The country of Hulumosi presented lions, leopards with gold spots, and large western horses. The country of Adan presented qilin of which the native name is culafa [a giraffe] as well as the long-horned animal maha [oryx antelope]. The country of Mugudushu presented huafu lu [zebras] as well as lions. The country of Bulawa [Brava] presented camels which run one thousand li as well as camel-birds [ostriches]. The countries of Zhaowa and Guli presented the animal miligao. They all vied in presenting the marvellous objects preserved in the mountains or hidden in the seas and the beautiful treasures buried in the sand or deposited on

---

[5] **false king Suganla**: Sekandar, who usurped the throne from the rightful ruler Zain Al'-Abidin. He is referred to as Cainu-liabiding in the next sentence.

the shores. Some sent a maternal uncle of the king, others a paternal uncle or a younger brother of the king in order to present a letter of homage written on gold leaf as well as tribute.

VI.   In the nineteenth year of Yongle (1421) commanding the fleet we conducted the ambassadors from Hulumosi and the other countries who had been in attendance at the capital for a long time back to their countries. The kings of all these countries prepared even more tribute than previously.

VII.   In the sixth year of Xuande (1431) once more commanding the fleet we have left for the barbarian countries in order to read to them (an Imperial edict) and to confer presents.

We have anchored in this port awaiting a north wind to take the sea, and recalling how previously we have on several occasions received the benefits of the protection of the divine intelligence we have thus recorded an inscription in stone.

READING AND DISCUSSION QUESTIONS

1.   What does the inscription suggest about the importance of overseas exploration to the Ming Dynasty?

2.   Describe the relationship between the Chinese explorers and the local populations that they encountered. How did the Chinese treat these populations? How did these people respond to the Chinese presence?

VIEWPOINTS

Exploration and Its Material Advantages

DOCUMENT 16-2

CHRISTOPHER COLUMBUS

Letter from the Third Voyage

1493

An Italian of modest birth, Christopher Columbus (1451–1506) was an experienced seafarer when he approached King Ferdinand and Queen Isabella of Spain. He sought their funding for an expedition across the Atlantic, which Columbus mistakenly believed was a shorter route to Asia than the journey east that Europeans typically made. In the end, Columbus did not reach Asia, but rather discovered two continents previously unknown to medieval Europeans. He described what he discovered in letters to the Spanish monarchs. The following is one from his third voyage, in which he defends the achievements of his explorations.

Most serene and most high and most powerful princes, the king and queen, our sovereigns: The Holy Trinity moved Your Highnesses to this enterprise of the Indies, and of His infinite goodness, He made me the messenger thereof, so that, being moved thereunto, I came with the mission to your royal presence, as being the most exalted of Christian princes and so ardently devoted to the Faith and to its increase. The persons who should have occupied themselves with the matter held it to be impossible, for they made of gifts of chance their riches and on them placed their trust.

On this matter I spent six or seven years of deep anxiety, expounding, as well as I could, how great service might in this be rendered to the Lord, by proclaiming abroad His holy name and His faith to so many peoples, which was all a thing of so great excellence and for the fair fame of great

Cecil Jane, ed. and trans., *Select Documents Illustrating the Four Voyages of Columbus* (Nendeln, Liechtenstein: Kraus Reprint Limited, 1967), 2:2–6, 14–16.

princes and for a notable memorial for them. It was needful also to speak of the temporal gain therein, foreshadowed in the writings of so many wise men, worthy of credence, who wrote histories and related how in these parts there are great riches. And it was likewise necessary to bring forward in this matter that which had been said and thought by those who have written of the world and who have described it. Finally, Your Highnesses determined that this enterprise should be undertaken.

Here you displayed that lofty spirit which you have always shown in every great affair, for all those who had been engaged on the matter and who had heard the proposal, one and all laughed it to scorn, save two friars who were ever constant.

I, although I suffered weariness, was very sure that this would not come to nothing, and I am still, for it is true that all will pass away, save the Word of God, and all that He has said will be fulfilled. And He spake so clearly of these lands by the mouth of Isaiah, in many places of his Book, affirming that from Spain His holy name should be proclaimed to them.

And I set forth in the name of the Holy Trinity, and I returned very speedily, with evidence of all, as much as I had said, in my hand. Your highnesses undertook to send me again, and in a little while I say that, . . . by the grace of God, I discovered three hundred and thirty-three leagues of Tierra Firme,[6] the end of the East, and seven hundred islands of importance, over and above that which I discovered on the first voyage, and I circumnavigated the island of Española, which in circumference is greater than all Spain, wherein are people innumerable, all of whom should pay tribute.

Then was born the defaming and disparagement of the undertaking which had been begun there, because I had not immediately sent caravels laden with gold, no thought being taken of the brevity of the time and the other many obstacles which I mentioned. And on this account, for my sins or, as I believe that it will be, for my salvation, I was held in abhorrence and was opposed in whatever I said and asked.

For this cause, I decided to come to Your Highnesses, and to cause you to wonder at everything, and to show you the reason that I had for all. And I told you of the peoples whom I had seen, among whom or from whom many souls may be saved. And I brought to you the service of the people of the island of Española, how they were bound to pay tribute and how they held you as their sovereigns and lords. And I brought to you abundant evidence of gold, and that there are mines and very great nuggets, and likewise of copper. And I brought to you many kinds of spices, of

---

[6] **Tierra Firme:** The mainland.

which it would be wearisome to write, and I told you of the great amount of brazil[7] and of other things, innumerable. . . .

[After describing the results of his first expeditions, Columbus turns to a narrative of his third voyage.]

On the following day there came from towards the east a large canoe with twenty-four men, all in the prime of life and very well provided with arms, bows and arrows and wooden shields, and they, as I have said, were all in the prime of life, well-proportioned and not negroes, but whiter than the others who have been seen in the Indies, and very graceful and with handsome bodies, and hair long and smooth, cut in the manner of Castile. They had their heads wrapped in scarves of cotton, worked elaborately and in colours, which, I believed, were *almaizares*.[8] They wore another of these scarves round the body and covered themselves with them in place of drawers.

When this canoe arrived, it hailed us from a great distance, and neither I nor anyone else could understand them. However, I ordered signs to be made to them that they should approach, and in this way more than two hours passed, and if they came a little nearer, they at once sheered off again. I caused pans and other things which shone to be shown to them in order to attract them to come, and after a good while they came nearer than they had hitherto done. And I greatly desired to have speech with them and it seemed to me that I had nothing that could be shown to them now which would induce them to come nearer. But I caused to be brought up to the castle of the poop[9] a tambourine, that they might play it, and some young men to dance, believing that they would draw near to see the festivity. And as soon as they observed the playing and dancing, they all dropped their oars and laid hand on their bows and strung them, and each one of them took up his shield, and they began to shoot arrows. I immediately stopped the playing and dancing, and then ordered some crossbows to be discharged. They left me and went quickly to another caravel and in haste got under its stern. And the pilot accosted them and gave a coat and a hat to a man who seemed to be one of the chief among them, and it was arranged that he should go to speak with them there on the shore, where they went at once in the canoe to wait for him. And he would not go without my permission, and when they saw him come to my ship in the boat, they entered their canoe again and went away, and I never saw any more of them or of the other inhabitants of this island.

---

[7] **brazil**: Brazilwood, a very expensive wood that was much sought after in Europe.

[8] *almaizares*: Head coverings worn by the Muslims who lived in Spain.

[9] **castle of the poop**: The raised section at the rear of the ship where the wheel was located.

READING AND DISCUSSION QUESTIONS

1. How does Columbus describe the people of the New World and their customs?

2. What seems to be Columbus's motivation for exploring these islands? What does Columbus believe were the results of his explorations? Why were they important?

3. What were some of the criticisms of Columbus's journeys?

4. What were Columbus's religious beliefs? What did he think was the role of Christianity in his voyages?

DOCUMENT 16-3

KING DOM MANUEL OF PORTUGAL
Grant of Rights of Trade
1500

Columbus was forced to sail west because Spain's rival, Portugal, controlled the known route to India along the coast of Africa. The Portuguese began exploring the west coast of Africa after capturing the Moroccan port of Ceuta in 1415. In 1488, Portuguese ships rounded the southern tip of Africa, and in 1498, Vasco da Gama reached India. As the Portuguese explored, they set up colonies and trading stations, like the one mentioned in this document at the island of São Thomé, which the Portuguese reached in 1473. Because most Portuguese exploration was financed by the Crown, the state had to grant all commercial contracts.

GRANT OF RIGHTS OF TRADE TO THE ISLANDERS OF SÃO THOMÉ.
26 MARCH 1500.

Dom Manuel [*etc.*]. To all to whom this letter shall come, we make known that we have made a grant to Fernam de Mello, a nobleman of our household, of the captaincy of the island of Samtome in the parts of Guinee[10] for

---

John William Blake, ed. and trans., *Europeans in West Africa* (Nendeln, Liechtenstein: Kraus Reprint Limited, 1967), 89–92.

[10] **Guinee**: Gulf of Guinea in West Africa.

him and his successors, as is contained in the said letter; and he now tells us that, since the said island is so remote from these our kingdoms, people are unwilling to go there to live, unless they have very great privileges and franchises; and we, observing the expenditure we have ordered for the peopling of the said island and likewise the great profits which would come from it to our kingdoms, if the island were peopled in perfection, as we hope with the help of Our Lord it will be, have resolved to grant him certain privileges and franchises, whereby the people and persons, who go there, may do this more willingly; and the privileges are as follows:

Item. Our will and pleasure is that the said inhabitants of the said island hereafter and always may have and hold licence, whenever they wish, to be able to go with ships to barter and to trade in all goods and articles, grown and produced in the said island, to the mainland — from that Rio Real and the island of Fernam de Poo as far as all the land of Manicomguo,[11] except that they cannot barter in the land where the gold is without our special command, and they may not barter in the said land any goods or articles, forbidden by the holy father or by us under the penalties already imposed by us. We will that they may thus trade in this land in the manner stated, without further approaching us or sending to us or our officers and others to ask or apply for licence for this purpose, or for clerks, so that they may have them with them to go to the said parts in their ships, according to our ordinance with reference to those who go there from our kingdoms; but we will that they ask and apply for the said licences and clerks from the customs officer or receiver, whom we command to be appointed there to be our deputy in order to collect and gather our dues, which are to be the fourth of all articles, which the inhabitants of the said island barter there in the said parts. And these, our officers, whom thus we appoint there in the said island, shall be ready and diligent to supply the said clerks to the said shippers, with the regulation that each shall carry one in the manner required in each ship which thus goes there, as is done in the ships which by our contracts go there to the said parts of Guinee. Thus, the said customs officer or receiver shall be ready to collect the said dues, which are to accrue to us, from the said ships which are equipped in the said island, as soon as they return from the said parts of Guinee. If the said officers are not thus ready to collect the said dues and to supply the said clerks, the said Fernam de Mello, the captain, shall in their absence supply and collect, and he shall keep these dues himself. When such happens,

---

[11] **from that Rio Real . . . Manicomguo**: A stretch along the coasts of modern-day Nigeria and Angola.

he shall advise us of it, so that we may send for them. These clerks, thus to be supplied, shall be fully competent and suitable for our service, and for their salaries they shall have double that which a mariner has; and you shall give them this from the day when the said ships leave the said island for the said trades up to the day when they return, and no more.

Furthermore, it is our will and pleasure, when the amount of our dues has been paid on all the said imported negroes and goods, that the said inhabitants of the said island may sell on their own accounts what remains to them to all persons, who want and desire them, not only there in the said island to others whatsoever but also in all our kingdoms and abroad; and if they sell in the said island, the buyers shall not have to pay on the said goods, in these kingdoms when they are brought here, either the tenth or any other dues; and if they do not sell them in the said island but wish to bring them to our kingdoms or to carry them to other parts, they may do this, because they are exempt from having to pay us the said dues.

They may do this, provided they carry a certificate from our officers, whom we shall thus appoint in the said island, showing that they have already paid our dues upon them there.

Furthermore, it is our will and pleasure that the inhabitants of the said island shall not be under obligation to us to carry or send our said dues, but that we are to send for them to the said island at our own charge and expense.

Furthermore, it is our will and pleasure, in the event of our farming out the said trades or a part thereof, that, should we do so, this licence, which we thus grant to the said inhabitants of the said island, shall not transgress or stay such a farm, and this is thus enacted so that we shall not be reminded of this.

Furthermore, it is our will and pleasure that hereafter and always the inhabitants of the said island shall be exempt and freed from the payment to us in all our kingdoms and lordships of the tenth of all goods, which they transport from the said island, not only of goods which are of their own inheritance and gathering, but also of goods which they buy in exchange for other things or in any manner whatsoever. Likewise, they shall be exempted from the payment to us of the tenth of all goods and articles, which they buy or sell or obtain in exchange for other things of their own in the islands of Cabo Verde, Samtiago, Canareas, Madeira, Porto Santo, and Açores, and all other islands of the ocean sea, and which they bring to our kingdoms.

This shall be, provided our officers are certified by letters from the said captain that the said persons are inhabitants of the said island.

Furthermore, it is our will and pleasure that the inhabitants and settlers of the said island may come to sell to the inhabitants of our city of
Sam Jorge all provisions, fruits and vegetables, which they have in the said
island, and they shall have gold in exchange. And this, provided all sales
are effected through our officers, according to the regulation governing
the manner in which are sold the provisions, which the mariners, who go
from our kingdoms to the said city, carry in our caravels and ships. Therefore, we command our overseers of our exchequer, officers of the Casa
de Guynee, and all accountants, treasurers, customs officers, receivers,
magistrates, judges and justices, and all our officers and others whatsoever,
to whom this our letter shall be shown and who are cognisant thereof, that
hereafter they shall fulfil and keep this our letter and cause it to be fulfilled and kept entirely as is contained therein; and should anyone wish to
disobey it, that they shall in no manner permit it, because this is our wish.
And for its security and our remembrance, we command them to be given
this our letter, signed by us and sealed with our pendent seal. Given in our
city of Lixboa, on the twenty-sixth day of the month of March in the year
of the birth of Our Lord Jesus Christ one thousand five hundred. Lopo
Fernamdez made this.

READING AND DISCUSSION QUESTIONS

1. Why did merchants want special privileges to trade at São Thomé?
   What privileges did they receive?

2. What kinds of goods did the merchant Fernam de Mello want to trade?
   What taxes did he have to pay on his goods?

3. What does this document tell us about the way the Portuguese ruled
   their empire?

BARTOLOMÉ DE LAS CASAS

From Brief Account of the Devastation of the Indies

1542

Bartolomé de Las Casas (1484–1566) was one of the most vocal opponents of the Spaniards' treatment of the native people of the West Indies. In particular, the Dominican missionary criticized the encomienda *system, which allowed Spanish colonists to force local peoples to work the colonists' land or mines — often under deplorable conditions. In his* Brief Account, *Las Casas discusses the detrimental impact that the arrival of the Europeans had on the West Indies. He pays significant attention to the steep depopulation of the islands of the Caribbean, one of the most dramatic events associated with the colonization of the West Indies.*

The [West] Indies were discovered in the year one thousand four hundred and ninety-two. In the following year a great many Spaniards went there with the intention of settling the land. Thus, forty-nine years have passed since the first settlers penetrated the land, the first so-claimed being the large and most happy isle called Hispaniola, which is six hundred leagues in circumference. Around it in all directions are many other islands, some very big, others very small, and all of them were, as we saw with our own eyes, densely populated with native peoples called Indians. This large island was perhaps the most densely populated place in the world. There must be close to two hundred leagues of land on this island, and the seacoast has been explored for more than ten thousand leagues, and each day more of it is being explored. And all the land so far discovered is a beehive of people; it is as though God had crowded into these lands the great majority of mankind.

And of all the infinite universe of humanity, these people are the most guileless, the most devoid of wickedness and duplicity, the most obedient and faithful to their native masters and to the Spanish Christians whom

Bartolomé de Las Casas, *The Devastation of the Indies: A Brief Account,* trans. Herma Briffault (New York: Seabury, 1974), 37–44, 51–52.

they serve. They are by nature the most humble, patient, and peaceable, holding no grudges, free from embroilments, neither excitable nor quarrelsome. These people are the most devoid of rancors, hatreds, or desire for vengeance of any people in the world. And because they are so weak and complaisant, they are less able to endure heavy labor and soon die of no matter what malady. The sons of nobles among us, brought up in the enjoyments of life's refinements, are no more delicate than are these Indians, even those among them who are of the lowest rank of laborers. They are also poor people, for they not only possess little but have no desire to possess worldly goods. For this reason they are not arrogant, embittered, or greedy. Their repasts are such that the food of the holy fathers in the desert can scarcely be more parsimonious, scanty, and poor. As to their dress, they are generally naked, with only their pudenda covered somewhat. And when they cover their shoulders it is with a square cloth no more than two varas [approximately 33 inches] in size. They have no beds, but sleep on a kind of matting or else in a kind of suspended net called hamacas. They are very clean in their persons, with alert, intelligent minds, docile and open to doctrine, very apt to receive our holy Catholic faith, to be endowed with virtuous customs, and to behave in a godly fashion. And once they begin to hear the tidings of the Faith, they are so insistent on knowing more and on taking the sacraments of the Church and on observing the divine cult that, truly, the missionaries who are here need to be endowed by God with great patience in order to cope with such eagerness. Some of the secular Spaniards who have been here for many years say that the goodness of the Indians is undeniable and that if this gifted people could be brought to know the one true God they would be the most fortunate people in the world.

Yet into this sheepfold, into this land of meek outcasts there came some Spaniards who immediately behaved like ravening wild beasts, wolves, tigers, or lions that had been starved for many days. And Spaniards have behaved in no other way during the past forty years, down to the present time, for they are still acting like ravening beasts, killing, terrorizing, afflicting, torturing, and destroying the native peoples, doing all this with the strangest and most varied new methods of cruelty, never seen or heard of before, and to such a degree that this Island of Hispaniola once so populous (having a population that I estimated to be more than three millions), has now a population of barely two hundred persons.

The island of Cuba is nearly as long as the distance between Valladolid and Rome; it is now almost completely depopulated. San Juan [Puerto Rico] and Jamaica are two of the largest, most productive and attractive islands; both are now deserted and devastated. On the northern side of Cuba and Hispaniola lie the neighboring Lucayos comprising more than sixty islands including those called Gigantes, beside numerous other islands, some small some large. The least felicitous of them were more fertile and beautiful than the gardens of the King of Seville. They have the healthiest lands in the world, where lived more than five hundred thousand souls; they are now deserted, inhabited by not a single living creature. All the people were slain or died after being taken into captivity and brought to the Island of Hispaniola to be sold as slaves. When the Spaniards saw that some of these had escaped, they sent a ship to find them, and it voyaged for three years among the islands searching for those who had escaped being slaughtered, for a good Christian had helped them escape, taking pity on them and had won them over to Christ; of these there were eleven persons and these I saw. . . .

As for the vast mainland, which is ten times larger than all Spain, even including Aragon and Portugal, containing more land than the distance between Seville and Jerusalem, or more than two thousand leagues, we are sure that our Spaniards, with their cruel and abominable acts, have devastated the land and exterminated the rational people who fully inhabited it. We can estimate very surely and truthfully that in the forty years that have passed, with the infernal actions of the Christians, there have been unjustly slain more than twelve million men, women, and children. In truth, I believe without trying to deceive myself that the number of the slain is more like fifteen million.

The common ways mainly employed by the Spaniards who call themselves Christian and who have gone there to extirpate those pitiful nations and wipe them off the earth is by unjustly waging cruel and bloody wars. Then, when they have slain all those who fought for their lives or to escape the tortures they would have to endure, that is to say, when they have slain all the native rulers and young men (since the Spaniards usually spare only the women and children, who are subjected to the hardest and bitterest servitude ever suffered by man or beast), they enslave any survivors. With these infernal methods of tyranny they debase and weaken countless numbers of those pitiful Indian nations.

Their reason for killing and destroying such an infinite number of souls is that the Christians have an ultimate aim, which is to acquire gold, and to swell themselves with riches in a very brief time and thus rise to a high estate disproportionate to their merits. It should be kept in mind that their insatiable greed and ambition, the greatest ever seen in the world, is the cause of their villainies. And also, those lands are so rich and felicitous, the native peoples so meek and patient, so easy to subject, that our

Spaniards have no more consideration for them than beasts. And I say this from my own knowledge of the acts I witnessed. But I should not say "than beasts" for, thanks be to God, they have treated beasts with some respect; I should say instead like excrement on the public squares. And thus they have deprived the Indians of their lives and souls, for the millions I mentioned have died without the Faith and without the benefit of the sacraments. This is a well known and proven fact which even the tyrant Governors, themselves killers, know and admit. And never have the Indians in all the Indies committed any act against the Spanish Christians, until those Christians have first and many times committed countless cruel aggressions against them or against neighboring nations. For in the beginning the Indians regarded the Spaniards as angels from Heaven. Only after the Spaniards had used violence against them, killing, robbing, torturing, did the Indians ever rise up against them. On the Island Hispaniola was where the Spaniards first landed, as I have said. Here those Christians perpetrated their first ravages and oppressions against the native peoples. This was the first land in the New World to be destroyed and depopulated by the Christians, and here they began their subjection of the women and children, taking them away from the Indians to use them and ill use them, eating the food they provided with their sweat and toil. The Spaniards did not content themselves with what the Indians gave them of their own free will, according to their ability, which was always too little to satisfy enormous appetites, for a Christian eats and consumes in one day an amount of food that would suffice to feed three houses inhabited by ten Indians for one month. And they committed other acts of force and violence and oppression which made the Indians realize that these men had not come from Heaven. And some of the Indians concealed their foods while others concealed their wives and children and still others fled to the mountains to avoid the terrible transactions of the Christians.

And the Christians attacked them with buffets and beatings, until finally they laid hands on the nobles of the villages. Then they behaved with such temerity and shamelessness that the most powerful ruler of the islands had to see his own wife raped by a Christian officer.

From that time onward the Indians began to seek ways to throw the Christians out of their lands. They took up arms, but their weapons were very weak and of little service in offense and still less in defense. (Because of this, the wars of the Indians against each other are little more than games played by children.) And the Christians, with their horses and swords and pikes began to carry out massacres and strange cruelties against them.

They attacked the towns and spared neither the children nor the aged nor pregnant women nor women in childbed, not only stabbing them and dismembering them but cutting them to pieces as if dealing with sheep in the slaughter house. They laid bets as to who, with one stroke of the sword, could split a man in two or could cut off his head or spill out his entrails with a single stroke of the pike. They took infants from their mothers' breasts, snatching them by the legs and pitching them headfirst against the crags or snatched them by the arms and threw them into the rivers, roaring with laughter and saying as the babies fell into the water, "Boil there, you offspring of the devil!" Other infants they put to the sword along with their mothers and anyone else who happened to be nearby. They made some low wide gallows on which the hanged victim's feet almost touched the ground, stringing up their victims in lots of thirteen, in memory of Our Redeemer and His twelve Apostles, then set burning wood at their feet and thus burned them alive. To others they attached straw or wrapped their whole bodies in straw and set them afire. With still others, all those they wanted to capture alive, they cut off their hands and hung them round the victim's neck, saying, "Go now, carry the message," meaning, Take the news to the Indians who have fled to the mountains. They usually dealt with the chieftains and nobles in the following way: they made a grid of rods which they placed on forked sticks, then lashed the victims to the grid and lighted a smoldering fire underneath, so that little by little, as those captives screamed in despair and torment, their souls would leave them. . . .

After the wars and the killings had ended, when usually there survived only some boys, some women, and children, these survivors were distributed among the Christians to be slaves. The repartimiento or distribution was made according to the rank and importance of the Christian to whom the Indians were allocated, one of them being given thirty, another forty, still another, one or two hundred, and besides the rank of the Christian there was also to be considered in what favor he stood with the tyrant they called Governor. The pretext was that these allocated Indians were to be instructed in the articles of the Christian Faith. As if those Christians who were as a rule foolish and cruel and greedy and vicious could be caretakers of souls! And the care they took was to send the men to the mines to dig for gold, which is intolerable labor, and to send the women into the fields of the big ranches to hoe and till the land, work suitable for strong men. Nor to either the men or the women did they give any food except herbs and legumes, things of little substance. The milk in the breasts of the women with infants dried up and thus in a short while the infants perished. And since men and women were separated, there could be no marital relations. And the men died in the mines and the women died on the ranches from the same causes, exhaustion and hunger. And thus was depopulated that island which had been densely populated.

READING AND DISCUSSION QUESTIONS

1. According to Las Casas, what motivated the Spaniards to settle the West Indies? What did they hope to gain?

2. Why did the West Indies experience a rapid depopulation when the Europeans arrived? According to Las Casas, how was this depopulation avoidable?

3. How does Las Casas suggest that the Christian mission to the New World had failed?

DOCUMENT 16-5

BERNAL DÍAZ DEL CASTILLO
From The True History of the Conquest of New Spain
1568

Initial Spanish occupation of the New World focused on exploiting native labor in the Caribbean. When the natives began to die off in large numbers because of disease and harsh treatment, some Spanish explorers (known as Conquistadors*) sought the conquest of new lands. One, Hernando Cortés, left his settlement at Cuba and landed in Central America in 1518. By 1519, he had collected a number of native tribes as allies and marched on the largest city in Mexico, Tenochtitlán, taking control of the entire area by 1521. This expedition is described by Bernal Díaz del Castillo, an eyewitness*

Bernal Díaz del Castillo, *The True History of the Conquest of New Spain*, trans. Alfred Percival Maudslay (London: Bedford Press, 1908), 257–263.

to the invasion. He wrote fifty years after participating in the conquest and named his work The True History *to distinguish it from earlier accounts that were not written by eyewitnesses.*

As Xicotenga was bad tempered and obstinate and proud, he decided to send forty Indians with food, poultry, bread and fruit and four miserable looking old Indian women, and much copal and many parrots' feathers. From their appearance we thought that the Indians who brought this present came with peaceful intentions, and when they reached our camp they fumigated Cortés with incense without doing him reverence, as was usually their custom. They said: "The Captain Xicotenga sends you all this so that you can eat. If you are savage Teules,[12] as the Cempoalans[13] say you are, and if you wish for a sacrifice, take these four women and sacrifice them and you can eat their flesh and hearts, but as we do not know your manner of doing it, we have not sacrificed them now before you; but if you are men, eat the poultry and the bread and fruit, and if you are tame Teules we have brought you copal (which I have already said is a sort of incense) and parrots' feathers; make your sacrifice with that."

Cortés answered through our interpreters that he had already sent to them to say that he desired peace and had not come to make war, but had come to entreat them and make clear to them on behalf of our Lord Jesus Christ, whom we believe in and worship, and of the Emperor Don Carlos, whose vassals we are, that they should not kill or sacrifice anyone as was their custom to do. That we were all men of bone and flesh just as they were, and not Teules but Christians, and that it was not our custom to kill anyone; that had we wished to kill people, many opportunities of perpetrating cruelties had occurred during the frequent attacks they had made on us, both by day and night. That for the food they had brought he gave them thanks, and that they were not to be as foolish as they had been, but should now make peace.

It seems that these Indians whom Xicotenga had sent with the food were spies sent to examine our huts and ranchos, and horses and artillery and [to report] how many of us there were in each hut, our comings and goings, and everything else that could be seen in the camp. They

---

[12] **Teules**: A series of divinities from central America. Occasionally they are considered wicked. Later, "Teules" virtually became a synonym for the Spanish.

[13] **Cempoalans**: A tribe in central America.

remained there that day and the following night, and some of them went with messages to Xicotenga and others arrived. Our friends whom we had brought with us from Cempoala looked on and bethought them that it was not a customary thing for our enemies to stay in the camp day and night without any purpose, and it was clear to them that they were spies, and they were the more suspicious of them in that when we went on the expedition to the little town of Tzumpantzingo, two old men of that town had told the Cempoalans that Xicotenga was all ready with a large number of warriors to attack our camp by night, in such a way that their approach would not be detected, and the Cempoalans at that time took it for a joke or bravado, and not believing it they had said nothing to Cortés; but Doña Marina[14] heard of it at once and she repeated it to Cortés.

So as to learn the truth, Cortés had two of the most honest looking of the Tlaxcalans taken apart from the others, and they confessed that they were spies; then two others were taken and they also confessed that they were spies from Xicotenga and the reason why they had come. Cortés ordered them to be released, and we took two more of them and they confessed that they were neither more nor less than spies, but added that their Captain Xicotenga was awaiting their report to attack us that night with all his companies. When Cortés heard this he let it be known throughout the camp that we were to keep on the alert, believing that they would attack as had been arranged. Then he had seventeen of those spies captured and cut off the hands of some and the thumbs of others and sent them to the Captain Xicotenga to tell him that he had had them thus punished for daring to come in such a way, and to tell him that he might come when he chose by day or by night, for we should await him here two days, and that if he did not come within those two days that we would go and look for him in his camp, and that we would already have gone to attack them and kill them, were it not for the liking we had for them, and that now they should quit their foolishness and make peace.

They say that it was at the very moment that those Indians set out with their hands and thumbs cut off, that Xicotenga wished to set out from his camp with all his forces to attack us by night as had been arranged; but when he saw his spies returning in this manner he wondered greatly and asked the reason of it, and they told him all that had happened, and from this time forward he lost his courage and pride, and in addition to this one

---

[14] **Doña Marina**: A native woman who learned Spanish. She served as a translator for Cortés and became his lover, giving birth to a son.

of his commanders with whom he had wrangles and disagreements during the battles which had been fought, had left the camp with all his men.

Let us get on with our story. . . .

While we were in camp not knowing that they would come in peace, as we had so greatly desired, and were busy polishing our arms and making arrows, each one of us doing what was necessary to prepare for battle, at that moment one of our scouts came hurrying in to say that many Indian men and women with loads were coming along the high road from Tlaxcala, and without leaving the road were making for our camp . . . Cortés and all of us were delighted at this news, for we believed that it meant peace, as in fact it did, and Cortés ordered us to make no display of alarm and not to show any concern, but to stay hidden in our huts. Then, from out of all those people who came bearing loads, the four chieftains advanced who were charged to treat for peace, according to the instructions given by the old caciques.[15] Making signs of peace by bowing the head, they came straight to the hut where Cortés was lodging and placed one hand on the ground and kissed the earth and three times made obeisance and burnt copal, and said that all the Caciques of Tlaxcala and their allies and vassals, friends and confederates, were come to place themselves under the friendship and peace of Cortés and of his brethren the Teules who accompanied him. They asked his pardon for not having met us peacefully, and for the war which they had waged on us, for they had believed and held for certain that we were friends of Montezuma and his Mexicans, who have been their mortal enemies from times long past, for they saw that many of his vassals who paid him tribute had come in our company, and they believed that they were endeavouring to gain an entry into their country by guile and treachery, as was their custom to do, so as to rob them of their women and children; and this was the reason why they did not believe the messengers whom we had sent to them. In addition to this they said that the Indians who had first gone forth to make war on us as we entered their country had done it without their orders or advice, but by that of the Chuntales Estomies [barbarous Otomís], who were wild people and very stupid, and that when they saw that we were so few in number, they thought to capture us and carry us off as prisoners to their lords and gain thanks for so doing; that now they came to beg pardon for their audacity, and had brought us food, and that every day they would bring more and

---

[15] **caciques**: Leaders.

trusted that we would receive it with the friendly feeling with which it was sent; that within two days the captain Xicotenga would come with other Caciques and give a further account of the sincere wish of all Tlaxcala to enjoy our friendship.

As soon as they had finished their discourse they bowed their heads and placed their hands on the ground and kissed the earth. Then Cortés spoke to them through our interpreters very seriously, pretending he was angry, and said that there were reasons why we should not listen to them and should reject their friendship, for as soon as we had entered their country we sent to them offering peace and had told them that we wished to assist them against their enemies, the Mexicans, and they would not believe it and wished to kill our ambassadors; and not content with that, they had attacked us three times both by day and by night, and had spied on us and held us under observation; and in the attacks which they made on us we might have killed many of their vassals, but he would not, and he grieved for those who were killed; but it was their own fault and he had made up his mind to go to the place where the old chiefs were living and to attack them; but as they had now sought peace in the name of that province, he would receive them in the name of our lord the King and thank them for the food they had brought. He told them to go at once to their chieftains and tell them to come or send to treat for peace with fuller powers, and that if they did not come we would go to their town and attack them.

He ordered them to be given some blue beads to be handed to their Caciques as a sign of peace, and he warned them that when they came to our camp it should be by day and not by night, lest we should kill them.

Then those four messengers departed, and left in some Indian houses a little apart from our camp, the Indian women whom they had brought to make bread, some poultry, and all the necessaries for service, and twenty Indians to bring wood and water. From now on they brought us plenty to eat, and when we saw this and believed that peace was a reality, we gave great thanks to God for it. It had come in the nick of time, for we were already lean and worn out and discontented with the war, not knowing or being able to forecast what would be the end of it. . . .

I will leave off here and will go on to tell what took place later, about some messengers sent by the great Montezuma.

READING AND DISCUSSION QUESTIONS

1. How does this source describe the various Mexican tribes? What does Castillo's description of these people reveal about how Europeans viewed the natives of Central America?

2. How are the Europeans, especially Cortés, able to converse with the Mexica?

3. Describe the meeting between Cortés and the native tribes. What kind of agreement is struck between them? How do the natives interact with Cortés?

DOCUMENT 16-6

From The Florentine Codex

ca. 1577–1580

A member of the Franciscan order, the Spaniard Bernardino de Sahagún (1499–1590) was one of the earliest missionaries to arrive in Mexico. Although committed to converting the native population of Mexico to Christianity, Sahagún learned the Aztec language of Nahuatl and helped compile an extensive study of Aztec culture and religious beliefs. This work raised concern among Sahagún's superiors for its sympathetic portrayal of the Aztec people. For this reason, his works were lost for more than 200 years until their eventual discovery in a library in Florence. The manuscript contains writing in Nahuatl, occasionally with a Spanish translation, in addition to numerous illustrations made by native artists. Even though the text has been influenced by European ideas — for example, the Mexica gods are called devils — it is one of the few sources written in a native language about the conquest. The illustrations here show the beginning of the conflict between the Spanish and the Mexica, when King Montezuma was captured and put in chains. At the lower left, another Mexica leader delivers an address prior to the scenes of fighting on the right.

Arthur J. O. Anderson and Charles E. Dibble, eds. and trans., *Book 12 — The Conquest of Mexico, Part XIII* (Santa Fe, N.M.: School of American Research and University of Utah, 1975), images 73–79.

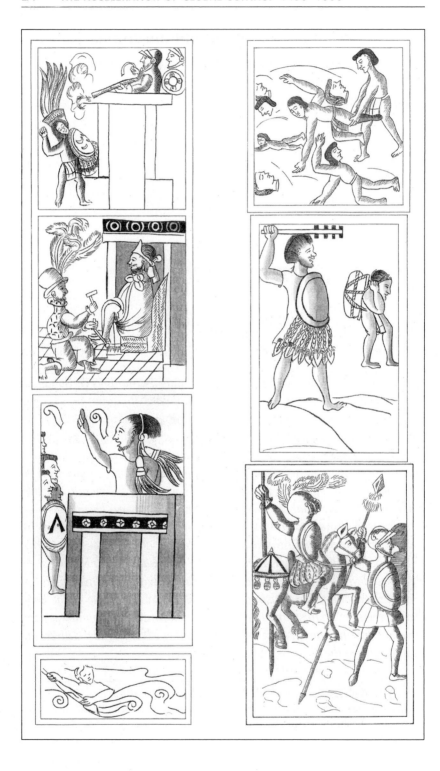

READING AND DISCUSSION QUESTIONS

1. How are the natives and the Spanish portrayed in this image, and does it suggest any bias? Explain your answer.

2. Judging from the drawings, why might the Spanish have had a military advantage over the natives?

DOCUMENT 16-7

MATTEO RICCI

From China in the Sixteenth Century

ca. 1607

Matteo Ricci (1552–1610) was an Italian Jesuit missionary to China. An exceptional scientist and mathematician, Ricci impressed China's scholars and eventually received an invitation from the emperor to visit the palace in Beijing. Ricci was an admirer of Chinese culture who learned the language and studied Confucian texts as part of his missionary work. He hoped to convert the Chinese by demonstrating the ultimate compatibility between the Christian and Chinese traditions. This reading comes from the journal that he wrote in for twenty-seven years. Published after his death, Ricci's journals were a major source of information about China for Europeans.

During 1606 and the year following, the progress of Christianity in Nancian[16] was in no wise retarded. . . . The number of neophytes [converts] increased by more than two hundred, all of whom manifested an extraordinary piety in their religious devotions. As a result, the reputation of the Christian religion became known throughout the length and breadth of this metropolitan city. . . .

From Matthew Ricci, *China in the Sixteenth Century*, trans. Louis J. Gallagher, S.J., copyright 1942, 1953, and renewed 1970 by Louis J. Gallagher, S.J. (New York: Random House, 1970).

[16] **Nancian:** Nanchang; a city in southeastern China founded during the Han Dynasty.

Through the efforts of Father Emanuele Dias another and a larger house was purchased, in August of 1607, at a price of a thousand gold pieces. This change was necessary, because the house he had was too small for his needs and was situated in a flood area. Just as the community was about to change from one house to the other, a sudden uprising broke out against them. . . .

At the beginning of each month, the Magistrates hold a public assembly . . . in the temple of their great Philosopher [Confucius]. When the rites of the new-moon were completed in the temple, and these are civil rather than religious rites,[17] one of those present took advantage of the occasion to speak on behalf of the others, and to address the highest Magistrate present. . . . "We wish to warn you," he said, "that there are certain foreign priests in this royal city, who are preaching a law, hitherto unheard of in this kingdom, and who are holding large gatherings of people in their house." Having said this, he referred them to their local Magistrate, . . . and he in turn ordered the plaintiffs to present their case in writing, assuring them that he would support it with all his authority, in an effort to have the foreign priests expelled. The complaint was written out that same day and signed with twenty-seven signatures. . . . The content of the document was somewhat as follows.

Matthew Ricci, Giovanni Soerio, Emanuele Dias, and certain other foreigners from western kingdoms, men who are guilty of high treason against the throne, are scattered amongst us, in five different provinces. They are continually communicating with each other and are here and there practicing brigandage on the rivers, collecting money, and then distributing it to the people, in order to curry favor with the multitudes. They are frequently visited by the Magistrates, by the high nobility and by the Military Prefects, with whom they have entered into a secret pact, binding unto death.

These men teach that we should pay no respect to the images of our ancestors, a doctrine which is destined to extinguish the love of future generations for their forebears. Some of them break up the idols, leaving the temples empty and the gods to be pitied, without any patronage. In the beginning they lived in small houses, but by this time they have bought up large and magnificent residences. The doctrine they teach is something infernal. It attracts the ignorant into its fraudulent meshes, and great crowds of this class are continually assembled at their houses. Their doctrine gets beyond the city walls and spreads itself through the neighboring towns and

---

[17] **civil rather than religious rites:** The Jesuits maintained that Confucian ceremonies were purely civil rather than religious in nature.

villages and into the open country, and the people become so wrapt up in its falsity, that students are not following their course, laborers are neglecting their work, farmers are not cultivating their acres, and even the women have no interest in their housework. The whole city has become disturbed, and, whereas in the beginning there were only a hundred or so professing their faith, now there are more than twenty thousand. These priests distribute pictures of some Tartar or Saracen,[18] who they say is God, who came down from Heaven to redeem and to instruct all of humanity, and who alone, according to their doctrine, can give wealth and happiness; a doctrine by which the simple people are very easily deceived. These men are an abomination on the face of the Earth, and there is just ground for fear that once they have erected their own temples, they will start a rebellion. . . . Wherefore, moved by their interest in the maintenance of the public good, in the conservation of the realm, and in the preservation, whole and entire, of their ancient laws, the petitioners are presenting this complaint and demanding, in the name of the entire province, that a rescript of it be forwarded to the King, asking that these foreigners be sentenced to death, or banished from the realm, to some deserted island in the sea. . . .

Each of the Magistrates to whom the indictment was presented asserted that the spread of Christianity should be prohibited, and that the foreign priests should be expelled from the city, if the Mayor saw fit, after hearing the case, and notifying the foreigners. . . . But the Fathers [Jesuit priests], themselves, were not too greatly disturbed, placing their confidence in Divine Providence, which had always been present to assist them on other such dangerous occasions.

[Father Emanuele is summoned before the Chief Justice.]

Father Emanuele, in his own defense, . . . gave a brief outline of the Christian doctrine. Then he showed that according to the divine law, the first to be honored, after God, were a man's parents. But the judge had no mind to hear or to accept any of this and he made it known that he thought it was all false. After that repulse, with things going from bad to worse, it looked as if they were on the verge of desperation, so much so, indeed, that they increased their prayers, their sacrifices, and their bodily penances, in petition for a favorable solution of their difficulty. Their adversaries appeared to be triumphantly victorious. They were already wrangling about the division of the furniture of the Mission residences, and to make results doubly certain, they stirred up the flames anew with added accusations and indictments. . . .

---

[18] **some Tartar or Saracen**: A reference to Jesus Christ.

The Mayor, who was somewhat friendly with the Fathers, realizing that there was much in the accusation that was patently false, asked the Magistrate Director of the Schools,[19] if he knew whether or not this man Emanuele was a companion of Matthew Ricci, who was so highly respected at the royal court, and who was granted a subsidy from the royal treasury, because of the gifts he had presented to the King. Did he realize that the Fathers had lived in Nankin [Nanjing] for twelve years, and that no true complaint had ever been entered against them for having violated the laws. Then he asked him if he had really given full consideration as to what was to be proven in the present indictment. To this the Director of the Schools replied that he wished the Mayor to make a detailed investigation of the case and then to confer with him. The Chief Justice then ordered the same thing to be done. Fortunately, it was this same Justice who was in charge of city affairs when Father Ricci first arrived in Nancian. It was he who first gave the Fathers permission, with the authority of the Viceroy, to open a house there. . . .

After the Mayor had examined the charges of the plaintiffs and the reply of the defendants, he subjected the quasi-literati[20] to an examination in open court, and taking the Fathers under his patronage, he took it upon himself to refute the calumnies of their accusers. He said he was fully convinced that these strangers were honest men, and that he knew that there were only two of them in their local residence and not twenty, as had been asserted. To this they replied that the Chinese were becoming their disciples. To which the Justice in turn replied: "What of it? Why should we be afraid of our own people? Perhaps you are unaware of the fact that Matthew Ricci's company is cultivated by everyone in Pekin [Beijing], and that he is being subsidized by the royal treasury. How dare the Magistrates who are living outside of the royal city expel men who have permission to live at the royal court? These men here have lived peacefully in Nankin for twelve years. I command," he added, "that they buy no more large houses, and that the people are not to follow their law." . . .

A few days later, the court decision was pronounced and written out . . . and was then posted at the city gates as a public edict. The following is a summary of their declaration. Having examined the cause of

---

[19] **Magistrate Director of the Schools**: The local Confucian academy. In this case, the director of the local academy was opposed to the Jesuit presence.

[20] **quasi-literati**: The local scholars who criticized Ricci and the Jesuits. Most of these scholars had passed only the first of the three Confucian civil service exams.

Father Emanuele and his companions, it was found that these men had come here from the West because they had heard so much about the fame of the great Chinese Empire, and that they had already been living in the realm for some years, without any display of ill-will. Father Emanuele should be permitted to practice his own religion, but it was not considered to be the right thing for the common people, who are attracted by novelties, to adore the God of Heaven. For them to go over to the religion of foreigners would indeed be most unbecoming. . . . It would therefore seem to be . . . [in] . . . the best interests of the Kingdom, to . . . [warn] . . . everyone in a public edict not to abandon the sacrifices of their ancient religion by accepting the cult of foreigners. Such a movement might, indeed, result in calling together certain gatherings, detrimental to the public welfare, and harmful also to the foreigner, himself. Wherefore, the Governor of this district, by order of the high Magistrates, admonishes the said Father Emanuele to refrain from perverting the people, by inducing them to accept a foreign religion. The man who sold him the larger house is to restore his money and Emanuele is to buy a smaller place, sufficient for his needs, and to live there peaceably, as he has done, up to the present. Emanuele, himself, has agreed to these terms and the Military Prefects of the district have been ordered to make a search of the houses there and to confiscate the pictures of the God they speak of, wherever they find them. It is not permitted for any of the native people to go over to the religion of the foreigners, nor is it permitted to gather together for prayer meetings. Whoever does contrary to these prescriptions will be severely punished, and if the Military Prefects are remiss in enforcing them, they will be held to be guilty of the same crimes. To his part of the edict, the Director of the Schools added, that the common people were forbidden to accept the law of the foreigners, and that a sign should be posted above the door of the Father's residence, notifying the public that these men were forbidden to have frequent contact with the people.

The Fathers were not too disturbed by this pronouncement, because they were afraid that it was going to be much worse. In fact, everyone thought it was rather favorable, and that the injunction launched against the spread of the faith was a perfunctory order to make it appear that the literati were not wholly overlooked, since the Fathers were not banished from the city, as the literati had demanded. Moreover it was not considered a grave misdemeanor for the Chinese to change their religion, and it was not customary to inflict a serious punishment on those violating such an order. The neophytes, themselves, proved this when they continued, as formerly, to attend Mass.

READING AND DISCUSSION QUESTIONS

1. What were the concerns of the officials in Nanchang regarding the Jesuit missionaries?

2. How did Father Emanuele try to convince the Chinese authorities that Christianity and the Jesuits did not pose a threat? What reasons did he give for the continued work of the missionaries?

3. Aside from their roles as missionaries, what other roles did the Jesuits play in China, as implied by this account?

COMPARATIVE QUESTIONS

1. Compare Zheng He's inscription and the Portuguese trade agreement. What do these sources suggest about the role that exploration played in strengthening the Spanish and Portuguese governments?

2. According to Las Casas and del Castillo, how did the Spaniards treat the native populations that they encountered? According to Zheng He's inscription, how did the Chinese treat local populations?

3. Compare Zheng He's inscription and the journals of Matteo Ricci. In what ways did the explorers and missionaries of this time feel that their actions were divinely compelled? What proof did they provide of divine favor?

4. Taking all the documents into consideration, what motivated the explorers of both the Western and Eastern worlds? What impact did this exploration have on the areas that they visited?

CHAPTER 17

European Power and Expansion

1500–1750

The seventeenth century was a time of deep crisis for Europe. The commercial and agricultural sectors suffered from prolonged economic stagnation, and many nations found themselves locked in expensive and devastating internal and external wars. In an effort to cope with these difficulties, European states instituted increased government growth and extended control over their populations through new forms of taxation, the military, and the state bureaucracy. The following documents reveal the different ways in which European governments engaged with the challenges of the seventeenth century. In countries like England, a system of constitutionalism envisioned political power as a careful balance of many forces. In France and eastern European states, the doctrine of absolutism stressed the divine and total power of the monarch. Despite their differences, both systems represented careful attempts to establish centralized states that claimed sovereignty over their territories and peoples.

VIEWPOINTS

Thoughts on Government

JACQUES-BENIGNE BOSSUET

On Divine Right

ca. 1675–1680

French absolutism developed in the seventeenth century as a response to a number of crises, including the French Wars of Religion (ca. 1562–1598) and a civil war known as the Fronde (1648–1653). A bishop in the French Catholic church and tutor to the son of Louis XIV, Jacques-Benigne Bossuet (1627–1704) was an important architect of French absolutism. Drawing on biblical sources, Bossuet argued in his treatises that monarchs' authority came directly from God. This concept of the divine right of kings implied that any challenge to royal authority was tantamount to sacrilege.

We have already seen that all power is of God. The ruler, adds St. Paul, "is the minister of God to thee for good. But if thou do that which is evil, be afraid; for he beareth not the sword in vain: for he is the minister of God, a revenger to execute wrath upon him that doeth evil" [Rom. 13:1–7]. Rulers then act as the ministers of God and as his lieutenants on earth. It is through them that God exercises his empire. Think ye "to withstand the kingdom of the Lord in the hand of the sons of David" [2 Chron. 13:8]? Consequently, as we have seen, the royal throne is not the throne of a man, but the throne of God himself. . . .

Moreover, that no one may assume that the Israelites were peculiar in having kings over them who were established by God, note what is said in Ecclesiasticus: "God has given to every people its ruler, and Israel is manifestly reserved to him" [Eccles. 17:14–15]. He therefore governs all

J. H. Robinson, ed., *Readings in European History*, 2 vols. (Boston: Ginn, 1906), 2:273–277.

peoples and gives them their kings, although he governed Israel in a more intimate and obvious manner.

It appears from all this that the person of the king is sacred, and that to attack him in any way is sacrilege. God has the kings anointed by his prophets with the holy unction in like manner as he has bishops and altars anointed. But even without the external application in thus being anointed, they are by their very office the representatives of the divine majesty deputed by Providence for the execution of his purposes. . . . Kings should be guarded as holy things, and whosoever neglects to protect them is worthy of death. . . .

But kings, although their power comes from on high, as has been said, should not regard themselves as masters of that power to use it at their pleasure; . . . they must employ it with fear and self-restraint, as a thing coming from God and of which God will demand an account. "Hear, O kings, and take heed, understand, judges of the earth, lend your ears, ye who hold the peoples under your sway, and delight to see the multitude that surround you. It is God who gives you the power. Your strength comes from the Most High, who will question your works and penetrate the depths of your thoughts, for, being ministers of his kingdom, ye have not given righteous judgments nor have ye walked according to his will. He will straightway appear to you in a terrible manner, for to those who command is the heaviest punishment reserved. The humble and the weak shall receive mercy, but the mighty shall be mightily tormented. For God fears not the power of any one, because he made both great and small and he has care for both" [Ws 6:2]. . . .

Kings should tremble then as they use the power God has granted them; and let them think how horrible is the sacrilege if they use for evil a power which comes from God. We behold kings seated upon the throne of the Lord, bearing in their hand the sword which God himself has given them. What profanation, what arrogance, for the unjust king to sit on God's throne to render decrees contrary to his laws and to use the sword which God has put in his hand for deeds of violence and to slay his children! . . .

The royal power is absolute. With the aim of making this truth hateful and insufferable, many writers have tried to confound absolute government with arbitrary government. But no two things could be more unlike, as we shall show when we come to speak of justice.

The prince need render account of his acts to no one. "I counsel thee to keep the king's commandment, and that in regard of the oath of God. Be not hasty to go out of his sight: stand not on an evil thing for he doeth whatsoever pleaseth him. Where the word of a king is, there is power:

and who may say unto him, What doest thou? Whoso keepeth the commandment shall feel no evil thing" [Eccles. 8:2–5]. Without this absolute authority the king could neither do good nor repress evil. It is necessary that his power be such that no one can hope to escape him, and, finally, the only protection of individuals against the public authority should be their innocence. This conforms with the teaching of St. Paul: "Wilt thou then not be afraid of the power? do that which is good" [Rom. 13:3].

I do not call majesty that pomp which surrounds kings or that exterior magnificence which dazzles the vulgar. That is but the reflection of majesty and not majesty itself. Majesty is the image of the grandeur of God in the prince.

God is infinite, God is all. The prince, as prince, is not regarded as a private person: he is a public personage, all the state is in him; the will of all the people is included in his. As all perfection and all strength are united in God, so all the power of individuals is united in the person of the prince. What grandeur that a single man should embody so much!

The power of God makes itself felt in a moment from one extremity of the earth to another. Royal power works at the same time throughout all the realm. It holds all the realm in position, as God holds the earth. Should God withdraw his hand, the earth would fall to pieces; should the king's authority cease in the realm, all would be in confusion.

Look at the prince in his cabinet. Thence go out the orders which cause the magistrates and the captains, the citizens and the soldiers, the provinces and the armies on land and on sea, to work in concert. He is the image of God, who, seated on his throne high in the heavens, makes all nature move. . . .

Finally, let us put together the things so great and so august which we have said about royal authority. Behold an immense people united in a single person; behold this holy power, paternal and absolute; behold the secret cause which governs the whole body of the state, contained in a single head: you see the image of God in the king, and you have the idea of royal majesty. God is holiness itself, goodness itself, and power itself. In these things lies the majesty of God. In the image of these things lies the majesty of the prince.

So great is this majesty that it cannot reside in the prince as in its source; it is borrowed from God, who gives it to him for the good of the people, for whom it is good to be checked by a superior force. Something of divinity itself is attached to princes and inspires fear in the people. The king should not forget this. "I have said," — it is God who speaks, — "I have said, Ye are gods; and all of you are children of the Most High. But ye shall die like men, and fall like one of the princes" [Ps. 82:6–7]. "I have said, Ye are gods"; that is to say, you have in your authority, and you bear on your forehead, a divine imprint. "You are the children of the Most High"; it is he who has established your power for the good of mankind. But, O gods of flesh and blood, gods of clay and dust, "ye shall die like men, and fall like princes." Grandeur separates men for a little time, but a common fall makes them all equal at the end.

O kings, exercise your power then boldly, for it is divine and salutary for human kind, but exercise it with humility. You are endowed with it from without. At bottom it leaves you feeble, it leaves you mortal, it leaves you sinners, and charges you before God with a very heavy account.

READING AND DISCUSSION QUESTIONS

1. According to Bossuet, what is the nature of monarchical authority? What are its sources and purposes?

2. Why must a prince wield his absolute power carefully?

3. To whom does the author seem to be addressing this treatise? What gives you that impression?

DOCUMENT 17-2

THOMAS HOBBES

From Leviathan: *Of the Natural Condition of Mankind as Concerning Their Felicity and Misery*

1651

Thomas Hobbes (1588–1679) was a major figure in Western political theory. Armed with a university education and years of study in Europe, he began to publish on natural law and social theory in the late 1630s, including a 1640 pamphlet that supported absolutist rule. He moved from England to Paris

---

Thomas Hobbes, *Leviathan* (England: Andrew Crooke, 1651), www.gutenberg.org/files/3207/3207-h/3207-h.htm.

in 1640 to escape political persecution by an anti-absolutist Parliament.
He remained in Paris until 1651, and it was there that he wrote Leviathan,
named for a biblical sea monster. In these excerpts, Hobbes explains both
the artificial nature of the state and its necessity, reflecting a fundamentally
pessimistic view of human nature.

Nature (the art whereby God hath made and governs the world) is by the
art of man, as in many other things, so in this also imitated, that it can
make an artificial animal. For seeing life is but a motion of limbs, the
beginning whereof is in some principal part within, why may we not say
that all automata (engines that move themselves by springs and wheels as
doth a watch) have an artificial life? For what is the heart, but a spring;
and the nerves, but so many strings; and the joints, but so many wheels,
giving motion to the whole body, such as was intended by the Artificer? Art
goes yet further, imitating that rational and most excellent work of Nature,
man. For by art is created that great LEVIATHAN called a COMMON-
WEALTH, or STATE (in Latin, CIVITAS), which is but an artificial man,
though of greater stature and strength than the natural, for whose protection and defence it was intended; and in which the sovereignty is an artificial soul, as giving life and motion to the whole body; the magistrates and
other officers of judicature and execution, artificial joints; reward and punishment (by which fastened to the seat of the sovereignty, every joint and
member is moved to perform his duty) are the nerves, that do the same
in the body natural; the wealth and riches of all the particular members
are the strength; salus populi (the people's safety) its business; counsellors,
by whom all things needful for it to know are suggested unto it, are the
memory; equity and laws, an artificial reason and will; concord, health;
sedition, sickness; and civil war, death. Lastly, the pacts and covenants, by
which the parts of this body politic were at first made, set together, and
united, resemble that fiat, or the Let us make man, pronounced by God
in the Creation. . . .

Nature hath made men so equal in the faculties of body and mind as
that, though there be found one man sometimes manifestly stronger in
body or of quicker mind than another, yet when all is reckoned together
the difference between man and man is not so considerable as that one
man can thereupon claim to himself any benefit to which another may
not pretend as well as he. For as to the strength of body, the weakest has
strength enough to kill the strongest, either by secret machination or by
confederacy with others that are in the same danger with himself.

And as to the faculties of the mind, setting aside the arts grounded upon words, and especially that skill of proceeding upon general and infallible rules, called science, which very few have and but in few things, as being not a native faculty born with us, nor attained, as prudence, while we look after somewhat else, I find yet a greater equality amongst men than that of strength. For prudence is but experience, which equal time equally bestows on all men in those things they equally apply themselves unto. That which may perhaps make such equality incredible is but a vain conceit of one's own wisdom, which almost all men think they have in a greater degree than the vulgar; that is, than all men but themselves, and a few others, whom by fame, or for concurring with themselves, they approve. For such is the nature of men that howsoever they may acknowledge many others to be more witty, or more eloquent or more learned, yet they will hardly believe there be many so wise as themselves; for they see their own wit at hand, and other men's at a distance. But this proveth rather that men are in that point equal, than unequal. For there is not ordinarily a greater sign of the equal distribution of anything than that every man is contented with his share.

. . . From this equality of ability ariseth equality of hope in the attaining of our ends. And therefore if any two men desire the same thing, which nevertheless they cannot both enjoy, they become enemies; and in the way to their end (which is principally their own conservation, and sometimes their delectation only) endeavour to destroy or subdue one another. And from hence it comes to pass that where an invader hath no more to fear than another man's single power, if one plant, sow, build, or possess a convenient seat, others may probably be expected to come prepared with forces united to dispossess and deprive him, not only of the fruit of his labour, but also of his life or liberty. And the invader again is in the like danger of another.

. . . And from this diffidence of one another, there is no way for any man to secure himself so reasonable as anticipation; that is, by force, or wiles, to master the persons of all men he can so long till he see no other power great enough to endanger him: and this is no more than his own conservation requireth, and is generally allowed. Also, because there be some that, taking pleasure in contemplating their own power in the acts of conquest, which they pursue farther than their security requires, if others, that otherwise would be glad to be at ease within modest bounds, should not by invasion increase their power, they would not be able, long time, by standing only on their defence, to subsist. And by consequence, such augmentation of dominion over men being necessary to a man's conservation, it ought to be allowed him.

Again, men have no pleasure (but on the contrary a great deal of grief) in keeping company where there is no power able to overawe them all. For every man looketh that his companion should value him at the same rate he sets upon himself, and upon all signs of contempt or undervaluing naturally endeavours, as far as he dares (which amongst them that have no common power to keep them in quiet is far enough to make them destroy each other), to extort a greater value from his contemners, by damage; and from others, by the example.

So that in the nature of man, we find three principal causes of quarrel. First, competition; secondly, diffidence; thirdly, glory.

The first maketh men invade for gain; the second, for safety; and the third, for reputation. The first use violence, to make themselves masters of other men's persons, wives, children, and cattle; the second, to defend them; the third, for trifles, as a word, a smile, a different opinion, and any other sign of undervalue, either direct in their persons or by reflection in their kindred, their friends, their nation, their profession, or their name.

... Hereby it is manifest that during the time men live without a common power to keep them all in awe, they are in that condition which is called war; and such a war as is of every man against every man. For war consisteth not in battle only, or the act of fighting, but in a tract of time, wherein the will to contend by battle is sufficiently known: and therefore the notion of time is to be considered in the nature of war, as it is in the nature of weather. For as the nature of foul weather lieth not in a shower or two of rain, but in an inclination thereto of many days together: so the nature of war consisteth not in actual fighting, but in the known disposition thereto during all the time there is no assurance to the contrary. All other time is peace.

... Whatsoever therefore is consequent to a time of war, where every man is enemy to every man, the same is consequent to the time wherein men live without other security than what their own strength and their own invention shall furnish them withal. In such condition there is no place for industry, because the fruit thereof is uncertain: and consequently no culture of the earth; no navigation, nor use of the commodities that may be imported by sea; no commodious building; no instruments of moving and removing such things as require much force; no knowledge of the face of the earth; no account of time; no arts; no letters; no society; and which is worst of all, continual fear, and danger of violent death; and the life of man, solitary, poor, nasty, brutish, and short.

It may seem strange to some man that has not well weighed these things that Nature should thus dissociate and render men apt to invade and destroy one another: and he may therefore, not trusting to this inference, made from the passions, desire perhaps to have the same confirmed by experience. Let him therefore consider with himself: when taking a journey, he arms himself and seeks to go well accompanied; when going to sleep, he locks his doors; when even in his house he locks his chests; and this when he knows there be laws and public officers, armed, to revenge all injuries shall be done him; what opinion he has of his fellow subjects, when he rides armed; of his fellow citizens, when he locks his doors; and of his children, and servants, when he locks his chests. Does he not there as much accuse mankind by his actions as I do by my words? But neither of us accuse man's nature in it. The desires, and other passions of man, are in themselves no sin. No more are the actions that proceed from those passions till they know a law that forbids them; which till laws be made they cannot know, nor can any law be made till they have agreed upon the person that shall make it.

It may peradventure be thought there was never such a time nor condition of war as this; and I believe it was never generally so, over all the world: but there are many places where they live so now. For the savage people in many places of America, except the government of small families, the concord whereof dependeth on natural lust, have no government at all, and live at this day in that brutish manner, as I said before. Howsoever, it may be perceived what manner of life there would be, where there were no common power to fear, by the manner of life which men that have formerly lived under a peaceful government use to degenerate into in a civil war. . . .

To this war of every man against every man, this also is consequent; that nothing can be unjust. The notions of right and wrong, justice and injustice, have there no place. Where there is no common power, there is no law; where no law, no injustice. Force and fraud are in war the two cardinal virtues. Justice and injustice are none of the faculties neither of the body nor mind. If they were, they might be in a man that were alone in the world, as well as his senses and passions. They are qualities that relate to men in society, not in solitude. It is consequent also to the same condition that there be no propriety, no dominion, no mine and thine distinct; but only that to be every man's that he can get, and for so long as he can keep it. And thus much for the ill condition which man by mere nature is actually placed in; though with a possibility to come out of it, consisting partly in the passions, partly in his reason.

READING AND DISCUSSION QUESTIONS

1. What is the significance of Hobbes's invocation of God and the monster Leviathan to support his argument?

2. What, according to Hobbes, is the "natural state" of humanity? What are the controls on this "natural state," and why are these important for a theory of government?

3. What sense of moral imperatives does Hobbes convey? Is there a "greater good" that he seeks? If so, what is it? If not, what is the significance of its absence?

4. How might Hobbes's excerpt be seen to endorse constitutionalism as well as absolutism?

DOCUMENT 17-3

JOHN LOCKE

From Two Treatises of Government: *Of the Ends of Political Society and Government*

1690

John Locke (1632–1704) was a physician, philosopher, and teacher with ties to the pro-parliamentary faction of the English government. His writings on political theory provided an important foundation for the development of constitutionalism in England. Under suspicion of taking part in a plot to assassinate Charles II, he fled to Holland in 1683. His return to England coincided with the Glorious Revolution of 1688, and he claimed that his Two Treatises *endorsed the ascension of William III to the English throne. The excerpt here from his second treatise shows Locke's interest in developing a philosophy of government through the careful investigation of human nature.*

Sec. 123. If man in the state of nature be so free, as has been said; if he be absolute lord of his own person and possessions, equal to the greatest, and subject to no body, why will he part with his freedom? Why will he give up

John Locke, *Two Treatises of Government* (London: A. Millar et al., 1764).

this empire, and subject himself to the dominion and control of any other power? To which it is obvious to answer, that though in the state of nature he hath such a right, yet the enjoyment of it is very uncertain, and constantly exposed to the invasion of others: for all being kings as much as he, every man his equal, and the greater part no strict observers of equity and justice, the enjoyment of the property he has in this state is very unsafe, very unsecure. This makes him willing to quit a condition, which, however free, is full of fears and continual dangers: and it is not without reason, that he seeks out, and is willing to join in society with others, who are already united, or have a mind to unite, for the mutual preservation of their lives, liberties, and estates, which I call by the general name, property.

Sec. 124. The great and chief end, therefore, of men's uniting into commonwealths, and putting themselves under government, is the preservation of their property. To which in the state of nature there are many things wanting.

First, There wants an established, settled, known law, received and allowed by common consent to be the standard of right and wrong, and the common measure to decide all controversies between them: for though the law of nature be plain and intelligible to all rational creatures; yet men being biassed by their interest, as well as ignorant for want of study of it, are not apt to allow of it as a law binding to them in the application of it to their particular cases.

Sec. 125. Secondly, In the state of nature there wants a known and indifferent judge, with authority to determine all differences according to the established law: for every one in that state being both judge and executioner of the law of nature, men being partial to themselves, passion and revenge is very apt to carry them too far, and with too much heat, in their own cases; as well as negligence, and unconcernedness, to make them too remiss in other men's.

Sec. 126. Thirdly, In the state of nature there often wants power to back and support the sentence when right, and to give it due execution. They who by any injustice offended, will seldom fail, where they are able, by force to make good their injustice; such resistance many times makes the punishment dangerous, and frequently destructive, to those who attempt it.

Sec. 127. Thus mankind, notwithstanding all the privileges of the state of nature, being but in an ill condition, while they remain in it, are quickly driven into society. Hence it comes to pass, that we seldom find any number of men live any time together in this state. The inconveniencies that they are therein exposed to, by the irregular and uncertain exercise of the power every man has of punishing the transgressions of others, make them take sanctuary under the established laws of government, and therein seek the preservation of their property. It is this makes them so willingly give up every one his single power of punishing, to be exercised by such alone, as shall be appointed to it amongst them; and by such rules as the community, or those authorized by them to that purpose, shall agree on. And in this we have the original right and rise of both the legislative and executive power, as well as of the governments and societies themselves.

Sec. 128. For in the state of nature, to omit the liberty he has of innocent delights, a man has two powers.

The first is to do whatsoever he thinks fit for the preservation of himself, and others within the permission of the law of nature: by which law, common to them all, he and all the rest of mankind are one community, make up one society, distinct from all other creatures. And were it not for the corruption and viciousness of degenerate men, there would be no need of any other; no necessity that men should separate from this great and natural community, and by positive agreements combine into smaller and divided associations.

The other power a man has in the state of nature, is the power to punish the crimes committed against that law. Both these he gives up, when he joins in a private, if I may so call it, or particular politic society, and incorporates into any commonwealth, separate from the rest of mankind.

Sec. 129. The first power, viz. of doing whatsoever he thought for the preservation of himself, and the rest of mankind, he gives up to be regulated by laws made by the society, so far forth as the preservation of himself, and the rest of that society shall require; which laws of the society in many things confine the liberty he had by the law of nature.

Sec. 130. Secondly, The power of punishing he wholly gives up, and engages his natural force, (which he might before employ in the execution of the law of nature, by his own single authority, as he thought fit) to assist the executive power of the society, as the law thereof shall require: for being now in a new state, wherein he is to enjoy many conveniencies, from the labor, assistance, and society of others in the same community, as well as protection from its whole strength; he is to part also with as much of his natural liberty, in providing for himself, as the good, prosperity, and safety of the society shall require; which is not only necessary, but just, since the other members of the society do the like.

Sec. 131. But though men, when they enter into society, give up the equality, liberty, and executive power they had in the state of nature, into the hands of the society, to be so far disposed of by the legislative, as the good of the society shall require; yet it being only with an intention in every one the better to preserve himself, his liberty and property; (for no rational creature can be supposed to change his condition with an intention to be worse) the power of the society, or legislative constituted by them, can never be supposed to extend farther, than the common good; but is obliged to secure every one's property, by providing against those three defects above mentioned, that made the state of nature so unsafe and uneasy. And so whoever has the legislative or supreme power of any commonwealth, is bound to govern by established standing laws, promulgated and known to the people, and not by extemporary decrees; by indifferent and upright judges, who are to decide controversies by those laws; and to employ the force of the community at home, only in the execution of such laws, or abroad to prevent or redress foreign injuries, and secure the community from inroads and invasion. And all this to be directed to no other end, but the peace, safety, and public good of the people.

READING AND DISCUSSION QUESTIONS

1. According to Locke, what powers do individuals have in the state of nature? What are some of the inevitable difficulties that arise when living in the state of nature?

2. Once individuals agree to form a government, what powers does the government have? What are its primary obligations?

3. In what ways does the treatise challenge the absolutist tendencies of seventeenth-century English monarchs?

DUC DE SAINT-SIMON

From Memoirs of Louis XIV: On the Early Life of Louis XIV

ca. 1730–1755

The Duc de Saint-Simon (1675–1755) was born Louis de Rouvroy in Paris. His father was a former page of Louis XIII, and his noble status gave the young de Rouvroy the opportunity to enter court life at Versailles after a brief military career. Incredibly, Saint-Simon's careful notes and the often scathing picture they paint of court life escaped the attention of his fellow courtiers, and they remained unpublished until well after his death. The writings excerpted here give an intimate portrait of the personal qualities of Louis XIV and, by extension, of absolutist rule in seventeenth-century Europe.

I shall pass over the stormy period of Louis XIV's minority. At twenty-three years of age he entered the great world as King, under the most favourable auspices. His ministers were the most skilful in all Europe; his generals the best; his Court was filled with illustrious and clever men, formed during the troubles which had followed the death of Louis XIII.

Louis XIV was made for a brilliant Court. In the midst of other men, his figure, his courage, his grace, his beauty, his grand mien, even the tone of his voice and the majestic and natural charm of all his person, distinguished him till his death as the King Bee, and showed that if he had only been born a simple private gentlemen, he would equally have excelled in fetes, pleasures, and gallantry, and would have had the greatest success in love. The intrigues and adventures which early in life he had been engaged in — when the Comtesse de Soissons lodged at the Tuileries, as superintendent of the Queen's household, and was the centre figure of the Court group — had exercised an unfortunate influence upon him: he received those impressions with which he could never after successfully struggle. From this time, intellect, education, nobility of sentiment, and high principle, in others, became objects of suspicion to him, and soon

Duc de Saint-Simon, *The Memoirs of Louis XIV, His Court and the Regency,* trans. Bayle St. John, chap. 73, www.gutenberg.org/files/3875/3875-h/3875-h.htm #2HCH0073.

of hatred. The more he advanced in years the more this sentiment was confirmed in him. He wished to reign by himself. His jealousy on this point unceasingly became weakness. He reigned, indeed, in little things; the great he could never reach: even in the former, too, he was often governed. The superior ability of his early ministers and his early generals soon wearied him. He liked nobody to be in any way superior to him. Thus he chose his ministers, not for their knowledge, but for their ignorance; not for their capacity, but for their want of it. He liked to form them, as he said; liked to teach them even the most trifling things. It was the same with his generals. He took credit to himself for instructing them; wished it to be thought that from his cabinet he commanded and directed all his armies. Naturally fond of trifles, he unceasingly occupied himself with the most petty details of his troops, his household, his mansions; would even instruct his cooks, who received, like novices, lessons they had known by heart for years. This vanity, this unmeasured and unreasonable love of admiration, was his ruin. His ministers, his generals, his mistresses, his courtiers, soon perceived his weakness. They praised him with emulation and spoiled him. Praises, or to say truth, flattery, pleased him to such an extent, that the coarsest was well received, the vilest even better relished. It was the sole means by which you could approach him. Those whom he liked owed his affection for them to their untiring flatteries. This is what gave his ministers so much authority, and the opportunities they had for adulating him, of attributing everything to him, and of pretending to learn everything from him. Suppleness, meanness, an admiring, dependent, cringing manner — above all, an air of nothingness — were the sole means of pleasing him.

This poison spread. It spread, too, to an incredible extent, in a prince who, although of intellect beneath mediocrity, was not utterly without sense, and who had had some experience. Without voice or musical knowledge, he used to sing, in private, the passages of the opera prologues that were fullest of his praises.

He was drowned in vanity; and so deeply, that at his public suppers — all the Court present, musicians also — he would hum these self-same praises between his teeth, when the music they were set to was played!

And yet, it must be admitted, he might have done better. Though his intellect, as I have said, was beneath mediocrity, it was capable of being formed. He loved glory, was fond of order and regularity; was by disposition prudent, moderate, discreet, master of his movements and his tongue. Will it be believed? He was also by disposition good and just! God had sufficiently gifted him to enable him to be a good King; perhaps even a tolerably great King! All the evil came to him from elsewhere. His early education was so neglected that nobody dared approach his apartment. He has often been heard to speak of those times with bitterness, and even to relate that, one evening he was found in the basin of the Palais Royal garden fountain, into which he had fallen! He was scarcely taught how to read or write, and remained so ignorant, that the most familiar historical and other facts were utterly unknown to him! He fell, accordingly, and sometimes even in public, into the grossest absurdities.

READING AND DISCUSSION QUESTIONS

1. How does Saint-Simon's description of Louis XIV's personality relate to Louis's historical role as a model of absolutist rule?

2. How does Saint-Simon's own presence as a courtier of Louis XIV complicate his assessment of the king's intolerance?

3. Saint-Simon claims that Louis was by nature "good and just" and that evil "came to him from elsewhere." What do these claims imply about the nature of absolutist rule?

4. What is Saint-Simon's tone, and how do you interpret it?

DOCUMENT 17-5

CATHERINE II OF RUSSIA

Two Decrees

1762, 1765

Catherine II, or Catherine the Great (1729–1796), led the Russian empire following the deposition of her husband, Peter III, in 1762. Born Sophia Augusta Frederica in Prussian-controlled Pomerania (in present-day Poland), Catherine converted to the Russian Orthodox Church and married the Russian tsarevich, or heir apparent, Peter in 1745. In 1762, her husband the tsar was deposed in a coup d'état and assassinated eight days later. Taking the

A Source Book for Russian History from Early Times to 1917, 3 vols. (New Haven: Yale University Press, 1972), 2:449, 453.

throne in his stead, Catherine oversaw an impressive expansion of Russian territory and embraced Enlightenment ideals, but her harsh treatment of Russia's peasant population — evidenced here in two decrees — may reveal her dependence on the support of the Russian landowning nobility and the practical limits of absolutism.

DECREE ON PEASANT DISTURBANCES, JULY 3, 1762

Upon our accession to the imperial throne of all Russia, we learned, to our great displeasure, that the peasants of some landlords, seduced and deluded by false rumors spread by unscrupulous people, had departed from the obedience due to their landlords and had proceeded to commit many unruly and defiant acts. We are firmly convinced that such false rumors will presently die away by themselves; the deluded peasants will recognize that from thoughtlessness they have fallen into grievous crime and will forthwith repent, endeavoring thereafter to earn forgiveness through mute submission to their masters. Nevertheless, in order to check the spread of such evil and to prevent any false rumors from being disseminated again and credulous peasants being corrupted thereby, we deem it right to make known herewith that . . . inasmuch as the welfare of the state, in accordance with divine and public laws, requires that each and every person be protected in the enjoyment of his well-earned property and his rights, and, conversely, that no one step beyond the bounds of his rank and office, we therefore intend to protect the landlords in their estates and possessions inviolably and to keep the peasants in their proper submission to them.

DECREE ON FORCED LABOR, JANUARY 17, 1765

To be announced for the information of the whole populace: In consequence of the confirmation given by Her Imperial Majesty, on the eighth of January [1765], to a report submitted by the Senate, it has been ordained that, should an estate owner desire to commit any of his people [i.e., serfs] who deserve just punishment for recalcitrance to penal servitude in Siberia, for the sake of stricter discipline, the College of the Admiralty shall take the same in charge and employ them at hard labor for as long as their estate owners wish; and during the time such people remain at hard labor they shall be provided with food and clothing from the treasury on the same basis as convicts; and whenever their estate owners desire to take them back, they shall be returned without argument, with the sole reservation that if such people during their stay have not worn their clothes and footwear for the full prescribed term, these shall be taken away from them and returned to the treasury.

READING AND DISCUSSION QUESTIONS

1. How do Catherine's decrees stand in relation to Enlightenment ideals?

2. These decrees give great power to estate owners and take power away from serfs. How might they have enhanced or decreased the power held by Catherine's own government?

DOCUMENT 17-6

EMILIAN IVANOVICH PUGACHEV

A Decree and a Manifesto

1773, 1774

Emilian Ivanovich Pugachev (1740s–1775) was a Cossack from the Don River area of southwest Russia. In 1773, claiming to be the deceased tsar Peter III, he led a massive rebellion of Cossacks, peasants, and others in central Russia. After several military victories and narrow escapes, Pugachev was seized by his own followers, handed over to Catherine the Great's government, and executed publicly in Moscow. Pugachev's success depended heavily on his appeals to popular discontent with the boyars, or local nobility. These two documents not only highlight popular discontent with Catherine's Russia, but also point to the popular support for centralized personal sovereignty in Russia.

DECREE, SEPTEMBER 17, 1773

From the autocratic emperor, our great sovereign Petr Feodorovich of all Russia, etcetera, etcetera, etcetera.

Through this, my sovereign decree, be it expressed to the Iaik [Ural] Cossacks: Just as you, my friends, and your grandfathers and fathers served former tsars to the last drop of blood, now should you serve me, the great sovereign and emperor Petr Feodorovich, for the good of your fatherland. For as you stand up for your fatherland, your Cossack glory and that of your children shall not pass away now or ever. And I, the great sovereign, shall

A Source Book for Russian History from Early Times to 1917, 3 vols. (New Haven: Yale University Press, 1972), 2:454–455.

bestow my bounty upon you: Cossacks[1] and Kalmyks and Tartars.[2] As for those of you who have been at fault before me, the sovereign and imperial majesty Petr Feodorovich, I, the sovereign Petr Feodorovich, forgive you these faults and confer upon you: the [Iaik, renamed Ural in the aftermath of the rebellion] river from its source to its mouth, and land, and meadows, and a monetary wage, and lead, and powder, and grain provisions.

I, the great sovereign and emperor Petr Feodorovich, bestow my bounty upon you.

Manifesto, July 31, 1774

By the grace of God we, Petr III, emperor and autocrat of all Russia, etcetera, etcetera, etcetera, announce the following tidings to all the world:

Through this sovereign decree we declare, in our monarchical and fatherly mercy, that all who were formerly peasants and subjected to landowners shall be faithful subjects and slaves of our crown; we grant you your ancient cross and prayers,[3] your heads and your beards, and bestow upon you freedom and liberty and the eternal rights of the Cossacks, including freedom from recruiting levies, the soul tax,[4] and other monetary taxes; we confer likewise the ownership of lands, forests, hayfields, fisheries, and salt lakes without purchase or rent; and we free the peasants and all the people from the taxes and oppression formerly imposed by the villainous nobles and the venal city judges. And we desire the salvation of your souls and a peaceful life on this earth, for which we have tasted and endured many wanderings and many hardships from the above-mentioned villainous nobles. But since our name now flourishes in Russia by the power of Almighty God, we therefore command through this, our sovereign decree: those who formerly were nobles on their estates and patrimonies, opposing our power, disturbing the empire, and despoiling the peasantry shall be caught, executed, and hanged, and treated just in the same fashion as they, lacking any Christian feeling, dealt with you, the peasants. After the extermination of which enemies and villainous nobles, every man may experience peace and a tranquil life, which shall forever endure.

---

[1] **Cossacks**: An ethnic group noted for their skills in mounted combat and traditionally employed by the Russian government in military campaigns.

[2] **Kalmyks and Tartars**: Two ethnic groups that flourished in the western and central Asian parts of the Russian empire.

[3] **we grant you . . . prayers**: Refers to the Old Believers, a sect of Russian Orthodoxy that separated from the official Russian church in the late 1600s, based on doctrinal differences.

[4] **the soul tax**: A tax levied on males by Peter the Great.

READING AND DISCUSSION QUESTIONS

1. How do Pugachev's proclamations combine the ideas of democracy and freedom, divinity, and absolutist rule?

2. What is the significance of Pugachev's consistent scapegoating of the nobility?

3. How would you summarize the political theory represented by Pugachev's decrees?

4. What was the significance of Pugachev's impersonation of Peter III for his rebellion? Are his ideas revolutionary? Why or why not?

COMPARATIVE QUESTIONS

1. Saint-Simon's indictment of Louis XIV's personality raises the question of human fallibility. How do the political theories of Locke, Hobbes, and Bossuet, as presented in this chapter, deal with the question of human frailties? How does the element of fallibility strengthen or weaken their arguments?

2. The question of divinity is conspicuously absent in Locke's excerpt. How might Locke have interpreted Bossuet's theologically based arguments about sovereignty? Is there room for religion in Locke's state of nature? What about in Hobbes's?

3. In what different ways do the texts in this chapter address political transformations away from the feudal system in the seventeenth century? How do the texts show continuity in old and new systems?

4. How would the political theorists Bossuet, Hobbes, and Locke analyze Catherine the Great's actions and policies? What advice would each give her in the face of the Pugachev rebellion?

CHAPTER 18

New Worldviews and Ways of Life

1540–1790

B eginning in the sixteenth century, Western Europe saw its religion-based notions of the natural and social worlds countered by arguments grounded in reason and observation. Leaders of the scientific revolution (ca. 1540–1690) drew on earlier European, Greek, and Arab insights to support their theories and challenge the church-dominated wisdom of the time. Advances in astronomy, physics, mathematics, and other fields were supported and promoted by the huge profits and increasing technological demands of growing European trade. Intellectuals in Europe and the United States next turned a critical eye toward society and politics. Those active in the period known as the Enlightenment, which stretched from the late seventeenth to the late eighteenth century, insisted on rational approaches to human relations, drawing on scientific arguments and existing critiques of organized religion in their calls for the reform of societies and governments.

GALILEO GALILEI

A Letter to the Grand Duchess Christina and "To the Discerning Reader"

1615, 1632

Perhaps the best-known thinker of early modern Europe, Galileo Galilei (1564–1642) is most famous for arguing that the sun, not the earth, is at the center of the solar system, which contradicted contemporary Catholic doctrine. His early works on telescopic observations provoked suspicion among church authorities, and in his letter to the grand duchess of Tuscany, excerpted here, he explained how he reconciled biblical passages with his own observations. In 1616, the church responded by forbidding works supporting heliocentrism. Galileo's later Dialogue Concerning the Two Chief World Systems *attempted to evade this prohibition by taking the form of a hypothetical conversation among two learned men and a skeptic called Simplicio. His critics were not amused, the* Dialogue *was banned, and in 1633 Galileo was found guilty of heresy and was forced to recant.*

FROM A LETTER TO THE GRAND DUCHESS CHRISTINA

Some years ago, as Your Serene Highness well knows,[1] I discovered in the heavens many things that had not been seen before our own age. The novelty of these things, as well as some consequences which followed from them in contradiction to the physical notions commonly held among academic philosophers, stirred up against me no small number of professors — as if I had placed these things in the sky with my own hands in order

---

Galileo Galilei, *Discoveries and Opinions of Galileo*, trans. Stillman Drake (New York: Random House, 1957); Galileo Galilei, *Dialogue Concerning the Two Chief World Systems*, trans. Stillman Drake (Berkeley: University of California Press, 1967), 5–7.

[1] **as your Serene Highness well knows**: Christina (1565–1637) was a member of the Medici family with whom Galileo had a good relationship. Galileo had tutored her son Cosimo in mathematics.

to upset nature and overturn the sciences. They seemed to forget that the increase of known truths stimulates the investigation, establishment, and growth of the arts; not their diminution or destruction.

Showing a greater fondness for their own opinions than for truth, they sought to deny and disprove the new things which, if they had cared to look for themselves, their own senses would have demonstrated to them. To this end they hurled various charges and published numerous writings filled with vain arguments, and they made the grave mistake of sprinkling these with passages taken from places in the Bible which they had failed to understand properly, and which were ill suited to their purposes.

Persisting in their original resolve to destroy me and everything mine by any means they can think of, these men are aware of my views in astronomy and philosophy. They know that as to the arrangement of the parts of the universe, I hold the sun to be situated motionless in the center of the revolution of the celestial orbs while the earth rotates on its axis and revolves about the sun. They know also that I support this position not only by refuting the arguments of Ptolemy[2] and Aristotle, but by producing many counterarguments; in particular, some which relate to physical effects whose causes can perhaps be assigned in no other way. In addition there are astronomical arguments derived from many things in my new celestial discoveries that plainly confute the Ptolemaic system while admirably agreeing with and confirming the contrary hypothesis. Possibly because they are disturbed by the known truth of other propositions of mine which differ from those commonly held, and therefore mistrusting their defense so long as they confine themselves to the field of philosophy, these men have resolved to fabricate a shield for their fallacies out of the mantle of pretended religion and the authority of the Bible. These they apply, with little judgment, to the refutation of arguments that they do not understand and have not even listened to.

First they have endeavored to spread the opinion that such propositions in general are contrary to the Bible and are consequently damnable and heretical. . . . Next, becoming bolder, . . . they began scattering rumors among the people that before long this doctrine would be condemned by the supreme authority [the pope]. They know, too, that official condemnation would not only suppress the two propositions which I have mentioned, but would render damnable all other astronomical and

---

[2] **Ptolemy**: Greek astronomer who spent most of his life (ca. 100–170 C.E.) in Alexandria, Egypt, and who advanced the idea that all planets revolved around the earth.

physical statements and observations that have any necessary relation or connection with these. . . .

To this end they make a shield of their hypocritical zeal for religion. They go about invoking the Bible, which they would have minister to their deceitful purposes. Contrary to the sense of the Bible and the intention of the holy Fathers, if I am not mistaken, they would extend such authorities until even in purely physical matters — where faith is not involved — they would have us altogether abandon reason and the evidence of our senses in favor of some biblical passage, though under the surface meaning of its words this passage may contain a different sense. . . .

The reason produced for condemning the opinion that the earth moves and the sun stands still is that in many places in the Bible one may read that the sun moves and the earth stands still. Since the Bible cannot err, it follows as a necessary consequence that anyone takes an erroneous and heretical position who maintains that the sun is inherently motionless and the earth movable.

With regard to this argument, I think in the first place that it is very pious to say and prudent to affirm that the holy Bible can never speak untruth — whenever its true meaning is understood. But I believe nobody will deny that it is often very abstruse, and may say things which are quite different from what its bare words signify. Hence in expounding the Bible if one were always to confine oneself to the unadorned grammatical meaning, one might fall into error. Not only contradictions and propositions far from true might thus be made to appear in the Bible, but even grave heresies and follies. Thus it would be necessary to assign to God feet, hands, and eyes, as well as corporeal and human affections, such as anger, repentance, hatred, and sometimes even the forgetting of things past and ignorance of those to come. These propositions uttered by the Holy Ghost were set down in that manner by the sacred scribes[3] in order to accommodate them to the capacities of the common people, who are rude and unlearned. . . .

This being granted, I think that in discussions of physical problems we ought to begin not from the authority of scriptural passages but from sense-experiences and necessary demonstrations; for the holy Bible and the phenomena of nature proceed alike from the divine Word, the former

---

[3] **These propositions . . . sacred scribes**: The Holy Ghost is part of the Holy Trinity, along with the Father and the Son. Christians believe the Holy Ghost wrote through the authors of the Bible.

as the dictate of the Holy Ghost and the latter as the observant executrix of God's commands. It is necessary for the Bible, in order to be accommodated to the understanding of every man, to speak many things which appear to differ from the absolute truth so far as the bare meaning of the words is concerned. But Nature, on the other hand, is inexorable and immutable; she never transgresses the laws imposed upon her, or cares a whit whether her abstruse reasons and methods of operation are understandable to men. For that reason it appears that nothing physical which sense-experience sets before our eyes, or which necessary demonstrations prove to us, ought to be called in question (much less condemned) upon the testimony of biblical passages which may have some different meaning beneath their words. For the Bible is not chained in every expression to conditions as strict as those which govern all physical effects; nor is God any less excellently revealed in Nature's actions than in the sacred statements of the Bible.

"To the Discerning Reader"

Several years ago there was published in Rome a salutary edict which, in order to obviate the dangerous tendencies of our present age, imposed a seasonable silence upon the Pythagorean opinion that the earth moves. There were those who impudently asserted that this decree had its origin not in judicious inquiry, but in passion none too well informed. Complaints were to be heard that advisers who were totally unskilled at astronomical observations ought not to clip the wings of reflective intellects by means of rash prohibitions.

Upon hearing such carping insolence, my zeal could not be contained. Being thoroughly informed about that prudent determination, I decided to appear openly in the theater of the world as a witness of the sober truth. I was at that time in Rome; I was not only received by the most eminent prelates of that Court, but had their applause; indeed, this decree was not published without some previous notice of it having been given to me. Therefore I propose in the present work to show to foreign nations that as much is understood of this matter in Italy, and particularly in Rome, as transalpine diligence can ever have imagined. Collecting all the reflections that properly concern the Copernican system, I shall make it known that everything was brought before the attention of the Roman censorship, and that there proceed from this clime not only dogmas for the welfare of the soul, but ingenious discoveries for the delight of the mind as well.

To this end I have taken the Copernican side in the discourse, proceeding as with a pure mathematical hypothesis and striving by every artifice to represent it as superior to supposing the earth motionless — not, indeed, absolutely, but as against the arguments of some professed Peripatetics.[4] These men indeed deserve not even that name, for they do not walk about; they are content to adore the shadows, philosophizing not with due circumspection but merely from having memorized a few ill-understood principles.

Three principal headings are treated. First, I shall try to show that all experiments practicable upon the earth are insufficient measures for proving its mobility, since they are indifferently adaptable to an earth in motion or at rest. I hope in so doing to reveal many observations unknown to the ancients. Secondly, the celestial phenomena will be examined, strengthening the Copernican hypothesis until it might seem that this must triumph absolutely. Here new reflections are adjoined which might be used in order to simplify astronomy, though not because of any necessity imposed by nature. In the third place, I shall propose an ingenious speculation. It happens that long ago I said that the unsolved problem of the ocean tides might receive some light from assuming the motion of the earth. This assertion of mine, passing by word of mouth, found loving fathers who adopted it as a child of their own ingenuity. Now, so that no stranger may ever appear who, arming himself with our weapons, shall charge us with want of attention to such an important matter, I have thought it good to reveal those probabilities which might render this plausible, given that the earth moves.

I hope that from these considerations the world will come to know that if other nations have navigated more, we have not theorized less. It is not from failing to take count of what others have thought that we have yielded to asserting that the earth is motionless, and holding the contrary to be a mere mathematical caprice, but (if for nothing else) for those reasons that are supplied by piety, religion, the knowledge of Divine Omnipotence, and a consciousness of the limitations of the human mind.

I have thought it most appropriate to explain these concepts in the form of dialogues, which, not being restricted to the rigorous observance of mathematical laws, make room also for digressions which are sometimes no less interesting than the principal argument.

---

[4] **Peripatetics**: The ancient Greek philosophers who studied with Aristotle and had a reputation for walking about as they philosophized.

Many years ago I was often to be found in the marvelous city of Venice, in discussions with Signore Giovanni Francesco Sagredo, a man of noble extraction and trenchant wit. From Florence came Signore Filippo Salviati, the least of whose glories were the eminence of his blood and the magnificence of his fortune. His was a sublime intellect which fed no more hungrily upon any pleasure than it did upon fine meditations. I often talked with these two of such matters in the presence of a certain Peripatetic philosopher whose greatest obstacle in apprehending the truth seemed to be the reputation he had acquired by his interpretations of Aristotle.

Now, since bitter death has deprived Venice and Florence of those two great luminaries in the very meridian of their years, I have resolved to make their fame live on in these pages, so far as my poor abilities will permit, by introducing them as interlocutors in the present argument. (Nor shall the good Peripatetic lack a place; because of his excessive affection toward the *Commentaries* of Simplicius, I have thought fit to leave him under the name of the author he so much revered, without mentioning his own.) May it please those two great souls, ever venerable to my heart, to accept this public monument of my undying love. And may the memory of their eloquence assist me in delivering to posterity the promised reflections.

READING AND DISCUSSION QUESTIONS

1. In his letter to the grand duchess, why does Galileo believe some people are opposed to his ideas? What actions does he say they have taken against him?

2. What is Galileo's position on the "truth" of biblical text?

3. How do you interpret Galileo's defense of the "salutary edict" that "imposed a reasonable silence upon the Pythagorean opinion that the earth moves"? What does his tone reveal?

4. According to these excerpts, what is Galileo's relationship with the church?

VIEWPOINTS

Changing Ideas of Science

DOCUMENT 18-2

FRANCIS BACON

From The Great Restoration: History of Life and Death

1623

Francis Bacon (1561–1626) is generally credited with establishing the "sci- entific method" of observing phenomena and generating new knowledge through the testing of hypotheses. He lived in England, where his career as a politician ended in disgrace. He turned seriously to writing and produced a great number of works on philosophical, social, and natural topics. He died of pneumonia, which he may have contracted in the process of an experiment in preserving meat through freezing. The work excerpted here is an excellent example both of Bacon's keen interest in the social value of knowledge and his careful approach to inquiry and the creation of knowledge.

TO THE PRESENT AND FUTURE AGES,
GREETING.

Although in my six monthly designations I placed the History of Life and Death last in order;[5] yet the extreme profit and importance of the subject, wherein even the slightest loss of time should be accounted precious, has decided me to make an anticipation, and advance it into the second place. For it is my hope and desire that it will contribute to the common good; that through it the higher physicians will somewhat raise their thoughts, and not devote all their time to common cures, nor be honoured for neces- sity only; but that they will become the instruments and dispensers of God's

The Works of Francis Bacon, ed. James Spedding, Robert Leslie Ellis, and Douglas Denon Heath (New York: Hurd and Houghton, 1864), 5:215–222.

[5] **last in order**: May refer to the publishing history of the work.

power and mercy in prolonging and renewing the life of man, the rather because it is effected by safe, convenient, and civil, though hitherto unattempted methods. For although we Christians ever aspire and pant after the land of promise,[6] yet meanwhile it will be a mark of God's favour if in our pilgrimage through the wilderness of this world, these our shoes and garments (I mean our frail bodies) are as little worn out as possible. . . .

There are . . . two subjects of inquiry; the one, the consumption or depredation of the human body; the other, the repair or refreshment thereof; with a view to the restraining of the one (as far as may be), and the strengthening and comforting the other. The first of these pertains principally to the spirits and external air, which cause the depredation; the second to the whole process of alimentation [eating and digesting], which supplies the renovation. With regard to the first part of the inquiry, touching consumption, it has many things in common with bodies inanimate. For whatever the native spirit (which exists in all tangible bodies whether with or without life) and the ambient or external air do to bodies inanimate, the same they try to do to bodies animate, though the presence of the vital spirit in part disturbs and restrains these operations, and in part intensifies and increases them exceedingly. For it is very evident that many inanimate bodies can last a very long time without repair, but animate bodies without aliment and repair at once collapse and die out like fire. The inquiry therefore should be twofold; regarding first the body of man as a thing inanimate and unrepaired by nourishment; and secondly as a thing animate and nourished. And with these prefatory remarks I now pass on to the Topics of Inquiry.

Particular Topics

Or, Articles of Inquiry Concerning Life and Death

1. Inquire into the Nature of Durable and Non-Durable inanimate bodies, and likewise in Vegetables; not in a full and regular inquiry, but briefly, summarily, and as it were only by the way.
2. Inquire more carefully touching the desiccation, arefaction [drying], and consumption of bodies inanimate and vegetable; of the ways and processes whereby they are effected, and withal the methods whereby they are prevented and retarded, and bodies are preserved in their own state. Also inquire touching the inteneration, softening, and renewal of bodies, after they have once commenced to become dry.

---

[6] **land of promise**: The Christian heaven; afterlife.

Neither however need this inquiry be perfect or exact; as these things should be drawn from the proper title of Nature Durable; and as they are not the principal questions in the present inquiry, but only shed a light on the prolongation and restoration of life in animals; wherein, as has been observed before, the same things generally happen, though in their own manner. From the inquiry concerning inanimate and vegetable bodies pass on to the inquiry of animals, not including man.

3. Inquire into the length and shortness of life in animals, with the proper circumstances which seem to contribute to either of them.

4. Since the duration of bodies is of two kinds, the one in their simple identity, the other by repair; whereof the former takes place only in bodies inanimate, the latter in vegetables and living creatures, and is performed by alimentation; inquire likewise touching alimentation, with its ways and process; yet this not accurately (for it belongs to the titles of Assimilation and Alimentation) but as before, in passing only.

From the inquiry concerning animals and things supported by nourishment pass on to that concerning man. And having now come to the principal subject of inquiry, that inquiry should be more accurate and complete on all points.

5. Inquire into the length and shortness of men's lives, according to the times, countries, climates, and places in which they were born and lived.

6. Inquire into the length and shortness of men's lives, according to their parentage and family (as if it were a thing hereditary); and likewise according to their complexion, constitution, habit of body, stature, manners and time of growth, and the make and structure of their limbs.

7. Inquire into the length and shortness of men's lives according to the times of their nativity; but so as to omit for the present all astrological and horoscopical observations. Admit only the common and manifest observations (if there be any); as, whether the birth took place in the 7th, 8th, 9th, or 10th month, whether by night or by day, and in what month of the year.

8. Inquire into the length and shortness of men's lives according to their food, diet, manner of living, exercise, and the like. With regard to the air in which they live and dwell, I consider that ought to be inquired under the former article concerning their places of abode.

9. Inquire into the length and shortness of men's lives according to their studies, kinds of life, affections of the mind, and various accidents.

10. Inquire separately into the medicines which are supposed to prolong life.
11. Inquire into the signs and prognostics of a long and short life; not into those which betoken that death is close at hand (for they belong to the history of medicine); but into those which appear and are observed even in health, whether taken from physiognomy or otherwise.

So far the inquiry touching the length and shortness of life is instituted in an unscientific and confused manner; but I have thought it right to add a systematic inquiry, bearing on practice by means of Intentions; which are of three kinds. Their more particular distributions I will set forth when I come to the inquiry itself. The three general intentions are: the prevention of consumption; the perfection of repair, and the renovation of that which is old.

12. Inquire into the things which preserve and exempt the body of man from arefaction and consumption, or at least which check and retard the tendency thereto.
13. Inquire into the things which belong to the general process of alimentation (whereby the body of man is repaired), that it may be good and with as little loss as possible.
14. Inquire into the things which clear away the old matter and supply new; and likewise those which soften and moisten the parts that have become hard and dry.

But since it will be difficult to know the ways to death, unless the seat and house (or rather cave) of death be first examined and discovered; of this too should inquiry be made; not however of every kind of death, but of such only as are caused, not by violence, but by privation and want. For these alone relate to the decay of the body from age.

15. Inquire into the point of death and the porches[7] which on all sides lead to it; provided it be caused by want and not by violence.

Lastly, since it is convenient to know the character and form of old age; which will be done best by making a careful collection of all the differences in the state and functions of the body between youth and old age, that by them you may see what it is that branches out into so many effects; do not omit this inquiry.

---

[7] **the porches**: Probably referring to transitional states; thresholds, gates (from the Latin *Porta*).

16. Inquire carefully into the differences of the state and faculties of the body in youth and old age; and see whether there be anything that remains unimpaired in old age.

READING AND DISCUSSION QUESTIONS

1. How does Bacon justify his investigation of life and death?

2. How does Bacon's scientific approach to life and death incorporate ideas of religion and church doctrine?

3. Bacon lays out a number of basic inquiries here. What is the relationship between them? Why does he proceed from inanimate objects through animals to people?

DOCUMENT 18-3

PETER THE GREAT
AND GOTTFRIED LEIBNIZ

On the Improvement of Arts and Sciences in Russia

ca. 1712–1718

Peter the Great (1672–1725), tsar of Russia, transformed his country from a minor state to a major European power. Peter traveled incognito throughout Europe early in his reign, studying a range of subjects. Upon his return to Russia, he implemented dramatic reforms ranging from the speech and appearance of his citizens to the founding of a new modern capital, St. Petersburg. Deeply concerned with what he perceived to be the ignorance of

A Source Book for Russian History from Early Times to 1917, ed. George Vernadsky (New Haven: Yale University Press, 1972), 2:367; and Anthony Anemone, "The Monsters of Peter the Great: The Culture of the St. Petersburg Kunstkamera in the Eighteenth Century," Slavic and East European Journal, 44:4 (Winter 2000), 592.

Russians, he enlisted the help of the great German mathematician and philosopher Gottfried Leibniz (1646–1716). Excerpted here is Peter's appointment of Leibniz, Leibniz's recommendation to Peter for the edification of his people, and Peter's explanation of the scientific value of specimens such as the ones that he himself collected and displayed at his Kunstkamera, or "chamber of curiosities."

DECREE ON THE ACCEPTANCE OF GOTTFRIED LEIBNIZ INTO RUSSIAN SERVICE, NOVEMBER 1, 1712

We, Peter I, tsar and autocrat of all Russia, etcetera, etcetera, etcetera.

We have most graciously judged it right that Gottfried Wilhelm von Leibniz, privy councillor in the judicature of the elector and duke of Brunswick-Lueneburg, be also appointed and confirmed as our privy councillor in the judicature, on account of his outstanding good qualities which have been praised to us and which we ourselves have found in him. Since we know that he can be of great help in the development of mathematics and of other arts, in historical research, and in the growth of learning in general, it is our intention to employ him, so that sciences and arts may flourish more and more in our realm. In consideration of the said rank of our privy councillor in the judicature it pleases us to appoint his yearly salary at one thousand Albertus-talers, which are to be paid out to him punctually every year on our behalf; for this we shall issue the necessary orders; his service begins from the date indicated below.

In confirmation whereof we issue these letters under our own signature and with our seal of state affixed.

Given at Karlsbad, November 1, 1712.

(Signed) Peter

(Countersigned) Count Golovkin

DRAFT OF LEIBNIZ'S MEMORANDUM ON THE IMPROVEMENT OF ARTS AND SCIENCES IN RUSSIA, 1716

The improvement of arts and sciences in a great empire involves:

1. Procurement of necessary equipment.
2. Training of men in sciences already established.
3. Discovery of new knowledge.

Equipment consists of books, museums ["curiosity collections"], instruments, and exhibits of works of nature and of human contrivance. . . .

Next to the library comes the museum ["collection of curiosities"], where one should find old and new medals, serving as a source and confirmation of history; remains of Roman, Greek, Hebrew, Chinese, and other antiquity; all kinds of rare objects from the three realms of nature, namely all sorts of mineral stones, ores, plants, insects, and strange animals; also all kinds of works of art — paintings and sculptures; as well as optical, astronomical, architectural, military, nautical, mechanical, and other inventions.

EXCERPT FROM A DECREE ON "MONSTERS," 1718

Ignoramuses think that such monsters are born from the action of the devil which is, however, impossible for there is only one creator of all creation, and that is God. And the Evil One has no power over any living creatures. For monsters are the result of internal damage, of fear and the thoughts of the mother during her pregnancy, of which fact there are many examples. For example, when the mother is frightened, hurt or injured in any way the child will be influenced.

READING AND DISCUSSION QUESTIONS

1. What are Leibniz's specific recommendations to Peter? What do they imply about the nature of knowledge, how it should be transmitted, and its value to society?

2. Given Peter's interest in modernizing Russia and bringing it into the European community of great powers, what do you imagine was the value of hiring a German scientist?

3. What does Peter's explanation of "monsters" suggest about the status of women in eighteenth-century Russia?

VOLTAIRE

From Dictionnaire Philosophique: *"Theist"*

1764

A major figure of the Enlightenment, Voltaire, or François-Marie Arouet (1694–1778), was a literary genius with a keen sense of social responsibility. His writings were immensely popular during his lifetime, although his satirical voice often earned him enemies among France's religious and political elite. The Dictionnaire Philosophique *(Philosophical Dictionary) of 1764 is less an encyclopedic reference than a compilation of Voltaire's critical musings on the nature of religion and intolerance in modern society. Here, his entry for "Theist" outlines the principles of theism (or deism, as it is more commonly known) and indicates his strong approval for the Enlightenment emphasis on secular humanism over sectarian doctrine.*

The theist is a man firmly persuaded of the existence of a Supreme Being equally good and powerful, who has formed all extended, vegetating, sentient, and reflecting existences; who perpetuates their species, who punishes crimes without cruelty, and rewards virtuous actions with kindness.

The theist does not know how God punishes, how he rewards, how he pardons; for he is not presumptuous enough to flatter himself that he understands how God acts; but he knows that God does act and that he is just. The difficulties opposed to a Providence do not stagger him in his faith, because they are only great difficulties, not proofs: he submits himself to that Providence, although he only perceives some of its effects and some appearances; and judging of the things he does not see from those he does see, he thinks that this Providence pervades all places and all ages.

United in this principle with the rest of the universe, he does not join any of the sects, who all contradict themselves; his religion is the most ancient and the most extended: for the simple adoration of a God has preceded all the systems in the world. He speaks a language which all nations understand, while they are unable to understand each other's. He has

M. de Voltaire, A *Philosophical Dictionary* (London: John and Henry L. Hunt, 1824), VI:258–259.

brethren from Pekin to Cayenne,[8] and he reckons all the wise his brethren. He believes that religion consists neither in the opinions of incomprehensible metaphysics, nor in vain decorations, but in adoration and justice. To do good — that is his worship: to submit oneself to God — that is his doctrine. The Mahometan [Muslim] cries out to him — "Take care of yourself, if you do not make the pilgrimage to Mecca." — "Woe be to thee," says a Franciscan, "if thou dost not make a journey to our Lady of Loretto."[9] He laughs at Loretto and Mecca; but he succours the indigent and defends the oppressed.

READING AND DISCUSSION QUESTIONS

1. What does Voltaire's treatment of the "theist" reveal about his general attitude toward religion?

2. Is Voltaire concerned more with the theist's beliefs about the divine or his actions in the world? Explain.

3. Based on this excerpt, what might Voltaire say about atheism? Explain.

DOCUMENT 18-5

IMMANUEL KANT

What Is Enlightenment?

1784

The Prussian professor Immanuel Kant (1724–1804) was perhaps the most influential philosopher of the Enlightenment. In Critique of Pure Reason *(1781), his best-known work, Kant sought to define what we can know*

Immanuel Kant, "What Is Enlightenment?" trans. Peter Gay, in *Introduction to Contemporary Civilization in the West* (New York: Columbia University Press, 1954), 1071–1076.

[8] **Pekin, Cayenne:** The cities of Peking (Beijing) and Cayenne, French Guiana.
[9] **Loretto:** Probably Loreto, a Catholic shrine in Italy and a popular destination for pilgrimages.

and how we know it, thereby reconciling the previous schools of rational-
ist and empiricist thought and inspiring philosophical trends to this day.
The following excerpt is taken from his "Answer to the Question: What Is
Enlightenment?" published in 1784 in a monthly periodical. The short work,
more accessible than his 800-page Critique, *marked his renewed status as a*
public thinker and spoke to his beliefs about intellectual freedom.

Enlightenment is man's emergence from his self-imposed nonage. Non-age is the inability to use one's understanding without another's guidance. This nonage is self-imposed if its cause lies not in lack of understanding but in indecision and lack of courage to use one's own mind without another's guidance. *Dare to know! (Sapere aude.)* "Have the courage to use your own understanding," is therefore the motto of the enlightenment.

Laziness and cowardice are the reasons why such a large part of mankind gladly remain minors all their lives, long after nature has freed them from external guidance. They are the reasons why it is so easy for others to set themselves up as guardians. It is so comfortable to be a minor. If I have a book that thinks for me, a pastor who acts as my conscience, a physician who prescribes my diet, and so on — then I have no need to exert myself. I have no need to think, if only I can pay; others will take care of that disagreeable business for me. The guardians who have kindly taken supervision upon themselves see to it that the overwhelming majority of mankind — among them the entire fair sex — should consider the step to maturity not only as hard, but as extremely dangerous. First, these guardians make their domestic cattle stupid and carefully prevent the docile creatures from taking a single step without the leading-strings to which they have fastened them. Then they show them the danger that would threaten them if they should try to walk by themselves. Now, this danger is really not very great; after stumbling a few times they would, at last, learn to walk. However, examples of such failures intimidate and generally discourage all further attempts.

Thus it is very difficult for the individual to work himself out of the nonage which has become almost second nature to him. He has even grown to like it and is at first really incapable of using his own understanding, because he has never been permitted to try it. Dogmas and formulas, these mechanical tools designed for reasonable use — or rather abuse — of his natural gifts, are the fetters of an everlasting nonage. The man who casts them off would make an uncertain leap over the narrowest ditch, because he is not used to such free movement. That is why there are only a few men who walk firmly, and who have emerged from nonage by cultivating their own minds.

It is more nearly possible, however, for the public to enlighten itself; indeed, if it is only given freedom, enlightenment is almost inevitable. There will always be a few independent thinkers, even among the self-appointed guardians of the multitude. Once such men have thrown off the yoke of nonage, they will spread about them the spirit of a reasonable appreciation of man's value and of his duty to think for himself. It is especially to be noted that the public which was earlier brought under the yoke by these men afterward forces these very guardians to remain in submission, if it is so incited by some of its guardians who are themselves incapable of any enlightenment. That shows how pernicious it is to implant prejudices: they will eventually revenge themselves upon their authors or their authors' descendants. Therefore, a public can achieve enlightenment only slowly. A revolution may bring about the end of a personal despotism or of avaricious and tyrannical oppression, but never a true reform of modes of thought. New prejudices will serve, in place of the old, as guidelines for the unthinking multitude.

This enlightenment requires nothing but *freedom* — and the most innocent of all that may be called "freedom": freedom to make public use of one's reason in all matters. Now I hear the cry from all sides: "Do not argue!" The officer says: "Do not argue — drill!" The tax collector: "Do not argue — pay!" The pastor: "Do not argue — believe!" Only one ruler in the world says: "Argue as much as you please, and about what you please, but obey!" We find restrictions on freedom everywhere. But which restriction is harmful to enlightenment? Which restriction is innocent, and which advances enlightenment? I reply: the public use of one's reason must be free at all times, and this alone can bring enlightenment to mankind.

On the other hand, the private use of reason may frequently be narrowly restricted without especially hindering the progress of enlightenment. By "public use of one's reason" I mean that use which a man, as *scholar*, makes of it before the reading public. I call "private use" that use which a man makes of his reason in a civic post that has been entrusted to him. In some affairs affecting the interest of the community a certain [governmental] mechanism is necessary in which some members of the community remain passive. This creates an artificial unanimity which will serve the fulfillment of public objectives, or at least keep these objectives from being destroyed. Here arguing is not permitted: one must obey. Insofar as a part of this machine considers himself at the same time a member of a universal community — a world society of citizens — (let us say that he thinks of himself as a scholar rationally addressing his public through his writings) he may indeed argue, and the affairs with which he is associated in part as a passive member will not suffer. Thus, it would be very unfortunate if an officer on duty and under orders from his superiors should want to criticize the appropriateness or utility of his orders. He must obey. But as a scholar he could not rightfully be prevented from taking notice of the mistakes in the military service and from submitting his views to his public for its judgment. The citizen cannot refuse to pay the taxes levied upon him; indeed, impertinent censure of such taxes could be punished as a scandal that might cause general disobedience. Nevertheless, this man does not violate the duties of a citizen if, as a scholar, he publicly expresses his objections to the impropriety or possible injustice of such levies. A pastor too is bound to preach to his congregation in accord with the doctrines of the church which he serves, for he was ordained on that condition. But as a scholar he has full freedom, indeed the obligation, to communicate to his public all his carefully examined and constructive thoughts concerning errors in that doctrine and his proposals concerning improvement of religious dogma and church institutions. This is nothing that could burden his conscience. For what he teaches in pursuance of his office as representative of the church, he represents as something which he is not free to teach as he sees it. He speaks as one who is employed to speak in the name and under the orders of another. He will say: "Our church teaches this or that; these are the proofs which it employs." Thus he will benefit his congregation as much as possible by presenting doctrines to which he may not subscribe with full conviction. He can commit himself to teach them because it is not completely impossible that they may contain hidden truth. In any event, he has found nothing in the doctrines that contradicts the heart of religion. For if he believed that such contradictions existed he would not be able to administer his office with a clear conscience. He would have to resign it. Therefore the use which a scholar makes of his reason before the congregation that employs him is only a private use, for, no matter how sizable, this is only a domestic audience. In view of this he, as preacher, is not free and ought not to be free, since he is carrying out the orders of others. On the other hand, as the scholar who speaks to his own public (the world) through his writings, the minister in the public use of his reason enjoys unlimited freedom to use his own reason and to speak for himself. That the spiritual guardians of the people should themselves be treated as minors is an absurdity which would result in perpetuating absurdities.

But should a society of ministers, say a Church Council, . . . have the right to commit itself by oath to a certain unalterable doctrine, in order to secure perpetual guardianship over all its members and through them over the people? I say that this is quite impossible. Such a contract, concluded to keep all further enlightenment from humanity, is simply null and void even if it should be confirmed by the sovereign power, by parliaments, and by the most solemn treaties. An epoch cannot conclude a pact that will commit succeeding ages, prevent them from increasing their significant insights, purging themselves of errors, and generally progressing in enlightenment. That would be a crime against human nature, whose proper destiny lies precisely in such progress. Therefore, succeeding ages are fully entitled to repudiate such decisions as unauthorized and outrageous. The touchstone of all those decisions that may be made into law for a people lies in this question: Could a people impose such a law upon itself? Now, it might be possible to introduce a certain order for a definite short period of time in expectation of a better order. But while this provisional order continues, each citizen (above all, each pastor acting as a scholar) should be left free to publish his criticisms of the faults of existing institutions. This should continue until public understanding of these matters has gone so far that, by uniting the voices of many (although not necessarily all) scholars, reform proposals could be brought before the sovereign to protect those congregations which had decided according to their best lights upon an altered religious order, without, however, hindering those who want to remain true to the old institutions. But to agree to a perpetual religious constitution which is not to be publicly questioned by anyone would be, as it were, to annihilate a period of time in the progress of man's improvement. This must be absolutely forbidden.

A man may postpone his own enlightenment, but only for a limited period of time. And to give up enlightenment altogether, either for oneself or one's descendants, is to violate and to trample upon the sacred rights of man. What a people may not decide for itself may even less be decided for it by a monarch, for his reputation as a ruler consists precisely in the way in which he unites the will of the whole people within his own. If he only sees to it that all true or supposed [religious] improvement remains in step with the civic order, he can for the rest leave his subjects alone to do what they find necessary for the salvation of their souls. Salvation is none of his business; it *is* his business to prevent one man from forcibly keeping another from determining and promoting his salvation to the best of his ability. Indeed, it would be prejudicial to his majesty if he meddled in these matters and supervised the writings in which his subjects seek to bring their [religious] views into the open, even when he does this from his own highest insight, because then he exposes himself to the reproach: *Caesar non est supra grammaticos*.[10] It is worse when he debases his sovereign power so far as to support the spiritual despotism of a few tyrants in his state over the rest of his subjects.

When we ask, Are we now living in an enlightened age? the answer is, No, but we live in an age of enlightenment. As matters now stand it is still far from true that men are already capable of using their own reason in religious matters confidently and correctly without external guidance. Still, we have some obvious indications that the field of working toward the goal [of religious truth] is now being opened. What is more, the hindrances against general enlightenment or the emergence from self-imposed nonage are gradually diminishing. In this respect this is the age of the enlightenment and the century of Frederick.[11]

A prince ought not to deem it beneath his dignity to state that he considers it his duty not to dictate anything to his subjects in religious matters, but to leave them complete freedom. If he repudiates the arrogant word *tolerant*, he is himself enlightened; he deserves to be praised by a grateful world and posterity as the man who was the first to liberate mankind from dependence, at least on the government, and let everybody use his own reason in matters of conscience. Under his reign, honorable pastors, acting as scholars and regardless of the duties of their office, can freely and openly publish their ideas to the world for inspection, although they deviate here and there from accepted doctrine. This is even more true of every other person not restrained by any oath of office. This spirit of freedom is spreading beyond the boundaries [of Prussia], even where it has to struggle against the external hindrances established by a government that fails to grasp its true interest. [Frederick's Prussia] is a shining example that freedom need not cause the least worry concerning public order or the unity of the community. When one does not deliberately attempt to keep men in barbarism, they will gradually work out of that condition by themselves.

---

[10] *Caesar non est supra grammaticos*: Latin for "Caesar is not above the grammarians."

[11] **the century of Frederick**: In the eighteenth century, Prussia was ruled by three Fredericks: Frederick I (r. 1701–1713), Frederick William I (r. 1713–1740), and Frederick II (r. 1740–1786).

I have emphasized the main point of the enlightenment — man's emergence from his self-imposed nonage — primarily in religious matters, because our rulers have no interest in playing the guardian to their subjects in the arts and sciences. Above all, nonage in religion is not only the most harmful but the most dishonorable. But the disposition of a sovereign ruler who favors freedom in the arts and sciences goes even further: he knows that there is no danger in permitting his subjects to make public use of their reason and to publish their ideas concerning a better constitution, as well as candid criticism of existing basic laws. We already have a striking example [of such freedom], and no monarch can match the one whom we venerate.

But only the man who is himself enlightened, who is not afraid of shadows, and who commands at the same time a well-disciplined and numerous army as guarantor of public peace — only he can say what [the sovereign of] a free state cannot dare to say: "Argue as much as you like, and about what you like, but obey!" Thus we observe here as elsewhere in human affairs, in which almost everything is paradoxical, a surprising and unexpected course of events: a large degree of civic freedom appears to be of advantage to the intellectual freedom of the people, yet at the same time it establishes insurmountable barriers. A lesser degree of civic freedom, however, creates room to let that free spirit expand to the limits of its capacity. Nature, then, has carefully cultivated the seed within the hard core — namely, the urge for and the vocation of free thought. And this free thought gradually reacts back on the modes of thought of the people, and men become more and more capable of acting in freedom. At last free thought acts even on the fundamentals of government, and the state finds it agreeable to treat man, who is now more than a machine, in accord with his dignity.

READING AND DISCUSSION QUESTIONS

1. Briefly summarize Kant's definition of *enlightenment*. Why is it so difficult for people to achieve enlightenment?

2. According to Kant, who is responsible for enlightening the populace?

3. What is the difference between "public" and "private" freedoms? What examples does Kant give of each?

4. How is Kant's definition limited to his time and place? How is it universally applicable?

DOCUMENT 18-6

PHILIP STANHOPE

From Letters to His Son

1748

Philip Stanhope (1694–1773), the fourth Earl of Chesterfield, served in the British Parliament and as secretary of state. From 1738 through 1768, Stanhope (also known as Chesterfield) corresponded frequently with his illegitimate son, giving him detailed advice on how to attain political and social influence despite the social stigma of his birth. The father's hopes were not realized, and his son (also named Philip Stanhope) achieved only minor success in political life before dying in 1768 at age thirty-six. His grieving father made provisions in his will for his grandchildren but not for his son's widow, and soon after the earl's death in 1773, she published his letters. The excerpts here, sent to his son while the latter was traveling in Europe, show the care with which he attempted to groom the young Stanhope in social mores and the craft of international diplomacy.

LETTER CXLIII

Bath, March 1. O. S. 1748

DEAR BOY,

. . . I find that you had been a great while without receiving any letters from me; but, by this time, I daresay you think you have received enough, and possibly more than you have read; for I am not only a frequent, but a prolix correspondent.

[Upon learning that his son is studying with an expert on European treaties:]

. . . I am extremely glad of it; for that is what I would have you particularly apply to, and make yourself perfect master of. The treaty part you must chiefly acquire by reading the treaties themselves, and the histories and memoirs relative to them; not but that inquiries and conversations upon those treaties will help you greatly, and imprint them better in your

Philip Dorner Stanhope, *Earl of Chesterfield, The Works of Lord Chesterfield* (New York: Harper & Brothers, 1838), 178–179, 223–225.

mind. In this course of reading, do not perplex yourself, at first, by the multitude of insignificant treaties which are to be found in the *Corps Diplomatique* [entire body of diplomatic works]; but stick to the material ones, which altered the state of Europe, and made a new arrangement among the great powers; such as the treaties of Munster, Nimeguen, Ryswick, and Utrecht.

But there is one part of political knowledge, which is only to be had by inquiry and conversation; that is, the present state of every power in Europe, with regard to the three important points, of strength, revenue, and commerce. You will, therefore, do well, while you are in Germany, to inform yourself carefully of the military force, the revenues, and the commerce of every prince and state of the empire; and to write down those informations in a little book, kept for that particular purpose. To give you a specimen of what I mean:

> *The Electorate of Hanover*
> The revenue is about £500,000 a year.
> The military establishment, in time of war, may be about 25,000 men;
>   but that is the utmost.
> The trade is chiefly linens, exported from Stade.
> There are coarse woolen manufactures for home-consumption.
> The mines of Hartz produce about £100,000 in silver, annually.

Such informations you may very easily get, by proper inquiries, of every state in Germany, if you will but prefer useful to frivolous conversations.

There are many princes in Germany, who keep very few or no troops, unless upon the approach of danger, or for the sake of profit, by letting them out for subsidies, to great powers: In that case, you will inform yourself what number of troops they could raise, either for their own defense, or furnish to other powers for subsidies.

There is very little trouble, and an infinite use, in acquiring of this knowledge. It seems to me even to be a more entertaining subject to talk upon, than *la pluie et le beau tems* [the weather].

Though I am sensible that these things cannot be known with the utmost exactness, at least by you yet, you may, however, get so near the truth, that the difference will be very immaterial.

Pray let me know if the Roman Catholic worship is tolerated in Saxony, anywhere but at Court; and if public mass-houses are allowed anywhere else in the electorate. Are the regular Romish clergy allowed; and have they any convents?

Are there any military orders in Saxony, and what? Is the White Eagle a Saxon or a Polish order? Upon what occasion, and when was it founded? What number of knights?

Adieu! God bless you; and may you turn out what I wish!

LETTER CLXVI

Bath, October 19. O. S. 1748

DEAR BOY,

Having, in my last, pointed out what sort of company you should keep, I will now give you some rules for your conduct in it; rules which my own experience and observation enable me to lay down, and communicate to you, with some degree of confidence. I have often given you hints of this kind before, but then it has been by snatches; I will now be more regular and methodical. I shall say nothing with regard to your bodily carriage and address, but leave them to the care of your dancing-master, and to your own attention to the best models; remember, however, that they are of consequence.

Talk often, but never long: in that case, if you do not please, at least you are sure not to tire your hearers. . . .

Tell stories very seldom, and absolutely never but where they are very apt and very short. Omit every circumstance that is not material, and beware of digressions. To have frequent recourse to narrative betrays great want of imagination.

Never hold anybody by the button or the hand, in order to be heard out; for, if people are not willing to hear you, you had much better hold your tongue than them.

Most long talkers single out some one unfortunate man in company (commonly him whom they observe to be the most silent, or their next neighbor) to whisper, or at least in a half voice, to convey a continuity of words to. This is excessively ill-bred, and in some degree a fraud; conversation-stock being a joint and common property. But, on the other hand, if one of these unmerciful talkers lays hold of you, hear him with patience (and at least seeming attention), if he is worth obliging; for nothing will oblige him more than a patient hearing, as nothing would hurt him more than either to leave him in the midst of his discourse, or to discover your impatience under your affliction.

Take, rather than give, the tone of the company you are in. If you have parts, you will show them, more or less, upon every subject; and if you have not, you had better talk sillily upon a subject of other people's than of your own choosing.

Avoid as much as you can, in mixed companies, argumentative, polemical conversations; which, though they should not, yet certainly do, indispose for a time the contending parties towards each other; and, if the controversy grows warm and noisy, endeavor to put an end to it by some genteel levity or joke. I quieted such a conversation-hubbub once, by representing to them that, though I was persuaded none there present would repeat, out of company, what passed in it, yet I could not answer for the discretion of the passengers in the street, who must necessarily hear all that was said.

Above all things, and upon all occasions, avoid speaking of yourself, if it be possible. Such is the natural pride and vanity of our hearts, that it perpetually breaks out, even in people of the best parts, in all the various modes and figures of the egotism. . . .

This principle of vanity and pride is so strong in human nature, that it descends even to the lowest objects; and one often sees people angling for praise, where, admitting all they say to be true (which, by the way, it seldom is), no just praise is to be caught. One man affirms that he has rode post an hundred miles in six hours; probably it is a lie: but supposing it to be true, what then? Why he is a very good post-boy, that is all. Another asserts, and probably not without oaths, that he has drunk six or eight bottles of wine at a sitting; out of charity, I will believe him a liar; for, if I do not, I must think him a beast. . . .

The only sure way of avoiding these evils, is never to speak of yourself at all. But when, historically, you are obliged to mention yourself, take care not to drop one single word that can directly or indirectly be construed as fishing for applause. Be your character what it will, it will be known; and nobody will take it upon your own word. . . . If you are silent upon your own subject, neither envy, indignation, nor ridicule, will obstruct or allay the applause which you may really deserve; but if you publish your own panegyric [praises] upon any occasion, or in any shape whatsoever, and however artfully dressed or disguised, they will all conspire against you, and you will be disappointed of the very end you aim at.

Take care never to seem dark and mysterious; which is not only a very unamiable character, but a very suspicious one too; if you seem mysterious with others, they will be really so with you, and you will know nothing. The height of abilities is to have *volto sciolto* and *pensieri stretti*; that is, a frank, open, and ingenuous exterior, with a prudent and reserved interior; to be upon your own guard, and yet, by a seeming natural openness, to put

people off theirs. . . . Always look people in the face when you speak to
them: the not doing it is thought to imply conscious guilt; besides that you
lose the advantage of observing by their countenances what impression
your discourse makes upon them. In order to know people's real sentiments, I trust much more to my eyes than to my ears: for they can say
whatever they have a mind I should hear; but they can seldom help looking, what they have no intention that I should know. . . .

Mimicry, which is the common and favorite amusement of little, low
minds, is in the utmost contempt with great ones. It is the lowest and most
illiberal of all buffoonery. Pray, neither practice it yourself, nor applaud
it in others. Besides that the person mimicked is insulted; and, as I have
often observed to you before, an insult is never forgiven.

I need not (I believe) advise you to adapt your conversation to the
people you are conversing with: for I suppose you would not, without this
caution, have talked upon the same subject, and in the same manner, to a
minister of state, a bishop, a philosopher, a captain, and a woman. A man
of the world must, like the chameleon, be able to take every different hue;
which is by no means a criminal or abject, but a necessary complaisance;
for it relates only to manners and not to morals.

One word only as to swearing, and that, I hope and believe, is more
than is necessary. You may sometimes hear some people in good company interlard their discourse with oaths, by way of embellishment, as they
think, but you must observe, too, that those who do so are never those who
contribute, in any degree, to give that company the denomination of good
company. They are always subalterns, or people of low education; for that
practice, besides that it has no one temptation to plead, is as silly and as
illiberal as it is wicked.

Loud laughter is the mirth of the mob, who are only pleased with silly
things; for true wit or good sense never excited a laugh since the creation
of the world. A man of parts and fashion is therefore only seen to smile,
but never heard to laugh.

READING AND DISCUSSION QUESTIONS

1.   Compare and contrast the content of these two letters. To what end is
     Stanhope's advice directed in each case?
2.   When the letters were published, several critics noted the pragmatic
     (and even cynical) quality of Stanhope's advice to his son. Why might

letters from a member of the British nobility to his illegitimate son offend the reading public?

3. What do these letters imply about the nature of power and influence in British society?

COMPARATIVE QUESTIONS

1. How do the documents in this chapter reflect a tension between individual thought and social order? In which document are these issues most prominent, and in which least? Explain.

2. Religion and spirituality are important components of several excerpts in this chapter. How does each author present religion, and to what end? What might the relative absence of religion in some of the texts signify?

3. How do the scientific investigations of Galileo, Bacon, and Peter the Great differ? Do they seem "scientific" to you? Why or why not?

4. Peter the Great, Stanhope, and Galileo all point in different ways to the importance of international awareness during the time of the Enlightenment. How do these documents show a pan-European sense of the Enlightenment and the scientific revolution?

5. To what extent are these authors concerned with a broad European identity, and to what extent with their own national or local concerns? Give examples.

CHAPTER 19

Africa and the World

1400–1800

T he fifteenth-century voyages of Portuguese mariners eager to identify and exploit new trade opportunities ushered in an era of violence, exploitation, and slavery on the African continent. However, Africa's story during these four centuries was not simply one of involuntary participation in a European-dominated system of colonization and enslavement. For centuries, diverse African states had played an important role in global trade, and foreign and indigenous influences combined to produce powerful and enduring cultures. Neither was slavery new to African culture. However, the traditional African idea of slavery was transformed by the dehumanizing profit motive of European capitalism and plantation economies. Many coastal societies facilitated the massive transatlantic slave trade by capturing people from the African interior and delivering them to European slave ships. The documents in this chapter depict both continuity and transformation in African society during this period of European incursion.

DOCUMENT 19-1

NZINGA MBEMBA (ALFONSO I)
From Letters to the King of Portugal
1526

King of the powerful central West African state of Kongo, Nzinga Mbemba ruled from around 1506 to 1543. Like his father, he was baptized a Catholic by Portuguese explorers in 1491, taking the Christian name Alfonso I. As king, he embraced many aspects of Portuguese society, including both

Basil Davidson, trans., *The African Past* (London: Curtis Brown, Ltd., 1964), 54–57.

Catholicism and material culture, which became important symbols of influence and power in his kingdom. In the 1520s, Alfonso noted with dismay the increasing Portuguese abuses of the thriving Kongolese slave markets and of his kingdom generally. The letters excerpted here represent his attempt to seek redress from his Portuguese counterpart.

Sir, Your Highness should know how our Kingdom is being lost in so many ways that it is convenient to provide for the necessary remedy, since this is caused by the excessive freedom given by your agents and officials to the men and merchants who are allowed to come to this Kingdom to set up shops with goods and many things which have been prohibited by us, and which they spread throughout our Kingdoms and Domains in such an abundance that many of our vassals, whom we had in obedience, do not comply because they have the things in greater abundance than we ourselves; and it was with these things that we had them content and subjected under our vassalage and jurisdiction, so it is doing a great harm not only to the service of God, but the security and peace of our Kingdoms and State as well.

And we cannot reckon how great the damage is, since the mentioned merchants are taking every day our natives, sons of the land and the sons of our noblemen and vassals and our relatives, because the thieves and men of bad conscience grab them wishing to have the things and wares of this Kingdom which they are ambitious of; they grab them and get them to be sold; and so great, Sir, is the corruption and licentiousness that our country is being completely depopulated, and Your Highness should not agree with this nor accept it as in your service. And to avoid it we need from those (your) Kingdoms no more than some priests and a few people to teach in schools, and no other goods except wine and flour for the holy sacrament. That is why we beg of Your Highness to help and assist us in this matter, commanding your factors that they should not send here either merchants or wares, because it is *our will that in these Kingdoms there should not be any trade of slaves nor outlet for them.* Concerning what is referred [to] above, again we beg of Your Highness to agree with it, since otherwise we cannot remedy such an obvious damage. Pray Our Lord in His mercy to have Your Highness under His guard and let you do forever the things of His service. I kiss your hands many times.

At our town of Kongo, written on the sixth day of July,
[secretary] João Teixeira did it in 1526.
The King. Dom [Lord] Alfonso.

* * *

Moreover, Sir, in our Kingdoms there is another great inconvenience which is of little service to God, and this is that many of our people, keenly desirous as they are of the wares and things of your Kingdoms, which are brought here by your people, and in order to satisfy their voracious appetite, seize many of our people, freed and exempt men, and very often it happens that they kidnap even noblemen and the sons of noblemen, and our relatives, and take them to be sold to the white men who are in our Kingdoms; and for this purpose they have concealed them; and others are brought during the night so that they might not be recognized.

And as soon as they are taken by the white men they are immediately ironed and branded with fire, and when they are carried to be embarked, if they are caught by our guards' men the whites allege that they have bought them but they cannot say from whom, so that it is our duty to do justice and to restore to the freemen their freedom, but it cannot be done if your subjects feel offended, as they claim to be.

And to avoid such a great evil we passed a law so that any white man living in our Kingdoms and wanting to purchase goods in any way should first inform three of our noblemen and officials of our court whom we rely upon in this matter, and these are Dom Pedro Manipanza and Dom Manuel Manissaba, our chief usher, and Gonçalo Pires our chief freighter, who should investigate if the mentioned goods are captives or free men, and if cleared by them there will be no further doubt nor embargo for them to be taken and embarked. But if the white men do not comply with it they will lose the aforementioned goods. And if we do them this favor and concession it is for the part Your Highness has in it, since we know that it is in your service too that these goods are taken from our Kingdom, otherwise we should not consent to this. . . .

* * *

Sir, Your Highness has been kind enough to write to us saying that we should ask in our letters for anything we need, and that we shall be provided with everything, and as the peace and the health of our Kingdom depend on us, and as there are among us old folks and people who have lived for many days, it happens that we have continuously many and different diseases which put us very often in such a weakness that we reach almost the last extreme; and the same happens to our children, relatives and natives owing to the lack in this country of physicians and surgeons who might know how to cure properly such diseases. And as we have got neither dispensaries nor drugs which might help us in this forlornness, many of those who had been already confirmed and instructed in the holy faith of Our Lord Jesus Christ perish and die; and the rest of the people in their majority cure themselves with herbs and breads and other ancient methods, so that they put all their faith in the mentioned herbs and ceremonies if they live, and believe that they are saved if they die; and this is not much in the service of God.

And to avoid such a great error and inconvenience, since it is from God in the first place and then from your Kingdoms and from Your Highness that all the good and drugs and medicines have come to save us, we beg of you to be agreeable and kind enough to send us two physicians and two apothecaries and one surgeon, so that they may come with their drugstores and all the necessary things to stay in our kingdoms, because we are in extreme need of them all and each of them. We shall do them all good and shall benefit them by all means, since they are sent by Your Highness, whom we thank for your work in their coming. We beg of Your Highness as a great favor to do this for us, because besides being good in itself it is in the service of God as we have said above.

READING AND DISCUSSION QUESTIONS

1. What complaints does Alfonso present to the Portuguese king, and what actions does he seek?

2. To justify his requests, Alfonso claims that the Portuguese are not acting "in the service of God." How might Alfonso's Christianity subject him to Portuguese control? How is it a useful tool for him?

3. Alfonso states that it is his will that the slave trade end in his country. Given the thriving slave markets that existed before contact with the Portuguese, what do you think about his decision to end the slave trade in Kongo? What seems to have motivated his choice?

DOCUMENT 19-2

LEO AFRICANUS
A Description of Timbuktu
1526

Leo Africanus (ca. 1465–1550) was one of thousands of Muslims expelled from the Iberian Peninsula after the "reconquest" of Spain by the Catholic monarchs Ferdinand and Isabella. Captured as a slave and given to Pope Leo X, Leo Africanus was baptized in 1519 and sent to Africa to observe and report back to the pope. The resulting work, published first in a larger collection by an Italian geographer, exemplified a new kind of travel writing that boasted careful research and meticulous, firsthand detail. In this excerpt, Leo Africanus relates his travels to the city of Timbuktu, which for centuries had been a center of international trade and Islamic higher learning.

The name of this kingdom is a modern one, after a city which was built by a king named Mansa Suleyman in the year 610 of the hegira[1] around twelve miles from a branch of the Niger River.

The houses of Timbuktu are huts made of clay-covered wattles [supports] with thatched roofs. In the center of the city is a temple built of stone and mortar, built by an architect named Granata, and in addition there is a large palace, constructed by the same architect, where the king lives. The shops of the artisans, the merchants, and especially weavers of cotton cloth are very numerous. Fabrics are also imported from Europe to Timbuktu, borne by Berber [North African] merchants.

The women of the city maintain the custom of veiling their faces, except for the slaves who sell all the foodstuffs. The inhabitants are very rich, especially the strangers who have settled in the country; so much so that the current king has given two of his daughters in marriage to two

---

Paul Brians, et al., *Reading About the World*, vol. 2, 3rd ed. (Harcourt Brace College Custom Books), 1999.

[1] **year 610 of the hegira**: Arabic for "migration," the *hegira (hijra)* was Muhammad's emigration to Medina in 622, the first year of the Islamic calendar. Therefore, Suleyman's city dates to the early thirteenth century.

brothers, both businessmen, on account of their wealth. There are many wells containing sweet water in Timbuktu; and in addition, when the Niger is in flood canals deliver the water to the city. Grain and animals are abundant, so that the consumption of milk and butter is considerable. But salt is in very short supply because it is carried here from Tegaza, some 500 miles from Timbuktu. I happened to be in this city at a time when a load of salt sold for eighty ducats. The king has a rich treasure of coins and gold ingots. One of these ingots weighs 970 pounds.

The royal court is magnificent and very well organized. When the king goes from one city to another with the people of his court, he rides a camel and the horses are led by hand by servants. If fighting becomes necessary, the servants mount the camels and all the soldiers mount on horseback. When someone wishes to speak to the king, he must kneel before him and bow down; but this is only required of those who have never before spoken to the king, or of ambassadors. The king has about 3,000 horsemen and infinity of foot-soldiers armed with bows made of wild fennel which they use to shoot poisoned arrows. This king makes war only upon neighboring enemies and upon those who do not want to pay him tribute. When he has gained a victory, he has all of them — even the children — sold in the market at Timbuktu.

Only small, poor horses are born in this country. The merchants use them for their voyages and the courtiers to move about the city. But the good horses come from Barbary. They arrive in a caravan and, ten or twelve days later, they are led to the ruler, who takes as many as he likes and pays appropriately for them.

The king is a declared enemy of the Jews. He will not allow any to live in the city. If he hears it said that a Berber merchant frequents them or does business with them, he confiscates his goods. There are in Timbuktu numerous judges, teachers and priests, all properly appointed by the king. He greatly honors learning. Many hand-written books imported from Barbary are also sold. There is more profit made from this commerce than from all other merchandise.

Instead of coined money, pure gold nuggets are used; and for small purchases, cowrie shells which have been carried from Persia, and of which 400 equal a ducat. Six and two-thirds of their ducats equal one Roman gold ounce.

The people of Timbuktu are of a peaceful nature. They have a custom of almost continuously walking about the city in the evening (except for those that sell gold), between 10 PM and 1 AM, playing musical instruments and dancing. The citizens have at their service many slaves, both men and women.

The city is very much endangered by fire. At the time when I was there on my second voyage, half the city burned in the space of five hours. But the wind was violent and the inhabitants of the other half of the city began to move their belongings for fear that the other half would burn.

There are no gardens or orchards in the area surrounding Timbuktu.

READING AND DISCUSSION QUESTIONS

1. Describe the tone that Leo Africanus uses. For whom do you imagine this work would be useful or interesting?

2. Leo Africanus notes that trade in books is worth more than any other form of commerce in the city. What does this suggest about life in Timbuktu?

DOCUMENT 19-3

OSEI BONSU

An Asante King Questions British Motives in Ending the Slave Trade

1820

Osei Bonsu was king of the Asante (also written Ashanti or Ashantee) state in West Africa from about 1801 to 1824. Under his rule, the Asante state expanded and solidified the sophisticated bureaucratic structure inaugurated by his predecessors in the late 1700s. The Asante export economy — based historically on the sale of gold, ivory, and slaves — flourished after initial contact with Europeans. His comments, presented here, were recorded by a British trader named Joseph shortly after the British abolition of the slave

David Robinson and Douglas Smith, *Sources of the African Past: Case Studies of Five Nineteenth-Century African Societies* (New York: Africana, 1979), 189–190.

trade. They indicate both the profound dependence of many African states on the European slave trade and the complex relationships fostered through that system.

"Now," said the king, after a pause, "I have another palaver [topic of discussion], and you must help me to talk it. A long time ago the great king [the king of England] liked plenty of trade, more than now; then many ships came, and they bought ivory, gold, and slaves; but now he will not let the ships come as before, and the people buy gold and ivory only. This is what I have in my head, so now tell me truly, like a friend, why does the king do so?" "His majesty's question," I replied, "was connected with a great palaver, which my instructions did not authorise me to discuss. I had nothing to say regarding the slave trade." "I know that too," retorted the king; "because, if my master liked that trade, you would have told me so before. I only want to hear what you think as a friend: this is not like the other palavers." I was confessedly at a loss for an argument that might pass as a satisfactory reason, and the sequel proved that my doubts were not groundless. The king did not deem it plausible, that this obnoxious traffic should have been abolished from motives of humanity alone; neither would he admit that it lessened the number either of domestic or foreign wars.

Taking up one of my observations, he remarked, "The white men who go to council with your master, and pray to the great God for him, do not understand my country, or they would not say the slave trade was bad. But if they think it bad now, why did they think it good before? Is not your law an old law, the same as the Crammo [Muslim] law? Do you not both serve the same God, only you have different fashions and customs? Crammos are strong people in fetische, and they say the law is good, because the great God made the book; so they buy slaves, and teach them good things, which they knew not before. This makes every body love the Crammos, and they go every where up and down, and the people give them food when they want it. Then these men come all the way from the great water [the Niger River], and from Manding, and Dagomba, and Killinga; they stop and trade for slaves, and then go home. If the great king would like to restore this trade, it would be good for the white men and for me too, because Ashantee is a country for war, and the people are strong; so if you talk that palaver for me properly, in the white country, if you go there, I will give you plenty of gold, and I will make you richer than all the white men."

READING AND DISCUSSION QUESTIONS

1. How does this document complicate your understanding of the racial politics of transatlantic slavery and of slavery in the United States?

2. In this document, Osei Bonsu uses Muslims (*Crammos*) as an example of moral behavior toward slaves. How does this illustrate his understanding of international affairs?

3. How does the king's description of how Muslims treat slaves compare with their treatment by European Christians?

4. The narrator notes that Osei Bonsu thought it "implausible" that the slave trade was abolished for purely humanitarian reasons. Do you agree, and why?

VIEWPOINTS

The Slave Trade

DOCUMENT 19-4

ANNA MARIA FALCONBRIDGE

From Narrative of Two Voyages to the River Sierra Leone

1794

Anna Maria Falconbridge (born 1769) was the first modern European woman to write about travels to Africa. She married surgeon and abolitionist Alexander Falconbridge in 1788, whose testimony before the British government became the basis for his 1788 abolitionist work, An Account of the Slave Trade on the Coast of Africa. *Anna Maria Falconbridge sailed with her husband to Sierra Leone, where a British company had established a settlement of "black poor," or African Americans who had fled the United States after the American Revolution. Her letters from these voyages were published as*

Anna Maria Falconbridge, *Narrative of Two Voyages to the River Sierra Leone*, ed. Christopher Fyfe (Liverpool: Liverpool University Press, 2000), 89–94.

the Narrative *upon her return to England in 1794. The excerpt here shows how her initial abolitionist views changed with her firsthand experience.*

We embarked and sailed on the ninth of June; nothing could have reconciled me to the idea of taking my passage in a slave ship . . . for I always entertained most horrid notions of being exposed to indelicacies, too offensive for the eyes of an English woman, on board these ships; however, I never was more agreeably disappointed in my life. In the centre of the ship a barricade was run across, to prevent any communication between the men and women; the men and boys occupied the forward part, and the women and girls, the after, so I was only liable to see the latter, who were full as well habited as they would have been in Africa. . . . Having heard such a vast deal of the ill treatment to slaves during the middle passage, I did not omit to make the nicest [closest] observations in my power. . . . I would declare I had not the slightest reason to suspect any inhumanity or mal-practice was shewn towards [the slaves], through the whole voyage; on the contrary, I believe they experienced the utmost kindness and care, and after a few days, when they had recovered from sea sickness, I never saw more signs of content and satisfaction, among any set of people, in their or any other country. . . . Regularly every day their rooms were washed out, sprinkled with vinegar, and well dried with chafing dishes of coal; during this operation the slaves were kept on deck, where they were allowed to stay the whole day (when the weather would permit) if they liked it. . . . Their provisions were excellent, consisting of boiled rice and English beans . . . and relished with a piece of beef, salt fish, or palm oil. . . . Great attention was paid the sick, of which, however, there were few. . . .

Whether slaves are equally well treated in common, I cannot pretend to say, but when one recollects how much the masters are interested in their well doing, it is natural to suppose such is the case, for self-interest so unalterably governs the human heart, that it alone must temper the barbarity of any man, and prevent him from committing violence on, or misusing his own property. . . .

For a length of time I viewed the Slave Trade with abhorrence — considering it a blemish on every civilized nation that countenanced or supported it, and that this, our happy enlightened country was more especially stigmatized for carrying it on, than any other; but I am not ashamed to confess, those sentiments were the effect of ignorance, and the prejudice of opinion, imbibed by associating with a circle of acquaintances, *bigoted for the abolition.* . . . So widely opposite are my ideas of the trade from what they were, that I now think it in no shape objectionable either to morality or religion, but on the contrary consistent with both, while neither are to be found in unhappy Africa; and while three-fourths of that populous country come into the world, like hogs or sheep, subject, at any moment, to be rob'd of their lives by the other fourth, I say, while this is the case, I cannot think the Slave Trade inconsistent with any moral, or religious law — in place of invading the happiness of Africa, tends to promote it; by pacifying the murdering, despotic Chieftains of that country, who only spare the lives of their vassals from a desire of acquiring the manufactures of this and other nations, and by saving millions from perdition, whose future existence is rendered comfortable, by the cherishing hands of Christian masters, who are not only restrained from exercising any improper or unjust cruelties over their slaves, by the fear of reciprocal injury, but by the laws of the land, and their religious tenets. . . .

Pray do not misinterpret my arguments, and suppose me a friend to slavery, or wholly an enemy to abolishing the Slave Trade; least you should, I must explain myself — by declaring from my heart I wish freedom to every creature formed by God, who knows its value — which cannot be the case with those who have not tasted its sweets; therefore, most assuredly, I must think favorably of the Slave Trade, while those innate prejudices, ignorance, superstition, and savageness, overspread Africa; and while the Africans feel no conviction by continuing it, but remove those errors of nature, teach them the purposes for which they were created, the ignominy of trafficking in their own flesh, and learn them to hold the lives of their fellow mortals in higher estimation, or even let me see a foundation laid, whereupon hopes itself may be built of their becoming proselytes to the doctrine of Abolition; then, no person on earth will rejoice more earnestly to see that trade suppressed in every shape.

READING AND DISCUSSION QUESTIONS

1. How does Falconbridge's letter depict the condition of slaves aboard the slave ship?

2. What is Falconbridge's rationale for her changed attitude toward the slave trade and abolition? Under what conditions would she support abolition?

3. How might an abolitionist respond to Falconbridge's assessment of the slave trade?

DOCUMENT 19-5

OLAUDAH EQUIANO

From The Interesting Narrative of Olaudah Equiano

1789

One of the few enslaved Africans able to purchase their freedom, Olaudah Equiano (ca. 1745–1797) drew on his remarkable education and experiences to write an autobiographical account of kidnapping and slavery in Africa and the Americas. It was published with the help of British abolitionists, and he promoted his work in Britain with the equivalent of a modern book tour. Recently discovered evidence suggests that Equiano may have been born in South Carolina and therefore would not have experienced life in Africa and the Middle Passage. However, his popular narrative is generally consistent with other accounts of the kidnapping and enslavement of Africans, and its power to inspire the abolitionist movement is unquestioned.

One day, when all our people were gone out to their works as usual, and only I and my dear sister were left to mind the house, two men and a woman got over our walls, and in a moment seized us both, and, without giving us time to cry out, or make resistance, they stopped our mouths, and ran off with us into the nearest wood. Here they tied our hands, and continued to carry us as far as they could, till night came on, when we reached a small house, where the robbers halted for refreshment, and spent the night. We were then unbound, but were unable to take any food; and, being quite overpowered by fatigue and grief, our only relief was some sleep, which allayed our misfortune for a short time. The next morning we left the house, and continued travelling all the day. For a long time we had kept [to] the woods, but at last we came to a road which I believed I knew. I now had some hopes of being delivered; for we had advanced but a little way before I discovered some people at a distance, on which I began to cry out for their assistance; but my cries had no other effect than to make them

Olaudah Equiano, *The Interesting Narrative of Olaudah Equiano* (London, 1789) in *The Atlantic Slave Trade*, ed. David Northrup (Lexington, Mass.: D. C. Heath, 1994), 78–79.

tie me faster and stop my mouth, and then they put me in a large sack. They also stopped my sister's mouth, and tied her hands; and in this manner we proceeded till we were out of sight of these people. When we went to rest the following night, they offered us some victuals, but we refused it; and the only comfort we had was in being in one another's arms all that night, and bathing each other with our tears. But alas! we were soon deprived of even the small comfort of weeping together.

The next day proved a day of greater sorrow than I had yet experienced; for my sister and I were then separated, while we lay clasped in each other's arms. It was in vain that we besought them not to part us; she was torn from me, and immediately carried away, while I was left in a state of distraction not to be described. I cried and grieved continually; and for several days did not eat anything but what they forced into my mouth. At length, after many days' travelling, during which I had often changed masters, I got into the hands of a chieftain, in a very pleasant country. This man had two wives and some children, and they all used me extremely well, and did all they could to comfort me; particularly the first wife, who was something like my mother. Although I was a great many days' journey from my father's house, yet these people spoke exactly the same language with us. . . .

From the time I left my own nation, I always found somebody that understood me till I came to the sea coast. The languages of different nations did not totally differ, nor were they so copious as those of the Europeans,[2] particularly the English. They were therefore easily learned; and, while I was journeying thus through Africa, I acquired two or three different tongues. In this manner I had been travelling for a considerable time, when, one evening, to my great surprise, whom should I see brought to the house where I was but my dear sister! As soon as she saw me, she gave a loud shriek, and ran into my arms — I was quite overpowered; neither of us could speak, but, for a considerable time, clung to each other in mutual embraces, unable to do anything but weep. Our meeting affected all who saw us; and, indeed, I must acknowledge, in honor of those sable destroyers of human rights, that I never met with any ill treatment, or saw any offered to their slaves, except tying them, when necessary, to keep them from running away.

When these people knew we were brother and sister, they indulged us to be together; and the man, to whom I suppose we belonged, lay with

---

[2] **nor were they so copious . . . Europeans**: Equiano is saying that African languages had less extensive vocabularies than European languages.

us, he in the middle, while she and I held one another by the hands across his breast all night; and thus for a while we forgot our misfortunes, in the joy of being together; but even this small comfort was soon to have an end; for scarcely had the fatal morning appeared when she was again torn from me forever! I was now more miserable, if possible, than before. The small relief which her presence gave me from pain, was gone, and the wretchedness of my situation was redoubled by my anxiety after her fate, and my apprehensions lest her sufferings should be greater than mine, when I could not be with her to alleviate them. . . .

I continued to travel, sometimes by land, sometimes by water, through different countries and various nations, till, at the end of six or seven months after I had been kidnapped, I arrived at the sea coast. . . .

The first object which saluted my eyes when I arrived on the coast, was the sea, and a slave ship, which was then riding at anchor, and waiting for its cargo. These filled me with astonishment, which was soon converted into terror, when I was carried on board. I was immediately handled, tossed up to see if I were sound, by some of the crew, and I was now persuaded that I had gotten into a world of bad spirits, and that they were going to kill me. Their complexions, too, differing so much from ours, their long hair, and the language they spoke (which was very different from any I had ever heard), united to confirm me in this belief. Indeed, such were the horrors of my views and fears at the moment, that, if ten thousand worlds had been my own, I would have freely parted with them all to have exchanged my condition with that of the meanest slave in my own country. When I looked round the ship too, and saw a large furnace of copper boiling, and a multitude of black people of every description chained together, every one of their countenances expressing dejection and sorrow. I no longer doubted of my fate, and, quite overpowered with horror and anguish, I fell motionless on the deck and fainted. When I recovered a little, I found some black people about me, who I believed were some of those who had brought me on board, and had been receiving their pay; they talked to me in order to cheer me, but all in vain. I asked them if we were not to be eaten by these white men with horrible looks, red faces, and long hair. They told me I was not, and one of the crew brought me a small portion of spirituous liquor in a wine glass; but being afraid of him, I would not take it out of his hand. One of the blacks therefore took it from him and gave it to me, and I took a little down my palate, which, instead of reviving me, as they thought it would, threw me into the greatest consternation at the strange feeling it produced, having never tasted any such liquor before.

Soon after this, the blacks who brought me on board went off, and left me abandoned to despair. . . .

At last, when the ship we were in, had got in all her cargo, they made ready with many fearful noises, and we were all put under deck, so that we could not see how they managed the vessel. But this disappointment was the least of my sorrow. The stench of the hold while we were on the coast was so intolerably loathsome, that it was dangerous to remain there for any time, and some of us had been permitted to stay on the deck for the fresh air; but now that the whole ship's cargo was confined together, it became absolutely pestilential. The closeness of the place, and the heat of the climate, added to the number in the ship, which was so crowded that each had scarcely room to turn himself, almost suffocated us. This produced copious perspirations, so that the air soon became unfit for respiration, from a variety of loathsome smells, and brought on a sickness among the slaves, of which many died — thus falling victims to the improvident avarice, as I may call it, of their purchasers. This wretched situation was again aggravated by the galling of the chains, now became insupportable, and the filth of the necessary tubs [latrines], into which the children often fell, and were almost suffocated. The shrieks of the women, and the groans of the dying, rendered the whole a scene of horror almost inconceivable. Happily, perhaps, for myself, I was soon reduced so low here that it was thought necessary to keep me almost always on deck, and from my extreme youth I was not put in fetters. In this situation I expected every hour to share the fate of my companions, some of whom were almost daily brought upon deck at the point of death, which I began to hope would soon put an end to my miseries. Often did I think of the many inhabitants of the deep much more happy than myself. I envied them [for] the freedom they enjoyed, and as often wished I could change my condition for theirs. Every circumstance I met with, served only to render my state more painful, and heightened my apprehensions, and my opinion of the cruelty of the whites.

One day they had taken a number of fishes; and when they had killed and satisfied themselves with as many as they thought fit, to our astonishment who were on deck, rather than give any of them to us to eat, as we expected, they tossed the remaining fish into the sea again, although we begged and prayed for some as well we could, but in vain. . . .

One day, when we had a smooth sea and a moderate wind, two of my wearied countrymen who were chained together (I was near them at the time), preferring death to such a life of misery, somehow made through the nettings and jumped into the sea; immediately, another quite dejected fellow, who, on account of his illness, was suffered to be out of irons, also followed their example; and I believe many more would have soon done the same, if they had not been prevented by the ship's crew, who were instantly alarmed. . . .

At last we came in sight of the island of Barbadoes, at which the whites on board gave a great shout, and made many signs of joy to us. We did not know what to think of this; but as the vessel grew nearer, we plainly saw the harbor, and other ships of different kinds and sizes, and we soon anchored among them, off Bridgetown. Many merchants and planters now came on board, though it was in the evening. They put us in separate parcels, and examined us attentively. They also made us jump, and pointed to the land, signifying we were to go there. We thought by this, we should be eaten by these ugly men, as they appeared to us; and, when soon after we were all put down under deck again, there was much dread and trembling among us, and nothing but bitter cries to be heard all the night from these apprehensions, insomuch, that at last the white people got some old slaves from the land to pacify us. They told us we were not to be eaten, but to work, and were soon to go on land, where we would see many of our country people. This report eased us much. And sure enough, soon after we were landed, there came to us Africans of all languages.

We were immediately conducted to the merchant's yard, where we were all pent up together, like so many sheep in a fold, without regard to sex or age. As every object was new to me, everything I saw filled me with surprise. What struck me first, was, that the houses were built with bricks and stories, and every other respect different from those I had seen in Africa; but I was still more astonished on seeing people on horseback.[3] I did not know what this could mean; and, indeed, I thought these people were full of nothing but magical arts. While I was in this astonishment, one of my fellow prisoners spoke to a countryman of his, about the horses, who said they were the same kind they had in their country. I understood them, though they were from a distant part of Africa; and I thought it odd I had not seen any horses there; but afterwards, when I came to converse with different Africans, I found they had many horses amongst them, and much larger than those I then saw.

---

[3] **people on horseback**: Equiano would have been unfamiliar with horses in West Africa, where they were susceptible to sleeping sickness, a lethal disease transmitted by the tsetse fly.

We were not many days in the merchant's custody, before we were sold in the usual manner, which is this: On a signal given (as the beat of a drum), the buyers rush at once into the yard where the slaves are confined, and make a choice of that parcel they like best. The noise and clamor with which this is attended, and the eagerness visible in the countenances of the buyers, serve not a little to increase the apprehension of terrified Africans, who may well be supposed to consider them as the ministers of that destruction to which they think themselves devoted. In this manner, without scruple, are relations and friends separated, most of them never to see each other again.

I remember, in the vessel in which I was brought over, in the men's apartment, there were several brothers, who, in the sale, were sold in different lots; and it was very moving on this occasion, to see and hear their cries at parting. O, ye nominal Christians! might not an African ask you — Learned you this from your God, who says unto you, Do unto all men as you would men should do unto you? Is it not enough that we are torn from our country and friends, to toil for your luxury and lust of gain? Must every tender feeling be likewise sacrificed to your avarice? Are the dearest friends and relations, now rendered more dear by their separation from their kindred, still to be parted from each other, and thus prevented from cheering the gloom of slavery, with the small comfort of being together, and mingling their sufferings and sorrows? Why are parents to lose their children, brothers their sisters, or husbands their wives? Surely, this is a new refinement in cruelty, which, while it has no advantage to atone for it, thus aggravates distress, and adds fresh horrors even to the wretchedness of slavery.

READING AND DISCUSSION QUESTIONS

1. How does Equiano contrast his experiences as a slave in Africa with his experiences aboard the slave ship?

2. To whom does Equiano appeal at the end of his narrative, and on what grounds?

3. At times, Equiano describes people as "white" or "black." At others, he distinguishes between people of his own nation and other "blacks," and elsewhere he refers to "Africans." What is the significance of these different categorizations?

DOCUMENT 19-6

Transportation of Slaves in Africa

ca. 1800–1900

This nineteenth-century painting depicts the dynamics of the African slave trade and particularly the internal conditions of that trade through the eighteenth and nineteenth centuries. The painting highlights not only the brutal conditions under which Africans were enslaved and transported to the coast, but also the multiple and diverse roles played by Africans in the slave trade. The slavers (the figures holding rifles, a hatchet, or a pistol) are guarding or visibly threatening the enslaved Africans, some of whom are yoked together with a forked wooden device. Victims of violence or deprivation are left alongside the trail, and women and children are clearly visible among the slave ranks.

READING AND DISCUSSION QUESTIONS

1. What differences and similarities are discernible between the traders and the captured slaves? What do their garments, postures, and expressions reveal?

2. What might the artist have intended to communicate with this illustration? To whom?

3. Note that at least two of the figures in the image are holding firearms. What, if anything, does the presence of firearms indicate about the nature of African slavery?

4. The group of enslaved Africans stretches in a line into the far distance and blurs as it recedes. What impression is created by this visual effect, and what does it communicate about the nature of African slavery?

COMPARATIVE QUESTIONS

1. What differences between African and European views of African slavery do the documents in this chapter reveal?

2. How might Falconbridge have interpreted the African slavery image? How might Equiano have interpreted the image? What about the two monarchs?

3. Falconbridge writes of the "ignorance, superstition, and savageness" of Africa based on her observations of Sierra Leone. In what ways does her assessment seem to support or refute the images presented by other sources?

4. What key differences, if any, exist between the two pro-slavery documents here?

5. Several of the authors in this chapter invoke morality to talk about the slave trade. What, specifically, are the moral standards cited in the various documents?

CHAPTER 20

The Islamic World Powers

1300–1800

With the decline of the Mongol Empire in the late thirteenth and fourteenth centuries, power shifted to a number of Turkish territories. By the sixteenth century, three areas had developed into major Islamic empires: the Safavid in Persia, the Ottoman in Anatolia, and the Mughal in India. Their collective territories stretched from eastern Europe and West Africa through present-day Bangladesh. As each state flourished, it made significant political, economic, intellectual, and artistic contributions. Islamic culture was enriched by the states' interactions with one another and with the increasingly mobile peoples of Christian Europe. However, the impressive extent of Islamic society and culture represented by the three states belies the sharp and often violent differences among them and the internal tensions in each society. The following documents reveal the splendor and troubled nature of the Ottoman, Safavid, and Mughal Empires, as well as their increasing interactions with western Europeans.

DOCUMENT 20-1

SULTAN SELIM I

From a Letter to Shah Ismail of Persia

1514

Sultan Selim I (r. 1512–1520) presided over a massive territorial expansion of the Ottoman Empire, conquering much of the Middle East, including the holy cities of Mecca and Medina. After defeating the Mamluk Dynasty in Egypt in 1517, Selim assumed the title of caliph — a political and religious successor to Muhammad — thereby declaring Sunni Ottoman leadership

John J. Saunders, ed. and trans., *The Muslim World on the Eve of Europe's Expansion* (Englewood Cliffs, N.J.: Prentice-Hall, 1966), 41–43.

*of the Muslim world. The excerpt that follows is from Selim's letter to Shah
Ismail of Persia, the young founder of the Shi'ite Safavid Empire and a
growing threat to Selim's power. The ensuing conflict in 1514 marked an
important moment in Sunni–Shi'ite power struggles in the Islamic world.*

The Supreme Being who is at once the sovereign arbiter of the destinies of
men and the source of all light and knowledge, declares in the holy book
[the Qur'an] that the true faith is that of the Muslims, and that whoever
professes another religion, far from being hearkened to and saved, will on
the contrary be cast out among the rejected on the great day of the Last
Judgment; He says further, this God of truth, that His designs and decrees
are unalterable, that all human acts are perforce reported to Him, and that
he who abandons the good way will be condemned to hell-fire and eternal
torments. Place yourself, O Prince, among the true believers, those who
walk in the path of salvation, and who turn aside with care from vice and
infidelity. . . .

    I, sovereign chief of the Ottomans, master of the heroes of the age; . . .
I, the exterminator of idolators, destroyer of the enemies of the true faith,
the terror of the tyrants and pharaohs of the age; I, before whom proud and
unjust kings have humbled themselves, and whose hand breaks the strongest scepters; I, the great Sultan-Khan, son of Sultan Bayezid-Khan, son
of Sultan Muhammad-Khan, son of Sultan Murad-Khan, I address myself
graciously to you, Emir Ismail, chief of the troops of Persia, comparable in
tyranny to Sohak and Afrasiab [legendary Asian kings], and predestined to
perish . . . in order to make known to you that the works emanating from
the Almighty are not the fragile products of caprice or folly, but make up
an infinity of mysteries impenetrable to the human mind. The Lord Himself says in his holy book: "We have not created the heavens and the earth
in order to play a game" [Qur'an, 21:16]. Man, who is the noblest of the
creatures and the summary of the marvels of God, is in consequence on
earth the living image of the Creator. It is He who has set up Caliphs on
earth, because, joining faculties of soul with perfection of body, man is the
only being who can comprehend the attributes of the divinity and adore
its sublime beauties; but he possesses this rare intelligence, he attains this
divine knowledge only in our religion and by observing the precepts of the
prince of prophets . . . the right arm of the God of Mercy [Muhammad];
it is then only by practicing the true religion that man will prosper in this
world and merit eternal life in the other. As to you, Emir Ismail, such a
recompense will not be your lot; because you have denied the sanctity

of the divine laws; because you have deserted the path of salvation and the sacred commandments; because you have impaired the purity of the dogmas of Islam; because you have dishonored, soiled, and destroyed the altars of the Lord, usurped the scepter of the East by unlawful and tyrannical means; because coming forth from the dust, you have raised yourself by odious devices to a place shining with splendor and magnificence; because you have opened to Muslims the gates of tyranny and oppression; because you have joined iniquity, perjury, and blasphemy to your sectarian impiety; because under the cloak of the hypocrite, you have sowed everywhere trouble and sedition; because you have raised the standard of irreligion and heresy; because yielding to the impulse of your evil passions, and giving yourself up without rein to the most infamous disorders, you have dared to throw off the control of Muslim laws and to permit lust and rape, the massacre of the most virtuous and respectable men, the destruction of pulpits and temples, the profanation of tombs, the ill-treatment of the ulama,[1] the doctors [teachers] and emirs [military commanders and princes] descended from the Prophet, the repudiation of the Quran, the cursing of the legitimate Caliphs.[2] Now as the first duty of a Muslim and above all of a pious prince is to obey the commandment, "O, you faithful who believe, be the executors of the decrees of God!" the ulama and our doctors have pronounced sentence of death against you, perjurer and blasphemer, and have imposed on every Muslim the sacred obligation to arm in defense of religion and destroy heresy and impiety in your person and that of all your partisans.

Animated by the spirit of this fatwa [religious decree], conforming to the Quran, the code of divine laws, and wishing on one side to strengthen Islam, on the other to liberate the lands and peoples who writhe under your yoke, we have resolved to lay aside our imperial robes in order to put on the shield and coat of mail [armor], to raise our ever victorious banner, to assemble our invincible armies, to take up the gauntlet of the avenger, to march with our soldiers, whose sword strikes mortal blows, and whose point will pierce the enemy even to the constellation of Sagittarius. In pursuit of this noble resolution, we have entered upon the campaign, and guided by the hand of the Almighty, we hope soon to strike down your

---

[1] **ulama**: Religious teachers and interpreters of the Qu'ran and Muslim law.
[2] **the legitimate Caliphs**: Shi'ites broke with mainstream Islam over a dispute about the early caliphate. They believe that Muhammad's cousin and son-in-law Ali (the fourth caliph) should have been the first caliph. Shi'ites thus believe that the first three caliphs are illegitimate.

DOCUMENT 20-2

ANTONIO MONSERRATE

From The Commentary of Father Monserrate: *On Mughal India*

ca. 1580

In 1580, Portuguese Jesuit missionary Antonio Monserrate (1536–1600) arrived in Mughal India. At the request of the sovereign, Akbar, who had a keen interest in other religions, Monserrate had been sent from Portuguese Goa with illustrated Bibles and other religious materials. He was appointed as a tutor to Akbar's son Murad, and he remained with Akbar for some years, accompanying him on military ventures and engaging with the sovereign on theological points. Monserrate's Commentary, *commissioned by his Jesuit superior, was never delivered and only resurfaced in the early 1900s in Calcutta. It offers invaluable insight into early modern European contact with Mughal India, demonstrating both the zeal of Jesuit missionaries and the tolerant nature of Akbar's rule.*

The wives of the Brachmans — a famous class of nobly-born Hindus — are accustomed, in accordance with an ancient tradition of their religion, to burn themselves on the same pyres as their dead husbands. The King ordered the priests to be summoned to see an instance of this. They went in ignorance of what was to take place; but when they found out, they plainly indicated by their saddened faces how cruel and savage they felt that crime to be. Finally Rudolf [a Jesuit] publicly reprimanded the King for showing openly by his presence there that he approved of such a revolting crime, and for supporting it by his weighty judgment and explicit approbation, (for he was heard to say that such fortitude could only come from God). Such was Zelaldinus' [Akbar's] kindness and favor towards the priests that he showed no resentment; and a certain chief, a great favorite of his, a Brahman by birth, who held the office of Superintendent of sacred observances, could no longer persuade him to attend such spectacles. The wretched women are rendered quite insensible by means of certain drugs, in order that

The Commentary of Father Monserrate, S.J., on His Journey to the Court of Akbar (London: Oxford University Press, 1922), 61–63.

they may feel no pain. For this purpose opium is used, or a soporific herb named bang, or — more usually — the herb "duturo," which is known to the Indians, although entirely unfamiliar alike to modern Europeans and to the ancients. Sometimes they are half-drugged: and, before they lose their resolution, are hurried to the pyre with warnings, prayers, and promises of eternal fame. On arriving there they cast themselves into the flames. If they hesitate, the wretched creatures are driven on to the pyre: and if they try to leap off again, are held down with poles and hooks. The nobles who were present were highly incensed at the Fathers' interference. They did not dare to gainsay the King; but they grumbled loudly amongst themselves, saying, "Away with you, black-clothed Franks." The whole city was filled with praise and admiration when news was brought that the Franks had dared to rebuke the King regarding this affair.

On one occasion, the Fathers met a crowd of worthless profligates [male prostitutes], some of those who dress and adorn themselves like women. The priests were rightly disgusted at this, and took the first opportunity of privately complaining to the King (since he was so favorable to them) about this disgraceful matter. They declared with the greatest emphasis that they were astonished at his permitting such a class of men to live in his kingdom, let alone in his city, and almost under his eyes. They must be banished, as though they were a deadly plague, to his most distant territories; even better, let them be burnt up by devouring flames. They never would have believed that such men could be found in the court itself and in the royal city, where lived a king of such piety, integrity, and prudence. Therefore let him give orders that these libertines should never again be seen in Fattepurum, seeing that his remarkable prophet [Muhammad] had guaranteed that good men should never suffer for their good actions. The King laughed at this piece of sarcasm and retired, saying that he would attend to the matter.

READING AND DISCUSSION QUESTIONS

1. What two phenomena does Monserrate describe?
2. What is Monserrate's opinion of the two phenomena? What type of language does he use to make this clear?
3. How does Monserrate present Akbar's interactions with the priests?
4. From Monserrate's account, what is the status of Catholic priests in Akbar's court? What level of influence do they have?

FARID UD-DIN ATTAR AND HABIBALLAH

Excerpt from and Illustration of The Conference of the Birds

1600

Following the brilliant military exploits of the young Shah Ismail and the conquest of Persia, the Safavid rulers quickly turned to consolidating their new state. Following the relocation of the royal capital to Isfahan in 1598 by Shah Abbas (r. 1587–1629) and his defeat of Ottoman forces, the Safavid state experienced a more stable and prosperous existence than ever before. Along with this stability came a flowering of culture; state sponsorship of architecture, painting, and literature helped strengthen the reputation of the Safavid as a cultural as well as military and economic power. Habiballah's illustration, reproduced in this selection, accompanied a manuscript of the famous Sufi epic poem entitled Manteq at-Tair *(The Conference of the Birds) by twelfth-century Persian poet Farid Ud-Din Attar. The poem, excerpted here, describes the mystical journey of birds to find their king, the Simurgh. The journey itself is an allegory for the trials and illusions of earthly existence, through which thirty birds come to realize that their mystical ruler is none other than themselves (the words* si murgh *mean "thirty birds").*

A Sage's Jest Concerning a Palace

A king built a palace which cost him a hundred thousand dinars. Outside it was adorned with gilded towers and cupolas, and the furniture and carpets made the interior a paradise. When it was finished he invited men from every country to visit him. They came and presented gifts, and he made them all sit down with him. Then he asked them: "Tell me what you think of my palace. Has anything been forgotten which mars its beauty?" They all protested that never had there been such a palace on Earth and never would its like be seen again. All, that is, except one, a Sage, who stood up and said: "Sire, there is one small crevice which to me seems a blemish. Were it not for this blemish, paradise itself would bring gifts to you from the invisible world."

Farid Ud-Din Attar, *The Conference of the Birds*, trans. S. C. Nott (London: Continuum, 2000), 76, 83, 144–147.

"I don't see this blemish," said the king angrily. "You are an ignorant person and you only wish to make yourself important." "No, proud King," replied the Sage. "This chink of which I speak is that through which Azrael, the angel of death, will come. Would to God you could stop it up, for otherwise, what use is your gorgeous palace, your crown and your throne? When death comes they will be as a handful of dust. Nothing lasts, and it is this which spoils the beauty of your dwelling. No art can make stable that which is unstable. Ah, do not put your hopes of happiness upon a palace! . . . If no one dares speak plainly to the king and remind him of his faults, that is a great misfortune." . . .

Excuse of the Eleventh Bird

Another bird said to the Hoopoe:[3] "O you whose faith is sincere, I have not a breath of good will. I have spent my life in vexation, desiring the ball of the world. There is such a sadness in my heart that I will never cease to mourn. I am always in a state of bewilderment and impotence; and when for a moment I have been content, then I am unbelieving. In consequence, I have become a dervish.[4] But now I hesitate to start out on the road of spiritual knowledge. If my heart were not so full of sorrow I would be charmed with this journey. As it is I am in a state of perplexity. Now that I have put my case before you tell me what I ought to do."

The Hoopoe said: "You, who are given over to pride, who are swallowed up in self-pity, you do well to be disturbed. Seeing that the world passes, you yourself should pass it by. Abandon it, for whoever becomes identified with transient things can have no part in the things that are lasting. The sufferings you endure can be made glorious and not humiliating. That which in outward appearance is suffering can be a treasure for the seer. A hundred blessings will come to you if you make effort on the Path. But as you are, you are only a skin covering a dull brain." . . .

Attitudes of the Birds

. . . In the end, only a small number of all this great company arrived at that sublime place to which the Hoopoe had led them. Of the thousands of birds almost all had disappeared. Many had been lost in the ocean, others had perished on the summits of the high mountains, tortured by thirst; others had had their wings burnt and their hearts dried up by the fire of the sun; others were devoured by tigers and panthers; others died of fatigue in the deserts and in the wilderness, their lips parched and their bodies

---

[3] **Hoopoe**: A type of bird.
[4] **dervish**: Devout practitioner of the Sufi tradition of Islam.

overcome by the heat; some went mad and killed each other for a grain of barley; others, enfeebled by suffering and weariness, dropped on the road unable to go further; others, bewildered by the things they saw, stopped where they were, stupefied; and many, who had started out from curiosity or pleasure, perished without an idea of what they had set out to find.

So then, out of all those thousands of birds, only thirty reached the end of the journey. . . . But now they were at the door of this Majesty that cannot be described, whose essence is incomprehensible — that Being who is beyond human reason and knowledge. Then flashed the lightning of fulfillment, and a hundred worlds were consumed in a moment. They saw thousands of suns each more resplendent than the other, thousands of moons and stars all equally beautiful, and seeing all this they were amazed and agitated like a dancing atom of dust. . . .

When . . . the door suddenly opened, there stepped out a noble chamberlain, one of the courtiers of the Supreme Majesty. He looked them over and saw that out of thousands only these thirty birds were left.

He said: "Now then, O Birds, where have you come from, and what are you doing here? What is your name? O you who are destitute of everything, where is your home? What do they call you in the world? What can be done with a feeble handful of dust like you?"

"We have come," they said, "to acknowledge the Simurgh as our king. Through love and desire for him we have lost our reason and our peace of mind." . . .

The Chamberlain replied: "O you whose minds and hearts are troubled, whether you exist or do not exist in the universe, the King has his being always and eternally. Thousands of worlds of creatures are no more than an ant at his gate. You bring nothing but moans and lamentations. Return then to whence you came, O vile handful of earth!"

At this, the birds were petrified with astonishment. . . .

Then the Chamberlain, having tested them, opened the door; and as he drew aside a hundred curtains, one after the other, a new world beyond the veil was revealed. Now was the light of lights manifested, and all of them sat down on the masnad, the seat of the Majesty and Glory. They were given a writing which they were told to read through; and reading this, and pondering, they were able to understand their state. When they were completely at peace and detached from all things they became aware that the Simurgh was there with them, and a new life began for them in the Simurgh. All that they had done previously was washed away. The sun of majesty sent forth his rays, and in the reflection of each other's faces these thirty birds [si murgh] of the outer world, contemplated the face of the Simurgh of the inner world. . . . At last, in a state of contemplation, they realized that they were the Simurgh and that the Simurgh was the thirty birds. When they gazed at the Simurgh they saw that it was truly the Simurgh who was there, and when they turned their eyes towards themselves they saw that they themselves were the Simurgh.

Image courtesy of The Metropolitan Museum of Art/Art Resource, N.Y.

READING AND DISCUSSION QUESTIONS

1. Attar's text illustrates not only a strong sense of self-denial — an important component of Sufism — but also the illusory nature of society and politics. How might this message have been received by Safavid rulers?

2. The illustration reflects various contemporary influences on Safavid art, including the familiar motif of a man with a firearm (upper right corner). How might such elements change the essential message of Attar's poem?

DOCUMENT 20-4

NURUDDIN SALIM JAHANGIR

From the Memoirs of Jahangir

ca. 1580–1600

Akbar's third son, Prince Salim (1569–1628), succeeded his father as the Mughal sovereign in 1605 and took the name Jahangir, or "World Conqueror." During his reign, he continued many of his father's policies, including (limited) religious tolerance and wars of territorial expansion. Jahangir found himself locked in a familiar pattern of Mughal succession when his son Khurram rebelled in 1622, just as Jahangir rebelled against his own father. The passages here are taken from Jahangir's autobiography. In the first section, he presents measures to promote justice and social welfare in the realm. In the second, he describes a hunting trip with his favorite wife, Nūr-Jahān Begam.

After my accession, the first order that I gave was for the fastening up of the Chain of Justice, so that if those engaged in the administration of justice should delay or practice hypocrisy in the matter of those seeking justice, the oppressed might come to this chain and shake it so that its noise might attract attention. Its fashion was this: I ordered them to make a chain of pure gold, 30 gaz in length and containing 60 bells. Its weight was 4 Indian

---

The Tūzuk-i-Jahāngīrī or *Memoirs of Jahāngīr*, ed. Alexander Rogers and Henry Beveridge (London: Royal Asiatic Society, 1909–1914), 2, 105.

maunds, equal to 42 'Irāqī maunds. One end of it they made fast to the battlements of the Shāh Burj of the fort at Agra and the other to a stone post fixed on the bank of the river. I also gave twelve orders to be observed as rules of conduct in all my dominions —

1. Forbidding the levy of cesses [taxes] under the names of tamghā and mīr baḥrī [river tolls], and other burdens which the jāgīrdārs[5] of every province and district had imposed for their own profit.
2. On roads where thefts and robberies took place, which roads might be at a little distance from habitations, the jāgīrdārs of the neighborhood should build sarā'īs [public rest houses], mosques, and dig wells, which might stimulate population, and people might settle down in those sarā'īs. If these should be near a khāliṣa estate,[6] the administrator of that place should execute the work.
3. The bales of merchants should not be opened on the roads without informing them and obtaining their leave.
4. In my dominions if anyone, whether unbeliever or Musalman, should die, his property and effects should be left for his heirs, and no one should interfere with them. If he should have no heir, they should appoint inspectors and separate guardians to guard the property, so that its value might be expended in lawful expenditure, such as the building of mosques and sarā'īs, the repair of broken bridges, and the digging of tanks and wells.
5. They should not make wine or rice-spirit or any kind of intoxicating drug, or sell them; although I myself drink wine, and from the age of 18 years up till now, when I am 38, have persisted in it. When I first took a liking to drinking I sometimes took as much as twenty cups of double-distilled spirit; when by degrees it acquired a great influence over me I endeavored to lessen the quantity, and in the period of seven years I have brought myself from fifteen cups to five or six. My times for drinking were varied; sometimes when three or four sidereal hours of the day remained I would begin to drink, and sometimes at night and partly by day. This went on till I was 30 years old. After that I took to drinking always at night. Now I drink only to digest my food.
6. They should not take possession of any person's house.

---

[5] jāgīrdārs: Regional rulers whose income came primarily from taxes imposed within their districts.
[6] khāliṣa estate: Land controlled by the state.

7. I forbade the cutting off the nose or ears of any person, and I myself made a vow by the throne of God that I would not blemish anyone by this punishment.

8. I gave an order that the officials of the Crown lands and the jāgīrdārs should not forcibly take the ryots' [farmers'] lands and cultivate them on their own account.

9. A government collector or a jāgīrdār should not without permission inter-marry with the people of the pargana [district] in which he might be.

10. They should found hospitals in the great cities, and appoint physicians for the healing of the sick; whatever the expenditure might be, should be given from the khāliṣa establishment.

11. In accordance with the regulations of my revered father, I ordered that each year from the 18th of Rabī'u-l-awwal, which is my birthday, for a number of days corresponding to the years of my life, they should not slaughter animals [for food]. Two days in each week were also forbid-den, one of them Thursday, the day of my accession, and the other Sunday, the day of my father's birth. He held this day in great esteem on this account, and because it was dedicated to the Sun, and also because it was the day on which the Creation began. Therefore it was one of the days on which there was no killing in his dominions.

12. I gave a general order that the offices and jāgīrs [land plots] of my father's servants should remain as they were. Later, the manṣabs [ranks or offices] were increased according to each one's circumstances by not less than 20 percent to 300 or 400 percent. The subsistence money of the aḥadīs was increased by 50 percent, and I raised the pay of all domestics by 20 percent. I increased the allowances of all the veiled ladies of my father's harem from 20 percent to 100 percent, according to their condition and relationship. By one stroke of the pen I con-firmed the subsistence lands of the holders of aimas [charity lands] within the dominions, who form the army of prayer, according to the deeds in their possession. I gave an order to Mīrān Ṣadr Jahān, who is one of the genuine Sayyids of India [descendants of Muhammad], and who for a long time held the high office of ṣadr [ecclesiastical officer] under my father, that he should every day produce before me deserv-ing people [worthy of charity]. I released all criminals who had been confined and imprisoned for a long time in the forts and prisons. . . .

On the 25th the contingent of I'timādu-d-daulah passed before me in review on the plain under the jharoka.[7] There were 2,000 cavalry well

---

[7] **jharoka:** Balcony used for architectural ornamentation and for spying.

horsed, most of whom were Moghuls, 500 foot [soldiers] armed with bows and guns, and fourteen elephants. The bakhshis reckoned them up and reported that this force was fully equipped and according to rule. On the 26th a tigress was killed. On Thursday, the 1st Urdībihisht, a diamond that Muqarrab Khān had sent by runners was laid before me; it weighed 23 surkh, and the jewellers valued it at 30,000 rupees. It was a diamond of the first water, and was much approved. I ordered them to make a ring of it. On the 3rd the mansab [military rank] of Yūsuf Khān was, at the request of Bābā Khurram, fixed at 1,000 with 1,500 horses, and in the same way the mansabs of several of the Amirs [nobles] and mansabdars [office holders] were increased at his suggestion.[8] On the 7th, as the huntsmen had marked down four tigers, when two watches and three gharis [a length of time] had passed I went out to hunt them with my ladies. When the tigers came in sight Nūr-Jahān Begam submitted that if I would order her she herself would kill the tigers with her gun. I said, "Let it be so." She shot two tigers with one shot each and knocked over the two others with four shots. In the twinkling of an eye she deprived of life the bodies of these four tigers. Until now such shooting was never seen, that from the top of an elephant and inside of a howdah [carriage atop an elephant] six shots should be made and not one miss, so that the four beasts found no opportunity to spring or move. As a reward for this good shooting I gave her a pair of bracelets of diamonds worth 100,000 rupees and scattered 1,000 ashrafis [over her].

READING AND DISCUSSION QUESTIONS

1. What is the purpose of Jahangir's Chain of Justice? What impression does it create of the sovereign?

2. Jahangir's twelve orders deal with a variety of issues. How would you categorize them? Which order is most striking to you, and why?

3. What is the effect of Jahangir's frequent references to gold and jewels in both of these excerpts? What image does that create of him and his realm?

4. Jahangir describes both military forces and a hunting expedition with his wives. How would you compare the tone of this passage with his comments about justice and social order?

---

[8] **fixed at 1,000 . . . suggestion**: System of military ranking that also determined compensation. High-ranking commanders were in one of three classes according to the proportion of horsemen in their unit.

VIEWPOINTS

Economics Micro and Macro

DOCUMENT 20-5

HALIME HATUN

Record of Two Petitions

1702

Muslim women in the Ottoman Empire enjoyed an impressive range of economic and social freedoms. Women could inherit property, lend and borrow money, and divorce; in order to defend and enforce these freedoms, they frequently petitioned the şeriat *(sharia) court of Islamic law. The petitions recorded here were presented in Istanbul by a woman named Halime Hatun, demanding the return of her* mehr, *or dowry, from her ex-husband. The* mehr *was the property of the wife, and only if she initiated divorce would it transfer to the husband. Here, Halime claims that she filed for divorce under duress and that her* mehr *should be returned.*

A *Hüküm* [ruling] to the *Kaimmakam* [governor] and *Kadi* [judge] of my threshold [i.e., Istanbul]: A lady named Halime has come complaining that her husband, Ahmet a resident of Istanbul has illegally taken from her goods worth 399 *kus*,[9] . . . another time has taken 100-cash,[10] and again has taken 40 *akches*[11] to purchase a shop. She has unwillingly reached an agreement with him, however, since a forced agreement is against the şeriat according to the *fetva*[12] of the *şeyhulislam*,[13] she has demanded via

---

Fariba Zarinebaf-Shahr, "Women, Law, and Imperial Justice in Ottoman Istanbul in the Late Seventeenth Century," in Amira El Azhary Sonbol, ed., *Women, the Family, and Divorce Laws in Islamic History* (Syracuse, N.Y.: Syracuse University Press, 1996), 92.

[9] *kus*: Probably *kuruş*, Ottoman currency until 1844.

[10] 100-cash: Possibly a reference to para, another unit of Ottoman currency.

[11] *akches*: Another unit of Ottoman currency; 120 *akche* (or *akçe*) made one *kuruş*.

[12] *fetva*: Fatwa, a legal decision of a Muslim authority.

[13] *şeyhulislam*: Ottoman empire religious authority.

her deputy the payment of all her due rights (*hakk*, read cash). This order is issued to you to act according to the *fetva* and the *şeriat*. . . .

To the *kadi* and *Kaimmakam* of my threshold: A lady named Halime has come claiming that her husband, Ahmet, a resident of Istanbul had forced her to sue for divorce and give up her *mehr*. . . . However, since the divorce is *kuhl*, that is, it has been forced upon her and therefore is against the *şeriat*, she is demanding her legally established *mehr* but he has refused to pay it to her deputy according to a *fetva*. This order is written to you to act according to the *şeriat*.

READING AND DISCUSSION QUESTIONS

1. Based on these petitions, what can you say about the legal status of Muslim women in the Ottoman Empire? What kind of social power do these petitions imply for Muslim women? What limitations do they imply, if any?

2. These petitions appealed to (and were made through) *şeriat*, or Islamic legal code. What protections are implied by *şeriat* for Muslim women in the Ottoman Empire?

DOCUMENT 20-6

THE DUTCH EAST INDIA COMPANY
AND SHAH ABBAS

Correspondences on Persian Trade
1647, 1648

With the help of the English East India Company's naval force, the Safavid Empire defeated Portuguese forces on the island of Hormoz in 1622, ending Portuguese dominance in the Persian Gulf. Following several unprofitable years, however, the English withdrew from Persian trade, leaving the Dutch

Willem Floor and Mohammad H. Faghfoory, *The First Dutch-Persian Commercial Conflict: The Attack on Qeshm Island, 1645* (Costa Mesa, Calif.: Mazda Publishers, 2004), 221–222, 232–233.

East India Company (the VOC) as the major European trade partner with the Safavid. The relationship was profitable but often troubled. The correspondence excerpted here shows the complex realities of international trade between the Safavid and the Dutch and demonstrates the Safavid Empire's role as an economic world power.

CORRESPONDENCE BETWEEN THE VOC REPRESENTATIVES IN ASIA AND SHAH ABBAS OF SAFAVID PERSIA, 1647

From the Dutch East India Company

First, we request Your Majesty to grant and open up to the Hon. Company the free unhindered trade for eternity, so that its servants may not be hindered in the least therein by His Majesty's subalterns as to their liking and may sell their imported merchandise wherever they please. Further, that they may buy or contract for storage as much silk and other goods, under whatever name, from private persons, as they deem necessary, and to transport there whatever they please. In return, we promise to purchase 100 to 125 cargas[14] of legia[15] silk (if it pleases His Majesty) annually at 38, maximum 40 tumans[16] per carga, provided these are delivered at Spahan [Isfahan] and (if possible) that payment of the silk will take place in Gamron.[17]

Safavid Reply

Regarding the silk price; this has varied in the past. In the days of Chia Soffhij [Shah Safi I, r. 1629–1642] you always have paid 50 tumans and you do not have a decree permitting you to buy silk from others without having to pay tolls. This year it will only be possible to contract silk with the shah, as before, at 45 tumans, otherwise His Majesty would lose money. However, if you buy this year 300 cargas from the shah at 45 tumans then you do not have to pay tolls and your nation will be allowed to trade throughout the kingdom, nobody being allowed to interfere, selling your imported goods to whomever and wherever you please. The tolls of 30 (per cent) of cargas of silk, which you have contracted with the shah (buying these from

---

[14] **cargas**: A measurement of weight, roughly 300 pounds.
[15] **legia**: A grade of silk, probably named after its origin in the city of Lahijan, Persia.
[16] **tumans**: A unit of Safavid currency.
[17] **Gamron**: Present-day Bandar Abbas, a port city on the Strait of Hormuz.

whomever you please) will be granted to you, while over the remainder you will have to pay imposts [taxes].

LETTERS FROM THE VOC DIRECTORS IN THE NETHERLANDS TO VOC REPRESENTATIVES IN ASIA, 1648

From the Council of the XVII to Governor-General and Councilors

Because of the uncertainty which is inherent to a war, as well as the fact that the Company's profitable trade must not come to a standstill, trade would remain open for the English and other nations, we are of the opinion that it would be bad policy to get into new trouble with the Persian. We would prefer to continue an uneasy trade with obnoxious vexations rather than have a better one with uncertainty. The more so, since all sensible people judge that His Majesty will never again grant the Dutch nation such a free trade as we had imagined enjoying there. For the Persian also wants to profit from this . . . (for this is what this avaricious and superb nation is out for).

From the Council of the XVII to Governor-General and Councilors

We have well observed from the previous Persian letters . . . that this nation is again obstructing the Company and will be the cause of much vexation, as they have already started to bring into practice. [Moreover] that you were of the opinion that, once again, arms had to [be] taken up to end all corruption, and we have also seen that you have passed a resolution to that effect, namely to start a war against Persia this year. . . . This has been considered by us, taking into account the importance of the Persian trade which by the sale of various goods yields such considerable profits each year, and we are worried whether the Company's objectives will be achieved by war. We are of the opinion that before embarking upon such an activity you should have asked for the advice of this Council so that this could have been done after communication between us. For we are well aware of the successes of war, how uncertain these are, as they may be begun with ease, but can only with difficulty be brought to an end. . . . If the profits are not so substantial as we would like, we have to exercise patience and wait for a better [time], without saying that we cannot exist in this way. . . . In consequence thereof, we in conclusion recommend and order you always to maintain the peace in this and similar affairs and that we will take up weapons only out of necessity.

READING AND DISCUSSION QUESTIONS

1. In the exchange between the Dutch East India Company and Safavid representatives, which side has the upper hand? Who controls Safavid-Dutch trade? What aspect of the language of either letter gives you that impression?

2. What does the correspondence from VOC headquarters to VOC representatives in Asia imply about the power balance between the Safavid and the Dutch?

3. What might be the "obnoxious vexations" described in the correspondence to the VOC governor-general in Asia? Why don't the vexations merit a military solution?

4. According to these letters, what were the fundamental goals of the Dutch? Of the Safavid?

COMPARATIVE QUESTIONS

1. Financial concerns play an important role in several of the documents in this chapter; other documents, like Sultan Selim I's letter, focus on religious values. What can you determine about the intersection of economic and religious concerns in each case? Is there a pattern?

2. What are the traditions — traditional values, traditional law, and traditional literature — displayed in these documents? How are these traditions upheld or challenged?

3. Several of the documents in this chapter touch on international relations among and beyond the Ottoman, Mughal, and Safavid Empires. What are the important concerns expressed in each case? What do they indicate about each state, and what do they suggest about the general nature of international relations in the modern era?

4. What do the Monserrate, Hatun, and Jahangir documents suggest about the status and opportunities available to women in their respective cultures? In what ways are women portrayed as equal to or unequal to men?

5. Father Monserrate and the representatives of the Dutch East India Company were both interacting with cultures that were not their own. What difficulties do cultural differences present in each case?

CHAPTER 21

Continuity and Change in East Asia

1400–1800

From 1400 to 1800, East Asian countries experienced important changes at all levels of society. Despite the growing presence of Europeans in East Asia, both China and Japan remained relatively free from the influence of European commercial expansion. Chinese thinkers in the Ming and early Qing periods were primarily concerned with internal development and regional conflicts involving other Asian states. In Japan, the work of the three great unifiers — Oda Nobunaga, Toyotomi Hideyoshi, and Tokugawa Ieyasu — ended the chaotic Warring States Period and led to the relative peace of the Tokugawa regime (1603–1867). In both countries, transitions from older to newer political orders were mirrored by changes in society and culture. In China, the fall of the Ming Dynasty and the founding of the Qing Dynasty (1644–1911) by Jurchen invaders from Manchuria (known as the Manchu) occasioned new unrest and social critique. In Japan, the stability of the Tokugawa family's rule fostered domestic economic and cultural advances, and — despite careful control of international contact — afforded Dutch merchants limited but important access to Japanese society. The documents here illustrate not only the political shifts in East Asia, but also new ways that the Chinese and Japanese tried to define gender and its role in their lives.

DOCUMENT 21-1

TOYOTOMI HIDEYOSHI
Letter to His Wife
1587

Toyotomi Hideyoshi (1536–1598, born Kinoshita Tokichirō) was a low-ranking foot soldier in the armies of Oda Nobunaga, the first of three major unifiers of Japan in the late 1500s. Hideyoshi's skills and cunning helped him rise in Nobunaga's service, and when Nobunaga was assassinated in 1582, Hideyoshi took effective control of his clan and its assets. His military and political successes helped him gain power over virtually all of Japan by 1590, but his plans to invade Korea and China ended as costly failures. He died in 1598. His letters offer astonishing insight into his private life and thoughts; here, a letter to his wife following his defeat of the Shimazu clan shows his political savvy, military ambitions, and human frailties.

I received your letter of the 10th of the 5th month today, the 28th, at Sashiki in Higo province. Tomorrow I shall go on to Yatsushiro, from where the troops of Shimazu have retreated [back into their home provinces]. We have arranged matters in the following way:

Item: As regards the hostage from Shimazu Yoshihisa, this should be a daughter of about 15 [years old]. . . .

Item: As for Yoshihisa himself, he should live in Kyoto.

Item: As regards the hostages of the Elder Councilors, about ten should be offered.

Item: As regards the hostages of Shimazu Hyōgo-no-kami, he should send his eldest son, who is now 15 years old, to Osaka to stay at the headquarters there, and should offer another [son], who is now eight, as a hostage.

Item: As for Shimazu Chūsho, I have granted him the two provinces of Satsuma and Ōsumi because he was in Osaka with his daughter on duty, and I have granted him complete remission. . . .

Yesterday we moved back to Higo province from Satsuma province. I plan to reach Hakata in Chikuzen province around the 5th day of the 6th month. We have thus already come back about halfway and we are halfway

101 *Letters of Hideyoshi: The Private Correspondence of Toyotomi Hideyoshi*, ed. and trans. Adriana Boscaro (Tokyo: Sophia University, 1975), 30–31.

to Osaka. At Hakata, I shall give orders for some construction work; then be assured that I shall be back in Osaka perhaps by the 6th month, or as late as the 10th day of the 7th month. I have received hostages from Iki and Tsushima and their submission. I have sent fast ships in order to urge even Korea to pay homage to the Emperor of Japan, stating that, if it does not, I shall conquer it next year. I shall take even China in hand, and have control of it during my lifetime; since [China] has become disdainful [of Japan], the work will be more exhausting.

After the last battle I feel older than I am; more and more white hairs have grown and I cannot pluck them out. I am very ashamed to be seen by anyone; only you will be tolerant of this, but I still complain.

READING AND DISCUSSION QUESTIONS

1. What are Hideyoshi's chief concerns, and what are his ambitions?
2. Hideyoshi takes care to allocate both rewards and punishment to members of the Shimazu clan. What are these, and how does he justify them?
3. Hideyoshi speaks casually of conquering Korea and China but then complains of battle-weariness and grey hair. What impression does this juxtaposition make?

DOCUMENT 21-2

HUANG ZONGXI

From Waiting for the Dawn: On the Prince and On Ministership

1662

Huang Zongxi (1610–1695) was a historian who lived through the tumultuous fall of the Ming Dynasty and the establishment of the Qing Dynasty. His father, a Ming official, died after imprisonment by politically influential eunuchs. Huang became a guerilla fighter against the Manchu; when they

Sources of Chinese Tradition, ed. Wm. Theodore de Bary and Richard Lufranco, 2 vols. (New York: Columbia University Press, 2000), 2:6–10.

succeeded in toppling the Ming and establishing the Qing Dynasty, Huang refused government employment and became an independent scholar. His Waiting for the Dawn, *excerpted here, shows both his mistrust of charismatic leadership and his interest in systemic order and constitutional law. While not widely read during his life, his writing found a sympathetic audience among reformers in the latter years of the Qing era.*

ON THE PRINCE

In the beginning of human life each man lived for himself and looked to his own interests. There was such a thing as the common benefit, yet no one seems to have promoted it; and there was common harm, yet no one seems to have eliminated it. Then someone came forth who did not think of benefit in terms of his own benefit but sought to benefit all-under-Heaven and who did not think of harm in terms of harm to himself but sought to spare all-under-Heaven from harm. Thus his labors were thousands of times greater than the labors of ordinary men. Now to work a thousand or ten thousand times harder without benefiting oneself is certainly not what most people in the world desire. Therefore in those early times some men worthy of ruling, after considering it, refused to become princes — Xu You and Wu Guang were such. Others undertook it and then quit — Yao and Shun, for instance. Still others, like Yu, became princes against their own will and later were unable to quit. How could men of old have been any different? To love ease and dislike strenuous labor has always been the natural inclination of man.

However, with those who later became princes it was different. They believed that since they held the power over benefit and harm, there was nothing wrong in taking for themselves all the benefits and imposing on others all the harm. They made it so that no man dared to live for himself or look to his own interests. Thus the prince's great self-interest took the place of the common good of all-under-Heaven. At first the prince felt some qualms about it, but his conscience eased with time. He looked upon the world as an enormous estate to be handed on down to his descendants, for their perpetual pleasure and well-being. . . .

This can only be explained as follows: In ancient times all-under-Heaven were considered the master and the prince was the tenant. The prince spent his whole life working for all-under-Heaven. Now the prince is master and all-under-Heaven are tenants. That no one can find peace and happiness anywhere is all on account of the prince. In order to get whatever he wants, he maims and slaughters all-under-Heaven and breaks up their families — all for the aggrandizement of one man's fortune. Without the least feeling of pity, the prince says, "I'm just establishing an estate for my descendants." Yet when he has established it, the prince still extracts the very marrow from people's bones and takes away their sons and daughters to serve his own debauchery. It seems entirely proper to him. It is, he says, the interest on his estate. Thus he who does the greatest harm in the world is none other than the prince. If there had been no rulers, each man would have provided for himself and looked to his own interests. How could the institution of rulership have turned out like this?

In ancient times men loved to support their prince, likened him to a father, compared him to Heaven, and truly this was not going too far. Now men hate their prince, look on him as a "mortal foe," call him "just another guy." And this is perfectly natural. But petty scholars have pedantically insisted that "the duty of the subject to his prince is utterly inescapable." . . . As if the flesh and blood of the myriads of families destroyed by such tyrants were no different from the "carcasses of dead rats." Could it be that Heaven and Earth, in their all-encompassing care, favor one man and one family among millions of men and myriads of families? . . .

If it were possible for latter-day princes to preserve such an estate and hand it down in perpetuity, such selfishness would not be hard to understand. But once it comes to be looked upon as a personal estate, who does not desire such an estate as much as the prince? Even if the prince could "tie his fortune down and lock it up tight," still the cleverness of one man is no match for the greed of all. At most it can be kept in the family for a few generations, and sometimes it is lost in one's own lifetime, unless indeed the life's blood spilled is that of one's own offspring. . . .

It is not easy to make plain the position of the prince, but any fool can see that a brief moment of excessive pleasure is not worth an eternity of sorrows.

ON MINISTERSHIP

Suppose there is someone who, in serving the prince, "sees [what to do] without being shown and hears without being told." Could he be called a [true] minister? I say no. Suppose that he sacrifices his life in the service of his prince. Could he then be called a [true] minister? I say no. "To see without being shown and hear without being told" is "to serve [one's prince] as one's father." To sacrifice one's life is the ultimate in selflessness. If these are not enough to fulfill this duty, then what should one do to fulfill the Way of the Minister?

The reason for ministership lies in the fact that the world is too big for one man to govern, so governance must be shared with colleagues. Therefore, when one goes forth to serve, it is for all-under-Heaven and not for the prince; it is for all the people and not for one family. . . .

But those who act as ministers today, not understanding this principle, think that ministership is instituted for the sake of the prince. They think that the prince shares the world with one so that it can be governed and that he entrusts one with its people so that they can be shepherded, thus regarding the world and its people as personal property in the prince's pouch [to be disposed of as he wills].

Today only if the toil and trouble everywhere and the strain on the people are grievous enough to endanger one's prince do ministers feel compelled to discuss the proper means for governing and leading the people. As long as these do not affect the dynasty's existence, widespread toil, trouble, and strain are regarded as trifling problems, even by supposedly true ministers. But was this the way ministers served in ancient times, or was it another way?

Whether there is peace or disorder in the world does not depend on the rise or fall of dynasties but upon the happiness or distress of the people. . . . If those who act as ministers ignore the "plight of the people," then even if they should succeed in assisting their prince's rise to power or follow him to final ruin, they would still be in violation of the true Way of the Minister. For governing the world is like the hauling of great logs. The men in front call out, "Heave!," those behind, "Ho!" The prince and his ministers should be log-haulers working together.

Alas, the arrogant princes of later times have only indulged themselves and have not undertaken to serve the world and its people. From the countryside they seek out only such people as will be servile errand boys. Thus from the countryside those alone respond who are of the servile errand-boy type; once spared for a while from cold and hunger, they feel eternally grateful for his majesty's kind understanding. Such people will not care whether they are treated by the prince with due respect . . . and will think it no more than proper to be relegated to a servant's status. . . .

It may be asked, Is not the term *minister* always equated with that of *child*? I say no. Father and child share the same vital spirit [psycho-physical forces, *qi*]. The child derives his own body from his father's body. Though a filial child is a different person bodily, if he can draw closer each day to his father in vital spirit, then in time there will be a perfect communion between them. An unfilial child, after deriving his body from his father's, drifts farther and farther from his parent, so that in time they cease to be kindred in vital spirit. The terms *prince* and *minister* derive from their relation to all-under-Heaven. If I take no responsibility for all-under-Heaven, then I am just another man on the street. If I come to serve him without regard for serving all-under-Heaven, then I am merely the prince's menial servant or concubine. If, on the other hand, I have regard for serving the people, then I am the prince's mentor and colleague. Thus with regard to ministership the designation may change. With father and child, however, there can be no such change.

READING AND DISCUSSION QUESTIONS

1. What is the relationship between ruler and ruled, according to Huang? How has it changed over time?

2. How does Huang's description of the ideal minister support his writings on the prince?

3. According to Huang, what is the greatest good? How can minister and prince serve that good, and how might they ignore or pervert it?

4. How might the new Qing rulers have viewed these critiques of government?

> DOCUMENT 21-3

ENGELBERT KAEMPFER

From History of Japan

1727

Engelbert Kaempfer (1651–1716) was a German physician who traveled extensively in Russia and Asia in the late 1600s. His writings on Japan were published posthumously in 1727 to great public interest, and his exhaustive descriptions of Japanese society, language, environment, culture, and history were so accurate — in many cases — that he earned the suspicion of a later

Engelbert Kaempfer, *Kaempfer's Japan: Tokugawa Culture Observed*, ed. and trans. Beatrice M. Bodart-Bailey (Honolulu: University of Hawaii Press, 1999), 132–133, 145, 187–188.

Japanese scholar, who warned in the early 1800s that Kaempfer's careful observations were proof that foreigners should be expelled to prevent espionage. The excerpts here outline his notes on commoners, his understanding of Confucianism, and his description of the Dutch in Japan and their commercial position there.

JUDŌ, THE TEACHING OR THE WAYS OF THE MORALISTS AND PHILOSOPHERS

Judō literally means the way or method of wise men. *Judōsha*, or *judōshū* in the plural, are their philosophers. They do not actually practice a religion but seek perfection and the greatest good in the contentment of the mind resulting from a virtuous and unblemished life and conduct. They believe in only secular punishment and reward, the consequence of virtue and vice. Thus one ought by necessity practice virtue as nature has given birth to us to lead the just life of people, as opposed to dumb animals.

Their founder, the first whose teaching was made public, was the famous Kōshi, born in China 2,238 years ago counting from this fifth year of Genroku, or the 1,692nd year after Christ. He used moral teachings to instruct his disciples in the greatest good and was the first to describe the *Shōgaku*, or book of living ethically, inflicting great damage on the opposing sect of Rōshi, flourishing at the time. After him this sect was continued by the much-praised teacher Mōshi, who established his philosophical Shisho, or Four Books, in this country. Up to this day they have their adherents in all countries where the characters of their writing system are understood.

Their moral philosophy consists of five articles, which they call *jin, gi, rei, chi, shin. Jin* teaches ethical living (consequently *jinsha*, virtuous person); *gi*, law and concern for justice; *rei*, politeness and civil behavior; *chi*, practical philosophy, politics, political judgment; *shin* concerns man's conscience and sincerity of heart.

They do not believe in the transmigration of souls but in a universal soul, or a force common to the entire world, which absorbs the souls of the dead, like the ocean takes back all water, and in the generation of matter permits them to depart again without differentiation. They associate this world soul, or universal nature, with the godhead and endow it with the attributes of the prime being. They use the word *ten*, heaven, or nature, in the actions and fortunes of life, thanking heaven or nature for their food. I have spoken to others who conceded an intellect or perfect incorporeal being as the governing agent, but not as the originator of nature. As the highest creation of nature it is produced by *in* and *yō*, that is, from the action of heaven and receptivity of the earth, the principles of generation and corruption. In this fashion they also accept other forces as spiritual and believe that the world is eternal and that men and animals were produced from the *in yō* of heaven and the five elements.

They have neither temple nor gods, but follow the traditions of their forefathers in observing the memory of and commemorating their dead friends. They venerate their dead friends' *byōsho*, or memorial tablet, according to the customs of their forefathers and in the fashion of other believers by placing meat in front of it, lighting candles, and bowing to the ground (as if they were alive). They celebrate their memory monthly and annually and prepare themselves three days in advance by abstaining from sexual intercourse and all sinful matter, cleaning their body, and putting on new clothes. All this they do as a human gesture, prompted by their grateful and virtuous heart. The body of the dead is kept for three days above ground and placed into a European-style coffin, flat on the back, but the head is raised a little. Presumably to prevent decomposition they sometimes also cover the body with spices and scented herbs. Then they accompany it to the place of burial, where they bury the body in the soil without prior cremation.

Suicide is not only permitted in this sect but is considered an extraordinary act of bravery when committed to preempt the enemy or a shameful death.

These atheistic philosophers will only perform heathen celebrations or special duties for the gods out of common politeness. Instead they strive for virtue, a clean conscience, and honorable behavior in accordance with the teaching of [Roman philosopher] Seneca or our Ten Commandments. Thus they are also capable of looking favorably at the Christian teaching and as a result have come under great suspicion. According to the new saws, which came into effect with the banishment of the Christians, they must, against their will, keep in their houses the image of a god or mount, or paste up, the characters of the name of a god with a pot of flowers and an incense burner placed in front of it. Generally they chose Kannon or Amida, whom, according to the custom of the country, they assign a place behind the hearth. Of their own free will they may have a picture of Kōshi in public places of learning or, in their own homes, the *byōsho* of their parents with the posthumous name of, or characters for, a learned man. In the past this now-suspicious sect comprised the greater part of the population and practically held a monopoly on the sciences and liberal arts. But after the martyrdom of the Christians, their numbers decreased yearly and their

Company, the Dutch, enticed by the fertile trade of the Portuguese, began making annual visits to this, the furthest empire of the world. They arrived at the city and island of Hirado and set up their warehouse and living quarters on a spit of land linked to the city by a bridge. Their admission to Japan was all the quicker and easier, the greater their enmity was toward those whom the ruler felt compelled to drive out of the country. Even though the Portuguese still had a lot of influence with the greatest lords of the country, and did much to prevent the entry of the Dutch, they were finally unable to stop the shogun Ieyasu — or Gongen, after his death — from giving the Dutch access to the country in the year of Christ 1611 with a special *goshuin*, which literally means "lofty cinnabar seal" and is a shogunal permit or pass. It is signed by the councilors of the empire and authorized by the red shogunal seal, from the color of which it also takes its name. With this document they were granted in very clear terms, or characters, free trade and access to all provinces and harbors with favorable recommendations to all subjects of the empire. After the death of the shogun they requested to have their privileges renewed and a new pass issued, against the practice of this nation, which considers upholding the laws of its forefathers a sacred duty. This they received, but while outwardly it appeared to be identical in form and shape, it contained much less advantageous conditions. Meanwhile, from the time they settled in Hirado, the Dutch did what they could to profit from the progressive decline of the Portuguese. They did everything possible to please the court, the source of success or failure, as well as the councilors, the lord of Hirado, and any other great men who might proffer help or hindrance. The Dutch spared no cost nor labor to seek out the world's rarest novelties to pay homage to the Japanese annually and to satisfy the ridiculous passion of the Japanese for various strange animals — which nature did not create the way they imagine them — by bringing in as many as possible from the most distant empires of India, Persia, and Europe. The Dutch showed the utmost subservience in everything, even wrongful impositions, to stay in the good books of this nation and conduct profitable trade. Since they valued their lives, they could show no objection when in 1638 the shogun ordered them to tear down as fast as if they were enemy property their own newly built residence and warehouse on the island of Hirado: valuable stone mansions such as Japan had never seen before. The reason was that the buildings were splendid beyond the custom of the country and had the year of the Christian era on the gable [of their roofs]. Soon afterward, in the same year of 1638, this heathen court had no qualms in inflicting upon them a cursed test to find out whether the orders of the shogun or the love for their fellow Christians had greater power over them. It was a matter of us serving the empire by helping to destroy the native Christians, of whom those remaining, some forty thousand people, in desperation over their martyrdom had moved into an old fortress in the province of Shimabara and made preparations to defend themselves. The head of the Dutch, Koekebecker, himself went to the location with the one remaining vessel (for in the face of the impudent demand the remainder had slipped out of the harbor the previous day) and in fourteen days treated the beleaguered Christians to 426 rough cannon salvos, both from land and sea. Although this assistance resulted neither in surrender nor complete defeat, it broke the strength of the besieged. And because the Japanese had the pleasure to order it, he stripped the vessel of a further six cannons (regardless of the fact that she still had to navigate dangerous seas) that the Japanese insisted had to be lent in addition to the first to carry out their cruel designs.

It is true that this show of total obedience was instrumental in keeping a foothold in the country when the court was considering completely closing it to all Christians. At the same time, however, they gained a bad reputation among the more high-minded at court and throughout the country, for they judged that people who so easily permitted themselves to be used in the destruction of those with whom they basically shared the same belief and the path of Christ — as they had been amply told by the padres from Portugal and Manila — could not be true of heart, honest, and loyal towards a foreign ruler. I was told this by the locals in these very same words. Thus far from earning the trust and deep friendship of this exceedingly suspicious nation by their compliance, the reputation of the Dutch was ruined unjustly, regardless of their merits. Shortly afterward, in 1641, the Dutch, having assisted in the confinement of the Portuguese by word and deed, were to undergo the same experience. For they were told to leave the island of Hirado with all their belongings and to exchange subordination to a lenient territorial lord for directions from a new and zealous administration directly responsible to the shogun, while retiring under strict guard and manifold supervision within the limits of the prison built for the Portuguese. Submission to these proud heathens into such servitude and imprisonment, forgoing all celebrations of feast days and Sundays, all devotion with religious song and prayer, the use of the name of Christ, the symbol of the cross, and all outward proof or signs of being a Christian, and, added to that, good-natured acceptance of their despicable impudence, an affront to any high-minded soul, all that for the love of profit and to gain control of the veins of ore in their mountains.

READING AND DISCUSSION QUESTIONS

1. Kaempfer was criticized for his favorable presentation of a "heathen" culture. How does he address religion in these excerpts?

2. According to Kaempfer, what role does religion play in Dutch and Japanese societies?

3. Kaempfer's description of Japan fascinated the European public. What might have particularly intrigued European readers in the early 1700s, and why?

4. Based on Kaempfer's accounts, what is his opinion of trade, particularly with Japan?

VIEWPOINTS

Gender in East Asia

DOCUMENT 21-4

KAIBARA EKIKEN AND KAIBARA TŌKEN

Common Sense Teachings for Japanese Children and Greater Learning for Women

ca. 1700

Kaibara Ekiken (1630–1714) was a physician, educator, and author from the samurai class during the enforced peace of the Tokugawa period (1603–1867). His works combined Neo-Confucian principles of self-reliance and humaneness with careful and practical attention to life in early modern Japan. His writings were printed and distributed widely, thanks to the vibrant publishing world of urban Tokugawa Japan. The following selections (the second probably coauthored with his wife, Tōken) show his concern with daily life and "common sense" and his interest in maintaining gender and social roles in the Confucian social order.

David J. Lu, *Japan: A Documentary History* (Armonk, N.Y.: M. E. Sharpe, 1997), 258–261.

Common Sense Teachings for Japanese Children

In January when children reach the age of six, teach them numbers one through ten, and the names given to designate 100, 1,000, 10,000, and 100,000,000. Let them know the four directions, East, West, North, and South. Assess their native intelligence and differentiate between quick and slow learners. Teach them Japanese pronunciation from the age of six or seven, and let them learn how to write. . . . From this time on, teach them to respect their elders, and let them know the distinctions between the upper and lower classes and between the young and old. Let them learn to use the correct expressions.

When the children reach the age of seven, do not let the boys and girls sit together, nor must you allow them to dine together. . . .

For the eighth year. This is the age when the ancients began studying the book *Little Learning*.[1] Beginning at this time, teach the youngsters etiquette befitting their age, and caution them not to commit an act of impoliteness. Among those which must be taught are: daily deportment, the manners set for appearing before one's senior and withdrawing from his presence, how to speak or respond to one's senior or guest, how to place a serving tray or replace it for one's senior, how to present a wine cup and pour rice wine and to serve side dishes to accompany it, and how to serve tea. Children must also learn how to behave while taking their meals.

Children must be taught by those who are close to them the virtues of filial piety and obedience. To serve the parents well is called filial piety, and to serve one's seniors well is called obedience. The one who lives close to the children and who is able to teach must instruct the children in the early years of their life that the first obligation of a human being is to revere the parents and serve them well. Then comes the next lesson which includes respect for one's seniors, listening to their commands and not holding them in contempt. One's seniors include elder brothers, elder sisters, uncles, aunts, and cousins who are older and worthy of respect. . . . As the children grow older, teach them to love their younger brothers and to be compassionate to the employees and servants. Teach them also the respect due the teachers and the behavior codes governing friends. The etiquette governing each movement toward important guests — such as standing, sitting, advancing forward, and retiring from their presence — and the language to be employed must be taught. Teach them how to pay respect to others according to the social positions held by them. Gradually the ways

---

[1] *Little Learning*: An instruction book for young children that contained rules of behavior.

of filial piety and obedience, loyalty and trustworthiness, right deportment and decorum, and sense of shame must be inculcated in the children's minds and they must know how to implement them. Caution them not to desire the possessions of others, or to stoop below one's dignity in consuming excessive amounts of food and drink. . . .

Once reaching the age of eight, children must follow and never lead their elders when entering a gate, sitting, or eating and drinking. From this time on they must be taught how to become humble and yield to others. Do not permit the children to behave as they please. It is important to caution them against "doing their own things."

At the age of ten, let the children be placed under the guidance of a teacher, and tell them about the general meaning of the five constant virtues and let them understand the way of the five human relationships.[2] Let them read books by the Sage [Confucius] and the wise men of old and cultivate the desire for learning. . . . When not engaged in reading, teach them the literary and military arts. . . .

Fifteen is the age when the ancients began the study of the *Great Learning*.[3] From this time on, concentrate on the learning of a sense of justice and duty. The students must also learn to cultivate their personalities and investigate the way of governing people. . . .

Those who are born in the high-ranking families have the heavy obligations of becoming leaders of the people, of having people entrusted to their care, and of governing them. Therefore, without fail, a teacher must be selected for them when they are still young. They must be taught how to read and be informed of the ways of old, of cultivating their personalities, and of the way of governing people. If they do not learn the way of governing people, they may injure the many people who are entrusted to their care by the Way of Heaven. That will be a serious disaster. . . .

GREATER LEARNING FOR WOMEN

Seeing that it is a girl's destiny, on reaching womanhood, to go to a new home, and live in submission to her father-in-law, it is even more incumbent upon her than it is on a boy to receive with all reverence her parents' instructions. Should her parents, through their tenderness, allow her to

---

[2] **five constant virtues . . . human relationships**: The *five virtues* are human heartedness, righteousness, propriety, wisdom, and good faith. The *five relationships* are ruler-subject, father-son, husband-wife, older brother-younger brother, and friend-friend.

[3] **Great Learning**: A chapter in the Record of Rituals, one of the four works that came to be known within the Confucian classics as the Four Books.

grow up self-willed, she will infallibly show herself capricious in her husband's house, and thus alienate his affection; while, if her father-in-law be a man of correct principles, the girl will find the yoke of these principles intolerable. She will hate and decry her father-in-law, and the end of those domestic dissensions will be her dismissal from her husband's house and the covering of herself with ignominy. Her parents, forgetting the faulty education they gave her, may indeed lay all the blame on the father-in-law. But they will be in error; for the whole disaster should rightly be attributed to the faulty education the girl received from her parents.

* * *

More precious in a woman is a virtuous heart than a face of beauty. The vicious woman's heart is ever excited; she glares wildly around her, she vents her anger on others, her words are harsh and her accent vulgar. When she speaks, it is to set herself above others, to upbraid others, to envy others, to be puffed up with individual pride, to jeer at others, to outdo others — all things at variance with the way in which a woman should walk. The only qualities that befit a woman are gentle obedience, chastity, mercy, and quietness.

From her earliest youth a girl should observe the line of demarcation separating women from men. The customs of antiquity did not allow men and women to sit in the same apartment, to keep their wearing apparel in the same place, to bathe in the same place, or to transmit to each other anything directly from hand to hand. A woman . . . must observe a certain distance in her relations even with her husband and with her brothers. In our days the women of lower classes, ignoring all rules of this nature, behave disorderly; they contaminate their reputations, bring down reproach upon the head of their parents and brothers, and spend their whole lives in an unprofitable manner. Is not this truly lamentable?

* * *

It is the chief duty of a girl living in the parental house to practice filial piety towards her father and mother. But after marriage her duty is to honor her father-in-law and mother-in-law, to honor them beyond her father and mother, to love and reverence them with all ardor, and to tend them with practice of every filial piety. . . . Even if your father-in-law and mother-in-law are inclined to hate and vilify you, do not be angry with them, and murmur not. If you carry piety towards them to its utmost limits, and minister to them in all sincerity, it cannot be but that they will end by becoming friendly to you.

* * *

The great lifelong duty of a woman is obedience. . . . When the husband issues his instructions, the wife must never disobey them. In a doubtful case, she should inquire of her husband and obediently follow his commands. . . .

Should her husband be roused at any time to anger, she must obey him with fear and trembling, and not set herself up against him in anger and forwardness. A woman should look upon her husband as if he were Heaven itself, and never weary of thinking how she may yield to her husband and thus escape celestial castigation.

Her treatment of her servant girls will require circumspection. Those low-born girls have had no proper education; they are stupid, obstinate, and vulgar in their speech. . . . Again, in her dealings with those lowly people, a woman will find many things to disapprove of. But if she be always reproving and scolding, and spend her time in hustle and anger, her household will be in a continual state of disturbance. When there is real wrongdoing, she should occasionally notice it, and point out the path of amendment, while lesser faults should be quietly endured without anger. . . .

READING AND DISCUSSION QUESTIONS

1. What values does Ekiken emphasize for children's education? How are they to be instilled?

2. How is concern for social hierarchy and propriety evident in Ekiken's work on children? In his work on women?

3. Based on these readings, what potential do you see for women to have power in Tokugawa society?

4. What assumptions, if any, does Ekiken make about his likely audience? What gives you that impression?

DOCUMENT 21-5

A Japanese Sake Brewer's Female Antipollution Pass

ca. 1603–1868

Tokugawa-era gender relations were marked by both continuity and change, as a variety of social and economic forces shaped the roles that were assigned to and performed by both men and women in various social contexts. In the

Joyce Chapman Lebra, "Women in an All-Male Industry: The Case of Sake Brewer Tatsu'uma Kiyo," in Gail Lee Bernstein, ed., *Recreating Japanese Women, 1600–1945* (Berkeley: University of California Press, 1991), 133.

realm of work, many occupations were identified with a certain gender. In the all-male industry that produced sake, a fermented rice drink, a powerful folk belief held that the female spirit of sake production was jealous; as a result, women were generally banned from working in the sake breweries. In the Aizu-Wakamatsu region of northern Japan, one sake producer found an ingenious way around the general prohibition by producing and issuing "antipollution passes" to women. Female workers wore these passes on their belts to counter the possible impurities associated with their gender.

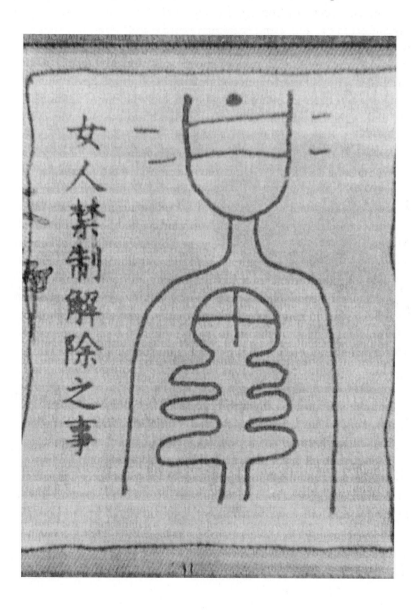

READING AND DISCUSSION QUESTIONS

1. This pass allowed women to work in an all-male industry by negating their female "impurity." Did its use liberate or limit women, and why?

2. Does the institution of the "antipollution pass" align with or move away from previous Tokugawa ideas about gender? Cite examples.

DOCUMENT 21-6

LI RUZHEN (LI JU-CHEN)
From Flowers in the Mirror
1827

Li Ruzhen (1763–1830) was a Chinese scholar and novelist in the Qing Dynasty. Objecting to the constraints of the Confucian examination system, he achieved only the lowest official rank of scholarship, but his work in linguistics earned him a reputation as an intellectual. His novel Flowers in the Mirror (Jing Hua Yuan) *is a fantastic and satirical take on Chinese society during the Tang Dynasty (618–907). In this excerpt, the main characters Tang Ao and Merchant Lin have traveled from the Kingdom on Earth to the Country of Women. Their experiences there call attention to gender dynamics during the Qing Dynasty, and especially the practice of foot binding, a popular but controversial procedure in which women's feet were crushed into a shape thought to be appealing to men.*

When Tang Ao heard that they had arrived at the Country of Women, he thought that the country was populated entirely by women, and was afraid to go ashore. But Old Tuo said, "Not at all! There are men as well as women, only they call men women, and women men. The men wear the skirts and take care of the home, while the women wear hats and trousers and manage affairs outside." . . .

"If the men dress like women, do they use cosmetics and bind their feet?" asked Tang Ao.

Li Ju-chen, *Flowers in the Mirror*, trans. and ed. Lin Tai-yi (Berkeley: University of California Press, 1965), 107–113.

"Of course they do!" cried Lin, and took from his pocket a list of the merchandise he was going to sell, which consisted of huge quantities of rouge, face powder, combs and other women's notions. "Lucky I wasn't born in this country," he said. "Catch me mincing around on bound feet!" . . .

Merchant Lin had been told by one of his customers that the "King's uncle" wanted to buy some of his goods. Following instructions, he went to the "Royal Uncle's" Residence in the Palace, and handed his list of merchandise to the gatekeeper. Soon, the gatekeeper came back and said that it was just what the "King" was looking for for his "concubines" and "maids," and asked Lin to be shown into the inner apartments. . . .

Merchant Lin followed the guard inside, and was soon in the presence of the "King." After making a deep bow, he saw that she was a woman of about thirty years old, with a beautiful face, fair skin and cherry-red lips. Around her there stood many palace "maids."

The "King" spoke to Lin in a light voice[,] . . . looking at him with interest as he answered her questions.

"I wonder what she is staring at me like this for," Merchant Lin thought to himself. "Hasn't she ever seen a man from the Kingdom on Earth before?" . . .

In a little time, Merchant Lin was ushered to a room upstairs, where victuals of many kinds awaited him. . . . Several palace "maids" ran upstairs soon, and calling him "Your Highness" kowtowed to him and congratulated him. Before he knew what was happening, Merchant Lin was being stripped completely bare by the maids and led to a perfumed bath. Against the powerful arms of these maids, he could scarcely struggle. Soon he found himself being anointed, perfumed, powdered and rouged, and dressed in a skirt. His big feet were bound up in strips of cloth and socks, and his hair was combed into an elaborate braid over his head and decorated with pins. . . .

Merchant Lin thought he must be drunk, or dreaming, and began to tremble. He asked the maids what was happening, and was told that he had been chosen by the "King" to be the Imperial Consort, and that a propitious day would be chosen for him to enter the "King's" chambers.

Before he could utter a word, another group of maids, all tall and strong and wearing beards, came in. One was holding a threaded needle. "We are ordered to pierce your ears," he said, as the other four "maids" grabbed Lin by the arms and legs. The white-bearded one seized Lin's right ear, and after rubbing the lobe a little, drove the needle through it.

"Ooh!" Merchant Lin screamed. . . .

Having finished what they came to do, the maids retreated, and a black-bearded fellow came in with a bolt of white silk. Kneeling down before him, the fellow said, "I am ordered to bind Your Highness's feet."

Two other maids seized Lin's feet as the black-bearded one sat down on a low stool, and began to rip the silk into ribbons. Seizing Lin's right foot, he set it upon his knee, and sprinkled white alum powder between the toes and the grooves of the foot. He squeezed the toes tightly together, bent them down so that the whole foot was shaped like an arch, and took a length of white silk and bound it tightly around it twice. One of the others sewed the ribbon together in small stitches. Again the silk went around the foot, and again, it was sewn up.

Merchant Lin felt as though his feet were burning, and wave after wave of pain rose to his heart. When he could stand it no longer, he let out his voice and began to cry. . . .

Before two weeks were over, Lin's feet had begun to assume a permanently arched form, and his toes begun to rot. Daily medical ablutions were given to them, and the pain persisted. . . .

In due course, his feet lost much of their original shape. Blood and flesh were squeezed into a pulp and then little remained of his feet but dry bones and skin, shrunk, indeed, to a dainty size. Responding to daily anointing, his hair became shiny and smooth, and his body, after repeated ablutions of perfumed water, began to look very attractive indeed. His eyebrows were plucked to resemble a new moon. With blood-red lipstick and powder adorning his face, and jade and pearl adorning his coiffure and ears, Merchant Lin assumed, at last, a not unappealing appearance.

READING AND DISCUSSION QUESTIONS

1. This excerpt from Li's novel offers, in excruciating detail, an account of the pain and harm that women endured through foot binding. What is the effect of Li's depiction of this practice being performed on a man rather than on a woman?

2. Li's novel is set during the Tang Dynasty. How do you imagine Li's work was received by his contemporaries?

3. How might Li's presentation of beauty call traditional standards of beauty into question?

COMPARATIVE QUESTIONS

1. Several of the documents in this chapter address, directly or indirectly, the construction of gender in East Asian societies. Based on these documents, what conclusions can you draw about how men and women related to one another in early modern China and Japan? How did these relations change, and why?

2. What might Kaibara Ekiken and Kaibara Tōken make of the "antipollution pass" and the controversy surrounding it?

3. Hideyoshi was, at the height of his influence, the most powerful man in Japan. How do you imagine Huang Zongxi would evaluate him and his leadership? Explain.

4. Both Kaempfer and Li write about the experience of being in a foreign culture. In Li's case, the fictional account is designed as a commentary on his own time and place. How might Kaempfer's writing say as much about his own culture as it does about early modern Japan? In what ways does his writing reflect a European perspective? How might it be different if written by a Japanese observer?

5. What evidence do these passages provide regarding an increasingly global perspective in East Asia? Which authors seemed most entrenched in their own cultures? Cite examples.

CHAPTER 22

Revolutions in the Atlantic World

1775–1815

B eginning with the American Revolution in 1775, the intellectual projects of the Enlightenment in Europe intersected with the economic logic of overseas colonial empires to generate optimism and upheaval in the Atlantic world. Colonists in British North America, members of the third estate in France, and slaves in the French colony of Saint-Domingue (Haiti) all used Enlightenment values to justify rebellion. The bloody expression of notions of freedom, equality, and national integrity in the American, French, and Haitian Revolutions, along with the Napoleonic wars of conquest in Europe, challenged many aspects of traditional European society at home and in the colonies. However, the endurance of sexual, class-based, and ethnic discrimination and the recurrence of violence and war complicate the era's story of egalitarianism and democracy. The following documents set forth the central ideologies of these revolutionary movements and some important critiques.

DOCUMENT 22-1

From the Declaration of Independence of the United States of America

1776

The Declaration of Independence formally announced the American colonies' intent to separate from Great Britain. It was authored primarily by Thomas Jefferson (1743–1826), a Virginia delegate to the Continental Congress and an adherent to Enlightenment ideals of human rights and freedom. From Jefferson's first draft, begun June 12, the document was revised

U.S. National Archives and Records Administration, Washington, D.C.

repeatedly both by the drafting committee and by the full Congress until its final printing on July 4, 1776. The declaration was quickly disseminated to the new states and printed in newspapers.

When, in the course of human events, it becomes necessary for one people to dissolve the political bands which have connected them with another, and to assume, among the powers of the earth, the separate and equal station to which the laws of nature and of nature's God entitle them, a decent respect to the opinions of mankind requires that they should declare the causes which impel them to the separation.

We hold these truths to be self-evident: That all men are created equal; that they are endowed by their Creator with certain unalienable rights; that among these are life, liberty, and the pursuit of happiness; that, to secure these rights, governments are instituted among men, deriving their just powers from the consent of the governed; that whenever any form of government becomes destructive of these ends, it is the right of the people to alter or to abolish it, and to institute a new government, laying its foundation on such principles, and organizing its powers in such form, as to them shall seem most likely to effect their safety and happiness. Prudence, indeed, will dictate that governments long established should not be changed for light and transient causes; and accordingly all experience hath shown that mankind are more disposed to suffer, while evils are sufferable, than to right themselves by abolishing the forms to which they are accustomed. But when a long train of abuses and usurpations, pursuing invariably the same object, evinces a design to reduce them under absolute despotism, it is their right, it is their duty, to throw off such government, and to provide new guards for their future security. Such has been the patient sufferance of these colonies; and such is now the necessity which constrains them to alter their former systems of government. The history of the present King of Great Britain is a history of repeated injuries and usurpations, all having in direct object the establishment of an absolute tyranny over these States. To prove this, let facts be submitted to a candid world.

READING AND DISCUSSION QUESTIONS

1. Who is the intended audience for the declaration?
2. Who is the "villain" here? To what are the colonists objecting?
3. How do Jefferson and the Congress justify their arguments?

Defining the Citizen

DOCUMENT 22-2

The Declaration of the Rights of Man
1789

On June 17, 1789, during a meeting of the Estates General, the traditional advisory body under the absolutist French monarchy, delegates of the third estate voted to form a new National Assembly of France. They were joined by clergy and noblemen from the first and second estates, one of whom, the Marquis de Lafayette (1757–1834), outlined the assembly's aims in the Declaration of the Rights of Man. The assembly approved the document in August, after the Revolution had begun, and trumpeted it throughout Europe and the world. This declaration, like the Declaration of Independence of the United States, is an important codification of Enlightenment ideas.

The representatives of the French people, organized as a National Assembly, believing that the ignorance, neglect, or contempt of the rights of man are the sole cause of public calamities and of the corruption of governments, have determined to set forth in a solemn declaration the natural, inalienable, and sacred rights of man, in order that this declaration, being constantly before all the members of the social body, shall remind them continually of their rights and duties; in order that the acts of the legislative power, as well as those of the executive power, may be compared at any moment with the objects and purposes of all political institutions and may thus be more respected; and, lastly, in order that the grievances of the citizens, based hereafter upon simple and incontestable principles, shall tend to the maintenance of the constitution and redound to the happiness of all. Therefore the National Assembly recognizes and proclaims, in the presence and under the auspices of the Supreme Being, the following rights of man and of the citizen:

James Harvey Robinson, ed., *Readings in European History* (Boston: Ginn, 1904), 2:409–411.

ARTICLE 1. Men are born and remain free and equal in rights. Social distinctions may be founded only upon the general good.

2. The aim of all political association is the preservation of the natural and imprescriptible rights of man. These rights are liberty, property, security, and resistance to oppression.

3. The principle of all sovereignty resides essentially in the nation. No body nor individual may exercise any authority which does not proceed directly from the nation.

4. Liberty consists in the freedom to do everything which injures no one else; hence the exercise of the natural rights of each man has no limits except those which assure to the other members of the society the enjoyment of the same rights. These limits can only be determined by law.

5. Law can only prohibit such actions as are hurtful to society. Nothing may be prevented which is not forbidden by law, and no one may be forced to do anything not provided for by law.

6. Law is the expression of the general will. Every citizen has a right to participate personally, or through his representative, in its formation. It must be the same for all, whether it protects or punishes. All citizens, being equal in the eyes of the law, are equally eligible to all dignities and to all public positions and occupations, according to their abilities, and without distinction except that of their virtues and talents.

7. No person shall be accused, arrested, or imprisoned except in the cases and according to the forms prescribed by law. Any one soliciting, transmitting, executing, or causing to be executed, any arbitrary order, shall be punished. But any citizen summoned or arrested in virtue of the law shall submit without delay, as resistance constitutes an offense.

8. The law shall provide for such punishments only as are strictly and obviously necessary, and no one shall suffer punishment except it be legally inflicted in virtue of a law passed and promulgated before the commission of the offense.

9. As all persons are held innocent until they shall have been declared guilty, if arrest shall be deemed indispensable, all harshness not essential to the securing of the prisoner's person shall be severely repressed by law.

10. No one shall be disquieted on account of his opinions, including his religious views, provided their manifestation does not disturb the public order established by law.

11. The free communication of ideas and opinions is one of the most precious of the rights of man. Every citizen may, accordingly, speak, write,

and print with freedom, but shall be responsible for such abuses of this freedom as shall be defined by law.

12. The security of the rights of man and of the citizen requires public military forces. These forces are, therefore, established for the good of all and not for the personal advantage of those to whom they shall be intrusted.

13. A common contribution is essential for the maintenance of the public forces and for the cost of administration. This should be equitably distributed among all the citizens in proportion to their means.

14. All the citizens have a right to decide, either personally or by their representatives, as to the necessity of the public contribution; to grant this freely; to know to what uses it is put; and to fix the proportion, the mode of assessment and of collection and the duration of the taxes.

15. Society has the right to require of every public agent an account of his administration.

16. A society in which the observance of the law is not assured, nor the separation of powers defined, has no constitution at all.

17. Since property is an inviolable and sacred right, no one shall be deprived thereof except where public necessity, legally determined, shall clearly demand it, and then only on condition that the owner shall have been previously and equitably indemnified.

READING AND DISCUSSION QUESTIONS

1. To what are the French citizens objecting in this document? What is the proposed solution, if any?

2. What is the role of law in this declaration? Who makes the laws, and whom do they protect?

3. Which of these rights seems most important to you? Which seems least applicable to your life? Why?

DOCUMENT 22-3

OLYMPE DE GOUGES

From the Declaration of the Rights of Woman

1791

Olympe de Gouges (1748–1793) was a French playwright who turned to political activism in the late 1780s. In plays and other writings, she advocated for the rights of enslaved people in France's colonies. After her initial enthusiasm with the Revolution, she became increasingly outspoken on gender equality. She continued to speak out against injustice, opposing the execution of Louis XVI and offering her opinion on factional revolutionary politics. She was arrested for the latter, and — thanks in part to her own refusal to plead ignorance — was executed in November 1793. The pamphlet excerpted here is her best-known work. In it, she skillfully reproduces the form of the Declaration of the Rights of Man and Citizen (see Document 22-2) to direct attention to women's rights.

For the National Assembly to decree in its last sessions, or in those of the next legislature:

Preamble

Mothers, daughters, sisters [and] representatives of the nation demand to be constituted into a national assembly. Believing that ignorance, omission, or scorn for the rights of woman are the only causes of public misfortunes and of the corruption of governments, [the women] have resolved to set forth in a solemn declaration the natural, inalienable, and sacred rights of woman in order that this declaration, constantly exposed before all the members of the society, will ceaselessly remind them of their rights and duties; in order that the authoritative acts of women and the authoritative acts of men may be at any moment compared with and respectful of the purpose of all political institutions; and in order that citizens' demands, henceforth based on simple and incontestable principles, will always support the constitution, good morals, and the happiness of all.

Darline G. Levy, Harriet B. Applewhite, and Mary D. Johnson, eds., *Women in Revolutionary Paris, 1789–1795* (Champaign: University of Illinois Press, 1979), 89–92.

Consequently, the sex that is as superior in beauty as it is in courage during the sufferings of maternity recognizes and declares in the presence and under the auspices of the Supreme Being, the following Rights of Woman and of Female Citizens.

Article I

Woman is born free an lives equal to man in her rights. Social distinctions can be based only on the common utility.

Article II

The purpose of any political association is the conservation of the natural and imprescriptible rights of woman and man; these rights are liberty, property, security, and especially resistance to oppression.

Article III

The principle of all sovereignty rests essentially with the nation, which is nothing but the union of woman and man; no body and no individual can exercise any authority which does not come expressly from it [the nation].

Article IV

Liberty and justice consist of restoring all that belongs to others; thus, the only limits on the exercise of the natural rights of woman are perpetual male tyranny; these limits are to be reformed by the laws of nature and reason.

Article V

Laws of nature and reason proscribe all acts harmful to society; everything which is not prohibited by these wise and divine laws cannot be prevented, and no one can be constrained to do what they do not command.

Article VI

The law must be the expression of the general will; all female and male citizens must contribute either personally or through their representatives to its formation; it must be the same for all: male and female citizens, being equal in the eyes of the law, must be equally admitted to all honors, positions, and public employment according to their capacity and without other distinctions besides those of their virtues and talents.

Article VII

No woman is an exception; she is accused, arrested, and detained in cases determined by law. Women, like men, obey this rigorous law.

Article VIII

The law must establish only those penalties that are strictly and obviously necessary, and no one can be punished except by virtue of a law established and promulgated prior to the crime and legally applicable to women.

Article IX

Once any woman is declared guilty, complete rigor is [to be] exercised by the law.

Article X

No one is to be disquieted for his very basic opinions; woman has the right to mount the scaffold; she must equally have the right to mount the rostrum [podium], provided that her demonstrations do not disturb the legally established public order.

Article XI

The free communication of thoughts and opinions is one of the most precious rights of woman, since that liberty assures the recognition of children by their fathers. Any female citizen thus may say freely, I am the mother of a child which belongs to you, without being forced by a barbarous prejudice to hide the truth; [an exception may be made] to respond to the abuse of this liberty in cases determined by the law.

Article XII

The guarantee of the rights of woman and the female citizen implies a major benefit; this guarantee must be instituted for the advantage of all, and not for the particular benefit of those to whom it is entrusted.

Article XIII

For the support of the public force and the expenses of administration, the contributions of woman and man are equal; she shares all the duties and all the painful tasks; therefore, she must have the same share in the distribution of positions, employment, offices, honors, and jobs.

Article XIV

Female and male citizens have the right to verify, either by themselves or through their representatives, the necessity of the public contribution. This can only apply to women if they are granted an equal share, not only of wealth, but also of public administration, and in the determination of the proportion, the base, the collection, and the duration of the tax.

Article XV

The collectivity of women, joined for tax purposes to the aggregate of men, has the right to demand an accounting of his administration from any public agent.

Article XVI

No society has a constitution without the guarantee of rights and the separation of powers; the constitution is null if the majority of individuals comprising the nation have not cooperated in drafting it.

Article XVII

Property belongs to both sexes whether united or separate; for each it is an inviolable and sacred right; no one can be deprived of it, since it is the true patrimony of nature, unless the legally determined public need obviously dictates it, and then only with a just and prior indemnity.

READING AND DISCUSSION QUESTIONS

1. De Gouges presents women as being equal to men under the laws of "nature and reason." What, if anything, does de Gouges say about these laws?

2. In her preamble, de Gouges mentions the superiority of women in beauty and "courage during the sufferings of maternity." What other distinctions between men and women does she make, if any?

3. How might this document be different if de Gouges had written it as a "declaration of the rights of men and women"?

DOCUMENT 22-4

MAXIMILIEN ROBESPIERRE
Revolutionary Speech
February 5, 1794

Maximilien Robespierre (1758–1794) was one of the most important figures during the French Revolution. His skills as an orator and his control of the influential Committee of Public Safety helped lead to the period known as the Reign of Terror, during which Robespierre and his political allies not only executed political rivals, but also encouraged the population through laws and example to practice their own persecution of fellow citizens deemed to be "counterrevolutionary." Thousands were executed by government tribunals without evidence, while many others were killed by mobs. Robespierre himself was executed by members of the National Convention on July 27, 1794. This excerpt from a speech he had delivered to the Convention several months earlier demonstrates Robespierre's extreme commitment to revolutionary values, even to the point of violence.

After having marched for a long time at hazard, and, as it were, carried away by the movement of contrary factions, the representatives of the people have at last formed a government. A sudden change in the nation's fortune announced to Europe the regeneration which had been operated in the national representation; but up to this moment, we must admit that *we have been rather guided in these stormy circumstances by the love of good, and by a sense of the country's wants, than by any exact theory, or precise rules of conduct.*

It is time to distinguish clearly the aim of the revolution, and the term to which we would arrive. It is time for us to render account to ourselves, both of the obstacles which still keep us from that aim, and of the means which we ought to take to attain it.

What is the aim to which we tend?

The peaceful enjoyment of liberty and equality; the reign of that eternal justice, of which the laws have been engraved, not upon marble, but upon the hearts of all mankind; even in the hearts of the slaves who forget

G. H. Lewes, ed., *The Life of Maximilien Robespierre: With Extracts of His Unpublished Correspondence* (Philadelphia: Carey and Hart, 1849), 270–273.

them, or of the tyrants who have denied them! We desire a state of things wherein all base and cruel passions shall be enchained; all generous and beneficent passions awakened by the laws; wherein ambition should be the desire of glory, and glory the desire of serving the country; wherein distinctions should arise but from equality itself; wherein the citizen should submit to the magistrate, the magistrate to the people, and the people to justice; wherein the country assures the welfare of every individual; wherein every individual enjoys with pride the prosperity and the glory of his country; wherein all minds are enlarged by the continual communication of republican sentiments, and by the desire of meriting the esteem of a great people; wherein arts should be the decorations of that liberty which they ennoble, and commerce the source of public wealth, and not the monstrous opulence of some few houses. We desire to substitute morality for egotism, probity for honor, principles for usages, duties for functions, the empire of reason for the tyranny of fashion, the scorn of vice for the scorn of misfortune, pride for insolence, greatness of soul for vanity, the love of glory for the love of money, good citizens for good society, merit for intrigue, genius for cleverness, truth for splendor, the charm of happiness for the *ennui* of voluptuousness, the grandeur of man for the pettiness of the great, a magnanimous people, powerful, happy, for a people amiable, frivolous, and miserable; that is to say, all the virtues and all the miracles of a republic, for all the vices and all the follies of a monarchy.

What is the nature of the government which can realize these prodigies? The democratic or republican government.

Democracy is that state in which the people, guided by laws which are its own work, executes for itself all that it can well do, and, by its delegates, all that it cannot do itself. But to found and consolidate democracy, we must first end the war of liberty against tyranny, and traverse the storm of the revolution. Such is the aim of the revolutionary system which you have organized; you ought, therefore, to regulate your conduct by the circumstances in which the republic finds itself; and the plan of your administration ought to be the result of the spirit of revolutionary government, combined with the general principles of democracy.

The great purity of the French revolution, the sublimity even of its object, is precisely that which makes our force and our weakness. Our force, because it gives us the ascendency of truth over imposture, and the rights of public interest over private interest. Our weakness, because it rallies against us all the vicious; all those who in their heart meditate the robbery of the people; all those who, having robbed them, seek impunity; and all those who have rejected liberty as a personal calamity, and those who have embraced the revolution as a trade, and the republic as a prey. Hence the defection of so many ambitious men, who have abandoned us on our route, because they did not commence the journey to arrive at the same object as we did. We must crush both the interior and exterior enemies of the republic, or perish with her. And in this situation, the first maxim of your policy should be to conduct the people by reason, and the enemies of the people by terror. If the spring of popular government during peace is virtue, the spring of popular government in rebellion is at once both virtue and terror; virtue, without which terror is fatal! terror, without which virtue is powerless! Terror is nothing else than justice, prompt, secure, and inflexible! It is, therefore, an emanation of virtue; it is less a particular principle, than a consequence of the general principles of democracy, applied to the most urgent wants of the country.

It has been said that terror is the instrument of a despotic government. Does yours then resemble despotism? Yes, as the sword which glitters in the hand of a hero of liberty, resembles that with which the satellites of tyranny are armed! The *government of a revolution is the despotism of liberty against tyranny*. Is force then only made to protect crime? Is it not also made to strike those haughty heads which the lightning has doomed? Nature has imposed upon every being the law of self-preservation. Crime massacres innocence to reign, and innocence struggles with all its force in the hands of crime. Let tyranny but reign one day, and on the morrow there would not remain a single patriot. Until when will the fury of tyranny continue to be called justice, and the justice of the people barbarity and rebellion? How tender they are to oppressors: how inexorable to the oppressed! Nevertheless, it is necessary that one or the other should succumb. Indulgence for the Royalist! exclaimed certain people. Pardon for wretches! No! Pardon for innocence, pardon for the weak, pardon for the unhappy, pardon for humanity!

READING AND DISCUSSION QUESTIONS

1. What are the aims of the French Revolution as Robespierre describes them? Are they achievable goals or unreasonable goals for society? Cite evidence to support your position.

2. How does Robespierre justify his vision of terror? Against whom should terror be directed?

3. Robespierre advocates for democracy. How might he define democracy? How does he imagine terror will help to achieve democracy?

DOCUMENT 22-5

MARY WOLLSTONECRAFT

From A Vindication of the Rights of Woman

1792

In response to a 1791 report to the French National Assembly by diplo-mat Charles Talleyrand (1754–1838), British author Mary Wollstonecraft (1759–1797) argued for the importance of equal educational opportunities for women. Her Vindication of the Rights of Woman *is viewed as an impor-tant early contribution to feminist theory, but it also provides insight on some of the controversy surrounding the French Revolution. It highlights how the revolution encouraged new debates and perspectives on gender rela-tions in modern societies.*

But, if strength of body be, with some show of reason, the boast of men, why are women so infatuated as to be proud of a defect? Rousseau has fur-nished them with a plausible excuse, which could only have occurred to a man, whose imagination had been allowed to run wild, and refine on the impressions made by exquisite senses; — that they might, forsooth, have a pretext for yielding to a natural appetite without violating a romantic spe-cies of modesty, which gratifies the pride and libertinism of man.

Women, deluded by these sentiments, sometimes boast of their weak-ness, cunningly obtaining power by playing on the *weakness* of men; and they may well glory in their illicit sway, for, like Turkish bashaws [i.e., pashas, or Lords], they have more real power than their masters: but virtue is sacrificed to temporary gratifications, and the respectability of life to the triumph of an hour.

Women, as well as despots, have now, perhaps, more power than they would have if the world, divided and subdivided into kingdoms and fami-lies, were governed by laws deduced from the exercise of reason; but in obtaining it, to carry on the comparison, their character is degraded, and licentiousness spread through the whole aggregate of society. The many become pedestal to the few. I, therefore, will venture to assert, that till

Mary Wollstonecraft, A *Vindication of the Rights of Woman: With Strictures on Political and Moral Subjects* (London: T. Fisher Unwin, 1891), 74–84.

women are more rationally educated, the progress of human virtue and improvement in knowledge must receive continual checks. And if it be granted that woman was not created merely to gratify the appetite of man, or to be the upper servant, who provides his meals and takes care of his linen, it must follow, that the first care of those mothers, or fathers, who really attend to the education of females, should be, if not to strengthen the body, at least, not to destroy the constitution by mistaken notions of beauty and female excellence; nor should girls ever be allowed to imbibe the pernicious notion that a defect can, by any chemical process of reasoning, become an excellence. . . .

But should it be proved that woman is naturally weaker than man, whence does it follow that it is natural for her to labor to become still weaker than nature intended her to be? Arguments of this cast are an insult to common sense, and savor of passion. The *divine right* of husbands, like the divine right of kings, may, it is to be hoped, in this enlightened age, be contested without danger, and, though conviction may not silence many boisterous disputants, yet, when any prevailing prejudice is attacked, the wife will consider, and leave the narrow-minded to rail with thoughtless vehemence at innovation.

The mother, who wishes to give true dignity of character to her daughter, must, regardless of the sneers of ignorance, proceed on a plan diametrically opposite to that which Rousseau has recommended with all the deluding charms of eloquence and philosophical sophistry: for his eloquence renders absurdities plausible, and his dogmatic conclusions puzzle, without convincing, those who have not ability to refute them.

Throughout the whole animal kingdom every young creature requires almost continual exercise, and the infancy of children, conformable to this intimation, should be passed in harmless gambols, that exercise the feet and hands, without requiring very minute direction from the head, or the constant attention of a nurse. In fact, the care necessary for self-preservation is the first natural exercise of the understanding, as little inventions to amuse the present moment unfold the imagination. But these wise designs of nature are counteracted by mistaken fondness or blind zeal. The child is not left a moment to its own direction, particularly a girl, and thus rendered dependent — dependence is called natural. . . .

Let not men then in the pride of power, use the same arguments that tyrannic kings and venal ministers have used, and fallaciously assert that woman ought to be subjected because she has always been so. But, when man, governed by reasonable laws, enjoys his natural freedom, let him despise woman, if she do not share it with him; and, till that glorious period arrives, in descanting on the folly of the sex, let him not overlook his own.

Women, it is true, obtaining power by unjust means, by practicing or fostering vice, evidently lose the rank which reason would assign them, and they become either abject slaves or capricious tyrants. They lose all simplicity, all dignity of mind, in acquiring power, and act as men are observed to act when they have been exalted by the same means.

It is time to effect a revolution in female manners — time to restore to them their lost dignity — and make them, as a part of the human species, labor by reforming themselves to reform the world. It is time to separate unchangeable morals from local manners. If men be demi-gods — why let us serve them! And if the dignity of the female soul be as disputable as that of animals — if their reason does not afford sufficient light to direct their conduct whilst unerring instinct is denied — they are surely of all creatures the most miserable! and, bent beneath the iron hand of destiny, must submit to be a *fair defect* in creation. But to justify the ways of [Divine] Providence respecting them, by pointing out some irrefragable reason for thus making such a large portion of mankind accountable and not accountable, would puzzle the subtlest casuist.[1]

READING AND DISCUSSION QUESTIONS

1. How does Wollstonecraft use the ideas of physical strength and exercise in her call for women's education?

2. How does Wollstonecraft connect the relationship between men and women to the relationship between ruler and ruled?

3. How does Wollstonecraft describe the ideal relationship between men and women? What is the level of equality in this relationship?

---

[1] **would puzzle the subtlest casuist**: A casuist attempts to solve moral problems. The author is suggesting that accepting that women are a weaker sex de facto is ludicrous and that any person capable of reason should be able to deduce as much.

DOCUMENT 22-6

The Haitian Declaration of Independence
1804

The Haitian Revolution represents one of modern history's most thorough political and social transformations. Beginning in 1791, slaves of African descent on the sugar and coffee plantations in the French colony of Saint-Domingue staged a series of uprisings against white plantation owners, ultimately forcing France to abolish slavery in its colonies. After Napoleonic forces sought to regain control of the colony and imprisoned Saint-Domingue's charismatic leader, Toussaint L'Ouverture (1743–1803), his lieutenant Jean-Jacques Dessalines (1758–1806) took command and expelled the French in 1803. His declaration of independence in 1804 invoked Enlightenment values and rhetoric to address racial inequality.

THE COMMANDER IN CHIEF TO THE PEOPLE OF HAITI

Citizens:

It is not enough to have expelled the barbarians who have bloodied our land for two centuries; it is not enough to have restrained those ever-evolving factions that one after another mocked the specter of liberty that France dangled before you. We must, with one last act of national authority, forever ensure liberty's reign in the country of our birth; we must take any hope of re-enslaving us away from the inhumane government that for so long kept us in the most humiliating stagnation. In the end we must live independent or die.

Independence or death . . . let these sacred words unite us and be the signal of battle and of our reunion.

Citizens, my countrymen, on this solemn day I have brought together those courageous soldiers who, as liberty lay dying, spilled their blood to save it; these generals who have guided your efforts against tyranny have not yet done enough for your happiness; the French name still haunts our land.

Thomas Madiou, *Histoire d'Haïti* (Port-au-Prince, 1847–1848), 3:146–150. Excerpted in *Slave Revolution in the Caribbean, 1789–1804: A Brief History with Documents,* Laurent Dubois and John D. Garrigus, eds. (Boston: Bedford/St. Martin's, 2006), 188–191.

Everything revives the memories of the cruelties of this barbarous people: our laws, our habits, our towns, everything still carries the stamp of the French. Indeed! There are still French in our island, and you believe yourself free and independent of that republic, which, it is true, has fought all the nations, but which has never defeated those who wanted to be free.

What! Victims of our [own] credulity and indulgence for fourteen years; defeated not by French armies, but by the pathetic eloquence of their agents' proclamations; when will we tire of breathing the air that they breathe? What do we have in common with this nation of executioners? The difference between its cruelty and our patient moderation, its color and ours, the great seas that separate us, our avenging climate, all tell us plainly that they are not our brothers, that they never will be, and that if they find refuge among us, they will plot again to trouble and divide us.

Native citizens, men, women, girls, and children, let your gaze extend on all parts of this island: look there for your spouses, your husbands, your brothers, your sisters. Indeed! Look there for your children, your suckling infants, what have they become? . . . I shudder to say it . . . the prey of these vultures.

Instead of these dear victims, your alarmed gaze will see only their assassins, these tigers still dripping with their blood, whose terrible presence indicts your lack of feeling and your guilty slowness in avenging them. What are you waiting for before appeasing their spirits? Remember that you had wanted your remains to rest next to those of your fathers after you defeated tyranny; will you descend into their tombs without having avenged them? No! Their bones would reject yours.

And you, precious men, intrepid generals, who, without concern for your own pain, have revived liberty by shedding all your blood, know that you have done nothing if you do not give the nations a terrible, but just example of the vengeance that must be wrought by a people proud to have recovered its liberty and jealous to maintain it. Let us frighten all those who would dare try to take it from us again; let us begin with the French. Let them tremble when they approach our coast, if not from the memory of those cruelties they perpetrated here, then from the terrible resolution that we will have made to put to death anyone born French whose profane foot soils the land of liberty.

We have dared to be free, let us be thus by ourselves and for ourselves. Let us imitate the grown child: his own weight breaks the boundary that has become an obstacle to him. What people fought for us? What people wanted to gather the fruits of our labor? And what dishonorable absurdity to conquer in order to be enslaved. Enslaved? . . . Let us leave this description for the French; they have conquered but are no longer free.

Let us walk down another path; let us imitate those people who, extending their concern into the future and dreading to leave an example of cowardice for posterity, preferred to be exterminated rather than lose their place as one of the world's free peoples.

Let us ensure, however, that a missionary spirit does not destroy our work; let us allow our neighbors to breathe in peace; may they live quietly under the laws that they have made for themselves, and let us not, as revolutionary firebrands, declare ourselves the lawgivers of the Caribbean, nor let our glory consist in troubling the peace of the neighboring islands. Unlike that which we inhabit, theirs has not been drenched in the innocent blood of its inhabitants; they have no vengeance to claim from the authority that protects them.

Fortunate to have never known the ideals that have destroyed us, they can only have good wishes for our prosperity.

Peace to our neighbors; but let this be our cry: "Anathema to the French name! Eternal hatred of France!"

Natives of Haiti! My happy fate was to be one day the sentinel who would watch over the idol to which you sacrifice; I have watched, sometimes fighting alone, and if I have been so fortunate as to return to your hands the sacred trust you confided to me, know that it is now your task to preserve it. In fighting for your liberty, I was working for my own happiness. Before consolidating it with laws that will guarantee your free individuality, your leaders, who I have assembled here, and I, owe you the final proof of our devotion.

Generals and you, leaders, collected here close to me for the good of our land, the day has come, the day which must make our glory, our independence, eternal.

If there could exist among us a lukewarm heart, let him distance himself and tremble to take the oath which must unite us. Let us vow to ourselves, to posterity, to the entire universe, to forever renounce France, and to die rather than live under its domination; to fight until our last breath for the independence of our country.

And you, a people so long without good fortune, witness to the oath we take, remember that I counted on your constancy and courage when I threw myself into the career of liberty to fight the despotism and tyranny you had struggled against for fourteen years. Remember that I sacrificed everything to rally to your defense; family, children, fortune, and now I am rich only with your liberty; my name has become a horror to all those who want slavery. Despots and tyrants curse the day that I was born. If ever you refused or grumbled while receiving those laws that the spirit guarding your fate dictates to me for your own good, you would deserve the fate of an ungrateful people. But I reject that awful idea; you will sustain the liberty that you cherish and support the leader who commands you. Therefore, vow before me to live free and independent and to prefer death to anything that will try to place you back in chains. Swear, finally, to pursue forever the traitors and enemies of your independence.

Done at the headquarters of Gonaïves, the first day of January 1804, the first year of independence.

READING AND DISCUSSION QUESTIONS

1. How does the Haitian Declaration of Independence inspire nationalist feelings in its audience?
2. How does the document justify the Haitian Revolution?
3. Describe the tone of the declaration. Who is speaking, and to whom?

COMPARATIVE QUESTIONS

1. Compare and contrast the four declarations excerpted in this chapter: the Declaration of Independence of the United States, the Declaration of the Rights of Man, the Declaration of the Rights of Woman, and the Haitian Declaration of Independence. How does each document describe past problems, and how does each present a vision of a new world? What values do all four embrace, and where do the documents diverge?
2. What is the role of violence in each of this chapter's documents? According to each, when is violence justified in order to enact positive social change? Which documents do not address the problem of violence?

3. Which is the most radical of these documents? Which is the most conservative? Why?

4. How might Robespierre have responded to the author of the Haitian Declaration of Independence? Would he have supported him? Why or why not?

5. De Gouges and Wollstonecraft were both supporters of women's rights and published around the same time. Compare and contrast their arguments. On what do you suspect they would have agreed? On what might they have disagreed?

CHAPTER 23

The Revolution in Energy and Industry

1760–1850

T he Industrial Revolution, though less visibly dramatic than the bloody political and social revolutions taking place in Europe and the Americas, did more to transform human societies around the world than any single development since the beginning of agriculture. Changes in farming, manufacturing, and domestic and foreign trade — first in Britain, and then in Europe and beyond — resulted in unprecedented economic growth. At the same time, shifts in social relations revealed obvious and disturbing inequalities between prosperous business owners and their often-abused workers. In the following documents, British politicians, workers, and intellectuals address some of the social effects of rapid modernization. Whether seeking protection for women and children in the workplace, demanding universal male suffrage, analyzing the challenges of a rapidly increasing population, or outlining the international effects of British industrialization, these texts show ways in which people tried to understand and navigate their changing social and economic worlds.

DOCUMENT 23-1

THOMAS ROBERT MALTHUS

From An Essay on the Principle of Population

1798

Anglican priest and scholar Thomas Robert Malthus (1766–1834) revised and republished his influential 1798 work on population numerous times to respond to critics and changing circumstances. His views on the relationships

---

Thomas Robert Malthus, "An Essay on the Principle of Population," in Walter Arnstein, ed., *The Past Speaks*, 2d ed. (Lexington, Mass.: D. C. Heath, 1993), 2:144–146.

between population, resources, and human happiness met with considerable opposition, especially from thinkers such as William Godwin (1756–1836), husband of the author Mary Wollstonecraft (Document 22-5) and author of a book that Malthus attacked directly. Malthus's attempts to fold natural and social sciences together, though frequently misunderstood or misappropriated, continue to inform debates over social policy and natural resources.

I have read some of the speculations on the perfectibility of man and of society with great pleasure. I have been warmed and delighted with the enchanting picture which they hold forth. I ardently wish for such happy improvements. But I see great, and, to my understanding, unconquerable difficulties in the way to them. These difficulties it is my present purpose to state; declaring, at the same time, that so far from exulting in them, as a cause of triumphing over the friends of innovation, nothing would give me greater pleasure than to see them completely removed. . . .

I think I may fairly make two postulata.

First, That food is necessary to the existence of man.

Secondly, That the passion between the sexes is necessary, and will remain nearly in its present state. . . .

Assuming, then, my postulata as granted, I say, that the power of population is indefinitely greater than the power in the earth to produce subsistence for man.

Population, when unchecked, increases in a geometrical ratio. Subsistence only increases in an arithmetical ratio. A slight acquaintance with numbers will show the immensity of the first power in comparison of the second.

By that law of our nature which makes food necessary to the life of man, the effects of these two unequal powers must be kept equal.

This implies a strong and constantly operating check on population from the difficulty of subsistence. This difficulty must fall some where; and must necessarily be severely felt by a large portion of mankind. . . .

The ultimate check to population appears then to be a want of food arising necessarily from the different ratios according to which population and food increase. But this ultimate check is never the immediate check, except in cases of actual famine.

The immediate check may be stated to consist in all those customs, and all those diseases which seem to be generated by a scarcity of the means of subsistence; and all those causes, independent of this scarcity, whether of a moral or physical nature, which tend prematurely to weaken and destroy the human frame.

In every country some of these checks are, with more or less force, in constant operation; yet, notwithstanding their general prevalence, there are few states in which there is not a constant effort in the population to increase beyond the means of subsistence. This constant effort as constantly tends to subject the lower classes of society to distress, and to prevent any great permanent melioration of their condition.

These effects, in the present state of society, seem to be produced in the following manner. We will suppose the means of subsistence in any country just equal to the easy support of its inhabitants. The constant effort toward population, which is found to act even in the most vicious societies, increases the number of people before the means of subsistence are increased. The food, therefore, which before supported eleven millions, must now be divided among eleven millions and a half. The poor consequently must live much worse, and many of them be reduced to severe distress. The number of laborers also being above the proportion of work in the market, the price of labor must tend to fall, while the price of provisions would at the same time tend to rise. The laborer therefore must do more work to earn the same as he did before. During this season of distress, the discouragements to marriage and the difficulty of rearing a family are so great, that the progress of population is retarded. In the meantime, the cheapness of labor, the plenty of laborers, and the necessity of an increased industry among them, encourage cultivators to employ more labor upon their land, to turn up fresh soil, and to manure and improve more completely what is already in tillage, till ultimately the means of subsistence may become in the same proportion to the population as at the period from which we set out. The situation of the laborer being then again tolerably comfortable, the restraints to population are in some degree loosened; and, after a short period, the same retrograde and progressive movements, with respect to happiness, are repeated. . . .

READING AND DISCUSSION QUESTIONS

1. According to Malthus, what features are constant in modern populations?

2. In Malthus's view, who bears the brunt of the cycle of human reproduction and food production? What seems to be Malthus's attitude toward these people?

3. What are possible solutions to the cycle that Malthus describes?

The Realities of Manufacturing

DOCUMENT 23-2

ROBERT OWEN

From Observations on the Effect of the Manufacturing System

1815

Robert Owen (1771–1858), a British socialist from a coal-rich area of Wales, first gained fame through his management of a cotton mill in New Lanark, Scotland. As part owner, Owen incorporated philanthropy with capitalism, and his concern for working conditions, education, and workers' lives helped establish New Lanark's international reputation as a model industrial community. Beginning in 1815, Owen lobbied the British Parliament for legislation to protect British workers, but the many concessions made to industrialists in the 1819 law left him disappointed. Owen penned his Observations *in 1815; although he would not develop utopian socialist ideals until later, his interest in public welfare and his distrust of naked capitalism are evident here.*

Those who were engaged in the trade, manufactures, and commerce of this country thirty or forty years ago, formed but a very insignificant portion of the knowledge, wealth, influence, or population of the Empire.

Prior to that period, Britain was essentially agricultural. But, from that time to the present, the home and foreign trade have increased in a manner so rapid and extraordinary as to have raised commerce to an importance, which it never previously attained in any country possessing so much political power and influence. This change has been owing chiefly to the mechanical inventions which introduced the cotton trade into this country, and to the cultivation of the cotton-tree in America. The wants,

Robert Owen, *Observations on the Effect of the Manufacturing System: With Hints for the Improvement of Those Parts of It Which Are Most Injurious to Health and Morals* (London: R. and A. Taylor, 1817), 3–6.

which this trade created for the various materials requisite to forward its multiplied operations, caused an extraordinary demand for almost all the manufactures previously established, and, of course, for human labour. The numerous fanciful and useful fabrics manufactured from cotton soon became objects of desire in Europe and America: and the consequent extension of the British foreign trade was such as to astonish and confound the most enlightened statesmen both at home and abroad.

The immediate effects of this manufacturing phenomenon were a rapid increase of the wealth, industry, population and political influence of the British empire; and by the aid of which it has been enabled to contend for five-and-twenty years against the most formidable military and *immoral* power that the world perhaps ever contained.[1]

These important results, however, great as they really are, have not been obtained without accompanying evils of such a magnitude as to raise a doubt whether the latter do not preponderate over the former.

Hitherto, legislators have appeared to regard manufactures only in one point of view, as a source of national wealth. The other mighty consequences, which proceed from extended manufactures, *when left to their natural progress*, have never yet engaged the attention of any legislature. Yet the political and moral effects to which we allude, well deserve to occupy the best faculties of the greatest and the wisest statesmen.

The general diffusion of manufactures throughout a country generates a new character in its inhabitants; and as this character is formed upon a principle quite unfavourable to individual or general happiness, it will produce the most lamentable and permanent evils, unless its tendency be counteracted by legislative interference and direction.

The manufacturing system has already so far extended its influence over the British empire, as to effect an essential change in the general character of the mass of the people. This alteration is still in rapid progress; and ere long, the comparatively happy simplicity of the agricultural peasant will be wholly lost amongst us: It is even now scarcely any where to be found, without a mixture of those habits, which are the offspring of trade, manufactures, and commerce.

The acquisition of wealth, and the desire which it naturally creates for a continued increase, have introduced a fondness for essentially injurious luxuries among a numerous class of individuals, who formerly never thought of them, and they have also generated a disposition which strongly

[1] **the most formidable . . . contained**: Owen is referring to Revolutionary and Napoleonic France.

impels its possessors to sacrifice the best feelings of human nature to this love of accumulation. To succeed in this career, the industry of the lower orders from whose labour this wealth is now drawn, has been carried by new competitors striving against those of longer standing, to a point of real oppression, reducing them by successive changes, as the spirit of competition increased, and the ease of acquiring wealth diminished, to a state more wretched than can be imagined by those who have not attentively observed the changes as they have gradually occurred. In consequence, they are at present in a situation infinitely more degraded and miserable than they were before the introduction of these manufactories, upon the success of which their bare subsistence now depends.

READING AND DISCUSSION QUESTIONS

1. What is the principal product that characterizes industry for Owen?

2. How does Owen situate British industry in the larger context of international relations?

3. What, in Owen's view, has been the attitude of government toward industry? What is government's implicit responsibility?

DOCUMENT 23-3

SADLER COMMITTEE AND
ASHLEY COMMISSION

Testimonies Before Parliamentary Committees on Working Conditions in England

1832, 1842

The Industrial Revolution depended on men, women, and children working under harsh and often deadly conditions. Troubled by the social changes wrought by Britain's rapid industrialization, politician Michael Sadler

John Bowditch, ed., Voices of the Industrial Revolution (Ann Arbor: University of Michigan Press, 1961), 82–90.

(1780–1835) *formed the Committee on the Labour of Children in the Mills and Factories of the United Kingdom. The committee's 1832 report shocked the public and mobilized support for labor reform. In 1840, another labor reform advocate, Lord Ashley (1801–1885), established the Children's Employment Commission. Its 1842 report shed light on the practice of child labor in coal mines, or "collieries." Both of these reports prompted legislation and raised public awareness of the human cost of the Industrial Revolution.*

TESTIMONY BEFORE THE SADLER COMMITTEE, 1832[2]

Elizabeth Bentley, Called in; and Examined

What age are you? — Twenty-three. . . .

What time did you begin to work at a factory? — When I was six years old. . . .

What kind of mill is it? — Flax-mill. . . .

What was your business in that mill? — I was a little doffer.[3]

What were your hours of labor in that mill? — From 5 in the morning till 9 at night, when they were thronged [busy].

For how long a time together have you worked that excessive length of time? — For about half a year.

What were your usual hours of labor when you were not so thronged? — From 6 in the morning till 7 at night.

What time was allowed for your meals? — Forty minutes at noon.

Had you any time to get your breakfast or drinking? — No, we got it as we could.

And when your work was bad, you had hardly any time to eat it at all? — No; we were obliged to leave it or take it home, and when we did not take it, the overlooker took it, and gave it to his pigs.

Do you consider doffing a laborious employment? — Yes.

Explain what it is you had to do. — When the frames are full, they have to stop the frames, and take the flyers off, and take the full bobbins off, and carry them to the roller; and then put empty ones on, and set the frames on again.

---

[2] **Testimony . . . 1832**: Michael Sadler first proposed a ten-hour workday in 1831; his bill was rejected by Parliament but prompted the formation of this investigative committee.

[3] **doffer**: A young child whose job was to clean the machinery.

Does that keep you constantly on your feet? — Yes, there are so many frames and they run so quick.

Your labor is very excessive? — Yes; you have not time for anything.

Suppose you flagged a little, or were too late, what would they do? — Strap us.

Are they in the habit of strapping those who are last in doffing? — Yes.

Constantly? — Yes.

Girls as well as boys? — Yes.

Have you ever been strapped? — Yes.

Severely? — Yes.

Could you eat your food well in that factory? — No, indeed, I had not much to eat, and the little I had I could not eat it, my appetite was so poor, and being covered with dust; and it was no use to take it home, I could not eat it, and the overlooker took it, and gave it to the pigs. . . .

Did you live far from the mill? — Yes, two miles.

Had you a clock? — No, we had not.

Supposing you had not been in time enough in the morning at the mills, what would have been the consequence? — We should have been quartered.

What do you mean by that? — If we were a quarter of an hour too late, they would take off half an hour; we only got a penny an hour, and they would take a halfpenny more. . . .

Were you generally there in time? — Yes, my mother has been up at 4 o'clock in the morning, and at 2 o'clock in the morning; the colliers used to go to their work about 3 or 4 o'clock, and when she heard them stirring she has got up out of her warm bed, and gone out and asked them the time, and I have sometimes been at Hunslet Car at 2 o'clock in the morning, when it was streaming down with rain, and we have had to stay till the mill was opened. . . .

TESTIMONY BEFORE THE ASHLEY COMMISSION ON THE CONDITIONS IN MINES, 1842[4]

Edward Potter

I am a coal viewer, and the manager of the South Hetton colliery. We have about 400 bound people (contract laborers), and in addition our

---

[4] **Testimony . . . 1842:** This testimony led to the Mines Act of 1842, which prohibited boys under the age of ten and women from working in the mines.

bank people (foremen), men and boys about 700. In the pits 427 men and boys; of these, 290 men. . . .

Of the children in the pits we have none under eight, and only three so young. We are constantly beset by parents coming making application to take children under the age, and they are very anxious and very dissatisfied if we do not take the children; and there have been cases in times of brisk trade, when the parents have threatened to leave the colliery, and go elsewhere if we did not comply. At every successive binding, which takes place yearly, constant attempts are made to get the boys engaged to work to which they are not competent from their years. In point of fact, we would rather not have boys until nine years of age complete. If younger than that, they are apt to fall asleep and get hurt; some get killed. It is no interest to the company to take any boys under nine. . . .

Hannah Richardson

I've one child that works in the pit; he's going on ten. He is down from 6 to 8. . . . He's not much tired with the work, it's only the confinement that tires him. He likes it pretty well, for he'd rather be in the pit than to go to school. There is not much difference in his health since he went into the pit. He was at school before, and can read pretty well, but can't write. He is used pretty well; I never hear him complain. I've another son in the pit, 17 years old. . . . He went into the pit at eight years old. It's not hurt his health nor his appetite, for he's a good size. It would hurt us if children were prevented from working till 11 or 12 years old, because we've not jobs enough to live now as it is. . . .

Mr. George Armitage

I am now a teacher at Hoyland school; I was a collier at Silkstone until I was 22 years old and worked in the pit above 10 years. . . . I hardly know how to reprobate the practice sufficiently of girls working in pits; nothing can be worse. I have no doubt that debauchery is carried on, for which there is every opportunity; for the girls go constantly, when hurrying, to the men, who work often alone in the bank-faces apart from every one. I think it scarcely possible for girls to remain modest who are in pits, regularly mixing with such company and hearing such language as they do — it is next to impossible. I dare venture to say that many of the wives who come from pits know nothing of sewing or any household duty, such as women ought to know — they lose all disposition to learn such things; they are rendered unfit for learning them also by being overworked and not being trained to the habit of it. I have worked in pits for above 10 years, where girls were constantly employed, and I can safely say it is an abominable system; indecent language is quite common. I think, if girls were trained properly, as girls ought to be, that there would be no more difficulty in finding suitable employment for them than in other places. Many a collier spends in drink what he has shut up a young child the whole week to earn in a dark cold corner as a trapper. The education of the children is universally bad. They are generally ignorant of common facts in Christian history and principles, and, indeed, in almost everything else. Little can be learned merely on Sundays, and they are too tired as well as indisposed to go to night schools. . . .

The Rev. Robert Willan, Curate of St. Mary's, Barnsley

I have been resident here as chief minister for 22 years. I think the morals of the working classes here are in an appalling state. . . . The ill manners and conduct of the weavers are daily presented to view in the streets, but the colliers work under ground and are less seen, and we have less means of knowing. . . . The master-sin among the youths is that of gambling; the boys may be seen playing at pitch-and-toss on the Sabbath and on weekdays; they are seen doing this in all directions. The next besetting sin is promiscuous sexual intercourse; this may be much induced by the manner in which they sleep — men, women, and children often sleeping in one bed-room. I have known a family of father and mother and 12 children, some of them up-grown, sleeping on a kind of sacking and straw bed, reaching from one side of the room to the other, along the floor; they were an English family. Sexual intercourse begins very young. This and gambling pave the way; then drinking ensues, and this is the vortex which draws in every other sin.

Thomas Wilson, Esq., Owner of Three Collieries

I object on general principles to government interference in the conduct of any trade, and I am satisfied that in the mines it would be productive of the greatest injury and injustice. The art of mining is not so perfectly understood as to admit of the way in which a colliery shall be conducted being dictated by any person, however experienced, with such certainty as would warrant an interference with the management of private business. I should also most decidedly object to placing collieries under the present provisions of the Factory Act[5] with respect to the education of children employed therein. First, because, if it is contended that coal-owners, as employers of children, are bound to attend to their education, this obligation extends equally to all other employers, and therefore it is unjust to single out one class only; secondly, because, if the legislature asserts a right to interfere to secure education, it is bound to make that interference general; and thirdly, because the mining population is in this neighborhood so intermixed with other classes, and is in such small bodies in any one place, that it would be impossible to provide separate schools for them.

READING AND DISCUSSION QUESTIONS

1. How do these testimonies present the realities of child labor? Give specific examples.

2. Both reports make particular note of the gender of workers. What is the effect of calling attention to female labor? Describe the attitudes toward gender differences conveyed in these reports.

3. Summarize the arguments presented in the Ashley Commission report for and against the regulation of female and child labor in mines. How is the issue of education used in each argument?

DOCUMENT 23-4

Chartism: The People's Petition

1838

In 1837, a group of twelve men — six members of Parliament and six members of the British working class — composed and circulated a list of demands

William Lovett, *The Life and Struggles of William Lovett* (New York: Knopf, 1920), 478–482.

[5] **Factory Act:** The Factory Act of 1833 restricted the workday to eight hours for children between the ages of nine and fourteen and twelve hours for those between fourteen and eighteen.

for electoral reforms including universal male suffrage. These demands were later incorporated into the People's Charter, from which the Chartist movement took its name. In 1838, the petition excerpted below was submitted to Parliament. Despite garnering more than a million signatures, the proposal met with little support from the rest of Parliament or from the middle classes, and it failed to pass on several occasions. Nevertheless, the Chartist movement was an important early milestone in the struggle for individual rights during the Industrial Revolution.

Unto the Honorable the Commons of the United Kingdom of Great Britain and Ireland in Parliament assembled, the Petition of the undersigned, their suffering countrymen.

HUMBLY SHEWETH,

That we, your petitioners, dwell in a land whose merchants are noted for enterprise, whose manufacturers are very skilful, and whose workmen are proverbial for their industry.

The land itself is goodly, the soil rich, and the temperature wholesome; it is abundantly furnished with the materials of commerce and trade; it has numerous and convenient harbors; in facility of internal communication it exceeds all others.

For three-and-twenty years we have enjoyed a profound peace.

Yet, with all these elements of national prosperity, and with every disposition and capacity to take advantage of them, we find ourselves overwhelmed with public and private suffering.

We are bowed down under a load of taxes; which, notwithstanding, fall greatly short of the wants of our rulers; our traders are trembling on the verge of bankruptcy; our workmen are starving; capital brings no profit, and labor no remuneration; the home of the artificer is desolate, and the warehouse of the pawnbroker is full; the workhouse is crowded, and the manufactory is deserted.

We have looked on every side, we have searched diligently in order to find out the causes of a distress so sore and so long continued.

We can discover none in nature, or in Providence.

Heaven has dealt graciously by the people; but the foolishness of our rulers has made the goodness of God of none effect.

The energies of a mighty kingdom have been wasted in building up the power of selfish and ignorant men, and its resources squandered for their aggrandizement.

The good of a party has been advanced to the sacrifice of the good of the nation; the few have governed for the interest of the few, while the interest of the many has been neglected, or insolently and tyrannously trampled upon.

It was the fond expectation of the people that a remedy for the greater part, if not for the whole, of their grievances, would be found in the Reform Act of 1832.

They were taught to regard that Act as a wise means to a worthy end; as the machinery of an improved legislation, when the will of the masses would be at length potential.

They have been bitterly and basely deceived.

The fruit which looked so fair to the eye has turned to dust and ashes when gathered.

The Reform Act has effected a transfer of power from one domineering faction to another, and left the people as helpless as before.

Our slavery has been exchanged for an apprenticeship to liberty, which has aggravated the painful feeling of our social degradation, by adding to it the sickening of still deferred hope.

We come before your Honorable House to tell you, with all humility, that this state of things must not be permitted to continue; that it cannot long continue without very seriously endangering the stability of the throne and the peace of the kingdom; and that if by God's help and all lawful and constitutional appliances, an end can be put to it, we are fully resolved that it shall speedily come to an end.

We tell your Honorable House that the capital of the master must no longer be deprived of its due reward; that the laws which make food dear, and those which by making money scarce, make labor cheap, must be abolished; that taxation must be made to fall on property, not on industry; that the good of the many, as it is the only legitimate end, so must it be the sole study of the Government.

As a preliminary essential to these and other requisite changes; as means by which alone the interests of the people can be effectually vindicated and secured, we demand that those interests be confided to the keeping of the people.

When the State calls for defenders, when it calls for money, no consideration of poverty or ignorance can be pleaded in refusal or delay of the call.

Required as we are, universally, to support and obey the laws, nature and reason entitle us to demand, that in the making of the laws, the universal voice shall be implicitly listened to.

We perform the duties of freemen; we must have the privileges of freemen.

WE DEMAND UNIVERSAL SUFFRAGE.

The suffrage to be exempt from the corruption of the wealthy, and the violence of the powerful, must be secret.

The assertion of our right necessarily involves the power of its uncontrolled exercise.

WE DEMAND THE BALLOT.

The connection between the representatives and the people, to be beneficial must be intimate.

The legislative and constituent powers, for correction and for instruction, ought to be brought into frequent contact.

Errors, which are comparatively light when susceptible of a speedy popular remedy, may produce the most disastrous effects when permitted to grow inveterate through years of compulsory endurance.

To public safety as well as public confidence, frequent elections are essential.

WE DEMAND ANNUAL PARLIAMENTS.

With power to choose, and freedom in choosing, the range of our choice must be unrestricted.

We are compelled, by the existing laws, to take for our representatives, men who are incapable of appreciating our difficulties, or who have little sympathy with them; merchants who have retired from trade, and no longer feel its harassings; proprietors of land who are alike ignorant of its evils and their cure; lawyers, by whom the honors of the senate are sought after only as means of obtaining notice in the courts.

The labors of a representative, who is sedulous in the discharge of his duty, are numerous and burdensome.

It is neither just, nor reasonable, nor safe, that they should continue to be gratuitously rendered.

We demand that in the future election of members of your Honorable House, the approbation of the constituency shall be the sole qualification; and that to every representative so chosen shall be assigned, out of the public taxes, a fair and adequate remuneration for the time which he is called upon to devote to the public service.

Finally, we would most earnestly impress on your Honorable House, that this petition has not been dictated by any idle love of change; that it springs out of no inconsiderate attachment to fanciful theories; but that it is the result of much and long deliberation, and of convictions, which the events of each succeeding year tend more and more to strengthen.

The management of this mighty kingdom has hitherto been a subject for contending factions to try their selfish experiments upon.

We have felt the consequences in our sorrowful experience — short glimmerings of uncertain enjoyment swallowed up by long and dark seasons of suffering.

If the self-government of the people should not remove their distresses, it will at least remove their repinings.

Universal suffrage will, and it alone can, bring true and lasting peace to the nation; we firmly believe that it will also bring prosperity.

May it therefore please your Honorable House to take this our petition into your most serious consideration; and to use your utmost endeavors, by all constitutional means, to have a law passed, granting to every male of lawful age, sane mind, and unconvicted of crime, the right of voting for members of Parliament; and directing all future elections of members of Parliament to be in the way of secret ballot; and ordaining that the duration of Parliaments so chosen shall in no case exceed one year; and abolishing all property qualifications in the members; and providing for their due remuneration while in attendance on their Parliamentary duties.

READING AND DISCUSSION QUESTIONS

1. What complaints does the People's Petition enumerate?
2. Do the authors of this document seem more concerned with the economic or political outcome of their demands? Support your conclusion with evidence from the document.
3. Explain which of the six specific demands would be relevant to your own life, and which would not.

DOCUMENT 23-5

The Treaty of Balta-Liman
August 16, 1838

The British Industrial Revolution led to increased demands for overseas markets. In 1838, the United Kingdom signed a treaty with the Ottoman Empire at Balta-Liman, near Istanbul. The treaty responded to complaints by British merchants that their goods were subject to a high tariff or other taxes when shipped into or across Egypt. Egypt, nominally a territory of the Ottoman Empire but virtually independent under the rule of Muhammad Ali (or Mehmet Ali), had embarked on its own efforts to industrialize, including high tariffs and state monopolies of important industrial sectors. These excerpts from the treaty show how the United Kingdom's demands and the Ottoman Empire's acquiescence helped destroy Egypt's industries by flooding its markets with cheap British goods.

Article I

All rights, privileges, and immunities which have been conferred on the subjects or ships of Great Britain by the existing Capitulations and Treaties, are confirmed now and for ever, except in as far as they may be specifically altered by the present Convention: and it is moreover expressly stipulated, that all rights, privileges, or immunities which the Sublime Porte[6] now grants, or may hereafter grant, to the ships and subjects of any other foreign Power, or which it may suffer the ships and subjects of any other foreign Power to enjoy, shall be equally granted to, and exercised and enjoyed by, the subjects and ships of Great Britain.

Article II

The subjects of Her Britannic Majesty, or their agents, shall be permitted to purchase at all places in the Ottoman Dominions (whether for the purposes of internal trade or exportation) all articles, without any exception

---

Convention of Commerce and Navigation Between Her Majesty and the Sultan of the Ottoman Empire (London: J. Harrison and Son, 1839), 3–6.

[6] **Sublime Porte:** Literally, the gate of the sultan's palace; the term refers to the sultan and his sovereignty.

whatsoever, the produce, growth, or manufacture of the said Dominions; and the Sublime Porte formally engages to abolish all monopolies of agricultural produce, or of any other articles whatsoever, as well as all *Permits* from the local Governors, either for the purchase of any article, or for its removal from one place to another when purchased; and any attempt to compel the subjects of Her Britannic Majesty to receive such *Permits* from the local Governors, shall be considered as an infraction of Treaties, and the Sublime Porte shall immediately punish with severity any Vizirs [ministers] and other officers who shall have been guilty of such misconduct, and render full justice to British subjects for all injuries or losses which they may duly prove themselves to have suffered. . . .

ADDITIONAL ARTICLES

Certain difficulties having arisen between the Ambassador of Her Britannick Majesty and the Plenipotentiaries of the Sublime Porte, in fixing the new conditions which should regulate the commerce in British goods imported into the Turkish Dominions, or passing through the same in transit, it is agreed between His Excellency the British Ambassador and the Plenipotentiaries of the Sublime Porte, that the present Convention should receive their signatures, without the articles which have reference to the above-mentioned subjects forming part of the body of the said Convention.

But at the same time it is also agreed, — the following Articles having been consented to by the Turkish Government, — that they shall be submitted to the approbation of Her Majesty's Government, and should they be approved and accepted by Her Majesty's Government, they shall then form an integral part of the Treaty now concluded.

The Articles in question are the following:

Article I

All articles being the growth, produce, or manufacture of the United Kingdom of Great Britain and Ireland and its dependencies, and all merchandize, of whatsoever description, embarked in British vessels, and being the property of British subjects, or being brought over land, or by sea, from other countries by the same, shall be admitted, as heretofore, into all parts of the Ottoman Dominions, without exception, on the payment of three per cent. duty, calculated upon the value of such articles.

And in lieu of all other and interior duties, whether levied on the purchaser or seller, to which these articles are at present subject, it is agreed that the importer, after receiving his goods, shall pay, if he sells them at the place of reception, or if he sends them thence to be sold elsewhere in the interior of the Turkish Empire, one fixed duty of two per cent.; after which such goods may be sold and resold in the interior, or exported, without any further duty whatsoever being levied or demanded on them.

But all goods that have paid the three per cent. import duty at one port, shall be sent to another free of any further duty, and it is only, when sold there or transmitted thence into the interior, that the second duty shall be paid.

It is always understood that Her Majesty's Government do not pretend, either by this Article or any other in the present Treaty, to stipulate for more than the plain and fair construction of the terms employed; nor to preclude, in any manner, the Ottoman Government from the exercise of its rights of internal administration, where the exercise of those rights does not evidently infringe upon the privileges accorded by ancient Treaties, or the present Treaty, to British merchandize or British subjects.

Article II

All foreign goods brought into Turkey from other countries, shall be freely purchased and traded in, in any manner, by the subjects of Her Britannic Majesty or the agents of the same, at any place in the Ottoman Dominions; and if such foreign goods have paid no other duty than the duty paid on importation, then the British subject or his agent shall be able to purchase such foreign goods on paying the extra duty of two per cent., which he will have to pay on the sale of his own imported goods, or on their transmission for sale into the interior; and after that such foreign goods shall be resold in the interior, or exported, without further duty; or should such foreign goods have already paid the amount of the two duties (*i. e.* the import duty and the one fixed interior duty,) then they shall be purchased by the British subject or his agent, and afterwards resold or exported, without being ever submitted to any further duty.

Article III

No charge whatsoever shall be made upon British goods, — (such being the growth, produce, or manufacture of the United Kingdom or its dependencies, or the growth, produce, or manufacture of any foreign country, and charged in British vessels and belonging to British subjects,) — passing through the straits of the Dardanelles, of the Bosphorus, and of the Black Sea, whether such goods shall pass through those straits in the ships that brought them, or are transshipped in those straits, or, destined to be sold elsewhere, are landed with a view to their being transferred to other vessels (and thus to proceed on their voyage) within a reasonable time. All merchandize imported into Turkey for the purpose of being transmitted to other countries, or which, remaining in the hands of the importer, shall be transmitted by him for sale to other countries, shall only pay the duty of three per cent. paid on importation, and no other duty whatsoever.

READING AND DISCUSSION QUESTIONS

1. The first article stipulates that any future concession to any other foreign power will be matched by a concession to Great Britain. This is known as a "most-favored nation clause." What does this clause tell you about this treaty? What does it tell you about international relations between the Ottoman Empire and other powers at this point in history?

2. What is the significance of eliminating Ottoman monopolies on any particular item? What is the significance of establishing lowered tariffs and shipping duties?

3. Does this treaty benefit both parties equally? Explain. If it provides benefit primarily to one party, then why might the other have signed it?

COMPARATIVE QUESTIONS

1. What is the relationship between the British government and British business in each document?

2. The Viewpoints documents in this chapter (Owen's *Observations* and the Sadler Committee and Ashley Commission testimonies) point to the effect of the modern age, and specifically the Industrial Revolution, on human society. How do the different documents describe this effect?

3. Which documents portray industry most positively? How so, and why?

4. Do Owen's observations support or refute Malthus's theory of population? Explain.

5. The Chartist petition and the Treaty of Balta-Liman were composed and published within a year of each other. What impression do they give of the relationship between British citizens and their government?

CHAPTER 24

Ideologies of Change in Europe

1815–1914

F ollowing the defeat of Napoleon and his imperial aspirations, a period of ideological development promised to transform the economic and political foundations of Europe. Born in part out of calls for national mobilization in revolutionary France, nationalism gained strength as cultural groups began to seek their own political identity as nation-states. While nationalist rhetoric in Europe often emphasized language, territory, or ethnicity as unifying principles, other movements coalesced around shared identities of gender or social class. In many cases, nationalism, socialism, and other ideologies led to uprisings, revolutions, and wars. In most cases, nationalist movements strengthened states through standardized culture, language, and history as they created both internal solidarity and external threats. Some nationalist movements fought unsuccessfully for recognition, and socialism threatened new nation-states and their nationalist ideologies with a universal call to recognize and respond to the social divisions wrought by the Industrial Revolution. The documents in this chapter present these ideologies as they were proposed and understood by European men and women.

DOCUMENT 24-1

KARL MARX AND FRIEDRICH ENGELS

From The Communist Manifesto

1848

Published in 1848, The Communist Manifesto was commissioned by the Communist League, an early socialist organization that advocated for workers' rights and societal reforms. Party members Karl Marx (1818–1883) and Friedrich Engels (1820–1895) set forth the group's analysis of social conditions under capitalism, their historical basis, and the roles of the bourgeoisie (middle-class property holders) and the proletariat (urban workers) in social change. Written in German, the document was translated into English in 1850 but received little attention. In later years, however, Marx's writings spurred great debate in England and around the world.

A specter is haunting Europe — the specter of communism. All the powers of old Europe have entered into a holy alliance to exorcise this specter: Pope and Czar, Metternich and Guizot,[1] French Radicals and German police-spies. . . .

Communism is already acknowledged by all European powers to be itself a power.

It is high time that Communists should openly, in the face of the whole world, publish their views, their aims, their tendencies, and meet this nursery tale of the specter of communism with a Manifesto of the party itself. . . .

The history of all hitherto existing society is the history of class struggles. . . .

Modern industry has established the world market, for which the discovery of America paved the way. This market has given an immense

Karl Marx and Friedrich Engels, "The Communist Manifesto," in Arthur P. Mendel, *The Essential Works of Marxism* (New York: Bantam, 1961), 13–17, 19, 23, 40–44.

[1] **Metternich and Guizot**: Prince Klemens von Metternich (1773–1859) was foreign minister and chancellor of the Austrian Empire (1809–1848); François Guizot (1787–1874) was a French politician who served as prime minister from 1847 to 1848.

development to commerce, to navigation, to communication by land. This development has, in its turn, reacted on the extension of industry; and in proportion as industry, commerce, navigation, railways extended, in the same proportion the bourgeoisie developed, increased its capital, and pushed into the background every class handed down from the Middle Ages. . . .

The bourgeoisie, historically, has played a most revolutionary part.

The bourgeoisie, wherever it has got the upper hand, has put an end to all feudal, patriarchal, idyllic relations. It has pitilessly torn asunder the motley feudal ties that bound man to his "natural superiors," and has left remaining no other nexus between man and man than naked self-interest, than callous "cash payment." It has drowned the most heavenly ecstasies of religious fervor, of chivalrous enthusiasm, of philistine sentimentalism, in the icy water of egotistical calculation. It has resolved personal worth into exchange value, and in place of the numberless indefeasible chartered freedoms, has set up that single, unconscionable freedom — Free Trade. In a word, for exploitation, veiled by religious and political illusions, it has substituted naked, shameless, direct, brutal exploitation.

The bourgeoisie has stripped of its halo every occupation hitherto honored and looked up to with reverent awe. It has converted the physician, the lawyer, the priest, the poet, and the man of science into its paid wage-laborers.

The bourgeoisie has torn away from the family its sentimental veil and has reduced the family relation to a mere money relation. . . .

The bourgeoisie has subjected the country to the rule of the towns. It has created enormous cities, greatly increased the urban population as compared with the rural, and thus rescued a considerable part of the population from the idiocy of rural life. . . .

The bourgeoisie, during its rule of scarcely one hundred years, has created more massive and more colossal productive forces than have all preceding generations together. . . .

But not only has the bourgeoisie forged the weapons that bring death to itself; it has also called into existence the men who are to wield those weapons — the modern working class — the proletariat.

In proportion as the bourgeoisie, i.e., capital, develops, in the same proportion the proletariat, the modern working class, develops — a class of laborers, who live only so long as they find work, and who find work only so long as their labor increases capital. These laborers, who must sell themselves piecemeal, are a commodity, like every other article of commerce, and are consequently exposed to all the vicissitudes of competition, to all the fluctuations of the market. . . .

Of all the classes that stand face to face with the bourgeoisie today, the proletariat alone is a really revolutionary class. The other classes decay and finally disappear in the face of modern industry; the proletariat is its special and essential product. . . .

The socialist and communist systems properly so called, those of Saint-Simon, Fourier, Owen[2] and others, spring into existence in the early undeveloped period, described above, of the struggle between proletariat and bourgeoisie. . . .

Such fantastic pictures of future society, painted at a time when the proletariat is still in a very undeveloped state and has but a fantastic conception of its own position, correspond with the first instinctive yearnings of that class for a general reconstruction of society.

But these socialist and communist publications contain also a critical element. They attack every principle of existing society. . . .

The Communists fight for the attainment of the immediate aims, for the enforcement of the momentary interests of the working class; but in the movement of the present, they also represent and take care of the future of that movement. . . .

The Communists turn their attention chiefly to Germany, because that country is on the eve of a bourgeois revolution that is bound to be carried out under more advanced conditions of European civilization, and with a much more developed proletariat, than that of England was in the seventeenth, and of France in the eighteenth century, and because the bourgeois revolution in Germany will be but the prelude to an immediately following proletarian revolution.

In short, the Communists everywhere support every revolutionary movement against the existing social and political order of things.

In all these movements they bring to the fore, as the leading question in each, the property question, no matter what its degree of development at the time.

Finally, they labor everywhere for the union and agreement of the democratic parties of all countries.

The Communists disdain to conceal their views and aims. They openly declare that their ends can be attained only by the forcible overthrow of all

---

[2] **Saint-Simon, Fourier, Owen:** French utopian socialists Henri de Saint-Simon (1760–1825) and Charles Fourier (1772–1837) and Welsh utopian socialist Robert Owen (1771–1858) believed that capitalists and workers could overcome their antagonism and work cooperatively for the common good.

existing social conditions. Let the ruling classes tremble at a Communistic revolution. The proletarians have nothing to lose but their chains. They have a world to win.

WORKING MEN OF ALL COUNTRIES, UNITE!

READING AND DISCUSSION QUESTIONS

1. Evaluate the actions of the bourgeoisie described by Marx and Engels. Which actions seem positive, and which seem negative?
2. What do Engels and Marx mean when they say that the bourgeoisie "has played a most revolutionary part" in history?
3. According to Marx and Engels, what is the purpose of their manifesto? How successful is it in achieving that purpose?

VIEWPOINTS
Visions of the Nation

DOCUMENT 24-2

JOHANN GOTTLIEB FICHTE
Address to the German Nation
1808

Johann Gottlieb Fichte (1762–1814) was a German philosopher who wrote and studied widely but is perhaps best known for his contributions to political theory. During the Napoleonic wars in the early nineteenth century, Fichte fled Berlin and the French forces attacking Prussia. Returning in 1807, he was disheartened to find French troops and a dispirited greater German public in the city. The anti-imperial (anti-French) sentiment of the

Johann Gottlieb Fichte, *Addresses to the German Nation*, trans. R. F. Jones and G. H. Turnbull (Chicago: Open Court Publishing, 1922), 2–4.

day found form in Fichte's celebration of German identity, which fostered German pride through an exaggerated litany of German accomplishments and virtues. His speeches (1807–1808) were published in 1808, inspiring citizens of German states to help fight and defeat Napoleon and laying the foundation for German nationalism.

Time is taking giant strides with us more than with any other age since the history of the world began. . . . At some point self-seeking has destroyed itself, because by its own complete development it has lost its self and the independence of that self; and since it would not voluntarily set itself any other aim but self, an external power has forced upon it another and a foreign purpose. He who has once undertaken to interpret his own age must make his interpretation keep pace with the progress of that age, if progress there be. It is, therefore, my duty to acknowledge as past what has ceased to be the present, before the same audience to whom I characterized it as the present.

. . . Whatever has lost its independence has at the same time lost its power to influence the course of events and to determine these events by its own will. If it remain in this state its age, and itself with the age, are conditioned in their development by that alien power which governs its fate. From now onwards it has no longer any time of its own, but counts its years by the events and epochs of alien nations and kingdoms. From this state, in which all its past world is removed from its independent influence and in its present world only the merit of obedience remains to it, it could raise itself only on condition that a new world should arise for it, the creation of which would begin, and its development fill, a new epoch of its own in history. . . . Now if, for a race which has lost its former self, its former age and world, such a world should be created as the means of producing a new self and a new age, a thorough interpretation of such a possible age would have to give an account of the world thus created.

Now for my part I maintain that there is such a world, and it is the aim of these addresses to show you its existence and its true owner, to bring before your eyes a living picture of it, and to indicate the means of creating it. . . .

I speak for Germans simply, of Germans simply, not recognizing, but setting aside completely and rejecting, all the dissociating distinctions which for centuries unhappy events have caused in this single nation. You, gentlemen, are indeed to my outward eye the first and immediate representatives who bring before my mind the beloved national characteristics, and are the visible spark at which the flame of my address is kindled. But my spirit gathers round it the educated part of the whole German nation, from all the lands in which they are scattered. It thinks of and considers our common position and relations; it longs that part of the living force, with which these addresses may chance to grip you, may also remain in and breathe from the dumb printed page which alone will come to the eyes of the absent, and may in all places kindle German hearts to decision and action. Only of Germans and simply for Germans, I said. In due course we shall show that any other mark of unity or any other national bond either never had truth and meaning or, if it had, that owing to our present position these bonds of union have been destroyed and torn from us and can never recur; it is only by means of the common characteristic of being German that we can avert the downfall of our nation which is threatened by its fusion with foreign peoples, and win back again an individuality that is self-supporting and quite incapable of any dependence upon others. With our perception of the truth of this statement its apparent conflict (feared now, perhaps, by many) with other duties and with matters that are considered sacred will completely vanish.

Therefore, as I speak only of Germans in general, I shall proclaim that many things concern us which do not apply in the first instance to those assembled here, just as I shall pronounce as the concern of all Germans other things which apply in the first place only to us. In the spirit, of which these addresses are the expression, I perceive that organic unity in which no member regards the fate of another as the fate of a stranger. I behold that unity (which shall and must arise if we are not to perish altogether) already achieved, completed, and existing.

READING AND DISCUSSION QUESTIONS

1. In 1808, there were more than two dozen German states, most of which had yielded to Napoleonic control in 1806. What does Fichte mean when he talks about "the whole German nation"?

2. What is the tone of Fichte's address? Who is his intended audience? What is the purpose of his address?

3. What does Fichte mean when he speaks of the "organic unity" that exists between Germans?

DOCUMENT 24-3

MAX NORDAU

On Zionism

1905

Max Nordau (1849–1923) cofounded, with Theodor Herzl, the World Zionist Organization in 1897. His first work, Die Conventionellen Lügen der Kulturmenschheit *(The Conventional Lies of Civilization, published in 1883) critiqued modern society for its failure to relate to humanity's "natural" characteristics. His* Entartung *(Degeneration, 1893) drew even more directly on his training as a physician by lamenting the effects of civilization on the healthy physiques of modern humans. Nordau saw Zionism as a means to combat the "degeneration" he identified in modern society. Excerpted here is his 1905 definition of Zionism.*

The generations that were under the influence of the Mendelssohnian rhetoric and enlightenment — of reform and assimilation — were followed in the last twenty years of the 19th century by a new generation which strove to secure for the Zionist question a different position from the traditional one. These new Jews shrug their shoulders at the talk of Rabbis and writers about a "Mission of Judaism" that has been in vogue these hundred years.

The Mission is said to consist in this, that the Jews must always live in dispersion among the nations in order to be unto them teachers and models of morality and to educate them gradually to a pure rationalism, to a universal brotherhood of man, and to an ideal cosmopolitanism. They declare this Mission to be a piece of presumption or folly. More modern and practical in their attitude, they demand for the Jewish people only the right to live and to develop in accordance with its own powers to the natural limits of its type. They have found, however, that this is impossible in a state of dispersion, as under such circumstances prejudice, hatred, contempt ever pursue and oppress them, and either inhibit their development

Max Nordau, "Zionism," from The English Zionist Federation, *Zionism, Its History and Its Aims,* trans. Israel Cohen (London: The English Zionist Federation, 1905), 3–20.

or else tend to reduce them to an ethnic mimicry. Thus, instead of their being originals worthy of their existence, this striving at imitation will mould them into mediocre or wretched copies of foreign models. They are therefore working systematically to make the Jewish people once again a normal people, which shall live on its own soil and discharge all the economic, spiritual, moral and political functions of a civilised people. . . .

This goal is not to be attained immediately. It lies in a near or a more distant future. It is an ideal, a wish, a hope, just as Messianic Zionism was and is. But the new Zionism, which is called political, is distinguished from the old religious Messianic Zionism in this, that it repudiates all mysticism, and does not rely upon the return to Palestine to be accomplished by a miracle, but is resolved to bring it about through its own efforts. . . .

The new Zionism has partly arisen out of the inner impulses of Jewry, out of the enthusiasm of modern educated Jews for their history and martyrology, out of the awakened consciousness of their racial fitness, out of their ambition to preserve the ancient stock to as distant a future as possible and to follow up the worthy deeds of ancestors with worthy deeds of descendants. . . .

But it is also partly the effect of two influences that have come from without: first, the national idea that has dominated European thought and feeling for half a century and determined international politics; secondly, Anti-Semitism, under which the Jews of all countries have to suffer more or less. . . .

The national idea has educated all nations to self-consciousness; it has taught them to feel that their peculiarities are so many valuable factors, and it has inspired them with the passionate wish for independence. It could not fail to exert a deep influence upon educated Jews. It stimulated them to reflect about themselves, to feel once again what they had unlearned, and to demand for themselves the normal destinies of a people. This task of re-discovering their national individuality, although not free from pain, was lightened for them by the attitude of the nations who isolated them as a foreign element and did not hesitate to emphasise the real and imagined contrasts, or rather differences, existing between them and the Jews. . . .

The national idea has, in its extravagances, deteriorated in different directions. It has been distorted into Chauvinism, transformed into an imbecile hatred of foreigners, besotted into grotesque self-deification. Jewish nationalism is quite secure from these self-caricatures. The Jewish nationalist does not suffer from vanity; on the contrary, he feels that he must put forth unremitting effort to render the name of Jew a name of honour. He discreetly recognises the good qualities of other nations, and eagerly strives to acquire them so far as they harmonise with his natural powers. He knows what terrible injuries have been wrought upon his originally proud and upright character by centuries of slavery and denial of rights, and he endeavours to heal them by strenuous self-education. But while Jewish nationalism is secure from distortion, it, moreover, is a natural phase of the process of development from barbarian self-seeking individualism to the status of noble manhood and altruism, a phase the justification and necessity of which can be denied only by him who knows nothing of the laws of organic evolution and is utterly void of historical sense. . . .

Anti-Semitism has likewise taught many educated Jews how to find the way back to their people. It has had the effect of a severe ordeal, which the weak cannot withstand, but from which the strong step forth stronger, or rather with a keener self-consciousness. It is not correct to say that Zionism is merely a gesture of defiance or an act of despair in the face of Anti-Semitism. Doubtless many an educated Jew has been constrained only through Anti-Semitism to attach himself again to Judaism, and he would again fall away if his Christian compatriots would welcome him as a friend. But in the case of most Zionists, Anti-Semitism was only a stimulus causing them to reflect upon their relation to the nations, and their reflection has led them to results that must remain for them a permanent intellectual and spiritual possession, even if Anti-Semitism were to vanish completely from the world. . . .

Let it be clearly understood. The Zionism that has hitherto been analysed is that of the free and educated Jews, the Jewish élite. The uneducated multitude that cling to old traditions are Zionistic without much reflection, out of sentiment, out of instinct, out of affliction and longing. They suffer too grievously from the misery of life, from the hatred of the nations, from legal restrictions and social proscriptions. They feel that they cannot hope for any permanent improvement of their position so long as they must live as a helpless minority in the midst of evil-disposed majorities. They want to be a people, to renew their youth in intimate touch with Mother Earth, and to become master of their own fate. A certain proportion of this Zionistic multitude are not altogether free from mystical tendencies. They allow Messianic reminiscences to flit through their Zionism, which they transfuse with religious emotions. They are quite clear about the goal, the national re-union, but not about the ways to attain it. Yet upon them, too, has been borne the necessity of putting forth their own efforts, and a vast difference exists between their organised activity with its voluntary labours and the prayerful passivity of the purely religious Messianist.

READING AND DISCUSSION QUESTIONS

1. How does Nordau differentiate between ancient and contemporary Zionism? For whom does the author seem to be defining Zionism?
2. According to Nordau, what role does evolution play in Zionism?
3. Does Nordau's Zionism seem like nationalism to you? Why or why not?

DOCUMENT 24-4

GIUSEPPE GARIBALDI
Speech to His Soldiers
1860

Giuseppe Garibaldi (1807–1882) was leader of the decades-long Risogimento (Resurgence), a movement for the unification of Italy. After taking part in local insurrections in mountainous northern Italy in the 1830s, Garibaldi fled to Latin America and took part in revolutionary and civil conflicts there. He returned to Italy in 1848 and again fought for various Italian states against the French army. While Garibaldi's bravery and skill as a fighter were of material importance in the wars for Italian unification, they also earned him a reputation as a symbol of modern nationalism. The 1860 speech excerpted here, delivered after declaring his support for Victor Emmanuel's control of the unified Italy and reprinted soon thereafter in the London Times, *displays his revolutionary zeal and his oratorical skills.*

The World's Famous Orations, ed. William Jennings Bryan, 10 vols. (New York: Funk and Wagnalls, 1906), 7:229–231.

We must now consider the period which is just drawing to a close as almost the last stage of our national resurrection, and prepare ourselves to finish worthily the marvelous design of the elect of twenty generations, the completion of which Providence has reserved for this fortunate age.

Yes, young men, Italy owes to you an undertaking which has merited the applause of the universe. You have conquered and you will conquer still, because you are prepared for the tactics that decide the fate of battles. . . . To this wonderful page in our country's history another more glorious still will be added, and the slave shall show at last to his free brothers a sharpened sword forged from the links of his fetters.

To arms, then, all of you! all of you! And the oppressors and the mighty shall disappear like dust. You, too, women, cast away all the cowards from your embraces; they will give you only cowards for children, and you who are the daughters of the land of beauty must bear children who are noble and brave. Let timid doctrinaires depart from among us to carry their servility and their miserable fears elsewhere. This people is its own master. It wishes to be the brother of other peoples, but to look on the insolent with a proud glance, not to grovel before them imploring its own freedom. It will no longer follow in the trail of men whose hearts are foul. No! No! No!

Providence has presented Italy with Victor Emmanuel. Every Italian should rally round him. By the side of Victor Emmanuel every quarrel should be forgotten, all rancor depart. Once more I repeat my battle-cry: "To arms, all — all of you!" If March, 1861, does not find one million of Italians in arms, then alas for liberty, alas for the life of Italy. Ah, no, far be from me a thought which I loathe like poison. March of 1861, or if need be February, will find us all at our post . . . and with us every man of this land who is not a coward or a slave. Let all of us rally round the glorious hero of Palestro[3] and give the last blow to the crumbling edifice of tyranny. Receive, then, my gallant young volunteers, at the honored conclusion of ten battles, one word of farewell from me.

I utter this word with deepest affection and from the very bottom of my heart. To-day I am obliged to retire, but for a few days only. The hour of battle will find me with you again, by the side of the champions of Italian liberty. Let those only return to their homes who are called by the imperative duties which they owe to their families, and those who by their

---

[3] **glorious hero of Palestro**: The northern Italian village of Palestro was the site of Victor Emmanuel's defeat of the Austrian army in 1859.

glorious wounds have deserved the credit of their country. These, indeed, will serve Italy in their homes by their counsel, by the very aspect of the scars which adorn their youthful brows. Apart from these, let all others remain to guard our glorious banners. We shall meet again before long to march together to the redemption of our brothers who are still slaves of the stranger. We shall meet again before long to march to new triumphs.

READING AND DISCUSSION QUESTIONS

1. Garibaldi speaks clearly of the roles of men and women in the fight for national unity. What are they?

2. Garibaldi links nationalism with military struggle. Describe the other elements of nationalism displayed here. Which is the most prominent? Why?

3. How does Garibaldi refer to family relations? How do those obligations work with or against those of nationalism?

DOCUMENT 24-5

Munich Bar Kochba Association

1902

The nineteenth century was a time of great preoccupation with physical training and the body. As politicians, scholars, and educators worked to craft visions of national identity in Europe and elsewhere, they turned to the human body as a symbolic and literal source of strength. New scientific methods of gymnastic training were paired with medical attention to health and wellness, and the bodies of citizens were understood to reflect the strength or weakness of the nations to which they belonged. The photograph here is from the Munich chapter of the Bar Kochba Association, a nationalist Jewish exercise and bodybuilding movement named after a biblical hero and founded by Max Nordau (see Document 24-3). Through such organizations, nationalist movements sought not only to improve but also to advertise the health of their nation.

bpk, Berlin/Art Resource, N.Y.

READING AND DISCUSSION QUESTIONS

1. Describe the people in the photograph. What might be the significance of their uniforms, and what effect do those uniforms produce?

2. What is the effect of representing a national movement specifically with male bodies?

3. What image of Jewish nationalism is produced by this photograph? What if anything marks this image as one of Jewish and not German nationalism?

DOCUMENT 24-6

BEATRICE WEBB

From My Apprenticeship: Why I Became a Socialist

1926

Beatrice Webb (1858–1943) cofounded the London School of Economics with her husband, Sidney. In the course of research into the urban poor of London, she met her future husband, with whom she would engage in a range of social reform efforts. From 1905 to 1909, she worked on the Royal Commission into the Operation of the Poor Laws and recommended the social safety net of a welfare state. Webb and her husband also wrote several works on socialism, trade unions, and other topics, and she is credited with inventing the term collective bargaining. *Webb's meditations on becoming a Socialist highlight not only a sense of social crisis, but her firm belief that socialism would provide an important remedy to many of the problems plaguing nineteenth-century Britain.*

The industrial revolution in Britain, which had its most intense phase in the latter end of the eighteenth and the beginning of the nineteenth century, cast out of our rural and urban life the yeoman cultivator and the copyholder, the domestic manufacturer and the independent handi-craftsman, all of whom owned the instruments by which they earned their livelihood; and gradually substituted for them a relatively small body of capitalist *entrepreneurs* employing at wages an always multiplying mass of propertyless men, women and children, struggling, like rats in a bag, for the right to live. This bold venture in economic reconstruction had now been proved to have been, so it seemed to me, at one and the same time, a stupendous success and a tragic failure. The accepted purpose of the pioneers of the new power-driven machine industry was the making of pecuniary profit; a purpose which had been fulfilled, as Dr. Johnson observed about his friend Thrale's brewery, "beyond the dreams of avarice."

Beatrice Webb, *My Apprenticeship* (London: Cambridge University Press, 1979), 346–349.

Commodities of all sorts and kinds rolled out from the new factories at an always accelerating speed with ever falling costs of production, thereby promoting what Adam Smith had idealised as *The Wealth of Nations*. The outstanding success of this new system of industry was enabling Great Britain, through becoming the workshop of the world, to survive the twenty years' ordeal of the Napoleonic Wars intact, and not even invaded, whilst her ruling oligarchy emerged in 1815 as the richest and most powerful government of the time.

On the other hand, that same revolution had deprived the manual workers — that is, four-fifths of the people of England — of their opportunity for spontaneity and freedom of initiative in production. It had transformed such of them as had been independent producers into hirelings and servants of another social class; and, as the East End of London in my time only too vividly demonstrated, it had thrust hundreds of thousands of families into the physical horrors and moral debasement of chronic destitution in crowded tenements in the midst of mean streets. There were, however, for the manual working class as a whole, certain compensations. The new organisation of industry had the merit of training the wage-earners in the art of team-work in manufacture, transport and trading. Even the oppressions and frauds of the capitalist profit-maker had their uses in that they drove the proletariat of hired men, which capitalism had made ubiquitous, to combine in Trade Unions and co-operative societies; and thus to develop their instinct of fellowship, and their capacity for representative institutions, alike in politics and in industry. Moreover, the contrast between the sweated workers of East London and the Lancashire textile operatives made me realise how the very concentration of wage-earners in the factory, the ironworks and the mine had made possible, in their cases, what the sweater's workshop, the independent craftsman's forge and the out-worker's home had evaded, namely, a collective regulation of the conditions of employment, which, in the Factory Acts and Mines Regulation Acts[4] on the one hand, and in the standard rates of wage and the normal working day of the Trade Unions on the other, had, during the latter part of the nineteenth century, wrought so great an improvement in the status of this regulated section of the World of Labour. It was, in fact, exactly this collective regulation of the conditions of employment, whether by

---

[4] **Factory Acts and Mines Regulation Acts**: Various laws passed by the British Parliament limiting hours worked by women and children in industrial jobs and by coal miners.

legislative enactment or by collective bargaining, that had raised the cotton operatives, the coal-miners and the workers of the iron trades into an effective democracy; or, at least, into one which, in comparison with the entirely unorganised workers of East London, was eager for political enfranchisement and education; and which, as the chapels, the co-operative societies and the Trade Unions had demonstrated, was capable of self-government. I wished to probe further this contrast between the wage-earners who had enjoyed the advantages of collective regulation and voluntary combinations, and those who had been abandoned to the rigours of unrestrained individual competition. But I wanted also to discover whether there was any practicable alternative to the dictatorship of the capitalist in industry, and his reduction of all the other participants in production to the position of subordinate "hands." For it was persistently asserted that there was such an alternative. In this quest I did not turn to the socialists. *Fabian Essays*[5] were still unwritten and unpublished; and such socialists as I had happened to meet at the East End of London belonged to the Social Democratic Federation, and were at that time preaching what seemed to me nothing but a catastrophic overturning of the existing order, by forces of whose existence I saw no sign, in order to substitute what appeared to me the vaguest of incomprehensible utopias.

There was, however, another alternative lauded by idealists of all classes: by leading Trade Unionists and the more benevolent employers, by revolutionary socialists and by Liberal and Conservative philanthropists: an experiment in industrial organisation actually, so it was reported, being brought into operation on a small scale by enthusiastic working men themselves. This was the ideal of "self-employment," and the peaceful elimination from industry of the capitalist *entrepreneur*; to be secured by the manual workers themselves acquiring the ownership, or at any rate the use, of the capital, and managing the industry by which they gained their livelihood. It was this ideal, so I was told, that animated the Co-operative Movement in the North of England and the Lowlands of Scotland — a movement barely represented in the London that I knew.

---

[5] *Fabian Essays*: *Fabian Essays in Socialism* by George Bernard Shaw et al., published in 1889, was an important collection of essays arguing for socialism through gradual reform.

READING AND DISCUSSION QUESTIONS

1. How does Webb link the Industrial Revolution to her own political beliefs? What is her argument?

2. What are the positive effects of industry, according to Webb?

3. How does Webb contrast herself to other Socialists? What form of socialism does she embrace, and why?

COMPARATIVE QUESTIONS

1. National identity was a major theme of the nineteenth century. How does each document in this chapter work either to produce or to discourage national identity?

2. Fichte, Nordau, and Garibaldi speak about the unity of the German, Jewish, and Italian nations, respectively. Compare and contrast the way that each document defines national unity and presents it as a motivating factor.

3. How does the communism presented by Marx and Engels relate to Webb's socialism? How are they similar, and how are they different?

4. What is the role of gender in each document? How is a person's gender a part of national or class identity, and why? Juxtapose Webb's perspective with that of the male authors and subjects of this chapter.

5. What social or political problem is defined in each document? What are the different ways in which each document presents a crisis, and what kind of language is used to motivate the intended audience?

CHAPTER 25

Africa, Southwest Asia, and the New Imperialism

1800–1914

The rise of industrial economies in Europe drove European nations to expand their empires in Africa and Asia. In search of markets, resources, and occasionally adventure, Europeans gained control of an increasingly large part of the globe by way of commerce and colonization. At the same time, states like the Ottoman Empire mixed western European notions of civilization with their own cultures to develop alternative visions of a "modern society." The documents in this chapter present different perspectives on the global progress of modernization and westernization: from the Ottoman Empire's government as it sought to draw on modern Western ideas to reform and strengthen its state, from a leading voice of British imperialism, from an African who fought and then submitted to British colonial rule, and from Africans who endured terrible abuses in the Belgian Congo. All of the documents offer insight on how non-Western peoples adapted and endured as nationalism, progress, and empire changed their worlds.

DOCUMENT 25-1

SULTAN ABDUL MEJID
Imperial Rescript
1856

Building on the work of previous rulers to enact military and administra-tive reforms, many of which were inspired by modern Western institutions, Sultan Abdul Mejid or Abdülmecid (r. 1839–1861) instituted a period of

E. A. Van Dyck, *Report upon the Capitulations of the Ottoman Empire Since the Year 1150*, pt. 1 (Washington, D.C : U.S. Government Printing Office, 1881, 1882), 106–108.

"reorganization," or Tanzimat, *in the aging Ottoman Empire. Various non-Turkish groups had been pulling away from Ottoman rule since the early 1800s, and large-scale violence against non-Muslim subjects was not uncommon. In this imperial rescript, or official proclamation, the sultan affirms his policy of "Ottomanism," or equal treatment of all citizens without regard to race, language, or religion. Ottomanism may be seen as a doomed and even hypocritical attempt to reassert central authority; however, the rescript represented real reform in Ottoman society.*

Let it be done as herein set forth. . . . It being now my desire to renew and enlarge still more the new Institutions ordained with the view of establishing a state of things conformable with the dignity of my Empire and . . . by the kind and friendly assistance of the Great Powers, my noble Allies.[1] . . . The guarantees promised on our part by the Hatti-Humaïoun of Gülhané,[2] and in conformity with the Tanzimat, . . . are today confirmed and consolidated, and efficacious measures shall be taken in order that they may have their full and entire effect.

All the privileges and spiritual immunities granted by my ancestors from time immemorial, and at subsequent dates, to all Christian communities or other non-Muslim persuasions established in my empire, under my protection, shall be confirmed and maintained.

Every Christian or other non-Muslim community shall be bound within a fixed period, and with the concurrence of a commission composed . . . of members of its own body, to proceed with my high approbation and under the inspection of my Sublime Porte,[3] to examine into its actual immunities and privileges, and to discuss and submit to my Sublime Porte the reforms required by the progress of civilization and of the age. The powers conceded to the Christian Patriarchs and Bishops[4] by the Sultan Mehmed II[5] and his successors, shall be made to harmonize with the new position which my generous and beneficent intentions ensure to

---

[1] **the Great Powers, my noble allies**: During the Crimean War (1853–1856), the Ottoman Empire fought with Great Britain and France against Russia.

[2] **The guarantees . . . Gülhané**: The Noble Rescript of 1839, also written by Sultan Abdul Mejid, guaranteed personal security, a fair tax system, controlled military conscriptions, and full rights to citizens regardless of faith.

[3] **Sublime Porte**: The term refers to the Sultan and his sovereignty.

[4] **Christian Patriarchs and Bishops**: Ruling officials of the Greek and Armenian churches in the Ottoman Empire.

[5] **Sultan Mehmed II**: Ottoman ruler from 1451 to 1481.

these communities. . . . The ecclesiastical dues, of whatever sort of nature they be, shall be abolished and replaced by fixed revenues of the Patriarchs and heads of communities. . . . In the towns, small boroughs, and villages, where the whole population is of the same religion, no obstacle shall be offered to the repair, according to their original plan, of buildings set apart for religious worship, for schools, for hospitals, and for cemeteries. . . .

Every distinction or designation tending to make any class whatever of the subjects of my Empire inferior to another class, on account of their religion, language, or race, shall be forever effaced from Administrative Protocol. The laws shall be put in force against the use of any injurious or offensive term, either among private individuals or on the part of the authorities. . . .

As all forms of religion are and shall be freely professed in my dominions, no subject of my Empire shall be hindered in the exercise of the religion that he professes. . . . No one shall be compelled to change their religion . . . and . . . all the subjects of my Empire, without distinction of nationality, shall be admissible to public employments. . . . All the subjects of my Empire, without distinction, shall be received into the civil and military schools of the government. . . . Moreover, every community is authorized to establish public schools of science, art, and industry. . . .

All commercial, correctional, and criminal suits between Muslims and Christian or other non-Muslim subjects, or between Christian or other non-Muslims of different sects, shall be referred to Mixed Tribunals. The proceedings of these Tribunals shall be public; the parties shall be confronted, and shall produce their witnesses, whose testimony shall be received, without distinction, upon an oath taken according to the religious law of each sect. . . .

Penal, correctional, and commercial laws, and rules of procedure for the Mixed Tribunals, shall be drawn up as soon as possible, and formed into a code. . . . Proceedings shall be taken, for the reform of the penitentiary system. . . .

The organization of the police . . . shall be revised in such a manner as to give to all the peaceable subjects of my Empire the strongest guarantees for the safety both of their persons and property. . . . Christian subjects, and those of other non-Muslim sects, . . . shall, as well as Muslims, be subject to the obligations of the Law of Recruitment [for military service]. The principle of obtaining substitutes, or of purchasing exemption, shall be admitted.

Proceedings shall be taken for a reform in the constitution of the Provincial and Communal Councils, in order to ensure fairness in the choice of the deputies of the Muslim, Christian, and other communities, and freedom of voting in the Councils. . . .

As the laws regulating the purchase, sale, and disposal of real property are common to all the subjects of my Empire, it shall be lawful for foreigners to possess landed property in my dominions. . . .

The taxes are to be levied under the same denomination from all the subjects of my Empire, without distinction of class or of religion. The most prompt and energetic means for remedying the abuses in collecting the taxes, and especially the tithes, shall be considered. The system of direct collection shall gradually, and as soon as possible, be substituted for the plan of farming,[6] in all the branches of the revenues of the state.

A special law having been already passed, which declares that the budget of the revenue and the expenditure of the state shall be drawn up and made known every year, the said law shall be most scrupulously observed. . . .

The heads of each community and a delegate, designated by my Sublime Porte, shall be summoned to take part in the deliberations of the Supreme Council of Justice on all occasions which might interest the generality of the subjects of my Empire. . . .

Steps shall be taken for the formation of banks and other similar institutions, so as to effect a reform in the monetary and financial system, as well as to create funds to be employed in augmenting the sources of the material wealth of my Empire.

Everything that can impede commerce or agriculture shall be abolished. To accomplish these objects means shall be sought to profit by science, the art, and the funds of Europe, and thus gradually to execute them.

READING AND DISCUSSION QUESTIONS

1. What specific measures does the sultan take to ensure religious and ethnic equality? What do these measures imply about life in the Ottoman Empire before the rescript was issued?

2. The sultan is careful to extend military service to people of all religious and ethnic backgrounds. How does this right compare to rights regarding public employment, education, taxation, and real estate?

---

[6] **farming**: Tax farming, in which the government contracted with private financiers who collected taxes for a profit.

3. The rescript mentions communities of Christian and non-Muslim people and villages or small areas where all people share a common religion. What does this imply about the integration of different religious groups in Ottoman society?

4. In explaining the purpose of his rescript, the sultan refers to the "dignity" of his empire and mentions the Ottoman Empire's relationship with European "Great Powers." How do you think the ideas of religious equality, social reform, and international relations and the dignity of the empire work together?

DOCUMENT 25-2

An Ottoman Government Decree on the "Modern" Citizen

1870

In June 1870, this official document was presented to Firhan Pasha, an Istanbul-educated sheikh of the Shammar tribe in what is now Iraq. The document drew on Western notions of "civilization" in order to push the local Bedouin population, a formerly nomadic people, into settled agricultural life. It demonstrates that the Ottoman Empire was challenged by divisions within its Muslim populations as well as those between Muslim and non-Muslim groups. With the rise of ethnic nationalisms in the late 1800s, the rift between Arab and Turkish populations in the Ottoman Empire would widen and further weaken the empire.

To the model of proverbs and peers, His Excellency Firhan Pasha Zayd 'Alwa. It is known that if one compares the tribes and people who live in the lifestyle of Bedouins with those urbane people who live in the cities and villages, one will note the complexity in the customs of city-folk. In contrast, it will be noted that in comparison to the original creation of

---

Ottoman Government Decree Issued to the Amir of Shamr, His Excellency Firhan Pasha, June 19, 1870, trans. Akram Khater. Ottoman Archives of Directorate General of State Archives at the Prime Ministry (Tapu Tahrir: Mosul, 1869–1872).

man and his internal self, the way of life of Bedouins is simple. In fact, the primitive and original state of man is most likely the same as that of the Bedouin. However, God has graced human beings with a characteristic that is absent from any other [species]. According to this characteristic, man cannot remain in his original state of creation but should prepare all that is needed for his food, drink, and clothing, and after this he must gather knowledge and develop commerce and other human necessities. He seeks to obtain other necessities as well, and every time he reaches a stage of acquisition, then he sees the need to advance and progress beyond what he had in the past. . . . Thus, it is apparent that even if the first state of man is to be a Bedouin, urbanity is a characteristic that cannot be separated from him. For the human being has become civilized . . . and the virtues of humanity cannot be attained except through the path of urbanization and civilization. Those who surpass their brethren and control all elements of this world, completely or partially, are those who live in the cities and who are civilized.

After proving that this is the case, we would like to explain and specify the reasons those people demand to remain in this state [of being Bedouins]. They remain in this state of deprivation of the virtues of humanity and the characteristics of civilization for several reasons. The first is that these people are ignorant of the state of the world and the nations. Because of their ignorance we have found our fathers desiring to stay unchanged in the state to which they were born. Secondly, the basis of the wealth of the tribes and clans is animals — in particular camels — and since it is difficult to manage and raise animals and camels in the cities — where they cannot find pasture — the people remain in their original state of being. . . . The third reason is that the mentioned peoples are like wild animals who enjoy what they have gotten used to in terms of stealing and raiding the property of others of their own people and killing them. This has become a reason for their wildness and their insistence on staying in the state of Bedouinism. It should be obvious that the first reason — which is ignorance and illiteracy — is an ugly and unacceptable characteristic in all the creatures of this world. And the second reason is the subordination [to tradition] characteristic of animals, and it is contrary to the image according to which man was created, for God has created the human being to be the most honorable of all creatures, and He made all breathing creatures subservient to him. He who is a Bedouin has become accustomed to the opposite of this natural order, so that although he used to be over other creatures, he has become subservient.

The truth is that this fallen state is an insult to humanity, and accordingly if we investigate the immense harm these tribes cause to each other, we will find that it has no equivalence in magnitude. For the human being has been commanded to protect those of his kind and treat them well, and is not commanded to do the opposite. In fact, all the religions command this [good treatment of others], and in particular the Mohammedan Shari'a [body of Islamic religious law]. After proving that this is contrary to what has been commanded and is prohibited in all religions and in the Mohammedan Shari'a, then anyone with intelligence will see that harming people and robbing them of their money and their cattle is contrary to humanity and Islam. He who dares to commit that which we have mentioned must be punished. In addition, we see that this implies that since living as a Bedouin . . . leads to these harmful results, then no one should stay in that state of being, especially since we have arrived at a time and epoch . . . where to stay in this fallen and immoral state of existence appears as an ugly habit in the eyes of the world. For these explained reasons, these people cannot stay even for a short period in this state, and these tribes and clans should be settled and gain good human characteristics. It is imperative upon the Sublime Government to facilitate the emergence of these moral characteristics. This is particularly the case since those tribes and clans that have been settled during the past two years have faced difficulties and material needs, and they have remained in their original state because they are deprived of access to agriculture and commerce. Thus, and in order to feed their children, they have dared to attack the fields belonging to the inhabitants of the cities and towns. And in that case the government will have to reimburse the farmers for their losses and to dispatch imperial troops to punish the perpetrators, all of which costs money. Thus, and before matters reach this state, we would advise to give the lands that extend from Tikrit [village in Iraq] to the borders of Mosul [main city in northern Iraq] and that are located east of the Tigris River to the Shamr clan. Furthermore, we recommend that these lands be designated as a Mutassarifiya [provincial government within the Ottoman Empire] and be named as Sandjak [province] of Shamr, and that they [the clan of Shamr] be settled in these lands until they dig the necessary canals to the Tigris and reclaim the lands and plant them like other people. Once it is apparent that they are settled, then this place should be designated as a Mutassarifiya, like the Mutassarifiya of al-Muntafak, and this Mutassarifiya should be placed under your authority, O, Pasha! . . . Because those [people] are used to being Bedouins, and because it will be difficult to sever those ties all at once, then we should grant some of them with animals a permit to pasture their animals on some of the lands, provided that they return to their places of residence. In order to encourage development of these lands, we should exempt those who reclaim the lands and dig the ditches and canals from all but the Miri tax. . . . Once this Sandjak is formed according to what has preceded, and a Mutassarifiya is subsequently established, then troops should be sent to keep the peace, and the Mutassarif should be assigned a deputy and a tax collector and all that he requires in terms of government officials. . . .

This official Ottoman decree has been issued by the ministry of the Vilayet of Baghdad, and let it be known to all.

READING AND DISCUSSION QUESTIONS

1. What is the motivation for this decree? What specific situation does the Ottoman government feel must be remedied?

2. The decree distinguishes between Bedouins and non-Bedouins. What are the assumptions behind these different definitions? Do you agree with them?

3. How does the document use religion to make its argument? How does it use the idea of civilization? How do the two ideas work together, or separately, to define both the Bedouin and those who have attained the "virtues of humanity"?

VIEWPOINTS

The Colonial Encounter in Africa

DOCUMENT 25-3

CECIL RHODES

From Confession of Faith

ca. 1877

Perhaps no single man exemplified European colonial exploitation of the African continent more than Cecil Rhodes (1853–1902). He was sent as a child from England to South Africa — then the British Cape Colony — for his health, and there he amassed a fortune by controlling diamond production. He entered politics in the Cape Colony and quickly parlayed his wealth and political influence into expanded colonial control of South African territories, one of which (comprising present-day Zambia and Zimbabwe) was named Rhodesia in his honor. Rhodes sent the following text to British journalist William Thomas Stead as representative of his thoughts on empire and race; it has survived as a marker of European pride and global ambitions in the late nineteenth century.

It often strikes a man to inquire what is the chief good in life; to one the thought comes that it is a happy marriage, to another great wealth, and as each seizes on his idea, for that he more or less works for the rest of his existence. To myself thinking over the same question the wish came to render myself useful to my country. I then asked myself how could I and after reviewing the various methods I have felt that at the present day we are actually limiting our children and perhaps bringing into the world half the human beings we might owing to the lack of country for them to inhabit that if we had retained America there would at this moment be millions more of English living. I contend that we are the finest race

John Flint, *Cecil Rhodes* (New York: Hachette, 1974), appendix.

in the world and that the more of the world we inhabit the better it is for the human race, just fancy those parts that are at present inhabited by the most despicable specimens of human beings what an alteration there would be if they were brought under Anglo-Saxon influence, look again at the extra employment a new country added to our dominions gives. I contend that every acre added to our territory means in the future birth to some more of the English race who otherwise would not be brought into existence. Added to this the absorption of the greater portion of the world under our rule simply means the end of all wars, at this moment had we not lost America I believe we could have stopped the Russian-Turkish war[7] by merely refusing money and supplies. Having these ideas what scheme could we think of to forward this object. I look into history and I read the story of the Jesuits[8] I see what they were able to do in a bad cause and I might say under bad leaders.

In the present day I become a member in the Masonic order[9] I see the wealth and power they possess the influence they hold and I think over their ceremonies and I wonder that a large body of men can devote themselves to what at times appear the most ridiculous and absurd rites without an object and without an end.

The idea gleaming and dancing before ones eyes like a will-of-the-wisp at last frames itself into a plan. Why should we not form a secret society with but one object the furtherance of the British Empire and the bringing of the whole uncivilised world under British rule for the recovery of the United States for the making the Anglo-Saxon race but one Empire. What a dream, but yet it is probable, it is possible. I once heard it argued by a fellow in my own college, I am sorry to own it by an Englishman, that it was a good thing for us that we have lost the United States. There are some subjects on which there can be no arguments, and to an Englishman this is one of them, but even from an American's point of view just picture what they have lost, look at their government, are not the frauds that yearly

---

[7] **Russian-Turkish war**: This 1870s conflict between the Ottoman Empire and Russia was spurred in part by various ethnic or religious nationalisms in Ottoman territories.
[8] **the Jesuits**: The Society of Jesus, or the Jesuits, was founded in 1534 as a missionary arm of the Roman Catholic Church and in partial response to the Protestant Reformation. Rhodes seems to be voicing anti-Catholic sentiments in his assessment of the "bad cause" and "bad leaders" of the Jesuits.
[9] **Masonic order**: A male fraternal organization largely centered in Great Britain, northwest Europe, and the United States.

come before the public view a disgrace to any country and especially theirs which is the finest in the world. Would they have occurred had they remained under English rule great as they have become how infinitely greater they would have been with the softening and elevating influences of English rule, think of those countless 000's of Englishmen that during the last 100 years would have crossed the Atlantic and settled and populated the United States. Would they have not made without any prejudice a finer country of it than the low class Irish and German emigrants? All this we have lost and that country loses owing to whom? Owing to two or three ignorant pig-headed statesmen of the last century, at their door lies the blame. Do you ever feel mad? do you ever feel murderous? I think I do with those men. I bring facts to prove my assertion. Does an English father when his sons wish to emigrate ever think of suggesting emigration to a country under another flag, never — it would seem a disgrace to suggest such a thing I think that we all think that poverty is better under our own flag than wealth under a foreign one.

Put your mind into another train of thought. Fancy Australia discovered and colonised under the French flag, what would it mean merely several millions of English unborn that at present exist we learn from the past and to form our future. We learn from having lost to cling to what we possess. We know the size of the world we know the total extent. Africa is still lying ready for us it is our duty to take it. It is our duty to seize every opportunity of acquiring more territory and we should keep this one idea steadily before our eyes that more territory simply means more of the Anglo-Saxon race more of the best the most human, most honourable race the world possesses.

READING AND DISCUSSION QUESTIONS

1. How is race a part of Rhodes's justification for empire? What does British society possess that he most admires?

2. What are the different races that Rhodes mentions? How do they relate to one another?

3. What is the purpose of the secret society that Rhodes proposes?

DOCUMENT 25-4

NDANSI KUMALO

On the British Incursion in Zimbabwe

1932

Ndansi Kumalo was a member of the Ndebele people who lived in what is now Zimbabwe, where the Ndebele had settled after years of struggle with Zulu and Dutch forces. The Ndebele sovereign, Lobengula, negotiated with the new wave of British colonizers intent on access to the region's mineral resources, but tensions mounted and conflict broke out in the 1890s. Kumalo, a witness to the British incursion, was hired to play the role of Lobengula in a 1932 British film about the life of colonizer Cecil Rhodes (see Document 25-3). While filming in England, Kumalo met the African scholar Margery Perham, who recorded the following firsthand account of British colonization.

We were terribly upset and very angry at the coming of the white men, for Lobengula . . . was under her . . . [the Queen's] protection and it was quite unjustified that white men should come with force into our country.[10] . . . Lobengula had no war in his heart: he had always protected the white men and been good to them. If he had meant war, would he have sent our regiments far away to the north at this moment? As far as I know the trouble began in this way. Gandani, a chief who was sent out, reported that some of the Mashona[11] had taken the king's cattle; some regiments were detailed to follow and recover them. They followed the Mashona to Ziminto's people. Gandani had strict instructions not to molest the white people established in certain parts and to confine himself to the people who had taken the cattle. The commander was given a letter which he had to produce to the Europeans and tell them what the object of the

---

Margery Perham, ed., *Ten Africans* (London: Faber and Faber, 1936).

[10] **under her . . . our country**: In an 1888 agreement Lobengula made with Cecil Rhodes, the British government guaranteed that there would be no incursion of English settlers on Ndebele land and that Lobengula's authority would continue. Unhappy with Lobengula's concessions, many Ndebele warriors began to press for war against the Europeans.

[11] **the Mashona**: A people who raised livestock and were ruled by the Ndebele.

party was. But the members of the party were restless and went without reporting to the white people and killed a lot of Mashonas. The pioneers were very angry and said, "You have trespassed into our part." They went with the letter, but only after they had killed some people, and the white men said, "You have done wrong, you should have brought the letter first and then we should have given you permission to follow the cattle." The commander received orders from the white people to get out, and up to a certain point which he could not possibly reach in the time allowed. A force followed them up and they defended themselves. When the pioneers turned out there was a fight at Shangani and at Bembezi. . . .

The next news was that the white people had entered Bulawayo; the King's kraal [stockade] had been burnt down and the King had fled. Of the cattle very few were recovered; most fell into the hands of the white people. Only a very small portion were found and brought to Shangani where the King was, and we went there to give him any assistance we could. . . . Three of our leaders mounted their horses and followed up the King and he wanted to know where his cattle were; they said they had fallen into the hands of the whites, only a few were left. He said, "Go back and bring them along." But they did not go back again; the white forces had occupied Bulawayo and they went into the Matoppos [hills]. Then the white people came to where we were living and sent word round that all chiefs and warriors should go into Bulawayo and discuss peace, for the King had gone and they wanted to make peace. . . . The white people said, "Now that your King has deserted you, we occupy your country. Do you submit to us?" What could we do? "If you are sincere, come back and bring in all your arms, guns, and spears." We did so. . . .

So we surrendered to the white people and were told to go back to our homes and live our usual lives and attend to our crops. But the white men sent native police who did abominable things; they were cruel and assaulted a lot of our people and helped themselves to our cattle and goats. These policemen were not our own people; anybody was made a policeman. We were treated like slaves. They came and were overbearing and we were ordered to carry their clothes and bundles. They interfered with our wives and our daughters and molested them. In fact, the treatment we received was intolerable. We thought it best to fight and die rather than bear it. How the rebellion started I do not know; there was no organization, it was like a fire that suddenly flames up. We had been flogged by native police and then they rubbed salt water in the wounds. There was much bitterness because so many of our cattle were branded and taken away from us; we had no property, nothing we could call our own. We said, "It is no good living under such conditions; death would be better — let us fight." Our King gone, we had submitted to the white people and they ill-treated us until we became desperate and tried to make an end of it all. We knew that we had very little chance because their weapons were so much superior to ours. But we meant to fight to the last, feeling that even if we could not beat them we might at least kill a few of them and so have some sort of revenge.

I fought in the rebellion. We used to look out for valleys where the white men were likely to approach. We took cover behind rocks and trees and tried to ambush them. We were forced by the nature of our weapons not to expose ourselves. I had a gun, a breech-loader [rear-loading gun]. They — the white men — fought us with big guns and Maxims [early machine guns] and rifles.

I remember a fight in the Matoppos when we charged the white men. There were some hundreds of us; the white men also were as many. We charged them at close quarters: we thought we had a good chance to kill them but the Maxims were too much for us. We drove them off at the first charge, but they returned and formed up again. We made a second charge, but they were too strong for us. I cannot say how many white people were killed, but we think it was quite a lot. . . . Many of our people were killed in this fight: I saw four of my cousins shot. One was shot in the jaw and the whole of his face was blown away — like this — and he died. One was hit between the eyes; another here, in the shoulder; another had part of his ear shot off. We made many charges but each time we were beaten off, until at last the white men packed up and retreated. But for the Maxims, it would have been different. . . .

So peace was made. Many of our people had been killed, and now we began to die of starvation; and then came the rinderpest [an infectious cow disease] and the cattle that were still left to us perished. We could not help thinking that all these dreadful things were brought by the white people. We struggled, and the Government helped us with grain; and by degrees we managed to get crops and pulled through. Our cattle were practically wiped out, but a few were left and from them we slowly bred up our herds again. We were offered work in the mines and farms to earn money and so were able to buy back some cattle. At first, of course, we were not used to going out to work, but advice was given that the chief should advise the young people to go out to work, and gradually they went. At first we received a good price for our cattle and sheep and goats. Then the tax came. It was 10s.[12] a year. Soon the Government

---

[12] **10s.**: Ten shillings.

said, "That is too little, you must contribute more; you must pay £1." We did so. Then those who took more than one wife were taxed; 10s. for each additional wife. The tax is heavy, but that is not all. We are also taxed for our dogs; 5s. for a dog. Then we were told we were living on private land; the owners wanted rent in addition to the Government tax; some 10s. some £1, some £2 a year. . . .

Would I like to have the old days back? Well, the white men have brought some good things. For a start, they brought us European implements — plows; we can buy European clothes, which are an advance. The Government has arranged for education and through that, when our children grow up, they may rise in status. We want them to be educated and civilized and make better citizens. Even in our own time there were troubles, there was much fighting and many innocent people were killed. It is infinitely better to have peace instead of war, and our treatment generally by the officials is better than it was at first. But, under the white people, we still have our troubles. Economic conditions are telling on us very severely. We are on land where the rainfall is scanty, and things will not grow well. In our own time we could pick our own country, but now all the best land has been taken by the white people. We get hardly any price for our cattle; we find it hard to meet our money obligations. If we have crops to spare we get very little for them; we find it difficult to make ends meet and wages are very low. When I view the position, I see that our rainfall has diminished, we have suffered drought and have poor crops and we do not see any hope of improvement, but all the same our taxes do not diminish. We see no prosperous days ahead of us. There is one thing we think an injustice. When we have plenty of grain the prices are very low, but the moment we are short of grain and we have to buy from Europeans at once the price is high. If when we have hard times and find it difficult to meet our obligations some of these burdens were taken off us it would gladden our hearts. As it is, if we do raise anything, it is never our own: all, or most of it, goes back in taxation. We can never save any money. If we could, we could help ourselves: we could build ourselves better houses; we could buy modern means of traveling about, a cart, or donkeys or mules.

As to my own life, I have had twelve wives altogether, five died and seven are alive. I have twenty-six children alive, five have died. Of my sons five are married and are all at work farming; three young children go to school. I hope the younger children will all go to school. I think it is a good thing to go to school.

There are five schools in our district. Quite a number of people are Christians, but I am too old to change my ways. In our religion we believe that when anybody dies the spirit remains and we often make offerings to the spirits to keep them good-tempered. But now the making of offerings is dying out rapidly, for every member of the family should be present, but the children are Christians and refuse to come, so the spirit-worship is dying out. A good many of our children go to the mines in the Union, for the wages are better there. Unfortunately a large number do not come back at all. And some send money to their people — others do not. Some men have even deserted their families, their wives, and children. If they cannot go by train they walk long distances.

READING AND DISCUSSION QUESTIONS

1. What reasons does Kumalo give for rebelling against British colonial forces? What caused the initial violence, and what was the outcome?

2. If the Ndebele leader Gandani had delivered the letter to the British and not acted in haste, do you think the British pioneers would have responded as violently as they did? What gives you that impression?

3. What is Kumalo's opinion of British colonial influence in Africa? Cite examples to support your answer.

DOCUMENT 25-5

ROGER CASEMENT AND DAVID ENGOHAHE

Victims of Belgian Congo Atrocities

ca. 1904–1905

In 1903, the British consul Roger Casement investigated abuses in the Congo Free State for the British government. The Congo Free State was the private holding of King Leopold II of Belgium from 1885 to 1908, and under Leopold's control the extraction of rubber led to gross human rights abuses.

Roger Anstey, "The Congo Rubber Atrocities: A Case Study," *African Historical Studies,* 4:1 (1971), 72.

Casement's report led to a public outcry in Europe. The report, upheld by an independent commission in 1905 and verified through later research, detailed the mutilation and murder practiced by Leopold's representatives in order to ensure rubber production. Here, an excerpt from Casement's report shows the testimony of eyewitness David Engohahe — a member of the Bolia ethnicity — detailing the violence employed to ensure the continued profits from rubber cultivation. The photograph of two young residents of the Congo Free State, Malo and Yoka, shows the human cost of the atrocities Engohahe describes.

At the time the district headquarters of the Basengele[13] was at Mbongo.[14] When the rubber was prepared you took it to Mbongo. . . . The State man[15] would stretch [the lengths of rubber] . . . out, and if they split he would reject them and throw them to one side. At the end of the count, if the rubber was bad, out of a village complement of 25 men he might shoot 5, out of 30, perhaps 10; and perhaps 20 out of 50. It was dreadful persecution. He then sent the rest of the men back to the forest to collect more rubber to make up the quota. . . . He forbad us to harvest the things in our own gardens so much so that our immediate forefathers did not eat manioc.[16] He forbad us the palm nuts in our own trees, and the plantains and all the garden produce, and sugar cane. It was all kept for his soldiers and his followers. . . . Many fled and some were mutilated. I myself saw a man at Likange who had had both his hands cut off. Sometimes they cut them at the wrist, sometimes farther up . . . with a machete. Also there is a Muboma[17] . . . who has a long scar across the back of his neck. There is another man called Botei at Ihanga with the same sort of scar, where they wounded him maliciously, expecting him to die. They didn't cut his head off, they didn't get to the bone, but expected him to bleed to death. It was sheer cruelty; the State treated us abominably.

---

[13] **Basengele**: A Bantu-language ethnic group.

[14] **Mbongo**: Near present-day Isoko, Democratic Republic of the Congo.

[15] **State man**: A representative of Leopold.

[16] **manioc**: A popular West African root crop, also called cassava.

[17] **Muboma**: An ethnic group.

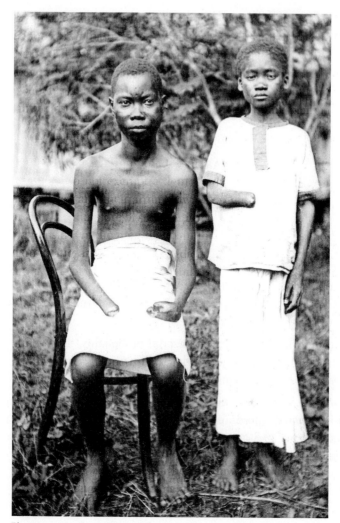

Photo courtesy of Anti-Slavery International.

READING AND DISCUSSION QUESTIONS

1. How does Engohahe connect the production of rubber to the presence or absence of subsistence agriculture?

2. How does the system of labor described here compare or contrast with your impression of slavery in the Americas?

3. Engohahe describes Leopold's representative as "the State man," but Leopold operated the territory as his own private holding rather than

as a colony of Belgium. How might Leopold's relationship to the territory change your impression of the abuses described here?

4. What is the effect of the photograph? Does it look posed or natural? What might have been the purpose of this photograph?

COMPARATIVE QUESTIONS

1. Most of the documents in this chapter are written from a non-Western point of view; two, however, present a European view of non-Europeans. How do the photograph and Rhodes's "Confession" each present Africans? What is the role of Africans in each document?

2. Each of these documents deals in some way with the intersection of non-Western cultures and modern (if not Western) ideas and influences. How does each present the idea of modernization? What is the influence of the modern world in each case?

3. Consider the 1856 Ottoman rescript on equality, the 1870 Ottoman decree on Bedouins, and Rhodes's 1877 "Confession." How does each present the idea of managing diverse populations?

4. Consider Engohahe's account in the context of other human rights abuses such as those inflicted upon the English workers and miners (Documents 23-3 and 23-4). How might Rhodes have responded to these accounts?

CHAPTER 26

Asia in the Era of Imperialism

1800–1914

Though not colonized as directly or thoroughly as Africa, Asia was heavily influenced by the imperial aspirations of Western industrial societies. British colonial rule directly reshaped the Indian economy and Indian culture, forcibly incorporating many Indians into the British-dominated world economy. In East Asia, treaties gave multiple Western powers — and Japan — economic, political, and military control over key areas of China. Spared the full brunt of Western attention, Japan incorporated Western ideas as it pushed to become an industrial power in its own right. But in every case, Asian nations wrestled with the presence of Westerners and Western ideas as well as their own domestic transformations. The documents in this chapter reflect the broad range of strategies that Asians used to appropriate and/or contest what they understood to be a new framework of international power.

Reactions to Imperialism and Modernity

DOCUMENT 26-1

LIN ZEXU

From a Letter to Queen Victoria

1839

Lin Zexu (1785–1850) was a Confucian scholar-bureaucrat of the highest rank, who was tapped by the Daoguang emperor in 1838 to stop the illegal importation of opium by Great Britain and other foreign powers. In 1839, he arrived in Guangzhou and, after increasingly hostile negotiations, seized and destroyed more than two million pounds of raw opium from British warehouses. This action, viewed as heroic by Chinese and Britons alike, ignited the First Opium War (1839–1842). Lin wrote to Queen Victoria, pleading with her to stop the British opium trade. Although his letter was never sent to the queen, it was published in Guangdong and later in Britain, where it aroused both outrage and sympathy.

It is only our high and mighty emperor, who alike supports and cherishes those of the Inner Land [China], and those from beyond the seas — who looks upon all mankind with equal benevolence — who, if a source of profit exists anywhere, diffuses it over the whole world — who, if the tree of evil takes root anywhere, plucks it up for the benefit of all nations: — who, in a word, hath implanted in his breast that heart (by which beneficent nature herself) governs the heavens and the earth! You, the queen of your honorable nation, sit upon a throne occupied through successive generations by predecessors, all of whom have been styled respectful and obedient. Looking over the public documents accompanying the tribute sent (by your predecessors) on various occasions, we find the following: — "All

The Chinese Repository, 20 vols. (Japan: Canton Press, 1840), 8:497–593.

the people of my (i. e. the king of England's) country, arriving at the Central Land for purposes of trade, have to feel grateful to the great emperor for the most perfect justice, for the kindest treatment," and other words to that effect. Delighted did we feel that the kings of your honorable nation so clearly understood the great principles of propriety, and were so deeply grateful for the heavenly goodness (of our emperor): — therefore, it was that we of the heavenly dynasty nourished and cherished your people from afar, and bestowed upon them redoubled proofs of our urbanity and kindness. It is merely from these circumstances, that your country — deriving immense advantage from its commercial intercourse with us, which has endured now two hundred years — has become the rich and flourishing kingdom that it is said to be!

But, during the commercial intercourse which has existed so long, among the numerous foreign merchants resorting hither, are wheat and tares, good and bad; and of these latter are some, who, by means of introducing opium by stealth, have seduced our Chinese people, and caused every province of the land to overflow with that poison. These then know merely to advantage themselves, they care not about injuring others! This is a principle which heaven's Providence repugnates; and which mankind conjointly look upon with abhorrence! Moreover, the great emperor hearing of it, actually quivered with indignation, and especially dispatched me, the commissioner, to Canton, that in conjunction with the viceroy and lieut.-governor of the province, means might be taken for its suppression! . . .

We find that your country is distant from us about sixty or seventy thousand [Chinese] miles, that your foreign ships come hither striving the one with the other for our trade, and for the simple reason of their strong desire to reap a profit. Now, out of the wealth of our Inner Land, if we take a part to bestow upon foreigners from afar, it follows, that the immense wealth which the said foreigners amass, ought properly speaking to be portion of our own native Chinese people. By what principle of reason then, should these foreigners send in return a poisonous drug, which involves in destruction those very natives of China? Without meaning to say that the foreigners harbor such destructive intentions in their hearts, we yet positively assert that from their inordinate thirst after gain, they are perfectly careless about the injuries they inflict upon us! And such being the case, we should like to ask what has become of that conscience which heaven has implanted in the breasts of all men?

We have heard that in your own country opium is prohibited with the utmost strictness and severity: — this is a strong proof that you know full well how hurtful it is to mankind. Since then you do not permit it to injure your own country, you ought not to have the injurious drug transferred to another country, and above all others, how much less to the Inner Land! Of the products which China exports to your foreign countries, there is not one which is not beneficial to mankind in some shape or other. There are those which serve for food, those which are useful, and those which are calculated for re-sale; — but all are beneficial. Has China (we should like to ask) ever yet sent forth a noxious article from its soil? Not to speak of our tea and rhubarb, things which your foreign countries could not exist a single day without, if we of the Central Land were to grudge you what is beneficial, and not to compassionate [pity] your wants, then wherewithal could you foreigners manage to exist? And further, as regards your woolens, camlets, and longells [all woolen, woven fabrics], were it not that you get supplied with our native raw silk, you could not get these manufactured! If China were to grudge you those things which yield a profit, how could you foreigners scheme after any profit at all? Our other articles of food, such as sugar, ginger, cinnamon, &c., and our other articles for use, such as silk piece-goods, chinaware, &c., are all so many necessaries of life to you; how can we reckon up their number! On the other hand, the things that come from your foreign countries are only calculated to make presents of, or serve for mere amusement. It is quite the same to us if we have them, or if we have them not. If then these are of no material consequence to us of the Inner Land, what difficulty would there be in prohibiting and shutting our market against them? It is only that our heavenly dynasty most freely permits you to take off her tea, silk, and other commodities, and convey them for consumption everywhere, without the slightest stint or grudge, for no other reason, but that where a profit exists, we wish that it be diffused abroad for the benefit of all the earth!

    . . . Now we have always heard that your highness possesses a most kind and benevolent heart, surely then you are incapable of doing or causing to be done unto another, that which you should not wish another to do unto you! We have at the same time heard that your ships which come to Canton do each and every of them carry a document granted by your highness' self, on which are written these words "you shall not be permitted to carry contraband goods"; this shows that the laws of your highness are in their origin both distinct and severe, and we can only suppose that because the ships coming here have been very numerous, due attention has not been given to search and examine; and for this reason it is that we now address you this public document, that you may clearly know how stern and severe are the laws of the central dynasty, and most certainly you will cause that they be not again rashly violated!

Moreover, we have heard that in London the metropolis where you dwell, as also in Scotland, Ireland, and other such places, no opium whatever is produced. It is only in sundry parts of your colonial kingdom of Hindostan, such as Bengal, Madras, Bombay, Patna, Malwa, Benares, Malacca, and other places where the very hills are covered with the opium plant, where tanks are made for the preparing of the drug; month by month, and year by year, the volume of the poison increases, its unclean stench ascends upwards, until heaven itself grows angry, and the very gods thereat get indignant! You, the queen of the said honorable nation, ought immediately to have the plant in those parts plucked up by the very root! Cause the land there to be hoed up afresh, sow in its stead the five grains, and if any man dare again to plant in these grounds a single poppy, visit his crime with the most severe punishment. By a truly benevolent system of government such as this, will you indeed reap advantage, and do away with a source of evil. Heaven must support you, and the gods will crown you with felicity! This will get for yourself the blessing of long life, and from this will proceed the security and stability of your descendants! . . .

Suppose the subject of another country were to come to England to trade, he would certainly be required to comply with the laws of England, then how much more does this apply to us of the celestial empire! Now it is a fixed statute of this empire, that any native Chinese who sells opium is punishable with death, and even he who merely smokes it, must not less die. Pause and reflect for a moment: if you foreigners did not bring the opium hither, where should our Chinese people get it to re-sell? It is you foreigners who involve our simple natives in the pit of death, and are they alone to be permitted to escape alive? If so much as one of those deprive one of our people of his life, he must forfeit his life in requital for that which he has taken: — how much more does this apply to him who by means of opium destroys his fellow-men? Does the havoc which he commits stop with a single life? Therefore it is that those foreigners who now import opium into the Central Land are condemned to be beheaded and strangled by the new statute, and this explains what we said at the beginning about plucking up the tree of evil, wherever it takes root, for the benefit of all nations.

We further find that during the second month of this present year, the superintendent of your honorable country, Elliot, viewing the law in relation to the prohibiting of opium as excessively severe, duly petitioned us, begging for "an extension of the term already limited, say five months for Hindostan and the different parts of India, and ten for England, after which they would obey and act in conformity with the new statute," and other words to the same effect. Now we, the high commissioner and colleagues, upon making a duly prepared memorial to the great emperor, have to feel grateful for his extraordinary goodness, for his redoubled compassion. Any one who within the next year and a half may by mistake bring opium to this country, if he will but voluntarily come forward, and deliver up the entire quantity, he shall be absolved from all punishment for his crime. If, however, the appointed term shall have expired, and there are still persons who continue to bring it, then such shall be accounted as knowingly violating the laws, and shall most assuredly be put to death! On no account shall we show mercy or clemency! This then may be called truly the extreme of benevolence, and the very perfection of justice!

Our celestial empire rules over ten thousand kingdoms! Most surely do we possess a measure of godlike majesty which ye cannot fathom! Still we cannot bear to slay or exterminate without previous warning, and it is for this reason that we now clearly make known to you the fixed laws of our land. If the foreign merchants of your said honorable nation desire to continue their commercial intercourse, they then must tremblingly obey our recorded statutes, they must cut off for ever the source from which the opium flows, and on no account make an experiment of our laws in their own persons! Let then your highness punish those of your subjects who may be criminal, do not endeavor to screen or conceal them, and thus you will secure peace and quietness to your possessions, thus will you more than ever display a proper sense of respect and obedience, and thus may we unitedly enjoy the common blessings of peace and happiness. What greater joy! What more complete felicity than this!

Let your highness immediately, upon the receipt of this communication, inform us promptly of the state of matters, and of the measures you are pursuing utterly to put a stop to the opium evil. Please let your reply be speedy. Do not on any account make excuses or procrastinate. A most important communication.

P. S. We annex an abstract of the new law, now about to be put in force. "Any foreigner or foreigners bringing opium to the Central Land, with design to sell the same, the principals shall most assuredly be decapitated, and the accessories strangled; — and all property (found on board the same ship) shall be confiscated. The space of a year and a half is granted, within the which, if any one bringing opium by mistake, shall voluntarily step forward and deliver it up, he shall be absolved from all consequences of his crime."

READING AND DISCUSSION QUESTIONS

1. Describe the tone of Lin's letter. What language or phrases establish Lin's understanding of the relationship between China and Great Britain?

2. According to Lin, what should motivate Queen Victoria to halt the opium trade? How will she be rewarded?

3. What does Lin say about trade between China and the world? In his opinion, whom does this trade benefit? How do you imagine a British trader would respond to Lin's assertions?

DOCUMENT 26-2

Two Proclamations of the Boxer Rebellion
1898, 1900

Following the Guangxu emperor's optimistic but unsuccessful attempt to modernize China during the 100 Days' Reform period of 1898, a local martial arts organization in Shandong village, the Society of Righteous and Harmonious Boxers, emerged as a violently antimodern, anti-Western, and anti-Christian force. Encouraged by the Qing government and eschewing modern military techniques, the Boxers killed thousands of foreign and Chinese Christians and in 1900 laid siege to the area in Beijing where foreign officials were quartered. A multinational force, including both Western and Japanese troops, ended the siege within two months, and the resulting Boxer Protocol of 1901 forced the Qing government to pay war reparations. The proclamations here outline the Boxers' beliefs and their exhortations to Chinese citizens.

The Society of Righteous and Harmonious Boxers, "The Gods Assist the Boxers" in the Peking and Tientsin *Times*, May 5, 1900. "Attention" in Ssu-ya Teng and John K. Fairbank, eds., *China's Response to the West* (Cambridge: Harvard University Press, 1954), 190.

1898 PROCLAMATION

The Gods assist the Boxers,
The Patriotic Harmonious corps,
It is because the "Foreign Devils" disturb the "Middle Kingdom"
    [China].
Urging the people to join their religion,
To turn their backs on Heaven,
Venerate not the Gods and forget the ancestors.
Men violate the human obligations,
Women commit adultery,
"Foreign Devils" are not produced by mankind,
If you do not believe,
Look at them carefully.
The eyes of all the "Foreign Devils" are bluish,
No rain falls,
The earth is getting dry,
This is because the churches stop Heaven,
The Gods are angry;
The Genii [minor spirits] are vexed;
Both come down from the mountain to deliver the doctrine.
This is no hearsay,
The practices of boxing[1] will not be in vain;
Reciting incantations and pronouncing magic words,
Burn up yellow written prayers,
Light incense sticks
To invite the Gods and Genii of all the grottoes.
The Gods come out from grottoes,
The Genii come down from mountains,
Support the human bodies to practice the boxing.
When all the military accomplishments or tactics
Are fully learned,
It will not be difficult to exterminate the "Foreign Devils" then.
Push aside the railway tracks,
Pull out the telegraph poles,
Immediately after this destroy the steamers.

---

[1] **practices of boxing**: Society members trained in Chinese martial arts techniques, which included intense physical and mental discipline and meditation techniques. Essentially, they believed that their physical prowess enabled them to deflect bullets.

The great France
Will grow cold and downhearted.
The English and Russians will certainly disperse.
Let the various "Foreign Devils" all be killed.
May the whole Elegant Empire of the Great Qing Dynasty[2] be ever
   prosperous!

1900 PROCLAMATION

Attention: all people in markets and villages of all provinces in China —
now, owing to the fact that Catholics and Protestants have vilified our gods
and sages, have deceived our emperors and ministers above, and oppressed
the Chinese people below, both our gods and our people are angry at
them, yet we have to keep silent. This forces us to practice the Yike[3] magic
boxing so as to protect our country, expel the foreign bandits and kill
Christian converts, in order to save our people from miserable suffering.
After this notice is issued to instruct you villagers, no matter which village
you are living in, if there are Christian converts, you ought to get rid of
them quickly. The churches which belong to them should be unreserv-
edly burned down. Everyone who intends to spare someone, or to disobey
our order by concealing Christian converts, will be punished according to
the regulation when we come to his place, and he will be burned to death
to prevent his impeding our program. We especially do not want to punish
anyone by death without warning him first. We cannot bear to see you suffer innocently. Don't disobey this special notice!

READING AND DISCUSSION QUESTIONS

1. What are the Boxers' complaints?

2. How do the Boxers characterize the distinction between the West and
    China?

3. How do you imagine Chinese citizens might have responded to the
    Boxers' proclamations?

---

[2] **Great Qing Dynasty**: Chinese imperial family between 1644 and 1912. The Qing
encouraged the Boxer uprising.
[3] **Yike**: The type of martial arts practiced by the Boxers.

DOCUMENT 26-3

SAIGŌ TAKAMORI

Letters on the Korean Question

1873

Saigō Takamori (1828–1877), one of the original leaders of the Meiji Resto-
ration of Japan and an ardent supporter of the samurai class and its values,
urged his colleagues in the new Meiji government (1868–1912) to provoke a
war in Korea and thereby secure Japanese influence there as a strategic move
against the threats of Russian and European encroachment in Asia. In his
1873 letters to his friend and colleague Itagaki Taisuke, he argues in clear,
blunt language for his plan to send an envoy to Korea in the hope that the
Koreans would be offended, kill the envoy, and thus justify Japan's strategic
war with and occupation of Korea. His plan was discarded, Saigō left the
government, and he was killed leading a rebellion against the Meiji govern-
ment in 1877.

JULY 29

Thank you so much for coming all the way to visit me the other day.

Has any decision been made on Korea, now that Soejima[4] is back? If
the meeting has yet to take place, I should like to be present despite my
illness if I am informed of what day I may attend. Please let me know.

When a decision is at last reached, what will it involve if we send
troops first? The Koreans will unquestionably demand their withdrawal,
and a refusal on our part will lead to war. We shall then have fomented a
war in a manner very different from the one you originally had in mind.
Wouldn't it be better therefore to send an envoy first? It is clear that if we
did so, the Koreans would resort to violence and would certainly give us
an excuse for attacking them.

In the event that it is decided to send troops first, difficulties may arise
in the future [elsewhere]. Russia has fortified Sakhalin and other islands,

---

Wm. Theodore De Bary, Carol Gluck, and Arthur E. Tiedemann, eds., *Sources of*
Japanese Tradition, 2 vols. (New York: Columbia University Press, 2006), 2:19–20.

[4]**Soejima**: Soejima Taneomi served as the foreign minister of the Meiji government.

and there have already been frequent incidents of violence. I am convinced that we should send troops to defend these places before we send them to Korea.

If it is decided to send an envoy officially, I feel sure that he will be murdered. I therefore beseech you to send me. I cannot claim to make as splendid an envoy as Soejima, but if it is a question of dying, that, I assure you, I am prepared to do.

AUGUST 14

Should there be any hesitation at your place with reference to my being sent, it will mean further and further delays. I ask you therefore please to cut short the deliberations and to speak out in favor of my being sent. If we fail to seize this chance to bring us into war, it will be very difficult to find another. By enticing the Koreans with such a gentle approach, we will certainly cause them to give us an opportunity for war. But this plan is doomed to fail if you feel it would be unfortunate for me to die before the war or if you have any thoughts of temporizing. The only difference is whether [my death comes] before or after the event. I shall be deeply grateful to you, even after death, if you exert yourself now on my behalf with the warm friendship you have always shown me.

READING AND DISCUSSION QUESTIONS

1. What, in short, is Saigō's plan for Japanese relations with Korea?

2. How does he justify his plan for war? How does his plan take international relations into account?

3. Saigō's plan was rejected, but Japan used the pretext of war with China to invade and occupy Korea in the 1894–1895 Sino-Japanese War. Why might Saigō's plan have met with disfavor from other members of the modernizing Meiji government?

DOCUMENT 26-4

SIR HENRY MONTGOMERY LAWRENCE

Letter to Lieutenant-Governor J. Colvin

June 13, 1857

Sir Henry Montgomery Lawrence (1806–1857) was an officer of the British army in India. Born in Ceylon to a British army officer, he was educated in Britain but posted to India in 1823, where he gained considerable military and political experience as part of the British colonial force. Appointed chief commissioner of the British territory of Awadh in 1857, Lawrence was nominated as the next governor-general of India by the British East India Company. Before he could fully assume that post, a popular revolt among Indian troops spread throughout India, and Lawrence was killed defending British control of the city of Lucknow (retaken by British and Nepalese forces in 1858). The rebellion marked the end of the East India Company's rule and the start of direct British state control of India. Lawrence's letters give an intimate account of how the British military saw the rebellion, the empire, and the indigenous people of India.

My dear Colvin,

I wrote a long letter yesterday telling you of the sad succession of misfortunes in this quarter. Today I have had confirmation of the fate of Sooltanpoor & Fyzabad.[5] A native letter bearing the stamp of truth tells that the troops rose & butchered the Europeans at Sooltanpoor. From Fyzabad Mr Bradford writes (no date, probably the 6th) that the officers & ladies had all been saved, that everything had been conducted with the utmost regularity, the native civil officer taking prominent places, & that the King of Delhi had been proclaimed. In all quarters we hear of similar method & regularity — at Duriabad, Secrora & Seetapoor individuals have been obliged

---

Letters of Sir Henry Montgomery Lawrence: Selections from the Correspondence of Sir Henry Montgomery Lawrence (1806–1857), ed. Sheo Bahadur Singh (New Delhi: Sagar, 1978), 28–30.

[5] **Sooltanpoor & Fyzabad**: Sultanpur, Faizabad, Daryabad, Sikrara, Sitapur, and Kanpur are place-names in present-day Uttar Pradesh. All were rendered according to British spelling in these documents.

to give up their plunder, & the treasure is carefully guarded. The quiet method bespeaks some [leading] influence. We cannot get certain tidings from Cawnpoor, altho' we have sent many messengers, but we have no reason to doubt that Gen. Wheeler still holds his grounds. The mutineers hold the river bank for many miles above & below Cawnpoor & search all papers. They at once seized all the boats and drew them to their own bank. Would that we could help the besieged, but our numbers, the distance and the heat forbid the thought — this is frightful weather for field operations for Europeans. Yesterday we lost two out of about 130 from exposure after 3 p.m. in our pursuit of the mutinous Police Battalions,[6] & yet Mr Gubbins would be continually sending 50 men on Elephants, 40, 50 and more miles off. He is perfectly insane on what he considers *energetic*, manly measures. His language has been so extravagant that were he not really useful I should be obliged to take severe measures against him. He is *the one* malcontent in the garrison — all others, I believe, are satisfied that as much energy has been evinced as circumstances permitted. Yesterday the mutineer police about 1000 strong were followed about 8 miles by 100 H.M. 32nd,[7] 2 guns, 50 Sikh horse & 20 European volunteers. It left for an hour the Residency Post[8] with only 100 Europeans, with the jail close by, over which these Policemen had held guard. Fortunately in an hour 100 Europeans came with Treasure from the Muchee Bawan[9] & were retained till the near return of the detached party. I had also instantly got up 2 companies of Irregulars[10] to the jail. All was quiet during the night, and the result of the pursuit has been good. This morning the zemindars [tax collectors] brought masses of musquets that the mutineers had thrown away. About 50 of them seem to have been killed. Our loss of 2

---

[6] **Police Battalions**: Indian troops employed as a police force by the British East India Company.

[7] **100 H.M. 32nd**: 100 members of Her Majesty's 32nd regiment, an armed forces unit.

[8] **Residency Post**: The complex of buildings occupied by the British resident, a representative of the British East India Company, which ruled the region indirectly. After the annexation of the region, the position of resident was replaced by the direct rule of a commissioner who continued to occupy and use the residency.

[9] **Muchee Bawan**: Macchi Bhawan, an area in the Agra Fort complex in Uttar Pradesh.

[10] **Irregulars**: Unlike "regular" troops, "irregulars" were variably trained, equipped on an ad hoc basis, and usually drawn from local populations. "Regular" troops were, by contrast, the official or formal members of a standing military force.

Europeans from the sun is a serious loss. 2 horsemen were killed, & Mr Thornhill, C.S, wounded. We have seen sad details of this butchery of officers & ladies who escaped from Jhaligshanpoor between Mohomdee and Seetapoor. Mr Thomason fell with them, Capt. Oor alone escaped, being protected by some men of his old Regiment. Of the Seetapoor party Sir M. Jackson, one of his sisters, Lt. Burn & a child of Mr Christians's escaped to the jungles beyond Seetapoor. Capt. Jester found his way here. All our Regulars except about 200 have taken leave to their homes, where many will go, for I believe their numbers were well purged on the 30th & 31st May, but there was a frantic fancy of Mr Gubbins to get rid of them all including those who have evinced unmistakeable fidelity, and to trust implicitly the Police & Irregulars, who have all gone with the herd. To my mind the Police have behaved in some respects the worst of all. I should have preferred keeping 500 of those men as more likely to be true than any other, but under Mr. Gubbin's pressure an order was issued when I was ill, to encourage all the Sikhs to be off. I have saved a few. We have still about 1000 Irregular Infantry, 200 Cavalry, 200 Regular Infantry, 30 Regular Cavalry & the Town Police, few of which can be expected to stand any severe pressure. We however hold our ground & daily strengthen both our Tower positions, bearing in mind that the Residency is to be the final point of concentration. The health of the troops is good & the weather propitious as long as there is not exposure to the sun. The conduct of the Europeans is beautiful. By God's help we can hold our own for a month, but there should be no delay in sending succour. The appearance of 2 European Regiments would soon enable us to settle the Province, but if succour be lost & this force destroyed, the difficulty would be vastly increased.

I have the honor to be yours,
H.M. Lawrence.

READING AND DISCUSSION QUESTIONS

1. How desperate does Lawrence seem in this letter? What language does he use to describe the seriousness of his position?

2. How does Lawrence describe the indigenous people of India and their behavior?

3. How does Lawrence describe the British military?

DOCUMENT 26-5

SUN YATSEN

On the Three People's Principles and the Future of the Chinese People

1906

Trained as a Western physician in Hong Kong, Sun Yatsen (1866–1925) studied and traveled extensively and became an important revolutionary during the final years of the Qing Dynasty (1644–1912). While in exile after a failed coup, he formed the Tongmenghui revolutionary organization and won support among Chinese expatriates through his "Three Principles of the People," presented in this excerpt from a 1906 speech in Tokyo. Although the 1911 revolution occurred in his absence, he was selected as provisional president of the new Republic of China, a post he occupied for less than three months. However, his legacy as founder of the Guomindang (Nationalist Party) and his position as an iconic figure of Chinese modernity remain strong.

Let us pause to consider for a moment: Where is the nation? Where is the political power? Actually, we are already a people without a nation! The population of the globe is only one billion, several hundred million; we Han,[11] being 400 million, comprise one-fourth of that population.

Our nation is the most populous, most ancient, and most civilized in the world, yet today we are a lost nation. Isn't that enormously bizarre? The African nation of the Transvaal has a population of only 200,000, yet when Britain tried to destroy it, the fighting lasted three years.[12] The Philippines have a population of only several million, but when America

---

Prescriptions for Saving China: Selected Writings of Sun Yat-sen, ed. Julie Lee Wei, Ramon H. Myers, and Donald G. Gillin (Palo Alto, Calif.: Hoover Institution Press, 1994).

[11] **Han**: The Chinese people.
[12] **The African nation . . . three years**: A reference to the South African War (1899–1902).

tried to subdue it, hostilities persisted for several years.[13] Is it possible that the Han will gladly be a lost nation?

We Han are now swiftly being caught up in a tidal wave of nationalist revolution, yet the Manchus continue to discriminate against the Han. They boast that their forefathers conquered the Han because of their superior unity and military strength and that they intend to retain these qualities so as to dominate the Han forever. . . . Certainly, once we Han unite, our power will be thousands of times greater than theirs, and the success of the nationalist revolution will be assured.

As for the Principle of Democracy, it is the foundation of the political revolution. . . . For several thousand years China has been a monarchical autocracy, a type of political system intolerable to those living in freedom and equality. A nationalist revolution is not itself sufficient to get rid of such a system. Think for a moment: When the founder of the Ming dynasty expelled the Mongols and restored Chinese rule, the nationalist revolution triumphed, but his political system was only too similar to those of the Han, Tang, and Song dynasties.[14] Consequently, after another three hundred years, foreigners again began to invade China. This is the result of the inadequacy of the political system, so that a political revolution is an absolute necessity. . . . The aim of the political revolution is to create a constitutional, democratic political system. . . .

* * *

Now, let me begin by discussing the origins of the Principle of the People's Livelihood, a principle that began to flourish only in the latter part of the nineteenth century. . . . As civilization advanced, people relied less on physical labor and more on natural forces, since electricity and steam could accomplish things a thousand times faster than human physical strength. For example, in antiquity a single man tilling the land could harvest at best enough grain to feed a few people, notwithstanding his toil and trouble. Now, however, as a result of the development of scientific agriculture, one man can grow more than enough to feed a thousand people because

---

[13] **The Philippines . . . several years**: Between 1899 and 1901, Filipinos fought against the United States after the United States took over the Philippines from Spain at the end of the Spanish-American War.

[14] **When the founder . . . dynasties**: The Ming Dynasty ruled from 1368 to 1644 C.E.; the Han (206 B.C.E.–220 C.E.), Tang (618–907 C.E.), and Song (960–1279 C.E.) were earlier Chinese dynasties.

he can use machinery instead of his limbs, with a consequent increase in efficiency. . . .

In view of this, everyone in Europe and America should be living in a state of plenty and happiness undreamed of in antiquity. If we look around, however, we see that conditions in those countries are precisely the opposite. Statistically, Britain's wealth has increased more than several thousandfold over the previous generation, yet poverty of the people has also increased several thousandfold over the previous generation. Moreover, the rich are extremely few, and the poor extremely numerous. This is because the power of human labor is no match for the power of capital. In antiquity, agriculture and industry depended completely on human labor; but now, with the development of natural forces that human labor cannot match, agriculture and industry have fallen completely into the hands of capitalists. The greater the amount of capital, the more abundant the resources that can be utilized. Unable to compete, the poor have naturally been reduced to destitution. . . .

Indeed, this constitutes a lesson for China. . . . Civilization yields both good and bad fruits, and we should embrace the good and reject the bad. In the countries of Europe and America, the rich monopolize the good fruits of civilization, while the poor suffer from its evil fruits. . . . Our current revolution will create a nation that not only belongs to the citizenry but is socially responsible. Certainly, there will be nothing comparable to it in Europe or America.

Why have Europe and America failed to solve their social problems? Because they have not solved their land problem. Generally speaking, wherever civilization is advanced, the price of land increases with each passing day. . . . In China capitalists have not yet emerged, so that for several thousand years there has been no increase in land prices. . . . After the revolution, however, conditions in China will be different. For example, land prices in Hong Kong and Shanghai are currently as much as several hundred times higher than those in the interior. This increment is the result of the advance of civilization and the development of communications. It is inevitable that, as the entire nation advances, land prices everywhere will rise accordingly. . . . Fifty years ago, land along the banks of the Huangpu River in Shanghai was worth up to a million dollars a *mou* [1.5 acres]. This is evidence of the clearest sort, from which we can see that in the future the rich will get richer every day, and the poor poorer. . . . Consequently, we must come up with a solution now. . . .

With respect to a solution, although the socialists have different opinions, the procedure I most favor is land valuation. For example, if a landlord has land worth 1,000 dollars, its price can be set at 1,000 or even 2,000 dollars. Perhaps in the future, after communications have been developed, the value of his land will rise to 10,000 dollars; the owner should receive 2,000, which entails a profit and no loss, and the 8,000 increment will go to the state. Such an arrangement will greatly benefit both the state and the people's livelihood. Naturally, it will also eliminate the shortcomings that have permitted a few rich people to monopolize wealth. This is the simplest, most convenient, and most feasible method. . . .

Once we adopt this method, the more civilization advances, the greater the wealth of the nation, and then we can be sure our financial problems will not become difficult to handle. After the excessive taxes of the present have been abolished, the price of consumer goods will gradually fall and the people will become increasingly prosperous. We will forever abolish the vicious taxation policies that have prevailed for several thousand years. . . . After China's social revolution is accomplished, private individuals will never again have to pay taxes. The collection of land revenues alone will make China the richest nation on earth. . . .

Obviously, . . . it is necessary to give considerable attention to what the constitution of the Republic of China should be. . . . The British constitution embodies the so-called separation of powers into executive, legislative, and judicial, all mutually independent. . . . The Frenchman[15] later embraced the British system and melded it with his own ideals to create his own school of thought. The American constitution was based on Montesquieu's theories but went further in clearly demarcating the separation of powers. . . . As to the future constitution of the Republic of China, I propose that we introduce a new principle, that of the "five separate powers."

Under this system, there will be two other powers in addition to the three powers just discussed. One is the examination power. . . . American officials are either elected or appointed. . . .

With respect to elections, those endowed with eloquence ingratiated themselves with the public and won elections, while those who had learning and ideals but lacked eloquence were ignored. Consequently, members of America's House of Representatives have often been foolish and

---

[15] **the Frenchman**: Montesquieu (1689–1755), a French political philosopher who argued that individual freedom is safest when the three powers of government — the judicial, executive, and legislative — are kept separate in a state.

ignorant people who have made its history quite ridiculous. As for appointees, they all come and go with the president. The Democratic and Republican parties have consistently taken turns holding power, and whenever a president is replaced, cabinet members and other officials, comprising no fewer than 60,000–70,000 people, including the postmaster general, are also replaced. As a result, the corruption and laxity of American politics are unparalleled among the nations of the world. . . . Therefore, the future constitution of the Republic of China must provide for an independent branch expressly responsible for civil service examinations. Furthermore, all officials, however high their rank, must undergo examinations in order to determine their qualifications. Whether elected or appointed, officials must pass those examinations before assuming office. This procedure will eliminate such evils as blind obedience, electoral abuses, and favoritism. . . .

The other power is the supervisory power, responsible for monitoring matters involving impeachment. For reasons that should be evident to all, such a branch is indispensable to any nation. The future constitution of the Republic of China must provide for an independent branch. Since ancient times, China had a supervisory organization, the Censorate,[16] to monitor the traditional social order. Inasmuch as it was merely a servant of the monarchy, however, it was ineffectual. . . .

With this added to the four powers already discussed, there will be five separate powers. That constitution will form the basis of the sound government of a nation that belongs to its own race, to its own citizens, and to its own society. This will be the greatest good fortune for our 400 million Han people. I presume that you gentlemen are willing to undertake and complete this task. It is my greatest hope.

READING AND DISCUSSION QUESTIONS

1. Sun presents his first principle only indirectly in the first three paragraphs of this speech. Describe what you think that principle is, based on your reading of the speech.

2. Sun mentions the Han and Manchu. Why do you think he uses ethnic groups to describe the situation in China?

---

[16] **the Censorate:** A unique feature of Chinese government during the Ming and Qing eras. Also called the Board of Censors, it was responsible for reviewing the conduct of officials and reporting any offences to the emperor.

3. What are Sun's second and third principles? What distinction does he make between the third principle and socialism?

4. How does Sun invoke Western countries to strengthen the argument for his three principles?

DOCUMENT 26-6

MOORFIELD STOREY AND JULIAN CODMAN
On American Imperialism in the Philippines
1902

During the 1898 Spanish-American War, American naval forces defeated the Spanish in the Philippines and, with Filipino revolutionaries, occupied most of the island nation. By 1899, however, the occupying U.S. forces were at war with the revolutionaries, who quickly recognized the American intention to retain control over the Philippines. The Philippine Army resorted to guerrilla warfare, and American forces responded brutally with tactics including concentration camps and indiscriminate killing. In 1902, the U.S. Anti-Imperialist League launched its Philippine Investigating Committee; excerpts of its reports on American wartime atrocities, focusing on Secretary of State Elihu Root and President Theodore Roosevelt, highlight both U.S. imperial policies and the domestic difficulties of implementing those policies in a democracy.

Let us pass now to Samar,[17] the scene of General Smith's[18] campaign.

Under date of August 20, 1901, General Hughes, in command of our forces on that island, reported as follows:

Moorfield Storey and Julian Codman, "Marked Severities," *Philippine Warfare: An Analysis of the Law and Facts Bearing on the Action and Utterances of President Roosevelt and Secretary Root* (Boston: Geo. H. Ellis, 1902), 29–33.

[17] **Samar**: An island in the Philippine archipelago.
[18] **General Smith**: General Jacob Hurd Smith (U.S. Army) directed brutal attacks against Filipino forces and civilians during the Philippine-American War, for which he was court-martialed.

The progress in Samar is satisfactory in some ways, and not in others. The subduing of the fighting propensities of the war faction is reduced almost to a nullity. The growth of our strength in the estimation of the people is also quite satisfactory. The fact is, their love for the flesh-pots,[19] and, incidentally, for the Americans, who represent said pots, is growing burdensome, as the securing of the hemp with which to pay for rice is becoming a heavy business. In nearly all our ports where the commander has exercised good judgment, colonies of natives have come in and settled, and concluded they would set up . . . under our wing. . . . The correspondence the troops have captured shows that the armed forces are deserting and breaking away from the military control of the Vicol [Philippine Army] leaders.

The unsatisfactory features are the slowness of the process of conversion, the failure to get rifles, and the slowness and the difficulty in making roads and trails; . . . and, while efforts have been made to push things faster, I am entirely satisfied with the results thus far secured.

This report on August 27 was forwarded to Washington by General Chaffee, with an indorsement which concluded: —

No estimate can be made of the time when the campaign in Samar is liable to close. It will have to be continued until the surrender of Lucban[20] is effected.

Captain H. L. Jackson on August 26 reported that on the 18th he had found Lucban with two officers, *"three riflemen and about twenty bolomen,"* that he charged them, killed three, wounded one officer, and captured the two officers, the wife and child of Lucban, some ammunition, and Lucban's "correspondence and personal effects." *Apparently, resistance was reduced to a minimum.*

On September 28 occurred the affair at Balangiga,[21] in which a detachment, consisting of three officers, one hospital corps man, and seventy men, were overpowered, and lost in action and retreat all but twenty-nine men, of whom twenty-two were wounded; while the enemy's loss was estimated at from fifty to one hundred and fifty killed.

---

[19] **flesh-pots**: Formal or informal areas where prostitution is practiced or condoned.
[20] **Lucban**: Likely a Philippine Army leader. Lucban is now the name of a city in the Philippines (possibly named after him).
[21] **Balangiga**: A city on the island of Samar.

One of the survivors of the garrison gave the history of the disaster before the Senate Committee. This was William J. Gibbs, of Springfield, Mass., who was promoted to be a corporal for his bravery in this fight, and was one of five recommended as deserving a medal of honor. He may therefore be regarded as a reliable witness. From his testimony it appeared that he had served in the Philippines for about three years, that he was one of the detachment sent to Balangiga, — a village of about two thousand inhabitants, living in some two hundred houses, who got their living by chopping down cocoanuts and fishing, — that, after landing, the commander, Captain Connell

> called the officials together, and told them he came there to establish peace and to keep out the surrounding bands of robbers. He told them he wanted them to be peaceable, and, if they were not, he was all ready and prepared to fight.

Then Captain Connell

> wanted to have things cleaned up around the town, and he went to work and issued a proclamation to have all the natives appear the next morning and clean out the town. The natives appeared to be somewhat reluctant in regard to that. They turned out, but they did not work very hard. And then the next morning they refused to come at all. So he went to work, and sent the men, — each man to a shack, — and forced them to come out, and had a guard placed over the men while they were working in the hot sun. He had two Sibley tents; and they put the ninety natives in the two Sibley tents, which only held about sixteen soldiers; they could not lie down; they had to stand up. There was not room enough to lie down. They stayed there for two or three days. In the morning Captain Connell would line the natives up, and would issue to them bolos[22] for the purpose of cutting down the underbrush.

Captain Connell began this cleaning up the day he arrived; and, when he sent the soldiers to get the inhabitants,

> everybody was brought out that was able to work, — every man. There were about ninety,

aged from forty-five to thirteen.

---

[22] **bolos**: Machete-like knives.

They had these bolos, and they were placed in the line, and had to cut down the underbrush and different stuff, and they stayed there right in the heat of the sun, with about twelve soldiers standing over them; and they were confined in the Sibley tents, about forty-five natives in each tent. The weather was damp, and of course it was the rainy season at that time; and it was very unpleasant all right for the natives, and they started to complain about it. They even wanted a little matting to put on the inside of the tent to keep them from the dampness, but he would not allow that at all.

After about four days of this treatment the men were allowed to go home and appear in the morning; and they did so, though they worked reluctantly all the while. This went on till about a week before the massacre, when the native chief of police brought seventy-five men from the mountains, who were confined for a week in the Sibley tents; and, though *"it rained more or less during the day," "no matting at all was given"* to them. They complained to the soldiers; *"they were afraid to make complaints to the officers,"* but were not relieved.

Gibbs was asked,

What sort of a man was Captain Connell? A. He did not seem to treat them right in one respect. While the natives were cleaning up the town, he sent out men from the company to destroy all the rice and fish and everything in the line of food that they possibly could. He thought they were taking them to the insurrectos[23] in the mountains.

This rice

was stored in about the same way as we store hay in the barn, perhaps fifteen or twenty bushels in some places. The work of cleaning up the town in the immediate locality was continued consecutively from the time we went there in July until the massacre occurred in September.

In a word, this Captain Connell came to a quiet village, and forced every man in the place, from forty-five to thirteen years of age, to work for months at cleaning the town with soldiers over them, while he destroyed all their food and confined them at night for the time and in the manner described by the witness. Suppose we had heard that a Spanish officer had done this. Truly, it was a strange way to assure them *"that full measure of*

---

[23] **insurrectos**: Guerrilla fighters, insurrectionists.

individual rights which is the heritage of free peoples," or to prove that the mission of the United States was *"one of benevolent assimilation, substituting the mild sway of justice and right for arbitrary rule."*

Singularly enough, these men rose upon their oppressors, and attacked them with the very bolos that the Americans had furnished them; and, singularly also, they tried to surprise them, perhaps remembering that bolos are a poor weapon against rifles. The result was that in this village the American force was cut to pieces, though, as Mr. Gibbs estimated, one hundred and fifty Filipinos were killed in the struggle. This is the massacre of Balangiga.

On the 10th of October General Jacob H. Smith was assigned to the command of the forces located on the island of Samar, with headquarters at Catbalogan. Either with knowledge of the facts just stated by the witness Gibbs or without investigation, he undertook to revenge the death of the soldiers killed at Balangiga upon the whole population of Samar, an island which, according to the American Encyclopaedia, had in 1881 a population of over 250,000 persons and an area of 5,000 square miles. Shortly afterward there appeared in the newspapers of this country a statement that he proposed to make of Samar *"a wilderness where not even a bird could live."* It is charitable, if difficult, to believe that Secretary Root did not see this despatch; but it is not possible to believe that no notice reached him of General Smith's purpose.

Certainly there was enough of vengeance foreshadowed in the reports from Manila to make it clear that a restraining hand from Washington was needed. On November 4 the Manila News, approving what it narrated, published the following: —

> The transport "Lawton" returned yesterday afternoon from a two weeks' cruise, touching at Catbalogan, Cebu, Perang-Perang, and Davao.[24] On her outward passage she took two hundred Ilocano scouts for the Samar service.
>
> On the arrival of the "Lawton" at Catbalogan, Brigadier-general Smith had been in Samar about ten days; and his strong policy was already making itself felt. He had already ordered all natives to present themselves in certain of the coast towns, saying that those who *were found outside would be shot and no questions asked.* The time limit had expired when the "Lawton" reached Catbalogan, and General Smith *was as good*

---

[24] **Catbalogan . . . Davao**: Various ports in the Philippines.

as his word. His policy of reconcentration is said to be the most effective thing of the kind ever seen in these islands under any flag. All suspects, including Spaniards and half-breeds, were rounded up in big stockades and kept under guard.

The dates show that General Smith gave this large scattered foreign population about ten days' notice to abandon their homes on pain of death. The time limit had expired, and he was enforcing the penalty.

Must we assume that this statement thus published broadcast at Manila did not reach the eye of General Chaffee nor the notice of the War Department? Was any step taken by any one to inquire or to stay General Smith?

The truth was worse even than the newspaper statement. To quote from Mr. Root's letter to the President of July 12, General Smith gave *"the following oral instructions"*: —

"I want no prisoners. I wish you to kill and burn: the more you kill and burn, the better you will please me," and, further, that he wanted all persons killed who were capable of bearing arms and in actual hostilities against the United States, and did, in reply to a question by Major Waller asking for an age limit, designate the limit as ten years of age.

It will be observed that the Secretary, after the words *"capable of bearing arms,"* interpolates the words *"and in actual hostilities against the United States."* These words do not appear in the statement of General Smith's orders made by his own counsel at this trial, as they were quoted in the despatches from Manila, which were never questioned. He said: —

General Smith did give instructions to Major Waller to "kill and burn" "and make Samar a howling wilderness," and he admits that he wanted everybody killed capable of bearing arms, and that he did specify all over ten years of age, as the Samar boys of that age were equally as dangerous as their elders.

On the 4th of February, 1902, the extract quoted from the Manila Newspaper as to General Smith's course was brought to the attention of the Senate in the petition of ex-Senator Edmunds and others. . . . These gentlemen asked that these charges be investigated, and that orders be given to stop such practices. Secretary Root can hardly plead ignorance of this demand from responsible citizens. Did he take any action either to investigate or to stop? So far as the record shows, none. The order to try General Smith by court-martial was not given till April 15.

READING AND DISCUSSION QUESTIONS

1. What tactic do Storey and Codman use to expose the atrocities committed by the U.S. military in the Philippines? What are they trying to prove, and whom do they blame?

2. This report was written at the request of a *nongovernment* committee. The Senate Committee on the Philippines had found the conduct of the military less objectionable. Based on this excerpt, why is that not surprising?

3. How well do you think Storey and Codman make their case? What is most convincing, and what is least convincing?

COMPARATIVE QUESTIONS

1. The documents in this chapter show different ways that Asian cultures engaged with Western modernity. Describe some of those forms of engagement.

2. Compare the attitudes of Lin Zexu, the Boxers, and Sun Yatsen toward the West. Compare also their approaches to both international and domestic affairs.

3. Several of the documents deal with the question of violence, either impending or ongoing. How does the position (or positions) taken in each document show a tolerance or distaste for violence? How is violence justified, and why? How and why is it condemned?

4. In Saigō Takamori's letter, imperialism is upheld as a legitimate mode of international contact. In Storey and Codman's account, imperialism is largely criticized. How might it change your understanding of imperialism and colonization in Asia to read a pro-imperialism document by an Asian author and an anti-imperialism document by American authors?

5. Sir Lawrence's letter and Storey and Codman's exposé depict British and U.S. imperialist forces as victims and victimizers, respectively. What evidence, taken from the documents, suggests why the power balance is so different in each case?

CHAPTER 27

Nation Building in the Americas and Australia

1770–1914

D uring the nineteenth century, rebellions and revolutions overturned long-established patterns of European colonial rule throughout the Americas and in Australia. The newly independent countries focused on nation building and economic development, struggled to establish systems of government and new trade patterns and to address issues of land management, urbanization, and regional and racial differences. Their struggles produced markedly different results. The United States, Canada, and Australia created stable democratic societies, whereas Latin American countries grappled with ongoing political and economic instability. The United States transformed into an industrial power rivaling those of Europe, while Canada and Australia remained largely agricultural economies. In every instance, however, national leaders — typically descendants of European settlers or settlers themselves — experienced status anxiety, which often manifested in discriminatory policies that ensured their higher standing and power over native populations.

DOCUMENT 27-1

SIMÓN BOLÍVAR

Jamaica Letter

1815

Simón Bolívar (1783–1830), the son of a wealthy colonial family whose ancestors had been in Venezuela since the sixteenth century, was educated in both Enlightenment ideals and military science. He rose to prominence

---

Guillermo A. Sherwell, *Simón Bolívar, El Libertado*r (Washington, D.C.: Byron S. Adams, 1921), 89–92.

during the 1810s, when American rebels took advantage of Napoleon's occupation of Spain by forming independent states in former Spanish colonies. Despite early revolutionary successes that earned him the title of El Libertador, or "the Liberator," Bolívar fled to Jamaica and then Haiti in 1815. Returning to Venezuela with Haitian support the following year, he launched the campaign that would liberate much of Latin America from Spanish rule. Bolívar's goals of freedom and equality were compromised in their execution by Latin American political and economic interests, and Bolívar died disenchanted with the "ungovernable" continent. His famous Jamaica Letter outlines his grievances and hopes for American independence.

Europe itself, . . . by reasons of wholesome policies, should have prepared and carried out the plan of American independence, not only because it is so required for the balance of the world, but because this is a legitimate and safe means of obtaining commercial posts on the other side of the ocean. . . .

I consider the actual state of America as when, after the collapse of the Roman Empire, each member constituted a political system in conformity with its interests and position, but with this great difference: that these scattered members reestablished the old nationalities with the alterations required by circumstances or events. But we, who scarcely keep a vestige of things of the past, and who, on the other hand, are not Indians nor Europeans, but a mixture of the legitimate owners of the country and the usurping Spaniards; in short, we, being Americans by birth and with rights equal to those of Europe, have to dispute these rights with the men of the country, and to maintain ourselves against the possession of the invaders. Thus, we find ourselves in the most extraordinary and complicated predicament. . . .

Americans, under the Spanish system now in vigor, have in society no other place than that of serfs fit for work, and, at the most, that of simple consumers; and even this is limited by absurd restrictions, such as prohibition of the cultivation of European products; the monopoly of certain goods in the hands of the king; the prevention of the establishment in America of factories not possessed by Spain; the exclusive privileges of trade, even regarding the necessities of life; the obstacles placed in the way of the American provinces so that they may not deal with each other, nor have understandings, nor trade. In short, do you want to know what was our lot? The fields, in which to cultivate indigo, cochineal,[1] coffee, sugar cane, cocoa, cotton; the solitary plains, to breed cattle; the deserts, to hunt the wild beasts; the bosom of the earth, to extract gold, with which that avaricious country was never satisfied.

We were never viceroys or governors except by very extraordinary reasons; archbishops and bishops, seldom; ambassadors, never; military men, only as subordinates; nobles, without privileges; lastly, we were neither magistrates nor financiers, and hardly merchants. All this we had to accept in direct opposition to our institutions.

The Americans have risen suddenly and without previous preparation and without previous knowledge and, what is more deplorable, without experience in public affairs, to assume in the world the eminent dignity of legislators, magistrates, administrators of the public treasury, diplomats, generals and all the supreme and subordinate authorities which form the hierarchy of an organized state.

The events of the mainland have proved that perfectly representative institutions do not agree with our character, habits, and present state of enlightenment. . . . So long as our fellow citizens do not acquire the talents and the political virtues which distinguish our brothers of the North, who have a system of government altogether popular in character, I am very much afraid these institutions might lead to our ruin instead of aiding us. . . .

I desire more than anybody else to see the formation in America of the greatest nation in the world, not so much as to its extension and wealth as to its glory and freedom.

READING AND DISCUSSION QUESTIONS

1. As Bolívar describes it, what is the advantage of American independence for Europe?

2. How did Europe (especially Spain) treat its American holdings, according to Bolívar?

3. What are the problems that Bolívar predicts for American self-governance? What kind of a system does he propose?

---

[1] **cochineal**: An insect from which valuable (and exportable) carmine dye is derived.

DOCUMENT 27-2

ALEXIS DE TOCQUEVILLE

From Democracy in America

1840

French thinker Alexis de Tocqueville (1805–1859) spent much of the early 1800s touring the United States and writing about the uniqueness of the American democratic experiment. His incisive observations revealed the strengths and inherent weaknesses of a political and economic system based on the notion of equality. One area in which democracy seemed to contradict itself was military service and the quest for peace. Tocqueville's comments on this topic were published a decade after the wars for independence in Latin and South America left parts of those regions under military rule and other areas plagued by violence and the need to recruit armies by force.

Book III
Chapter XXII
Why Democratic Nations Naturally Desire Peace, and Democratic Armies, War

The same interests, the same fears, the same passions that deter democratic nations from revolutions deter them also from war; the spirit of military glory and the spirit of revolution are weakened at the same time and by the same causes. The ever increasing numbers of men of property who are lovers of peace, the growth of personal wealth which war so rapidly consumes, the mildness of manners, the gentleness of heart, those tendencies to pity which are produced by the equality of conditions, that coolness of understanding which renders men comparatively insensible to the violent and poetical excitement of arms, all these causes concur to quench the military spirit. I think it may be admitted as a general and constant rule that among civilized nations the warlike passions will become more rare and less intense in proportion as social conditions are more equal.

Alexis de Tocqueville, *Democracy in America*, 3d ed., ed. Francis Bowen, trans. Henry Reeve (Cambridge: Sever and Francis, 1863), 2:326–332.

War is nevertheless an occurrence to which all nations are subject, democratic nations as well as others. Whatever taste they may have for peace, they must hold themselves in readiness to repel aggression, or, in other words, they must have an army. Fortune, which has conferred so many peculiar benefits upon the inhabitants of the United States, has placed them in the midst of a wilderness, where they have, so to speak, no neighbors; a few thousand soldiers are sufficient for their wants. But this is peculiar to America, not to democracy.

The equality of conditions and the manners as well as the institutions resulting from it do not exempt a democratic people from the necessity of standing armies, and their armies always exercise a powerful influence over their fate. It is therefore of singular importance to inquire what are the natural propensities of the men of whom these armies are composed. . . .

In democratic armies all the soldiers may become officers, which makes the desire of promotion general and immeasurably extends the bounds of military ambition. The officer, on his part, sees nothing that naturally and necessarily stops him at one grade more than at another; and each grade has immense importance in his eyes because his rank in society almost always depends on his rank in the army. Amongst democratic nations it often happens that an officer has no property but his pay and no distinction but that of military honors; consequently, as often as his duties change, his fortune changes and he becomes, as it were, a new man. What was only an appendage to his position in aristocratic armies has thus become the main point, the basis of his whole condition.

Under the old French monarchy officers were always called by their titles of nobility; they are now always called by the title of their military rank. This little change in the forms of language suffices to show that a great revolution has taken place in the constitution of society and in that of the army.

In democratic armies the desire of advancement is almost universal: it is ardent, tenacious, perpetual; it is strengthened by all other desires and extinguished only with life itself. But it is easy to see that, of all armies in the world, those in which advancement must be slowest in time of peace are the armies of democratic countries. As the number of commissions is naturally limited while the number of competitors is almost unlimited, and as the strict law of equality is over all alike, none can make rapid progress; many can make no progress at all. Thus the desire of advancement is greater and the opportunities of advancement fewer there than elsewhere. All the ambitious spirits of a democratic army are consequently ardently desirous of war, because war makes vacancies and warrants the violation of that law of seniority which is the sole privilege natural to democracy.

We thus arrive at this singular consequence, that, of all armies, those most ardently desirous of war are democratic armies, and of all nations, those most fond of peace are democratic nations; and what makes these facts still more extraordinary is that these contrary effects are produced at the same time by the principle of equality.

All the members of the community, being alike, constantly harbor the wish and discover the possibility of changing their condition and improving their welfare; this makes them fond of peace, which is favorable to industry and allows every man to pursue his own little undertakings to their completion. On the other hand, this same equality makes soldiers dream of fields of battle, by increasing the value of military honors in the eyes of those who follow the profession of arms and by rendering those honors accessible to all. In either case the restlessness of the heart is the same, the taste for enjoyment is insatiable, the ambition of success as great; the means of gratifying it alone are different. . . .

Moreover, as amongst democratic nations (to repeat what I have just remarked) the wealthiest, best-educated, and ablest men seldom adopt the military profession, the army, taken collectively, eventually forms a small nation by itself, where the mind is less enlarged and habits are more rude than in the nation at large. Now, this small uncivilized nation has arms in its possession and alone knows how to use them; for, indeed, the pacific temper of the community increases the danger to which a democratic people is exposed from the military and turbulent spirit of the army. Nothing is so dangerous as an army in the midst of an unwarlike nation; the excessive love of the whole community for quiet continually puts the constitution at the mercy of the soldiery.

It may therefore be asserted, generally speaking, that if democratic nations are naturally prone to peace from their interests and their propensities, they are constantly drawn to war and revolutions by their armies. Military revolutions, which are scarcely ever to be apprehended in aristocracies, are always to be dreaded among democratic nations. These perils must be reckoned among the most formidable that beset their future fate, and the attention of statesmen should be sedulously applied to find a remedy for the evil.

When a nation perceives that it is inwardly affected by the restless ambition of its army, the first thought which occurs is to give this inconvenient ambition an object by going to war. I do not wish to speak ill of war:

war almost always enlarges the mind of a people and raises their character. In some cases it is the only check to the excessive growth of certain propensities that naturally spring out of the equality of conditions, and it must be considered as a necessary corrective to certain inveterate diseases to which democratic communities are liable.

War has great advantages, but we must not flatter ourselves that it can diminish the danger I have just pointed out. That peril is only suspended by it, to return more fiercely when the war is over; for armies are much more impatient of peace after having tasted military exploits. War could be a remedy only for a people who were always athirst for military glory.

I foresee that all the military rulers who may rise up in great democratic nations will find it easier to conquer with their armies than to make their armies live at peace after conquest. There are two things that a democratic people will always find very difficult, to begin a war and to end it.

Again, if war has some peculiar advantages for democratic nations, on the other hand it exposes them to certain dangers which aristocracies have no cause to dread to an equal extent. I shall point out only two of these.

Although war gratifies the army, it embarrasses and often exasperates that countless multitude of men whose minor passions every day require peace in order to be satisfied. Thus there is some risk of its causing, under another form, the very disturbance it is intended to prevent.

No protracted war can fail to endanger the freedom of a democratic country. Not indeed that after every victory it is to be apprehended that the victorious generals will possess themselves by force of the supreme power, after the manner of Sulla and Caesar;[2] the danger is of another kind. War does not always give over democratic communities to military government, but it must invariably and immeasurably increase the powers of civil government; it must almost compulsorily concentrate the direction of all men and the management of all things in the hands of the administration. If it does not lead to despotism by sudden violence, it prepares men for it more gently by their habits. All those who seek to destroy the liberties of a democratic nation ought to know that war is the surest and the shortest means to accomplish it. This is the first axiom of the science. . . .

---

[2] **Sulla and Caesar**: Sulla refers to Lucius Cornelius Sulla, a dictator who claimed power in Rome from 82 to 79 B.C.E.; Caesar is Julius Caesar, dictator of Rome from 45 to 44 B.C.E., when he was murdered by political leaders who feared his growing sense of self-importance.

The remedy for the vices of the army is not to be found in the army itself, but in the country. Democratic nations are naturally afraid of disturbance and of despotism; the object is to turn these natural instincts into intelligent, deliberate, and lasting tastes. When men have at last learned to make a peaceful and profitable use of freedom and have felt its blessings, when they have conceived a manly love of order and have freely submitted themselves to discipline, these same men, if they follow the profession of arms, bring into it, unconsciously and almost against their will, these same habits and manners. The general spirit of the nation, being infused into the spirit peculiar to the army, tempers the opinions and desires engendered by military life, or represses them by the mighty force of public opinion. Teach the citizens to be educated, orderly, firm, and free and the soldiers will be disciplined and obedient.

Any law that, in repressing the turbulent spirit of the army, should tend to diminish the spirit of freedom in the nation and to overshadow the notion of law and right would defeat its object; it would do much more to favor than to defeat the establishment of military tyranny. After all, and in spite of all precautions, a large army in the midst of a democratic people will always be a source of great danger. The most effectual means of diminishing that danger would be to reduce the army, but this is a remedy that all nations are not able to apply.

READING AND DISCUSSION QUESTIONS

1. How is military rank determined in democratic countries? What is the effect of this system?

2. According to Tocqueville, the principle of equality inspires different motivations among the soldiers and citizens of a democracy. What are these motivations, and why might they be a source of conflict?

3. Tocqueville says that laws won't keep armies from seeking to wage war. What does he see as the key to a lasting peace?

Federal Dispossession in the United States and Australia

DOCUMENT 27-3

Cherokee Nation Versus the State of Georgia

1831

The economic development of the United States in the nineteenth century rested, in part, on expanding the nation's landholdings westward onto Indian lands, even if that meant violating earlier treaties. In 1828, Georgia passed several laws to remove the Cherokee from their homeland. Cherokee chief John Ross fought back, appealing first to Congress and, after passage of the federal Cherokee Removal Act, by filing suit in 1830 on behalf of his tribe. In 1831, Supreme Court Justice John Marshall wrote the following opinion dismissing the case, thereby denying self-governance to the Cherokee. Seven years later, President Martin Van Buren enforced his predecessor Andrew Jackson's decision to resettle the Cherokee from Georgia to Oklahoma in a forced march that became known as the Trail of Tears.

Mr. Chief Justice MARSHALL delivered the opinion of the Court:

This bill is brought by the Cherokee Nation, praying an injunction to restrain the state of Georgia from the execution of certain laws of that state, which as is alleged, go directly to annihilate the Cherokees as a political society, and to seize, for the use of Georgia, the lands of the nation which have been assured to them by the United States in solemn treaties repeatedly made and still in force.

If courts were permitted to indulge their sympathies, a case better calculated to excite them can scarcely be imagined. A people once numerous, powerful, and truly independent, found by our ancestors in the quiet and uncontrolled possession of an ample domain, gradually sinking beneath

Cherokee Nation v. Georgia, 30 U.S. 1 (1831).

our superior policy, our arts, and our arms, have yielded their lands by successive treaties, each of which contains a solemn guarantee of the residue, until they retain no more of their formerly extensive territory than is deemed necessary to their comfortable subsistence. To preserve this remnant the present application is made.

Before we can look into the merits of the case, a preliminary inquiry presents itself. Has this Court jurisdiction of the cause?

The 3rd Article of the Constitution describes the extent of the judicial power. The 2nd Section closes an enumeration of the cases to which it is extended, with controversies between a state or the citizens thereof, and foreign states, citizens, or subjects. A subsequent clause of the same section gives the Supreme Court original jurisdiction in all cases in which a state shall be a party. The party defendant may then unquestionably be sued in this Court. May the plaintiff sue in it? Is the Cherokee Nation a foreign state in the sense in which that term is used in the Constitution?

The counsel for the plaintiffs have maintained the affirmative of this proposition with great earnestness and ability. So much of the argument as was intended to prove the character of the Cherokees as a state, as a distinct political society separated from others, capable of managing its own affairs and governing itself, has, in the opinion of a majority of the judges, been completely successful. They have been uniformly treated as a state from the settlement of our country. The numerous treaties made with them by the United States recognize them as a people capable of maintaining the relations of peace and war, of being responsible in their political character for any violation of their engagements, or for any aggression committed on the citizens of the United States by any individual of their community. Laws have been enacted in the spirit of these treaties. The acts of our government plainly recognize the Cherokee Nation as a state, and the courts are bound by those acts.

A question of much more difficulty remains. Do the Cherokees constitute a foreign state in the sense of the Constitution?

The counsel have shown conclusively that they are not a state of the Union, and have insisted that individually they are aliens, not owing allegiance to the United States. An aggregate of aliens composing a state must, they say, be a foreign state. Each individual being foreign, the whole must be foreign.

This argument is imposing, but we must examine it more closely before we yield to it. The condition of the Indians in relation to the United States is perhaps unlike that of any other two people in existence. In the general, nations not owing a common allegiance are foreign to each other.

The term foreign nation is, with strict propriety, applicable by either to the other. But the relation of the Indians to the United States is marked by peculiar and cardinal distinctions which exist nowhere else.

The Indian Territory is admitted to compose part of the United States. In all our maps, geographical treatises, histories, and laws, it is so considered. In all our intercourse with foreign nations, in our commercial regulations, in any attempt at intercourse between Indians and foreign nations, they are considered as within the jurisdictional limits of the United States, subject to many of those restraints which are imposed upon our own citizens. They acknowledge themselves in their treaties to be under the protection of the United States; they admit that the United States shall have the sole and exclusive right of regulating the trade with them and managing all their affairs as they think proper; and the Cherokees in particular were allowed by the Treaty of Hopewell,[3] which preceded the Constitution, to send a deputy of their choice, whenever they think fit, to Congress. Treaties were made with some tribes by the state of New York under a then unsettled construction of the Confederation, by which they ceded all their lands to that state, taking back a limited grant to themselves in which they admit their dependence.

Though the Indians are acknowledged to have an unquestionable and, heretofore, unquestioned right to the lands they occupy until that right shall be extinguished by a voluntary cession to our government, yet it may well be doubted whether those tribes which reside within the acknowledged boundaries of the United States can, with strict accuracy, be denominated foreign nations. They may more correctly, perhaps, be denominated domestic dependent nations. They occupy a territory to which we assert a title independent of their will, which must take effect in point of possession when their right of possession ceases. Meanwhile, they are in a state of pupilage. Their relation to the United States resembles that of a ward to his guardian.

They look to our government for protection; rely upon its kindness and its power; appeal to it for relief to their wants; and address the President as their great father. They and their country are considered by foreign nations, as well as by ourselves, as being so completely under the sovereignty and dominion of the United States that any attempt to acquire their lands or to form a political connection with them would be considered by all as an invasion of our territory and an act of hostility.

---

[3] **Treaty of Hopewell**: Signed on November 28, 1785, this treaty between the United States and the Cherokee defined the westernmost boundary for white settlement.

These considerations go far to support the opinion that the framers of our Constitution had not the Indian tribes in view when they opened the courts of the Union to controversies between a state or the citizens thereof and foreign states.

In considering this subject, the habits and usages of the Indians in their intercourse with their white neighbors ought not to be entirely disregarded. At the time the Constitution was framed, the idea of appealing to an American court of justice for an assertion of right or a redress of wrong had perhaps never entered the mind of an Indian or of his tribe. Their appeal was to the tomahawk, or to the government. This was well understood by the statesmen who framed the Constitution of the United States, and might furnish some reason for omitting to enumerate them among the parties who might sue in the courts of the Union. Be this as it may, the peculiar relations between the United States and the Indians occupying our territory are such that we should feel much difficulty in considering them as designated by the term foreign state were there no other part of the Constitution which might shed light on the meaning of these words. But we think that in construing them, considerable aid is furnished by that clause in the 8th Section of the 3rd Article, which empowers Congress to regulate commerce with foreign nations, and among the several states, and with the Indian tribes.

In this clause they are as clearly contradistinguished by a name appropriate to themselves from foreign nations as from the several states composing the Union. They are designated by a distinct appellation; and as this appellation can be applied to neither of the others, neither can the appellation distinguishing either of the others be in fair construction applied to them. The objects to which the power of regulating commerce might be directed are divided into three distinct classes: foreign nations, the several states, and Indian tribes. When forming this article, the Convention considered them as entirely distinct. We cannot assume that the distinction was lost in framing a subsequent article, unless there be something in its language to authorize the assumption.

Foreign nations is a general term, the application of which to Indian tribes, when used in the American Constitution, is at best extremely questionable. In one article in which a power is given to be exercised in regard to foreign nations generally, and to the Indian tribes particularly, they are mentioned as separate in terms clearly contradistinguishing them from each other. We perceive plainly that the Constitution in this article does not comprehend Indian tribes in the general term foreign nations; not, we presume, because a tribe may not be a nation but because it is not foreign to the United States. When, afterward, the term foreign state is introduced, we cannot impute to the Convention the intention to desert its former meaning and to comprehend Indian tribes within it, unless the context force that construction on us. We find nothing in the context and nothing in the subject of the article which leads to it.

The Court has bestowed its best attention on this question and, after mature deliberation, the majority is of opinion that an Indian tribe or nation within the United States is not a foreign state in the sense of the Constitution, and cannot maintain an action in the courts of the United States.

A serious additional objection exists to the jurisdiction of the Court. Is the matter of the bill the proper subject for judicial inquiry and decision? It seeks to restrain a state from the forcible exercise of legislative power over a neighboring people, asserting their independence; their right to which the state denies. On several of the matters alleged in the bill, for example on the laws making it criminal to exercise the usual powers of self-government in their own country by the Cherokee Nation, this Court cannot interpose, at least in the form in which those matters are presented.

That part of the bill which respects the land occupied by the Indians, and prays the aid of the Court to protect their possession, may be more doubtful. The mere question of right might perhaps be decided by this Court in a proper case with proper parties. But the Court is asked to do more than decide on the title. The bill requires us to control the legislature of Georgia, and to restrain the exertion of its physical force. The propriety of such an interposition by the Court may be well questioned. It savors too much of the exercise of political power to be within the proper province of the Judicial Department. But the opinion on the point respecting parties makes it unnecessary to decide this question.

If it be true that the Cherokee Nation have rights, this is not the tribunal in which those rights are to be asserted. If it be true that wrongs have been inflicted and that still greater are to be apprehended, this is not the tribunal which can redress the past or prevent the future.

The motion for an injunction is denied.

READING AND DISCUSSION QUESTIONS

1. How does Chief Justice Marshall define "foreign nation"?
2. What are the unique qualities of the U.S. relationship with Indians according to Marshall?

3. Why does Marshall use the phrase "domestic dependent nations" in relation to Native Americans?

4. Why does Marshall say that the Supreme Court is not the place to address the rights of the Cherokee in this matter?

DOCUMENT 27-4

From the Aborigines Protection Act

1909

Beginning in 1869, Australian officials adopted new laws that reflected the uneasy coexistence of the island's native Aborigine and settler populations. The Aborigines Protection Act, which was amended several times through 1943, on the surface attempted to protect the native nomadic peoples. In reality, it sought to regulate their lives in numerous ways, including outlining where they could work and live. The most controversial aspect of the law was its application to Aborigine children, who could legally be taken from their parents — sometimes forcibly and permanently — at the discretion of the state.

ACT NO. 25, 1909

An Act to provide for the protection and care of aborigines; to repeal the Supply of Liquors to Aborigines Prevention Act; to amend the Vagrancy Act, 1902, and the Police Offences (Amendment) Act, 1908; and for purposes consequent thereon or incidental thereto. [Assented to, 20th December, 1909.]

Be it enacted by the King's Most Excellent Majesty, by and with the advice and consent of the Legislative Council and Legislative Assembly of New South Wales in Parliament assembled, and by the authority of the same, as follows: . . .

Public Acts of New South Wales, 1824–1957, ed. R. J. McKay, O. M. L. Davies, and S. G. O. Martin (Sydney: Law Book Co. of Australia, 1958).

3.   In this Act, unless the context or subject matter otherwise indicates or requires: —

"Aborigine" means any full-blooded or half-caste aboriginal who is a native of Australia and who is temporarily or permanently resident in New South Wales.

"Adopted boarder" means a child who, if under the maximum age up to which he is compelled by law to attend school, is allowed by authority of the board to remain with a foster parent without payment of an allowance or, if over the maximum age up to which he is compelled by law to attend school, is allowed by authority of the board to remain with the foster parent on terms and conditions which do not require that the whole or any part of any wages earned by the child be paid to the board on behalf of such child,

"Board" means the Aborigines Welfare Board, constituted under this Act. . . .

"Reserve" means area of land heretofore or hereafter reserved from sale or lease under any Act dealing with Crown lands, or given by or acquired from any private person, for the use of aborigines. . . .

"Ward" means a child who has been admitted to the control of the board or committed to a home constituted and established under section eleven of this Act. . . .

7.   (1) It shall be the duty of the board —

   (a) to, with the consent of the Minister, apportion, distribute, and apply as may seem most fitting, any moneys voted by Parliament, and any other funds in its possession or control, for the relief or benefit of aborigines or for the purpose of assisting aborigines in obtaining employment and of maintaining or assisting to maintain them whilst so employed, or otherwise for the purpose of assisting aborigines to become assimilated into the general life of the community;

   (b) To distribute blankets, clothing, and relief to aborigines at the discretion of the board;

   (c) To provide for the custody and maintenance of the children of aborigines;

   (d) To manage and regulate the use of reserves;

   (e) To exercise a general supervision and care over all aborigines and over all matters affecting the interests and welfare of aborigines, and to protect them against injustice, imposition, and fraud;

(f) to arrange for the inspection at regular intervals of each station and training school under the control of the board, by the Superintendent of Aborigines Welfare and one or more of the other members of the board, or by one or more of such other members. . . .

(2) The board may on the application of the parent or guardian of any child admit such child to the control of the board.

8. (1) All reserves shall be vested in the board, and it shall not be lawful for any person other than an aborigine, or an officer under the board, or a person acting under the board's direction, or under the authority of the regulations, or a member of the police force, to enter or remain upon or be within the limits of a reserve upon which aborigines are residing, for any purpose whatsoever:

Provided that the board may, by permit in the prescribed form, authorize, subject to such terms and conditions as it may think fit, any person apparently having an admixture of aboriginal blood to enter or remain upon or be within the limits of any such reserve.

(2) The board may remove from a reserve any aborigine or other person who is guilty of any misconduct, or who, in the opinion of the board, should be earning a living away from such reserve.

(3) Any building erected on a reserve shall be vested in and become the property of the board, also all cattle, horses, pigs, sheep, machinery, and property thereon purchased or acquired for the benefit of aborigines.

8A. (1) Where an aborigine or a person apparently having an admixture of aboriginal blood is, in the opinion of the board, living in insanitary or undesirable conditions, or should in the opinion of the board be placed under control, a stipendiary or police magistrate may, on the application of the board, order such aborigine or person to remove to a reserve or place controlled by the board, or, if such aborigine or person is but temporarily resident in this State, to return to the State whence he came within a time specified in the order. . . .

(3) Until such an order is cancelled every aborigine or other person named therein in that behalf shall be and remain under the control of the board while he is in this State. . . .

11. The board may constitute and establish under this Act homes for the reception, maintenance, education, and training of wards and may assign a name or names to such homes.

11A. (1) The board may, by indenture, bind or cause to be bound any ward as an apprentice or may, where apprenticeship conditions are not applicable or desirable, place any ward in other suitable employment. . . .

(3) All wages earned by any ward except such part thereof as the employer is required to pay to the ward personally as pocket money, shall be paid by the employer to the board on behalf of such ward and shall be applied as prescribed. . . .

11B. (1) Where a ward is not regarded by the board as ready for placement in employment or for apprenticeship, such ward may be placed in a home for the purpose of being maintained, educated, and trained.

(2) Where the board is satisfied that any ward is not likely to succeed in his employment or as an apprentice, the board may, with the approval of the employer or guardian of such ward, cancel any indenture of apprenticeship or agreement, and may place such ward in a home for the purpose of being maintained, educated, and trained.

11C. Upon complaint made by the board or any officer authorized by the board in that behalf, that any person with whom any ward has been placed in employment or apprenticed is not observing or performing the conditions of any indenture of apprenticeship or agreement or is unfit to have the further care of such ward any magistrate or justice may call upon such person to answer such complaint, and on proof thereof a children's court established under the Child Welfare Act, 1939, may order such agreement to be terminated and may direct that the ward be sent to a home constituted and established under section eleven of this Act pending arrangements for further employment or apprenticeship.

11D. (1) The board shall be the authority to —

(a) admit a child to its control;

(b) provide for the accommodation and maintenance of any child admitted to its control until he is apprenticed, placed in employment, boarded-out, or placed as an adopted boarder;

(c) pay foster parents such rates as may be prescribed;

(d) direct the removal or transfer of any ward (other than a ward who has been committed to an institution for a specified term);

(e) apprentice, place in employment, board-out, or place as an adopted boarder any ward (other than a ward who has been committed to an institution for a specified term);

(f) approve of persons applying for the custody of wards and of the homes of such persons;

(g) arrange the terms and conditions of the custody of any ward;

(h) direct the restoration of any ward (other than a ward who has been committed to an institution for a specified term) to the care of his parent or of any other person;

(i) direct the absolute discharge of any ward (other than a ward who has been committed to an institution for a specified term) from supervision and control.

(2) (a) The board may, under and in accordance with subsection one of this section, board out any child to the person for the time being in charge of any charitable depot, home, or hostel and may make to the person in charge of such charitable depot, home, or hostel, payments in respect of such child at the rates prescribed for payments under paragraph (c) of that subsection. . . .

13B. In any case where an aborigine is living with, or employed by, any other person, and the board has reason to believe that such aborigine is not receiving fair and proper treatment, and is not being paid a reasonable wage, or the board is of opinion that his moral or physical well-being is likely to be impaired by continuance in such employment, or that he is being influenced to continue in such employment, the board shall have the power to terminate same and remove the aborigine concerned to such reserve, home, or other place as it may direct. For the purposes of this section any officer of the board, or member of the police force, shall have access to such aborigine at all reasonable times for the purpose of making such inspection and inquiries as he may deem necessary.

13C. In any case where it appears to the board to be in the best interests of the aborigine concerned and/or of his wife and/or children the board may direct employers or any employer to pay the wages of the aborigine to the Superintendent of Aborigines Welfare or some other officer named by him, and any employer who fails to observe such directions shall be deemed to have not paid such wages. The wages so collected shall be expended solely on behalf of the aborigine to whom they were due and/or of his wife and/or children, and an account kept of such expenditure. . . .

14A. The board may authorize the medical examination of any aborigine or person having apparently an admixture of aboriginal blood and may have such aborigine or person so examined, removed to and kept in a public hospital or other institution for appropriate curative treatment, or may require such aborigine or person to undergo such treatment as and where provided.

Any such examination shall be performed only by a medical practitioner authorized in that behalf either generally or in a particular case by the Chief Medical Officer of the Government. . . .

READING AND DISCUSSION QUESTIONS

1. What duties does the board established by this act have in "protecting" the Aborigines?

2. Under what circumstances can a child be removed from the reserve (reservation) by government representatives? What powers does this act give the government regarding the treatment of such wards?

3. What notions of race and caste does this legislation reveal?

DOCUMENT 27-5

N. C. ADOSSIDES

Villa, the Bandit General

1914

Doroteo Arango, known as Francisco "Pancho" Villa (1878–1923), was a charismatic bandit-turned-general and perhaps the best-known figure of the Mexican Revolution. After an early life of banditry and military activity, Villa became a rebel leader against his former superior, Victoriano Huerta, who seized dictatorial power in 1913. Villa commanded the Northern Division, a well-supplied and successful rebel army from the wealthy Chihuahua region, and gained international fame as a dashing revolutionary acting

"Villa, the Bandit General," *California Outlook* 16:19 (May 9, 1914), 15.

against corrupt Mexican governments. This excerpt from the U.S. journal
The California Outlook *not only highlights the bravado and chaos of the*
Mexican Civil War, but also conveys the voyeuristic pleasure of the U.S.
media in depicting the glamorous side of nation building.

Interesting and romantic is the fact that the presiding genius of this rebel
campaign is the notorious bandit, Pancho Villa. It was at Mapimi[4] that I
had the doubtful pleasure of meeting this Fra Diavalo of Mexico. Then
a war correspondent with Madero's[5] Federal army, I found myself at the
little mining town in the company of Raoul Madera.[6] Madero[7] was awaiting Villa's return from the battle of Parral.[8] There were rumors of his
defeat. The suspense was ended by the arrival of the defeated Colonel
Villa, who, had, before evacuating Parral, robbed its bank of 180,000 pesos
and annexed one thousand sheep.

Clad in picturesque charro costume, with eyes bright and cunning, he
looked a robust representative of the lower regions disguised just enough
to visit a more civilized realm.

"Are the sacks really filled with flour?" I asked.

He grinned. "Flour from the bank of Parral — Terrazas's[9] flour that
financed Orozco's[10] revolution," was the reply. "I took Parral and was the
master of the town, but, receiving no reinforcements, I decided to abandon
it. Before evacuating, however, I went to the Banco Miniero, owned by
Louis Terrazas, and approached the cashier's window. 'My name is Pancho
Villa,' I said. 'How much cash have you on hand?' 'One hundred and eighty
thousand pesos, Senor.' 'I need them right away,' said I. 'Fill the sacks that
are loaded on the mules outside of your building and muy pronto.'

"Obeying, the man begged me for a receipt for his personal protection. I handed him one that read: 'I have received from the Banco Miniero
of Parral the sum of 180,000 pesos as a booty of war which the Federal
authorities will not have to repay.' Then I patted the little man, gave him
the receipt and a cigarette, and left him with a 'Muchas gracias, Senor.'"

---

[4] **Mapimi**: City in the Mexican state of Durango.

[5] **Madero**: Francisco Madero, president of Mexico from 1911 to 1913.

[6] **Raoul Madera**: Not to be confused with Madero, Raoul Madera was a revolutionary
leader.

[7] **Madero**: Probably a typo for Madera.

[8] **Parral**: City in the Mexican state of Chihuahua.

[9] **Terrazas**: Luis Terrazas, a wealthy landowner in Chihuahua.

[10] **Orozco**: Pascual Orozco, a Mexican revolutionary.

At the death of his father, Francisco, or Pancho, was left in charge of the Villa ranch in the state of Chihuahua and with it the responsibility of his mother and a young sister. Becoming enamored of the sheriff of Chihuahua, the girl eloped with him. Forgetful of the marriage ceremony the couple fled to the mountains. The enraged Villa, with an escort of cowboys and a priest, pursued the runaways. Overtaking them, he forced matrimony upon the unwilling sheriff, then handing him a shovel, commanded his brother-in-law to dig a grave. That horrid task completed, Pancho shot down the terrified bridegroom and rolled his body into the pit.

With that began his life of bandit and marauder. For fifteen years he roamed the Durango and Chihuahua Sierras. Porfirio Diaz[11] had bid $20,000 for his head and the inspired rurales[12] tracked him from hiding-place to hiding-place. "I had forty-eight encounters with the rurales and killed thirty-seven," said he.

Villa's Animus Against Huerta

Huerta had the ex-bandit arrested and threatened with death. Madero saved his life, but Huerta threw him into jail again, whence he contrived to escape. Again he took to the mountains.

In March, 1913, Villa joined the Constitutionalist revolution with a borrowed mule, a few sacks of flour, and nine men. In a short time he gathered an army of several thousand volunteers. Now he revenges himself upon Huerta. He has won battle after battle, dislodged the Federals from their strong positions, conquered villages, towns and states. He has captured enormous quantities of ammunition, artillery batteries and quick-firing guns, trains of war supplies and provisions and millions of dollars in currency and property. The most important strongholds in Northern Mexico — Tierra Blanca, Juarez, Ojinaga, Chihuahua, Torreon and San Pedro — have fallen into his hands. He has driven the enemy southward and remains in control of Northern Mexico from the Pacific to the Atlantic.

Whether or not his magical successes will continue remains to be seen, but on one point I am certain, namely, that Pancho Villa, drunk with victory as he must be today, will not be truly gratified until he has personally solved the problem of Huerta, and I am convinced that Villa does not aspire to the position from which he plots to dislodge the provisional president. Ambitious he is, but he is astute enough to realize that

---

[11] **Porfirio Diaz**: Former dictator of Mexico, against whom Francisco Madero launched the Mexican Revolution in 1910.

[12] **rurales**: Mounted police, members of the Mexican Rural Guard.

for his undisciplined and untutored self the presidency is not the place. Vain he is, but not vain enough to reason that his variety of popularity would cushion the thorny throne of Mexico. Illiterate he is, and yet not so illiterate as to miss the ominous writing on the wall, and so suspicious is he that never would he risk his life by seating himself under the sword of Damocles. — Condensed from "Pancho Villa, Man and Soldier," by N. C. Adossides, in the "American Review of Reviews" for May.

READING AND DISCUSSION QUESTIONS

1. What is the overall tone of the journalist's representation of Villa? How is it different from the American press's depictions of rebel leaders in modern conflicts?

2. What is the effect of presenting Huerta as Villa's mortal enemy?

3. Judging by this account, how would you describe the interest of the U.S. media and reading public in Mexican nation building? Is it literary? Political? Personal? What are other possible reasons for U.S. interest in the Mexican Revolution?

DOCUMENT 27-6

Advertisement for Rail Travel to Canada

1885

In 1885, the Canadian Pacific Railway Company completed the first Canadian transcontinental railroad. The company was formed in 1881, in part to address the political scandals associated with lucrative rail contracts and emphasize an all-Canada railroad. However, other ventures such as the St. Paul, Minneapolis, and Manitoba Railway (advertised here) continued to build and maintain their own lines, many of which took advantage of established United States routes. This advertisement shows not only how Canadian railroads sought to attract "colonists" from Canada and abroad to populate huge tracts of land awarded to railroad companies, but also the international nature of Canadian railroad development.

Canadian Pacific Archives A6409.

READING AND DISCUSSION QUESTIONS

1. To whom is the advertisement designed to appeal? How might that influence the nature of the new Canadian nation?

2. Based on the advertisement, where do colonists board the rail and what are their likely destinations?

COMPARATIVE QUESTIONS

1. What tone does each document in this chapter adopt in describing the creation of a nation? In each case, what are the priorities, and what is the basic motivation for nation building?

2. How does each document present general principles (freedom, equality, or solidarity) as a part of nation building?

3. How might de Tocqueville have analyzed the upheaval of nation building as it is presented in Bolívar's Jamaica Letter and the article on Pancho Villa? What similarities and differences are there between Bolívar and Villa and their forms of revolution?

4. What is the effect of associating nation building with one specific person or group of people? Cite examples from the documents.

5. How are indigenous people made a part of the nation-building process in *Cherokee Nation Versus the State of Georgia* and the Aborigines Protection Act? What strikes you most about each document? What similarities and differences do you discern between the two acts of dispossession?

6. What is the role of land and territory conveyed through the *Cherokee* case, the Aborigines Protection Act, and the advertisement for rail travel to Canada? What is spoken and unspoken in each document?

CHAPTER 28

World War and Revolution

1914–1929

orld War I (1914–1918) changed the global balance of economic, military, and political power. Though the conflict started as a dispute between two small Eastern European nations over a political assassination, a web of national alliances and long-suppressed hostilities over lost territory helped escalate it into four years of war that involved most major countries. The "Great War" led to a rise in Asian nationalism, the decline of Great Britain, France, and Germany as world powers, and the ascent of the United States as a global force. People everywhere seized opportunities created by the war as an opportunity for change. Russia was transformed by a social revolution at home and Zionists across Europe sought support for a national homeland in Palestine.

DOCUMENT 28-1

From A War Nurse's Diary

1918

The declaration of war in August 1914 electrified the British populace. Among the civilians who volunteered to serve were more than 100,000 women. As casualties mounted, the initially class-segregated women's services began to recruit women from lower social classes to serve in paramilitary or military organizations both at home and in continental Europe. Women enlisted in such services for many reasons, including a desire to escape menial or difficult labor at private employers, a simple need for income, a romantic interest in travel to France and the Mediterranean, and patriotism. Among the women who enlisted, nurses occupied a special position both for their

---

A War Nurse's Diary: Sketches from a Belgian Field Hospital (New York: Macmillan, 1918), 18–26.

talents and their professional status, and they frequently found themselves at the front lines of action. The following excerpt from a British nurse's diary recording her service in Belgium presents an immediate account not only of war, but of the important role of women in it.

By the end of the fourth week we had become accustomed to the constant influx of mangled and bleeding forms, and it was only upon the failure of our water supply that we clearly realized the proximity of the enemy, who was daily creeping nearer and nearer, as fort after fort fell, a mass of ruins and dead men. The Fort of Walaem[1] witnessed a fiercely contested battle, because, not only was it an important strategic position, but there was the reservoir which supplied the city with water. The dead British and Belgians were piled up against the walls of the reservoir, forming a ghastly barricade. The resourceful citizens immediately filled a dry-dock with the salt water of the Scheldt [River], purifying the water to a certain extent and connecting it with the main pipes. A notice was sent round that the taps could be used for half-an-hour each day when the supply for twenty-four hours must be drawn. Our pails and tubs were very limited, whilst our household consisted of over two hundred people, one hundred and seventy of whom were wounded men needing water in large quantities. The [operating] theatre alone used many gallons for sterilization.

As the reader perhaps knows, treating wounds in a home-hospital under surgically clean conditions is a very different thing from dealing with mangled and shattered flesh where the wounds are filled with mud, torn clothing and shrapnel. Often these men had received no first-aid treatment, and their wounds had remained uncovered for as long as two or three days. With few exceptions all these cases were septic. Our treatment for this, as a rule, was fomentations. This meant an endless supply of boiling water and constant renewal. On our floor we just placed a large tin wash-basin on a petrol stove and kept it boiling all the time. It sterilized the dressing, and the same water-supply did for every one and was always boiling. The first day we left off washing those white marble floors, the following days we stopped washing the patients, and we just kept that brackish water for medical purposes, soup and coffee. . . .

Walaem fell five days before the bombardment of Antwerp. During that week there was a huge explosion which filled many of the hospitals

---

[1] **Walaem**: The village of Walem, some 15 miles south of Antwerp, Belgium.

in Antwerp with burnt men. Some of our wards were full of them. The injuries were confined to their faces, heads and hands, and they were often ghastly. Some were so terribly burned that it was difficult to tell where their faces were; how they lived is a marvel to us, for no features seemed left to them. We had sometimes to force an opening where the mouth had been to insert a tube to feed them. Each man's dressing took over an hour, as even each finger had to be treated separately.

Towards the end of the first week in October a message came for all the staff to assemble in the central-hall. There our Commandant told us that the last mail boat was leaving that night, and any desirous to return to England must take the last chance. Two nurses went, and one married man.

Shortly after this another message arrived, from the Germans this time. All civilians desirous of escaping in safety must do so within the next twenty-four hours, as twenty-four hours later, at midnight, they would commence to shell the city. We never believed it, much less realized it. Already the news had spread that an Expeditionary Force was on its way to supplement the Marines and save the city. Meanwhile, things became fast and furious; there was no time to think of bombardments; it was a case of sending on all men who could possibly travel on a stretcher to make room for all who came.

Wednesday night, October 6th, as we took our usual little journey up the Boulevard to the R — 's house, we noticed solitary figures with little bags furtively hurrying along under the cover of darkness. There was no panic; each fugitive was ashamed to leave. . . .

There was a change in the R — 's house. All the handsome pile carpets had been rolled up and placed across the marble first floor to form a presumably bomb-proof shelter of the cellars. We went to our bed-room as usual and settled down to sleep. Our boulevard was a main road leading through one of the great city gates to the battle field. All day the roar of traffic, hoots of cars going at top speed, and lumbering of heavy lorries made a constant roar. Gradually the noise died down, whilst one heavy dray drawn by a horse rumbled over the paved street.

The city clock struck midnight, when simultaneously we heard a boom far away, immediately followed by a new whistling scream increasing in volume and intensity till it became the roar of a train in a tunnel. It skimmed over our heads, literally raising our hair in its passage. This ended in a large, full explosion. Then all was silence for a breathless second, — when the terrified roar of a wounded animal rent the air, like that of a great bull bellowing. A pistol shot followed, and silence ensued again. I was seized with an uncontrollable ague [trembling], whilst my friend reached out her hand and said, "Remember we are British women, not emotional continentals. We've got to keep our heads."

As we lay quite still in the darkness we became aware of stealthy movements outside. There was a soft knock at our door, and one of the boys said in broken English, "I sink you had better dress and come down to ze caves." We dressed and packed our holdalls, going down the back-stairs to the wine-vaults where carpets and arm-chairs had been placed. No sooner had we sat down than we realized that our place was beside our wounded. The dear old lady and gentleman urged us to stay, but after a hurried farewell, two of the sons took up our baggage and quickly escorted us to our hospital.

Twenty minutes at most had elapsed since the first shell fell. Shells were now falling at two minute intervals. Yet in that short space of time the whole of the third floor, about fifty wounded, had been quietly and methodically brought down on stretchers and placed along the network of underground passages. It was done in darkness because the roof of our house was glass. We quickly started in applying strong restoratives,[2] after all three floors had been removed to what we deemed was safety.

About 2.00 A. M. all the patients had been settled below, with two night nurses, and the rest of us sat on some marble stairs under a colonnade until morning. As sleep was impossible, and the noise terrific, we just started singing "Tipperary," "Dixie," and other ragtime choruses to drown the explosions and buck us all up.

When morning came there was trouble in the camp. There were no servants, just one dear old woman who worked gratuitously as cook. Even she was in tears, longing to go. There was not much chance of nursing in those narrow passages, so our Chief gave me leave to help in the kitchen. Among our men were several Tommies [British soldiers] with slight wounds; I explained the situation to them and they were fine — full of Cockney[3] jokes and humour. I sent them all to peel the vegetables for soup. We caught four noisy fowls who were intruders in our back yard, killed them and hung them up to the gymnasium poles to pluck. Each time a shell burst we just hopped inside, and when the pieces had scattered came out and went on with our job. We also collected the fragments of bread, for we felt we might be hungry before the end. I made four huge bread-puddings and put them in the oven. The Germans had those half baked puddings, likewise the four chickens!

---

[2] **restoratives**: An outdated term for life-giving or energy-giving treatments.

[3] **Cockney**: The people or culture of London's working class.

I put our escape down to the German passion for system. They shelled Antwerp methodically, block by block; fortunately our section was not the object of immediate attention, only shells that fell short dropped in our locality. . . .

It was represented to us that it was a most dangerous adventure to try to escape, but that we must save some of the more seriously wounded. Who would volunteer to attend the patients? My friend and I were standing near, so we offered. Quickly the men were packed in, as the shells fell thicker and nearer. Just at the last minute I remembered one of our patients who came in with the first batch. He was precious because he owed his life to us. When those first one hundred and seventy arrived five weeks before he was laid aside, white and pulseless, as too far gone to operate upon. We gave him restorative injections, and at last felt a feeble flutter. Running to the theatre, we begged the surgeons to give him a chance.

There was a great gash beneath his chest, and his stomach was literally lying outside of him, ripped open and covered with mud. He had been lying in that condition out on a field for two days, and according to all human calculations should have died long ago. When we asked the surgeon to operate he justly said, "We have more patients to treat than we can really get through. Those will probably live after, but it is wasting precious time to operate on your man." Finally we prevailed. They operated on him. For three days he was to have nothing by mouth, not even water. Before two days were over he had grabbed his neighbour's brown bread and bolted it greedily!

Well, this is the man I wanted to save, so I ran along to a glass house which at any minute might be wiped out by a shell, and tried to drag him along. It took some time. When we got to the front door the first convoy had gone. Standing there I watched a dwelling opposite, six stories high, come clattering down like a card house. The shell just went in at the roof and out at the area-grating, first exploding in the cellar. (All Antwerp was living in the cellars.) So there was not much chance for that household. Just the dismantled skeleton of the outer walls was left.

Fetching in the wounded meant constant excursions to the front door. One of the pitiful sights was the little pet dogs that came running in, looking up with pleading eyes and wagging their tails for a welcome. Just down our street, outside a closed house, from which the occupants had flown, sat a fox terrier of good breed. He was shivering with terror, but still he guarded the house whose faithless owner had forsaken him. Just then a bomb crashed near by, I whipped him up under my arm and tied him to a table leg, meaning to adopt him. We afterwards named him "Bombe."

READING AND DISCUSSION QUESTIONS

1. According to this account, what are the nurse's most pressing concerns while living and working at the front?

2. Does the author's identity as a British citizen seem to matter in this excerpt? What about her identity as a woman? If so, how? If not, what inference can you draw from this? What would you say is the most important facet of the author's identity?

3. How does the author present the German enemy?

DOCUMENT 28-2

Correspondence of Evelyn and Fred Albright

1917

Even for the millions of civilians fortunate enough to live far from the front lines, the First World War presented dramatic interruptions to the daily lives of men and women at home. The correspondence of Evelyn and Fred Albright, two Canadian citizens, spanned the years from 1910 through 1917 and included over 550 letters. Fred, a lawyer, enlisted in 1916 and was sent to England for training in 1917. He shared vivid details of his overseas posting in letters to his wife. In letters back to her husband, Evelyn chronicled the challenges and triumphs of her life at home, including her work at Fred's law office. These excerpts show how the war touched lives far from Europe, capturing not only their individual experiences but also the Albright's great love and, following Fred's death at the Second Battle of Passchendaele, Belgium, in late October 1917, Evelyn's grief.

An Echo in My Heart: The Letters of Elnora Evelyn (Kelly) Albright and Frederick Stanley Albright, comp. and ed. Lorna Brooks, http://sites.google.com/site/echoinmy heartsite/home.

Fred to Evelyn

France
Mon evening,
Oct. 1 1917

My darling wife, —

It is one of those beautiful clear evenings which have been our almost invariable portion since coming here. By daylight saving time, which still prevails with the army in France, it is 6.30 and a soft twilight haze has followed the setting of the sun. I went outside and stretched myself out on the bank, when before I started to write, I heard the distant hum of a German aeroplane and immediately after came the order "Get under cover," so we all hurried to our dugouts and now I am sitting at the entrance to the dugout which has been my home for the past 4 days and which we are leaving tonight for a while back of the lines.

We don't rush to cover from aeroplanes because of danger but because the aircraft are out for reconnaissance and the least movement on the ground is discernable. Naturally we don't want Heine[4] to know what positions we occupy. Of course he knows this and where most of the other trenches now held by us are, both because he can see them and because a large number of them were once occupied by him. But such matters are employed to conceal the guns, dispositions of troops etc. that Fritz[5] doesn't know where our strong points are, so on every available opportunity he sends over his aeroplanes for observation purposed, just as we do over Fritz's lines.

Later.

Since writing the above we had to put on our equipment and stand to, ready to move out. But as we have a wait of no one knows how long, I am back in the dugout writing by candle light. One has to snatch such odd moments if he would write at all. I haven't written any since last Friday. . . .

I haven't had any parcels from you since about a week prior to leaving Eng. I find that papers & boxes are sent up to the front line trenches however, when possible. Several of the fellows got parcels today. It really is wonderful to think that daily mail can be delivered even to the front line trenches. Yes — and hot tea and occasionally boiled rice or potatoes.

---

[4] **Heine**: Slang for German.
[5] **Fritz**: Slang for German.

The grub here is remarkably good and there is no stint. Every night ration parties go out for the grub to the head of a narrow gauge railway about a mile away. Drinking water has to be carried rather farther. In some places it is almost impossible to get water for washing purposes at all but here we are unusually fortunate in having right at hand a spring well at the bottom of what Fritz had intended for a dugout before the water appeared.

Wed. evening, Oct 3/17

Once again my abode has changed. On Monday night we came out of the line and while the battalion is still considered as being in support we are back 4 or 5 miles — quite beyond the range of all but the largest guns — and they rarely put a shell over this way except when firing at one of our captive balloons so we feel absolutely safe here.

Though freer from danger this place is in many respects less desirable than the line. There the grub is of the best & unstinted. Here we have a piece of bread a slice of bacon & tea for breakfast. Bully beef, bread jam & cheese for dinner & mulligan bread & tea for supper. There the quarters were much more commodious & comfortable. . . . The dugout from which I last wrote was about from 4 to 5 feet in height. The ceiling & walls were all carefully timbered and planked by Fritz and it was dry & quite comfortable. Of course there were lice — they are everywhere here — but they didn't trouble much. Most of the boys have already been attacked but as far as I know I am still free.

There were a few rats which we could plainly hear in the walls & ceiling but I never saw any inside. As for our present abode it is more a hut than a dugout for it is not really underground. Made of sandbags with a roof of loose sheets of corrugated iron it is situated on the side of a steep slope facing west. The floor is of chalk clay.

Rat holes in the sand bags abound and the rodents themselves can be seen scurrying all around at any time of day or night. The night before last when I was up for a visit to the latrine I saw 2 of the night cooks out on a rat hunting expedition. One wouldn't so much mind them outside, but when they play hide and seek around and over you while you are sleeping, and even nibble at one's toes, as they did the other night to the serj. maj. [sergeant major], they may truly be considered a pest.

Monday night I left a little bread & cheese in my mess tin for morning and as a result there are now 2 holes in the canvas cover and 2 distinct dents in the tin itself where Mr. Rat's teeth endeavored to punch a hole through the metal.

As for the mansion(?) itself — it is of such dimensions that when McKenzie, Edwards & I are in at night we have to put our packs & equipment outside. During the day we reverse the process. In plain figures, its inside dimensions are nearly 5' 10" long, 4½' wide & 3½' high — quite a snug little apartment for 3. Of course we sleep with our clothes on. We use our greatcoats for bedding, and the first night we each had a blanket over us but yesterday while we were out on a working party someone relieved us of 2 and now we have only 1 blanket for the 3 of us.

Fortunately the weather is mild, although the air becomes quite chilly before morning. However I always sleep warm. I haven't slept with my clothes off — I mean my outer clothes for 10 days. When we were in the line, of course we had to keep our puttees & boots on and wear our box respirators — and were supposed to keep all equipment on. In the front line everything is worn but in the support line where I was most of the fellows slept with their equipment off.

. . . I told you the night before we left the line we got back here about 3 a.m. had something to eat & got to bed about 3.30. Then 15 of us — among whom were McK. [McKenzie], Edwards & I had to get up at 6, breakfast at 6.30 & start at 7 on a working party. We marched back to within a mile of where we had been in the line — our work was under cover & needless to say we didn't work very hard. About 3.30 we quit & marched back — arriving here about 5.30. After supper I had a rub bath, & a shave and by the time I read your letter, & one from Don [Albright], I was ready for bed. Today we were on the same work and the same place.

It takes us about 2 hours each way going and coming, & the marching is all in trenches which wind and twist and turn. Nearly all the way the bottom is covered with trench matting — ie — a walk about 2 feet wide made of small slots laid crosswise on 2" x 4" scantling. This is a great boon in wet weather but makes hard walking in dry weather.

We have just been warned for the same working party tomorrow for which I am very glad. If we didn't go on the day party we'd be on a night one, and its nicer to work in the day and have the night for sleep. Don't worry about me darling. Though my time is full and I sometimes get tired, I'm hard as nails and never felt in better health in my life. I'm never too tired to sleep or rest and I'm sure I can hold up my end with the best of them.

Do you remember Mr. Lucas who was in the 191 & was with me at Sarcee? His son was killed last Thursday night. I wish you would see or phone Mrs. Lucas and assure her that her boy didn't suffer. He was killed instantaneously by a big shell which killed 1 other and wounded 2. This was the first night we were in the line. McKenzie helped to carry him out and he is buried near here in a little cemetery where the 50th now inter all their dead. If I get time I'll write the Lucases a short letter. Anyhow I know they would appreciate your telling them what I have just written.

Oh my darling, I am so glad you have been feeling better, and that you had a good visit at Beamsville. The other fellows have come in now and we must turn in so goodnight my own darling wife.

Your Ferd.[6]

EVELYN TO FRED

Calgary,
Nov. 11 1917

Dearest Ferd: —

One year ago to-day was the Sunday when the gas was off. That was a memorable day, wasn't it? And to-day was so warm that I didn't even wear my little fur around my neck, much less carry my muff.

I took David to church this morning and Mr. and Mrs. Peters kindly brought us home. David kicked up a row, but I did not tell his parents as they would have felt very much humiliated, and I'm not sure that a spanking would have done him any good. I gave him a good talking to tonight when he was in bed. He needs a <u>very</u> firm hand, and he's just at a very saucy age.

Mr. Dagleish preached this morning about the halo on common things. It was a good enough sermon, freely interspersed with quotations from the poets, Ruskin, etc. I wonder why that stuff seems so academic to me now, whereas it used to appeal to me very much. The church was very well filled this morning and the music was good. Wilfred gave an Organ Recital yesterday afternoon, which I did not attend, but if he keeps them up all winter I hope to go often. . . .

Last night, in the night I woke up, and an utterable longing for you swept over me, and so dearest, I prayed for you, and then I went to sleep again. I had just received your letter telling me you were reading the 46th Psalm, the night we read the bad Russian news, and I read it and felt comforted. . . .

There are some things I'd like to tell Wray, yet I do not want to preach at him, and I can't say some of them without making him think we were discussing him at Beamsville, which as you very well know we were, so I had better keep my mouth shut.

---

[6] **Ferd**: Fred's pet name, often used in their correspondence.

Well dearie, I'll have a birthday this week. How funny you should think it was in October. . . .

Mr. Clarke told Miss Playter she was to get $40 after she had been there two months, the same as they gave me, but I was there 5 months before they gave me $40. And if she gets $40, then why shouldn't I get what Fitch, Roy and Bryenton have been getting? You don't think me mercenary, do you dear? Of course, I know I'm not worth very much to the office just now, but that's not my fault; I'll work if I get it to do.

I had a good story to tell you, but I've forgotten what it was. Maybe I'll remember it to tell you tomorrow. Goodnight dearest. I'm going up to get in bed now, and I'll write to my parents there. You seem far away tonight dearest. I wonder why. You are ever uppermost in my thoughts.

Your wife.

Evelyn to Fred, After His Death in Late October

Taber, Alta

Nov. 23, 1917

Dearest: —

It is not yet two weeks since I wrote my last letter to you, not two weeks since I read that awful telegram that told me you were gone from me.

I suppose it seems silly for me to write to you, but if you know, you'll understand, and nobody else need know. But it has come to me that time might dim your image and the knowledge of your dear companionship, and I cannot bear to think of that. Then too, my darling, oh my darling, I sometimes cannot believe that you are gone, and I go on pretending as I have ever since you went away last March, that you were coming home again. And if you should — why then you'd be glad of a link between the times. It is so easy, sweetheart, to lose myself in dreaming, for whenever hard unpleasant things have come, I have always made believe things were as I would have them. But in this case, the coming back to Earth is hard.

I think it has been like this, sweetheart. I could not, would not face the thought that you would not come back: I interpreted those psalms we read together, as meaning that you would be kept safe from accident, danger and death. When I knew that you were in the thick of things, I went calmly to sleep at night, believing that you were in God's hands and that He would keep you safe, for I could not, and do not yet believe that it is His will that any of you should fall. Some of the time, while I so calmly slept and went about my work, you were lying dead Dead! Oh my darling, as I have so often called you — the light of my life.

I have thought of late dear one, that I did not fully realize what it meant to you to go. I was so filled with my own grief, with the thought of my loneliness, and with the dread of what you would have to face, that I did not fully realize what it meant to you to give up all you did and to leave me, fearing that you might never come back. You have always said I wrote cheerful letters; I am glad if you thought they were, for I tried to make them so for you had enough to bear, without me making your lot harder.

The woman is coming up to sweep, so I'll stop. But my dear one, it almost seems as if you'll read this some day. Or is it that you are reading it over my shoulder as I write? In any case, you know I adore you, my sweetheart and my friend. Oh darling, I shall try to live on cheerfully and well, but it seems that I am like a tree, half killed my [sic] lightning. Such a tree, I suppose is not expected to give the shade of a whole one — but the question always comes, why should it have been marred and blighted? Do you know now?

Your wife, for wherever you are, my darling, I shall always be that.

READING AND DISCUSSION QUESTIONS

1. From the tone of their letters, how frequent do you imagine contact was between Fred and Evelyn? How might the frequency of contact affect the war experiences of those at the front and those at home?

2. What does the correspondence reveal about Evelyn's life without her husband? What had changed, and how had she adjusted to her new circumstances?

3. What is the role of religion in these letters? When is it mentioned, and how?

DOCUMENT 28-3

VLADIMIR ILYICH LENIN
All Power to the Soviets!
1917

Vladimir Ilyich Ulyanov (1870–1924), better known by his nom de guerre Lenin, was a central intellectual and political force behind the uprisings that made up the Russian Revolution (1905–1917). Following years of exile and a triumphant return to Russia with the assistance of the German government, Lenin capitalized on the fall of the tsar by pushing for further revolution under the guidance of his Bolshevik faction of what would become the Russian Communist Party. In the months leading to the October 1917 revolution and Bolshevik power, Lenin took control of the popular newspaper Pravda *(Truth) and used its editorial pages to powerful effect. The speech reproduced here demonstrates both the political infighting that marked the Russian Revolution and Lenin's relentless use of propaganda to outmaneuver his opponents.*

"Drive nature out of the door and she will rush back through the window." It seems that the Socialist-Revolutionary and Menshevik parties[7] have to "learn" this simple truth time and again by their own experience. They under took to be "revolutionary democrats" and found themselves in the shoes of revolutionary democrats — they are now forced to draw the conclusions which every revolutionary democrat must draw.

Democracy is the rule of the majority. As long as the will of the majority was not clear, as long as it was possible to make it out to be unclear,

---

"All Power to the Soviets!" *Pravda*, no. 99 (July 18, 1917). Republished in *Lenin Collected Works*, 45 vols. (Moscow: Progress, 1977), 25:155–156.

[7] **Socialist-Revolutionary and Menshevik parties**: Russian political factions during the Russian Revolutions. The Mensheviks, with the Bolsheviks, made up the Russian Marxist Party; the Mensheviks were more inclusive and favored more compromise than did their Bolshevik counterparts. They were banned by the Bolsheviks in 1921. The Socialist-Revolutionary Party emphasized rural peasants more than either wing of the Russian Marxists did; despite success at the polls, they were outmaneuvered by the Bolsheviks and largely dissolved.

at least with a grain of plausibility, the people were offered a counter-revolutionary bourgeois government disguised as "democratic." But this delay could not last long. During the several months that have passed since February 27[8] the will of the majority of the workers and peasants, of the overwhelming majority of the country's population, has become clear in more than a general sense. Their will has found expression in mass organisations — the Soviets of Workers', Soldiers' and Peasants' Deputies.

How, then, can anyone oppose the transfer of all power in the state to the Soviets? Such opposition means nothing but renouncing democracy! It means no more no less than imposing on the people a government which *admittedly* can neither come into being nor hold its ground *democratically*, i.e., as a result of truly free, truly popular elections.

It is a fact, strange as it may seem at first sight, that the Socialist-Revolutionaries and Mensheviks have *forgotten* this perfectly simple, perfectly obvious and palpable truth. Their position is so false, and they are so badly confused and bewildered, that they are unable to "recover" this truth they have lost. Following the elections in Petrograd[9] and in Moscow, the convocation of the All-Russia Peasant Congress, and the Congress of Soviets,[10] the classes and parties throughout Russia have shown what they stand for so clearly and specifically that people who have not gone mad or deliberately got themselves into a mess and simply cannot have any illusions on this score.

To tolerate the Cadet Ministers or the Cadet government or Cadet policies[11] means challenging democrats and democracy. This is the source of the political crises since February 27, and this also the source of the shakiness and vacillation of our government system. At every turn, daily and even hourly, appeals are being made to the people's revolutionary spirit and to their democracy on behalf of the most authoritative government institutions and congresses. Yet the government's policies in particular, are all departures from revolutionary principles, and breaches in democracy.

This sort of thing will not do.

It is inevitable that a situation like the present should show elements of instability now for one reason, now for another. And it is not exactly a

---

[8] **February 27**: This date marked the initial revolution that toppled the Russian tsar and brought the Provisional Government to power.

[9] **Petrograd**: Later Leningrad, and now St. Petersburg.

[10] **All-Russia Peasant Congress . . . Congress of Soviets**: Meetings in 1918 that codified and strengthened Bolshevik control of the Russian government.

[11] **Cadet Ministers . . . Cadet policies**: Members of the Constitutional Democratic (Konstitutionnaya Demokraticheskaya) Party prominent in the Provisional Government.

clever policy of jib. Things are moving by fits and starts towards a point where power will be transferred to the Soviets, which is what our Party called for long ago.

READING AND DISCUSSION QUESTIONS

1. What is the main point of Lenin's speech, and how does he argue his point?

2. According to Lenin, who are the opponents to his call for Soviet power?

3. How does Lenin characterize those who are not directly in line with his thinking? To what end?

VIEWPOINTS

Zionist, German, and Japanese Views on the End of WWI

DOCUMENT 28-4

THE ZIONIST ORGANIZATION

Memorandum to the Peace Conference in Versailles: On the Establishment of a Jewish State in Palestine

February 3, 1919

Zionists who had long sought to establish a Jewish state in the Middle East saw the Paris Peace Conference as an opportunity to gain support for their quest. Already backed by Great Britain, Zionist leaders recognized that the Allied powers would be addressing the redistribution of colonies around the globe and the future of the Middle East. Members of the Zionist Organization — an umbrella organization that merged Zionist groups in Europe and

David Hunter Miller, *My Diary at the Conference of Paris* (New York: Appeal Printing, 1924), 5:15–29.

elsewhere — and their Arab counterparts were concerned about what this might mean for them, and Jewish leaders drafted a memo that made their case to the Allies for the creation of a Jewish state in Palestine.

The Zionist Organization respectfully submits the following draft resolutions for the consideration of the Peace Conference:

1. The High Contracting Parties recognize the historic title of the Jewish people to Palestine and the right of the Jews to reconstitute in Palestine their National Home.
2. The boundaries of Palestine shall be as declared in the Schedule annexed hereto.
3. The sovereign possession of Palestine shall be vested in the League of Nations and the Government entrusted to Great Britain as mandatary of [mandated by] the League.
4. (Provision to be inserted relating to the application in Palestine of such of the general conditions attached to mandates as are suitable to the case.)
5. The mandate shall be subject also to the following special conditions:
    I. Palestine shall be placed under such political, administrative, and economic conditions as will secure the establishment there of the Jewish National Home and ultimately render possible the creation of an autonomous Commonwealth, it being clearly understood that nothing shall be done which may prejudice the civil and religious rights of existing non-Jewish communities in Palestine or the rights and political status enjoyed by Jews in any other country.
    II. To this end the Mandatary Power shall *inter alia* ["among other things"]
        a. Promote Jewish immigration and close settlement on the land, the established rights of the present non-Jewish population being equitably safeguarded.
        b. Accept the co-operation in such measures of a Council representative of the Jews of Palestine and of the world that may be established for the development of the Jewish National Home in Palestine and entrust the organization of Jewish education to such Council.
        c. On being satisfied that the constitution of such Council precludes the making of private profit, offer to the Council in

priority any concession for public works or for the development of natural resources which may be found desirable to grant.

III. The Mandatary Power shall encourage the widest measure of self-government for localities practicable in the conditions of the country.

IV. There shall be for ever the fullest freedom of religious worship for all creeds in Palestine. There shall be no discrimination among the inhabitants with regard to citizenship and civil rights, on the grounds of religion or of race.

V. (Provision to be inserted relating to the control of the Holy Places.)

THE BOUNDARIES OF PALESTINE SCHEDULE

The boundaries of Palestine shall follow the general lines set out below:

Starting on the North at a point on the Mediterranean Sea in the vicinity of Sidon and following the watersheds of the foothills of the Lebanon as far as Jisr El Karaon, thence to El Bire, following the dividing line between the two basins of the Wadi El Korn and the Wadi Et Teim thence in a southerly direction following the dividing line between the Eastern and Western slopes of the Hermon, to the vicinity West of Beit Jenn, thence Eastward following the northern watersheds of the Nahr Mughaniye close to and west of the Hedjaz Railway.

In the East a line close to and West of the Hedjaz Railway terminating in the Gulf of Akaba.

In the South a frontier to be agreed upon with the Egyptian Government. In the West the Mediterranean Sea.

The details of the delimitations, or any necessary adjustments of detail, shall be settled by a Special Commission on which there shall be Jewish representation.

STATEMENT

The Historic Title

The claims of the Jews with regard to Palestine rest upon the following main considerations:

1. The land is the historic home of the Jews; there they achieved their greatest development, from that center, through their agency, there emanated spiritual and moral influences of supreme value to mankind. By violence they were driven from Palestine, and through the ages they have never ceased to cherish the longing and the hope of a return.

2. In some parts of the world, and particularly in Eastern Europe, the conditions of life of millions of Jews are deplorable. Forming often a congested population, denied the opportunities which would make a healthy development possible, the need of fresh outlets is urgent, both for their own sake and in the interest of the population of other races, among whom they dwell. Palestine would offer one such outlet. To the Jewish masses it is the country above all others in which they would most wish to cast their lot. By the methods of economic development to which we shall refer later, Palestine can be made now as it was in ancient times, the home of a prosperous population many times as numerous as that which now inhabits it.

3. But Palestine is not large enough to contain more than a proportion of the Jews of the world. The greater part of the fourteen millions or more scattered through all countries must remain in their present localities, and it will doubtless be one of the cares of the Peace Conference to ensure for them, wherever they have been oppressed, as for all peoples, equal rights and humane conditions. A Jewish National Home in Palestine will, however, be of high value to them also. Its influence will permeate the Jewries of the world: it will inspire these millions, hitherto often despairing, with a new hope; it will hold out before their eyes a higher standard; it will help to make them even more useful citizens in the lands in which they dwell.

4. Such a Palestine would be of value also to the world at large, whose real wealth consists in the healthy diversities of its civilizations.

5. Lastly the land itself needs redemption. Much of it is left desolate. Its present condition is a standing reproach. Two things are necessary for that redemption — a stable and enlightened Government, and an addition to the present population which shall be energetic, intelligent, devoted to the country, and backed by the large financial resources that are indispensable for development. Such a population the Jews alone can supply.

Inspired by these ideas, Jewish activities particularly during the last thirty years have been directed to Palestine within the measure that the Turkish administrative system allowed. Some millions of pounds sterling have been spent in the country particularly in the foundation of Jewish agricultural settlements. Those settlements have been for the most part highly successful.

With enterprise and skill the Jews have adopted modern scientific methods and have shown themselves to be capable agriculturalists. Hebrew has been revived as a living language, it is the medium of instruction in the schools and the tongue is in daily use among the rising generation. The foundations of a Jewish University have been laid at Jerusalem and considerable funds have been contributed for the creation of its building and for its endowment. Since the British occupation, the Zionist Organization has expended in Palestine approximately £50,000 a month upon relief, education, and sanitation. To promote the future development of the country great sums will be needed for drainage, irrigation, roads, railways, harbors, and public works of all kinds, as well as for land settlement and house building. Assuming a political settlement under which the establishment of a Jewish National Home in Palestine is assured the Jews of the world will make every effort to provide the vast sums of money that will be needed. . . .

[Here follow a recital of the Balfour Declaration[12] and of its endorsement by the French foreign minister and reference to support of Zionism and the Balfour Declaration by other allied governments.]

Great Britain as Mandatary of the League of Nations

We ask that Great Britain shall act as Mandatary of the League of Nations for Palestine. The selection of Great Britain as Mandatary is urged on the ground that this is the wish of the Jews of the world and the League of Nations in selecting a Mandatary will follow as far as possible, the popular wish of the people concerned.

The preference on the part of the Jews for a British Trusteeship is unquestionably the result of the peculiar relationship of England to the Jewish Palestinian problem. The return of the Jews to Zion has not only been a remarkable feature in English literature, but in the domain of statecraft it has played its part, beginning with the readmission of the Jews under Cromwell.[13] It manifested itself particularly in the 19th century in the instructions given to British Consular representatives in the Orient

---

[12] **Balfour Declaration**: The 1917 endorsement of a Jewish homeland in Palestine by the British government.

[13] **readmission of the Jews . . . Cromwell**: In 1290, under King Edward I, Jews were cast out of England. In 1656, during his rule as Lord Protector of the Commonwealth of England, Scotland, and Ireland (1653–1658), Oliver Cromwell allowed them to return, in part due to his religious tolerance and in part to stimulate the British economy.

after the Damascus Incident;[14] in the various Jewish Palestinian projects suggested by English non-Jews prior to 1881; in the letters of endorsement and support given by members of the Royal Family and Officers of the Government to Lawrence Oliphant and finally, in the three consecutive acts which definitely associated Great Britain with Zionism in the minds of the Jews viz. — the El Arish offer in 1901; the East African offer in 1903, and lastly the British Declaration in favor of a Jewish National Home in Palestine in 1917.[15] Moreover, the Jews who have gained political experience in many lands under a great variety of governmental systems, wholeheartedly appreciate the advanced and liberal policies adopted by Great Britain in her modern colonial administration. . . .

[Here follows an account of the selection of Great Britain as mandatary power by the American Jewish Congress and a conference of Palestine Jews at Jaffa.]

BOUNDARIES

The boundaries above outlined are what we consider essential for the necessary economic foundation of the country. Palestine must have its natural outlets to the seas and the control of its rivers and their headwaters. The boundaries are sketched with the general economic needs and historic traditions of the country in mind, factors which necessarily must also be considered by the Special Commission in fixing the definite boundary lines. This Commission will bear in mind that it is highly desirable, in the interests of economical administration[,] that the geographical area of Palestine should be as large as possible so that it may eventually contain a large and thriving population which could more easily bear the burdens of modern civilized government than a small country with a necessary limitation of inhabitants.

The economic life of Palestine, like that of every other semi-arid country depends on the available water supply. It is, therefore, of vital importance not only to secure all water resources already feeding the country, but also to be able to conserve and control them at their sources.

The Hermon[16] is Palestine's real "Father of Waters" and cannot be severed from it without striking at the very root of its economic life. The

---

[14] **Damascus Incident**: In 1840, the Jews of Damascus were unjustly accused of ritual murder and imprisoned. England spearheaded a successful effort to rescue them.

[15] **various Jewish Palestinian projects . . . 1917**: Events in which England lent its support to the establishment of a Jewish homeland.

[16] **the Hermon**: A mountain range in Palestine with a vast waterfall at its base.

Hermon not only needs reforestation but also other works before it can again adequately serve as the water reservoir of the country. It must therefore be wholly under the control of those who will most willingly as well as most adequately restore it to its maximum utility. Some international arrangement must be made whereby the riparian rights of the people dwelling south of the Litani River may be fully protected. Properly cared for these head waters can be made to serve in the development of the Lebanon as well as of Palestine.

The fertile plains east of the Jordan, since the earliest Biblical times, have been linked economically and politically with the land west of the Jordan. The country which is now very sparsely populated, in Roman times supported a great population. It could now serve admirably for colonization on a large scale. A just regard for the economic needs of Palestine and Arabia demands that free access to the Hedjaz Railway throughout its length be accorded both Governments.

An intensive development of the agriculture and other opportunities of Transjordania make it imperative that Palestine shall have access to the Red Sea and an opportunity of developing good harbors on the Gulf of Akaba. Akaba, it will be recalled, was the terminus of an important trade route of Palestine from the days of Solomon onwards. The ports developed in the Gulf of Akaba should be free ports through which the commerce of the Hinterland may pass on the same principle which guides us in suggesting that free access be given to the Hedjaz Railway.

PROPOSALS TO THE MANDATARY POWER

In connection with the Government to be set up by the Mandatary of the League of Nations until such time as the people of Palestine shall be prepared to undertake the establishment of representative and responsible Government proposals will be made in due course to the Mandatary Power to the following effect:

1. In any instrument establishing the constitution of Palestine the Declarations of the Peace Conference shall be recited as forming an integral part of that constitution.
2. The Jewish people shall be entitled to fair representation in the executive and legislative bodies and in the selection of public and civil servants. In giving such representation the Mandatary Power shall consult the Jewish Council hereinafter mentioned.

    Neither law nor custom shall preclude the appointment of a citizen of Palestine as chief of the executive.

3. That in encouraging the self government of localities the Mandatary Power shall secure the maintenance by local communities of proper standards of administration in matters of education, communal, or regional activities. In granting or enlarging local autonomy regard shall be had to the readiness and ability of the community to attain such standards. Local autonomous communities shall be empowered and encouraged to combine and cooperate for common purposes.

4. Education without distinction of race shall be assisted from public funds.

5. Hebrew shall be one of the official languages of Palestine and shall be employed in all documents, decrees, and announcements and on all stamps, coins, and notes issued by the Government.

6. The Jewish Sabbath and Holy Days shall be recognized as legal days of rest.

7. All inhabitants continuing to reside in Palestine who on the ____ day of ____, 19____, have their domicile in Palestine, except those who elect in writing within six months from such date to retain their foreign citizenship, shall become citizens of Palestine, and they and all persons in Palestine or naturalized under the laws of Palestine after the ____ day of ____, 19____, shall be citizens thereof and entitled to the protection of the Mandatary Power on behalf of the Government of Palestine.

Land Commission

Recognizing that the general progress of Palestine must begin with the reform of the conditions governing land tenure and settlement, the Mandatary Power shall appoint a Commission (upon which the Jewish Council shall have representation) with power:

a. To make survey of the land and to schedule all lands that may be made available for close settlement, intensive cultivation, and public use.

b. To propose measures for determining and registering titles of ownership of land.

c. To propose measures for supervising transactions in land with a view of preventing land speculation.

d. To propose measures for the close settlement, intensive cultivation, and public use of land, where necessary by compulsory purchase at a fair pre-war price and further by making available all waste lands unoccupied and inadequately cultivated lands or lands without legal owners, and state lands.

e. To propose measures for the taxation and the tenure of land and in general any progressive measures in harmony with the policy of making the land available for close settlement and intensive cultivation.

f. To propose measures whereby the Jewish Council may take over all lands available for close settlement and intensive cultivation.

g. In all such measures the established rights of the present population shall be equitably safeguarded.

THE JEWISH COUNCIL FOR PALESTINE

1. A Jewish Council for Palestine shall be elected by a Jewish Congress representative of the Jews of Palestine and of the entire world, which shall be convoked in Jerusalem on or before the First day of January, 1920, or as soon thereafter as possible, by the Provisional Jewish Council hereinafter mentioned.

    The Jewish Congress shall determine its functions as well as the constitution and functions of the Jewish Council in conformity with the purpose and spirit of the Declarations of the Peace Conference and of the powers conferred by the Mandatary Power upon the Jewish Council.

2. The Jewish Council shall be recognized as a legal entity and shall have power:

    a. To co-operate and consult with and to assist the Government of Palestine in any and all matters affecting the Jewish people in Palestine and in all such cases to be and to act as the representative of the Jewish people.

    b. To participate in the development and administration of immigration, close land settlement, credit facilities, public works, services, and enterprises, and every other form of activity conducive to the development of the country. The organization of Jewish education to be entrusted to such Council.

    c. To acquire and hold Real Estate.

    d. To acquire and exercise concessions for public works and the development of natural resources.

    e. With the consent of the Jewish inhabitants concerned or their accredited representatives, to assess such inhabitants for the purpose of stimulating and maintaining education, communal, charitable, and other public institutions (including the Jewish Council) and other activities primarily concerned with the welfare of the Jewish people in Palestine.

    f.   With the approval of the Mandatary Power and upon such terms and conditions as the Mandatary Power may prescribe, to administer the immigration laws of Palestine in so far as they affect Jewish immigration.

    g.   With the approval of the Mandatary Power, to issue bonds, debentures, or other obligations, the proceeds of any or all of which to be expended by the Jewish Council for the benefit of the Jewish people or for the development of Palestine.

    h.   The Jewish Council shall hold all of its property and income in trust for the benefit of the Jewish people.

3.   A provisional Jewish Council of representatives of the Zionist Organization, of the Jewish population in Palestine, and of such other approved Jewish organizations as are willing to co-operate in the development of a Jewish Palestine shall be formed forthwith by the Zionist Organization. Such Provisional Jewish Council shall exercise all of the powers and perform all of the duties of the Jewish Council until such time as the Jewish Council shall be formally constituted by the Jewish Congress.

4.   Finally when in the opinion of the Mandatary Power, the inhabitants of Palestine shall be able to undertake the establishment of Representative and Responsible Government, such steps shall be taken as will permit the establishment of such government through the exercise of a democratic franchise, without regard to race or faith; and the inhabitants of Palestine under such government, shall continue to enjoy equal civil and political rights as citizens irrespective of race or faith.

READING AND DISCUSSION QUESTIONS

1.   How does the Zionist Organization justify its claims to a portion of Palestinian land as the Jewish National Home?

2.   How do the authors of this memorandum seek to address the fears that the creation of a Jewish homeland might inspire in Palestinians and others?

3.   According to the Zionists, what is the symbolic importance for Jews everywhere of a national homeland?

4.   Why do the Zionists want Great Britain to oversee this operation as the "Mandatary Power"?

DOCUMENT 28-5

GERMAN DELEGATION TO THE
PARIS PEACE CONFERENCE
On the Conditions of Peace
October 1919

The Treaty of Versailles, signed at the 1919 Paris Peace Conference, formally brought World War I to an end and set the conditions for peace. Orchestrated by the Allied powers — the United States, Great Britain, and France — the treaty blamed the war on Germany and ordered it to pay $33 billion in repa-rations, cede all of its colonies, dismantle its air force, and greatly reduce other military operations. It also established the League of Nations as an international peacekeeping organization. Russia did not attend the confer-ence, and Germany — the nation most impacted by the treaty — was not permitted to contribute to the negotiations. Fearing invasion, Germany ulti-mately signed the treaty despite continued protests.

Although President Wilson, in his speech of October 20th, 1916, has acknowledged that "no single fact caused the war, but that in the last analy-sis the whole European system is in a deeper sense responsible for the war, with its combination of alliances and understandings, a complicated tex-ture of intrigues and espionage that unfailingly caught the whole family of nations in its meshes,". . . Germany is to acknowledge that Germany and her allies are responsible for all damages which the enemy Governments or their subjects have incurred by her and her allies' aggression. . . . Apart from the consideration that there is no incontestable legal foundation for the obligation for reparation imposed upon Germany, the amount of such compensation[17] is to be determined by a commission nominated solely by Germany's enemies, Germany taking no part. . . . The commis-sion is plainly to have power to administer Germany like the estate of a bankrupt.

"Comments of the German Delegation to the Paris Peace Conference on the Condi-tions of Peace, Oct., 1919," in *International Conciliation*, no. 143 (October 1919).

[17] **amount of such compensation:** A reparations commission appointed by the Peace Conference determined the final sum to be $33 billion in 1921.

As there are innate rights of man, so there are innate rights of nations. The inalienable fundamental right of every state is the right of self-preservation and self-determination. With this fundamental right the demand here made upon Germany is incompatible. Germany must promise to pay an indemnity, the amount of which at present is not even stated. The German rivers are to be placed under the control of an international body upon which Germany's delegates are always to be but the smallest minority. Canals and railroads are to be built on German territory at the discretion of foreign authorities.

These few instances show that that is not the just peace we were promised, not the peace "the very principle of which," according to a word of President Wilson, "is equality and the common participation in a common benefit. . . ."

In such a peace the solidarity of human interests, which was to find its expression in a League of Nations, would have been respected. How often Germany has been given the promise that this League of Nations would unite the belligerents, conquerors as well as conquered, in a permanent system of common rights! . . .

But in contradiction to them, the Covenant of the League of Nations has been framed without the cooperation of Germany. Nay, still more. Germany does not even stand on the list of those States that have been invited to join the League of Nations. . . . What the treaty of peace proposes to establish, is rather a continuance of the present hostile coalition which does not deserve the name of "League of Nations." . . . The old political system based on force and with its tricks and rivalries will thus continue to thrive!

Again and again the enemies of Germany have assured the whole world that they did not aim at the destruction of Germany. . . .

In contradiction to this, the peace document shows that Germany's position as a world power is to be utterly destroyed. The Germans abroad are deprived of the possibility of keeping up their old relations in foreign countries and of regaining for Germany a share in world commerce, while their property, which has up to the present been confiscated and liquidated, is being used for reparation instead of being restored to them. . . .

In this war, a new fundamental law has arisen which the statesmen of all belligerent peoples have again and again acknowledged to be their aim: the right of self-determination. To make it possible for all nations to put this privilege into practice was intended to be one achievement of the war. . . .

Neither the treatment described above of the inhabitants of the Saar region[18] as accessories to the [coal] pits nor the public form of consulting the population in the districts of Eupen, Malmédy, and Prussian Moresnet[19] — which, moreover, shall not take place before they have been put under Belgian sovereignty — comply in the least with such a solemn recognition of the right of self-determination.

The same is also true with regard to Alsace-Lorraine. If Germany has pledged herself "to right the wrong of 1871," this does not mean any renunciation of the right of self-determination of the inhabitants of Alsace-Lorraine. A cession of the country without consulting the population would be a new wrong, if for no other reason, because it would be inconsistent with a recognized principle of peace.

On the other hand, it is incompatible with the idea of national self-determination for two and one-half million Germans to be torn away from their native land against their own will. By the proposed demarcation of the boundary, unmistakably German territories are disposed of in favor of their Polish neighbors. Thus, from the Central Silesian districts of Guhrau and Militsch certain portions are to be wrenched away, in which, beside 44,900 Germans, reside at the utmost 3,700 Poles. . . .

This disrespect of the right of self-determination is shown most grossly in the fact that Danzig[20] is to be separated from the German Empire and made a free state. Neither historical rights nor the present ethnographical conditions of ownership of the Polish people can have any weight as compared with the German past and the German character of that city. . . . Likewise the cession of the commercial town of Memel, which is to be exacted from Germany, is in no way consistent with the right of self-determination. The same may be said with reference to the fact that millions of Germans in German-Austria are to be denied the union with Germany which they desire and that, further, millions of Germans dwelling along our frontiers are to be forced to remain part of the newly created Czecho-Slovakian State.

---

[18] **inhabitants of the Saar region**: After fifteen years, Saar inhabitants would vote in a plebiscite to decide if they would stay under the administration of a League of Nations commission or become part of France or Germany. In 1935, they voted to join Germany.

[19] **Prussian Moresnet**: Moresnet was annexed outright by Belgium. In Eupen and Malmédy, those who objected to transferring the areas to Belgium could sign their names in a public registry. Both areas became Belgian.

[20] **Danzig**: Danzig was administered by the League of Nations.

Even as regards that part of the national territory that is to be left to Germany, the promised right of self-determination is not observed. A Commission for the execution of the indemnity shall be the highest instance for the whole State. Our enemies claim to have fought for the great aim of the democratization of Germany. To be sure, the outcome of the war has delivered us from our former authorities, but instead of them we shall have in exchange a foreign, dictatorial power whose aim can and must be only to exploit the working power of the German people for the benefit of the creditor states.[21] . . .

The fact that this is an age in which economic relations are on a world scale, requires the political organization of the civilized world. The German Government agrees with the Governments of the Allied and Associated Powers in the conviction that the horrible devastation caused by this war requires the establishment of a new world order, an order which shall insure the "effective authority of the principles of international law," and "just and honorable relations between the nations." . . .

There is no evidence of these principles in the peace document which has been laid before us. Expiring world theories, emanating from imperialistic and capitalistic tendencies, celebrate in it their last horrible triumph. As opposed to these views, which have brought unspeakable disaster upon the world, we appeal to the innate sense of right of men and nations, under whose token the English State developed, the Dutch People freed itself, the North American nation established its independence, France shook off absolutism. The bearers of such hallowed traditions cannot deny this right to the German people, that now for the first time has acquired in its internal polities the possibility of living in harmony with its free will based on law.

READING AND DISCUSSION QUESTIONS

1. What does the German delegation say is the real cause of the war?
2. What does the delegation mean when it invokes the "innate rights of nations"?

---

[21] **Commission for the execution . . . states**: After the Germans fell behind in their payments in 1923, the French-controlled reparations commission sent French, Belgian, and Italian technicians into Germany's Ruhr region to collect coal to make up for the delinquent payments.

3. How does the peace proposed by the treaty differ from that which Germany expected and says it was promised, particularly by Wilson?

4. According to the Germans, in what ways does the treaty violate the right of self-determination?

DOCUMENT 28-6

KONOE FUMIMARO

Against a Pacifism Centered on England and America

1918

Konoe Fumimaro (1891–1945) held a range of political and diplomatic positions in modern Japan, including three terms as prime minister. As a member of the delegation to the Paris Peace Conference in 1918, Konoe argued for the inclusion of a "racial equality clause" in the charter of the League of Nations, a proposal that won majority support but was defeated through lack of support from Woodrow Wilson and active opposition from member states of the British Empire, such as Australia. Konoe's outspoken argument here, written before his departure for the Paris conference, foreshadows Japanese nationalist rhetoric against Anglo-British power during the Second World War.

In my view, the European war has been a conflict between established powers and powers not yet established, a conflict between countries that found upholding the status quo convenient and countries that found overthrowing the status quo convenient. The countries that found upholding the status quo convenient clamored for peace, while the countries that found overthrowing the status quo convenient cried out for war. Pacifism does not always serve justice and humanism, and militarism does not always violate justice and humanism. All depends on the nature of the status quo. If the prewar status quo was the best possible and was consonant with justice and humanism, he who would destroy it is the enemy of justice and humanism; but if the status quo did not meet the criteria of justice

---

Sources of Japanese Tradition, ed. Wm. Theodore de Bary, Carol Gluck, and Arthur E. Tiedemann, 2 vols. (New York: Columbia University Press, 2006), 2:291–293.

and humanism, its destroyer is not necessarily the enemy of justice and humanism. By the same token, the pacifist countries that would uphold this status quo are not necessarily qualified to pride themselves on being the champions of justice and humanity.

Although England and America may have regarded Europe's prewar status as ideal, an impartial third party cannot acknowledge it to have been ideal in terms of justice and humanism. As the colonial history of England and France attests, they long ago occupied the less civilized regions of the world, made them into colonies, and had no scruples about monopolizing them for their own profit. Therefore not only Germany but all late-developing countries were in the position of having no land to seize and being unable to find any room for expansion. This state of affairs contravenes the principle of equal opportunity for all humanity, jeopardizes all nations' equal right to survival, and is a gross violation of justice and humanity. Germany's wish to overthrow this order was quite justified; the means it chose, however, were unfair and immoderate, and because they were based on militarism, with its emphasis on armed might, Germany received the world's opprobrium. Nevertheless, as a Japanese, I cannot help feeling deep sympathy for what Germany has to do.

. . . At the coming peace conference, in joining the League of Nations Japan must insist at the very least, that repudiation of economic imperialism and nondiscriminatory treatment of Orientals and Caucasians be agreed upon from the start. Militarism is not the only thing injurious to justice and humanism. Although the world has been saved from the smoke of gunpowder and the hail of bullets by Germany's defeat, military might is not all that threatens nations' equal right to survival. We must realize that there is invasion through money, conquest through wealth. Just as we repudiate military imperialism, so in the same spirit we should naturally repudiate economic imperialism, which seeks to profit by monopolizing enormous capital and abundant natural resources and suppressing other nations' free growth without recourse to arms. I cannot avoid grave misgivings as to how far economic imperialism can be repudiated at the coming peace conference, led as it is by England and America, which I fear will unsheathe the sword of their economic imperialism after the war.

If we cannot subdue this rampant economic imperialism at the peace conference, England and America, which have profited most from the war, will promptly unify the world under their economic dominance and will rule the world, using the League of Nations and arms limitations to fix the status quo that serves their purpose. How will other countries endure this? Deprived of arms to express their revulsion and indignation, they will have no choice but to follow England and America, bleating in their wake like a flock of meek sheep. England has lost no time in trumpeting a policy of self-sufficiency, and many are advocating that other countries be denied access to its colonies. Such are the contradictions between what England and America say and what they do. This, indeed, is why I am wary of those who glorify England and America. If such a policy is carried out, needless to say it would be a great economic blow to Japan. Japan is limited in territory, [is] poor in natural resources, and has a small population and thus a meager market for manufactured products. If England closed off its colonies, how would we be able to assure the nation's secure survival? In such a case, the need to ensure its survival would compel Japan to attempt to overthrow the status quo as Germany did before the war. If this is the fate awaiting all late-developing countries with little territory and no colonies, not only for the sake of Japan but for the sake of establishing the equal right to life of all nations of the world on the basis of justice and humanism, we must do away with economic imperialism and see that countries do not monopolize their colonies but accord other countries equal use of them both as markets for manufactured products and as suppliers of natural resources.

The next thing that the Japanese, especially, should insist upon is the elimination of discrimination between Caucasians and Orientals. There is no need to dwell on the fact that the United States, along with the English colonies of Australia and Canada, opens its doors to Caucasians but looks down on the Japanese and on Orientals in general and rejects them. This is something at which the Japanese have long chafed. Not only are Orientals barred from employment and forbidden to lease houses and farmland, but still worse, it is reported that in some places an Oriental wishing to spend the night at a hotel is required to have a Caucasian guarantor. This is a grave humanitarian problem that no defender of justice, Oriental or otherwise, should overlook.

At the coming peace conference, we must see that the English and Americans show deep remorse for their past sins and change their arrogant and insulting attitude, and we must insist, from the standpoint of justice and humanism, that they revise all laws that call for discriminatory treatment of Orientals, including of course rescinding immigration restrictions against Orientals. I believe that the coming peace conference will be the great test of whether the human race can bring itself to reconstruct a world based on justice and humanism. If Japan does not rashly endorse a pacifism centered on England and America but steadfastly asserts its position from the standpoint of justice and humanism in the true sense, it will long be celebrated in history as the champion of justice.

READING AND DISCUSSION QUESTIONS

1. What are Konoe's arguments against British and American pacifism? How does he describe the "status quo" supported by this pacifism?

2. What are the kinds of imperialism described by Konoe, and how does he use them to make his argument?

3. How do you respond to Konoe's call for "the elimination of discrimination between Caucasians and Orientals"? Do his complaints seem justified? Why or why not?

COMPARATIVE QUESTIONS

1. The documents in this chapter range from intensely personal to geopolitical in nature. What connections can you draw between the emotions and experiences presented in the memoirs and letters of the British war nurse and the Albrights and the political stances of the other authors?

2. How might the British nurse and the Albrights have responded to the claims of Lenin, the Zionist Organization, the German delegation, and Konoe Fumimaro? How might the authors of the latter documents have addressed the individuals whose voices we heard in the first two documents?

3. What vision of the postwar world is offered in each document? How narrow or broad is its focus?

4. The Zionist Organization, the German delegation, and Konoe each argue that the Treaty of Versailles presented an opportunity to reshape the political landscape. Compare the language and intent of these three documents. How does each document use ideas of freedom and self-determination to justify its claims? How does each address the question of foreign territories or peoples? How does each deal with the question of guilt or justice?

5. The Konoe and Zionist documents reflect Japanese and Jewish positions in the aftermath of the First World War and its dramatic challenge to the prewar international order of empires and colonies. Compare these documents to the writings of Max Nordau (Document 24-3) and Saigō Takamori (Document 26-3). How have the political positions and aspirations of Japanese and Jewish leaders changed to fit the postwar world? What continuities, if any, can you detect?

CHAPTER 29

Nationalism in Asia

1914–1939

T hough the First World War is often cast as a European conflict, it reflected and exacerbated tensions throughout the world. The global network of empires and colonies that had formed by the turn of the century drew Asian peoples into the conflict, and the rhetoric of freedom and democracy mobilized during the war inspired nationalist sentiments in many contexts. For some in Asia, the war was an opportunity to fight for national sovereignty against imperial control. For others, the war created an opportunity to link their own popular nationalist causes with the stated goals of the victors. For Asians, the material and human cost of the war and the ensuing geopolitical reorganization was manifest in new ways of thinking about national identity. The documents in this chapter present a range of personal and political views on nations and national identity in Asia, exploring the complex mix of fear, hope, disappointment, and resolve of Asians who sought to build national identities out of the chaos of the early twentieth century.

DOCUMENT 29-1

MARY L. GRAFFAM

An Account of Turkish Violence
Against Armenians

1915

As young Turkish revolutionaries rose to power in Turkey after 1908, they sought to enforce a narrowly defined national identity that erased the country's multiculturalism and instead focused on Turkish language, culture,

Mary L. Graffam, reprinted from the *Missionary Herald* (Boston), December 1915.

and race. Their efforts to consolidate what was left of the Ottoman Empire led to genocide against the Armenians. During World War I, while the international community was distracted by the war, the Turks massacred thousands of Armenians and deported others. Mary Graffam, a missionary from Massachusetts, was among the hundreds of U.S. and European workers and diplomats in Turkey who recorded the killings, starvation, and brutal deportations. These eyewitness accounts were later printed in newspapers around the world.

When we were ready to leave Sivas,[1] the Government gave forty-five ox-carts for the Protestant townspeople and eighty horses, but none at all for our pupils and teachers; so we bought ten ox-carts, two horse arabas [wagons], and five or six donkeys, and started out. In the company were all our teachers in the college, about twenty boys from the college and about thirty of the girls'-school. It was as a special favor to the Sivas people, who had not done anything revolutionary, that the Vali [provincial governor] allowed the men who were not yet in prison to go with their families.

The first night we were so tired that we just ate a piece of bread and slept on the ground wherever we could find a place to spread a yorgan [blanket]. It was after dark when we stopped, anyway. We were so near Sivas that the gendarmes [Armed Ottoman police] protected us, and no special harm was done; but the second night we began to see what was before us. The gendarmes would go ahead and have long conversations with the villagers, and then stand back and let them rob and trouble the people until we all began to scream, and then they would come and drive them away. Yorgans and rugs, and all such things, disappeared by the dozen, and donkeys were sure to be lost. Many had brought cows; but from the first day those were carried off, one by one, until not a single one remained.

We got accustomed to being robbed, but the third day a new fear took possession of us, and that was that the men were to be separated from us at Kangal. . . . Our teacher from Mandjaluk was there, with his mother and sisters. They had left the village with the rest of the women and children, and when they saw that the men were being taken off to be killed the teacher fled to another village, four hours away, where he was found by the police and brought safely with his family to Kangal, because the tchaoush [officer] who had taken them from Mandjaluk wanted his sister. I found

---

[1] **Sivas**: City in North Central Turkey, where Mary Graffam was the principal of a girls' school.

them confined in one room. I went to the Kaimakam [district official] and got an order for them all to come with us.

At Kangal some Armenians had become Mohammedans, and had not left the village, but the others were all gone. . . . They said that a valley near there was full of corpses. At Kangal we also began to see exiles from Tokat. The sight was one to strike horror to any heart; they were a company of old women, who had been robbed of absolutely everything. At Tokat the Government had first imprisoned the men, and from the prison had taken them on the road. . . . After the men had gone, they arrested the old women and the older brides, perhaps about thirty or thirty-five years old. There were very few young women or children. All the younger women and children were left in Tokat. . . .

When we looked at them we could not imagine that even the sprinkling of men that were with us would be allowed to remain. We did not long remain in doubt; the next day we . . . had come to Hassan Tehelebi . . . and it was with terror in our hearts that we passed through that village about noon. But we encamped and ate our supper in peace, and even began to think that perhaps it was not so, when the Mudir [official in charge] came round with gendarmes and began to collect the men. . . .

The night passed, and only one man came back to tell the story of how every man was compelled to give up all his money, and all were taken to prison. The next morning they collected the men who had escaped the night before and extorted forty-five liras from our company, on the promise that they would give us gendarmes to protect us. One "company" is supposed to be from 1,000 to 3,000 persons. Ours was perhaps 2,000, and the greatest number of gendarmes would be five or six. In addition to these they sewed a red rag on the arm of a Kurdish villager and gave him a gun, and he had the right to rob and bully us all he pleased.[2]

Broken-hearted, the women continued their journey. . . .

As soon as the men left us, the Turkish drivers began to rob the women, saying: "You are all going to be thrown into the Tokma Su [river], so you might as well give your things to us, and then we will stay by you and try to protect you." Every Turkish woman that we met said the same thing. The worst were the gendarmes, who really did more or less bad things. One of our schoolgirls was carried off by the Kurds twice, but her companions made so much fuss that she was brought back. . . .

---

[2] **sewed a red rag . . . he pleased**: The "red rag" was an arm band that gave the Kurds special status.

As we approached the bridge over the Tokma Su, it was certainly a fearful sight. As far as the eye could see over the plain was this slow-moving line of ox-carts. For hours there was not a drop of water on the road, and the sun poured down its very hottest. As we went on we began to see the dead from yesterday's company, and the weak began to fall by the way. The Kurds working in the fields made attacks continually, and we were half-distracted. I piled as many as I could on our wagons, and our pupils, both boys and girls, worked like heroes. One girl took a baby from its dead mother and carried it until evening. Another carried a dying woman until she died. We bought water from the Kurds, not minding the beating that the boys were sure to get with it. I counted forty-nine deaths, but there must have been many more. One naked body of a woman was covered with bruises. I saw the Kurds robbing the bodies of those not yet entirely dead. . . .

The hills on each side were white with Kurds, who were throwing stones on the Armenians, who were slowly wending their way to the bridge. I ran ahead and stood on the bridge in the midst of a crowd of Kurds, until I was used up [exhausted]. I did not see anyone thrown into the water, but they said, and I believe it, that a certain Elmas, who has done handwork for me for years, was thrown over the bridge by a Kurd. Our Badvelli's wife was riding on a horse with a baby in her arms, and a Kurd took hold of her to throw her over, when another Kurd said: "She has a baby in her arms," and they let her go. . . .

The police for the first time began to interfere with me here, and it was evident that something was decided about me. The next morning after we arrived at this bridge, they wanted me to go to Malatia; but I insisted that I had permission to stay with the Armenians. During the day, however, they said that [I had been ordered] to come to Malatia, and that the others were going to Kiakhta. Soon after we heard that they were going to Ourfa, there to build villages and cities, &c.

In Malatia I went at once to the commandant, a captain who they say has made a fortune out of these exiles. I told him how I had gone to Erzeroum last winter, and how we pitied these women and children and wished to help them, and finally he sent me to the Mutessarif [district official]. The latter is a Kurd, apparently anxious to do the right thing; but he has been sick most of the time since he came, and the "beys" [Kurdish chiefs] here have had things more or less their own way, and certainly horrors have been committed. . . .

My friends here are very glad to have me with them, for they have a very difficult problem on their hands and are nearly crazy with the horrors they have been through here. The Mutessarif and other officials here and at Sivas have read me orders from Constantinople again and again to the effect that the lives of these exiles are to be protected, and from their actions I should judge that they must have received such orders; but they certainly have murdered a great many in every city. Here there were great trenches dug by the soldiers for drilling purposes. Now these trenches are all filled up, and our friends saw carts going back from the city by night. A man I know told me that when he was out to inspect some work he was having done, he saw a dead body which had evidently been pulled out of one of these trenches, probably by dogs. . . . The Beledia Reis [village chief] here says that every male over ten years old is being murdered, that not one is to live, and no woman over fifteen. The truth seems to be somewhere between these two extremes.

READING AND DISCUSSION QUESTIONS

1. What happened to the men after Graffam's group left Tokat?

2. How were the women treated on this exile from Turkey?

3. Where were the Armenian exiles sent (and for what purpose) after Graffam was separated from them?

4. What do you suppose was the intended use of the trenches?

DOCUMENT 29-2

ARTHUR JAMES BALFOUR

Debating the Balfour Declaration: The British Government Supports a Jewish Homeland in Palestine

1917

The decision to support a Jewish homeland in Palestine posed a diplomatic dilemma for Great Britain. Though Lord Balfour, the British foreign secretary (1916–1919), would ultimately be authorized to endorse a Jewish

---

"The Balfour Declaration," *Times* (London), November 9, 1917, p. 1.

homeland, the behind-the-scenes discussions excerpted below illustrate the War Department's concern about the consequences of such support. On the one hand, England hoped its actions might enlist American Zionists to push the U.S. Congress to back Britain in the war and would help Britain retain control of the Suez Canal. On the other, it risked its alliance with Arab leaders, who saw a separate Jewish state as contradictory to its government by majority rule.

THE BALFOUR DECLARATION, 1917

Foreign Office
November 2nd, 1917
Dear Lord Rothschild,[3]

I have much pleasure in conveying to you, on behalf of His Majesty's Government, the following declaration of sympathy with Jewish Zionist aspirations which has been submitted to, and approved by, the Cabinet.

"His Majesty's Government view with favor the establishment in Palestine of a national home for the Jewish people, and will use their best endeavors to facilitate the achievement of this object, it being clearly understood that nothing shall be done which may prejudice the civil and religious rights of existing non-Jewish communities in Palestine, or the rights and political status enjoyed by Jews in any other country."

I should be grateful if you would bring this declaration to the knowledge of the Zionist Federation.[4]
Yours sincerely,
Arthur James Balfour

CAMBON LETTER TO SOKOLOW,[5] JUNE 4, 1917

You were good enough to present the project to which you are devoting your efforts, which has for its object the development of Jewish colonization in Palestine. You consider that, circumstances permitting, and the independence of the Holy Places being safeguarded on the other hand, it

---

[3] **Lord Rothschild**: Walter Lord Rothschild was a former member of Parliament (1899–1910) and an ardent English Zionist who was influential in shaping the Balfour Declaration.
[4] **Zionist Federation**: The British Federation of Zionists, an organization that lobbied the British government to support a Jewish homeland in Palestine.
[5] **Cambon . . . Sokolow**: Jules Cambon, secretary-general of the French Foreign Ministry; Nahum Sokolow, head of the Zionist Organization based in London.

would be a deed of justice and of reparation to assist, by the protection of the Allied Powers, in the renaissance of the Jewish nationality in that Land from which the people of *Israel* were exiled so many centuries ago.

The French Government, which entered this present war to defend a people wrongfully attacked, and which continues the struggle to assure the victory of right over might, can but feel sympathy for your cause, the triumph of which is bound up with that of the Allies.

I am happy to give you herewith such assurance.

OFFICIAL ZIONIST FORMULA, 18 JULY 1917

H. M. Government, after considering the aims of the Zionist Organization,[6] accepts the principle of recognizing Palestine as the National Home of the Jewish people and the right of the Jewish people to build up its National life in Palestine under a protection to be established at the conclusion of Peace, following upon the successful issue of the war.

H. M. Government regards as essential for the realization of this principle the grant of internal autonomy to the Jewish nationality in Palestine, freedom of immigration for Jews, and the establishment of a Jewish National Colonizing Corporation for the re-settlement and economic development of the country.

The conditions and forms of the internal autonomy and a charter for the Jewish National Colonizing Corporation should, in the view of H. M. Government, be elaborated in detail and determined with the representatives of the Zionist Organization.

MINUTES OF WAR CABINET MEETING NO. 227, MINUTE NO. 2, 3 SEPTEMBER 1917

The War Cabinet had under consideration correspondence which had passed between the Secretary of State for Foreign Affairs and Lord Rothschild on the question of the policy to be adopted towards the Zionist movement. In addition to the draft declaration of policy included in the above correspondence, they had before them an alternative draft prepared by Lord Milner. They had also before them a Memorandum by Mr. Montagu entitled "The Anti-Semitism of the present Government."

It was suggested that a question raising such important issues as to the future of Palestine ought, in the first instance, to be discussed with our Allies, and more particularly with the United States.

---

[6] **Zionist Organization**: An umbrella organization that merged Zionist groups in Europe and elsewhere to establish a Jewish state in Palestine.

On the question of submitting Lord Milner's draft for the consideration of the United States Government, Mr. Montagu urged that the use of the phrase "the home of the Jewish people" would vitally prejudice the position of every Jew elsewhere and expand the argument contained in his Memorandum. Against this it was urged that the existence of a Jewish State or autonomous community in Palestine would strengthen rather than weaken the situation of Jews in countries where they were not yet in possession of equal rights, and that in countries like England, where they possessed such rights and were identified with the nation of which they were citizens, their position would be unaffected by the existence of a national Jewish community elsewhere. The view was expressed that, while a small influential section of English Jews were opposed to the idea, large numbers were sympathetic to it, but in the interests of Jews who wished to go from countries where they were less favorably situated, rather than from any idea of wishing to go to Palestine themselves.

With reference to a suggestion that the matter might be postponed, the Acting Secretary of State for Foreign Affairs pointed out that this was a question on which the Foreign Office had been very strongly pressed for a long time past. There was a very strong and enthusiastic organization, more particularly in the United States, who were zealous in this matter, and his belief was that it would be of most substantial assistance to the Allies to have the earnestness and enthusiasm of these people enlisted on our side. To do nothing was to risk a direct breach with them, and it was necessary to face this situation.

The War Cabinet decided that —

The views of [U.S.] President Wilson should be obtained before any declaration was made, and requested the Acting Secretary of State for Foreign Affairs to inform the Government of the United States that His Majesty's Government were being pressed to make a declaration in sympathy with the Zionist movement, and to ascertain their views as to the advisability of such a declaration being made.

MINUTES OF WAR CABINET MEETING NO. 245, MINUTE NO. 18, 4 OCTOBER 1917

With reference to War Cabinet 227, Minute 2, the Secretary of State for Foreign Affairs stated that the German Government were making great efforts to capture the sympathy of the Zionist Movement. This Movement, though opposed by a number of wealthy Jews in this country, had behind it the support of a majority of Jews, at all events in Russia and America, and possibly in other countries. He saw nothing inconsistent between the establishment of a Jewish national focus in Palestine and the complete assimilation and absorption of Jews into the nationality of other countries. Just as English emigrants to the United States became, either in the first or subsequent generations, American nationals, so, in future, should a Jewish citizenship be established in Palestine, would Jews become either Englishmen, Americans, Germans, or Palestinians. What was at the back of the Zionist Movement was the intense national consciousness held by certain members of the Jewish race. They regarded themselves as one of the great historic races of the world, whose original home was Palestine, and these Jews had a passionate longing to regain once more this ancient national home. Other Jews had become absorbed into the nations among whom they and their forefathers had dwelt for many generations. Mr. Balfour then read a very sympathetic declaration by the French Government which had been conveyed to the Zionists, and he stated that he knew that President Wilson was extremely favorable to the Movement.

Attention was drawn to the contradictory telegrams received from Colonel House and Justice Brandeis.

The Secretary was instructed to take the necessary action.

The War Cabinet further decided that the opinions received upon this draft declaration should be collated and submitted to them for decision.

Minutes of War Cabinet Meeting No. 259, Minute No. 12, 25 October 1917

With reference to War Cabinet 245, Minute 18, the Secretary mentioned that he was being pressed by the Foreign Office to bring forward the question of Zionism, an early settlement of which was regarded as of great importance.

Lord Curzon[7] stated that he had a Memorandum on the subject in course of preparation.

The question was adjourned until Monday, 29th October, or some other day early next week.

Minutes of War Cabinet Meeting No. 261, Minute No. 12, 31 October 1917

With reference to War Cabinet 245, Minute 18, the War Cabinet had before them a note by the Secretary, and also a memorandum by Lord Curzon on the subject of the Zionist movement.

---

[7] **Lord Curzon**: George Nathaniel Curzon served in the British War Cabinet as Lord President of the Council (1916–1919).

The Secretary of State for Foreign Affairs stated that he gathered that everyone was now agreed that, from a purely diplomatic and political point of view, it was desirable that some declaration favorable to the aspirations of the Jewish nationalists should now be made. The vast majority of Jews in Russia and America, as, indeed, all over the world, now appeared to be favorable to Zionism. If we could make a declaration favorable to such an ideal, we should be able to carry on extremely useful propaganda both in Russia and America. He gathered that the main arguments still put forward against Zionism were twofold: —

(*a.*) That Palestine was inadequate to form a home for either the Jewish or any other people.
(*b.*) The difficulty felt with regard to the future position of Jews in Western countries.

With regard to the first, he understood that there were considerable differences of opinion among experts regarding the possibility of the settlement of any large population in Palestine, but he was informed that, if Palestine were scientifically developed, a very much larger population could be sustained than had existed during the period of Turkish misrule. As to the meaning of the words "national home," to which the Zionists attach so much importance, he understood it to mean some form of British, American, or other protectorate, under which full facilities would be given to the Jews to work out their own salvation and to build up, by means of education, agriculture, and industry, a real center of national culture and focus of national life. It did not necessarily involve the early establishment of an independent Jewish State, which was a matter for gradual development in accordance with the ordinary laws of political evolution.

With regard to the second point, he felt that, so far from Zionism hindering the process of assimilation in Western countries, the truer parallel was to be found in the position of an Englishman who leaves his country to establish a permanent home in the United States. In the latter case there was no difficulty in the Englishman or his children becoming full nationals of the United States, whereas, in the present position of Jewry, the assimilation was often felt to be incomplete, and any danger of a double allegiance or non-national outlook would be eliminated.

Lord Curzon stated that he admitted the force of the diplomatic arguments in favor of expressing sympathy, and agreed that the bulk of the Jews held Zionist rather than anti-Zionist opinions. He added that he did not agree with the attitude taken up by Mr. Montagu. On the other hand, he could not share the optimistic views held regarding the future of Palestine. These views were not merely the result of his own personal experiences of travel in that country, but of careful investigations from persons who had lived for many years in the country. He feared that by the suggested declaration we should be raising false expectations which could never be realized. He attached great importance to the necessity of retaining the Christian and Moslem Holy Places in Jerusalem and Bethlehem, and, if this were to be effectively done, he did not see how the Jewish people could have a political capital in Palestine. However, he recognized that some expression of sympathy with Jewish aspirations would be a valuable adjunct to our propaganda, though he thought that we should be guarded in the language used in giving expression to such sympathy.

READING AND DISCUSSION QUESTIONS

1. What do the various leaders envision will be the impact of creating a Jewish state on Jews living in other countries?

2. What reasons do the leaders give for the urgency to act on this matter and show support for Zionism?

3. What are their concerns about establishing a Jewish settlement within Palestine?

4. Why might some historians see the Balfour Declaration as the cause of later Palestinian-Jewish conflicts? Based on these excerpts, what might support that claim?

DOCUMENT 29-3

SAROJINI NAIDU

From The Agony and Shame of the Punjab:
An Indian Nationalist Condemns the
British Empire

1920

Despite British concerns, the First World War provoked strong support for Britain among the Indian population. Indians rallied around the British war effort, offering soldiers, food, and other essential resources. After the war, however, Indian nationalism grew rapidly, due in large part to disillusionment with Britain's continuing imperialist policies toward its colonies. In 1919, British troops were ordered to use live ammunition to disperse a peaceful crowd of men, women, and children celebrating a Sikh festival in the city of Amritsar. Hundreds were killed and more than a thousand wounded. Indian feminist and nationalist leader Sarojini Naidu (1879–1949) used this incident and other examples of British hypocrisy to justify Indian independence and self-rule.

I speak to you today as standing arraigned because of the blood-guiltiness of those who have committed murder in my country. I need not go into the details. But I am going to speak to you as a woman about the wrongs committed against my sisters. Englishmen, you who pride yourselves upon your chivalry, you who hold more precious than your imperial treasures the honor and chastity of your women, will you sit still and leave unavenged the dishonor, and the insult and agony inflicted upon the veiled women of the Punjab?

The minions of Lord Chelmsford, the Viceroy, and his martial authorities rent the veil from the faces of the women of the Punjab. Not only were men mown down as if they were grass that is born to wither; but they tore asunder the cherished Purdah,[8] that innermost privacy of the chaste womanhood of India. My sisters were stripped naked, they were flogged, they were outraged. These policies left your British democracy betrayed,

---

Sarojini Naidu, "The Agony and Shame of the Punjab" [speech], in Padmini Sengupta, *Sarojini Naidu: A Biography* (London: Asia Publishing House, 1966), 161–162.

[8] **Purdah**: Practice in which Indian women hide themselves from view behind veils or in special building enclosures.

dishonored, for no dishonor clings to the martyrs who suffered, but to the tyrants who inflicted the tyranny and pain. Should they hold their Empire by dishonoring the women of another nation or lose it out of chivalry for their honor and chastity? The Bible asked, "What shall it profit a man to gain the whole world and lose his own soul?" You deserve no Empire. You have lost your soul; you have the stain of blood-guiltiness upon you; no nation that rules by tyranny is free; it is the slave of its own despotism.

READING AND DISCUSSION QUESTIONS

1. Why is Naidu angry?

2. According to Naidu, how does the treatment of Indian women by British officials differ from their treatment of English women?

3. Why does she say that the English "deserve no Empire"? What might this reveal about Indian values at the time?

VIEWPOINTS

Prescriptions for National Improvement in China and Siam

DOCUMENT 29-4

JIANG JIESHI

The New Life Movement

1934

Following the death of Nationalist Party leader Sun Yatsen (see Document 26-5), his protégé Jiang Jieshi (better known as Chiang Kai-shek, 1887–1975) took control of the Nationalist movement. By 1927, Jiang had established control of a precariously unified China by defeating or eliminating

Sources of Chinese Tradition, ed. Wm. Theodore de Bary and Richard Lufrano, 2 vols. (New York: Columbia University Press, 2001), 2:341–344.

his opposition, including his former allies, the Communists. Jiang's rule focused on the unification and "education" of China, which he felt necessary before democracy could be practiced. To those ends, in 1934 Jiang gave a speech proclaiming his New Life Movement. Enforced with the help of Jiang's secret and quasi-fascist Blue Shirt Society, the New Life Movement set forth tradition, anti-individualism, and personal morality and hygiene as the foundation for a stronger, better China.

The Object of the New Life Movement

Why Is a New Life Needed?

The general psychology of our people today can be described as spiritless. What manifests itself in behavior is this: lack of discrimination between good and evil, between what is public and what is private, and between what is primary and what is secondary. Because there is no discrimination between good and evil, right and wrong are confused; because there is no discrimination between public and private, improper taking and giving [of public funds] occur; and because there is no distinction between primary and secondary, first and last are not placed in the proper order. As a result, officials tend to be dishonest and avaricious, the masses are undisciplined and calloused, youth become degraded and intemperate, adults are corrupt and ignorant, the rich become extravagant and luxurious, and the poor become mean and disorderly. Naturally it has resulted in disorganization of the social order and national life, and we are in no position either to prevent or to remedy natural calamities, disasters caused from within, or invasions from without. The individual, society, and the whole country are now suffering. . . . In order to develop the life of our nation, protect the existence of our society, and improve the livelihood of our people, it is absolutely necessary to wipe out these unwholesome conditions and to start to lead a new and rational life.

The Content of the New Life Movement

The Principles of the New Life Movement

The New Life Movement aims at the promotion of a regular life guided by the four virtues, namely, *li, yi, lian,* and *chi.* Those virtues must be applied to ordinary life in the matter of food, clothing, shelter, and action. The four virtues are the essential principles for the promotion of morality. They form the major rules for dealing with men and human affairs, for cultivating oneself, and for adjustment to one's surroundings. Whoever violates these rules is bound to fail, and a nation that neglects them will not survive.

There are two kinds of skeptics:

First, some hold that the four virtues are merely rules of good conduct. No matter how good they may be, they are not sufficient to save a nation whose knowledge and technique are inferior to others.

Those who hold this view do not seem to understand the distinction between matters of primary and secondary importance. People need knowledge and technique because they want to do good. Otherwise, knowledge and technique can only be instruments of dishonorable deeds. *Li, yi, lian,* and *chi* are the principal rules alike for the community, the group, or the entire nation. Those who do not observe these rules will probably utilize their knowledge and ability to the detriment of society and ultimately to their own disadvantage. Therefore, these virtues not only can save the nation but also can rebuild the nation.

Second, there is another group of people who argue that these virtues are merely formal refinements that are useless in dealing with hunger and cold. . . . [Yet] when these virtues prevail, even if food and clothing are insufficient, they can be produced by human labor; or, if the granary is empty, it can be filled through human effort. On the other hand, when these virtues are not observed, if food and clothing are insufficient, they will not be made sufficient by fighting and robbing; or, if the granary is empty, it will not be filled by stealing and begging. The four virtues, which rectify the misconduct of men, are the proper methods of achieving abundance. Without them, there will be fighting, robbing, stealing, and begging among men. . . .

The Meaning of Li, Yi, Lian, and Chi

Although *li, yi, lian,* and *chi* have always been regarded as the foundations of the nation, yet the changing times and circumstances may require that these principles be given a new interpretation. As applied to our life today, they may be interpreted as follows:

Li means "regulated attitude."

Yi means "right conduct."

Lian means "clear discrimination."

Chi means "real self-consciousness."

The word *li* (decorum) means *li* (principle). It becomes natural law when applied to nature; it becomes a rule when applied to social affairs;

and it signifies discipline when used in reference to national affairs. A man's conduct is considered regular if it conforms with the above law, rule, and discipline. When one conducts oneself in accordance with the regular manner, one is said to have the regulated attitude.

The word *yi* means "proper." Any conduct that is in accordance with *li* — i.e., natural law, social rule, and national discipline — is considered proper. To act improperly, or to refrain from acting when one knows it is proper to act, cannot be called *yi*.

The word *lian* means "clear." It denotes distinction between right and wrong. What agrees with *li* and *yi* is right, and what does not agree is wrong. To take what we recognize as right and to forgo what we recognize as wrong constitute clear discrimination.

The word *chi* means "consciousness." When one is conscious of the fact that his own actions are not in accordance with *li*, *yi*, *lian*, and *chi*, one feels ashamed.

From the above explanations, it is clear that *chi* governs the motive of action, that *lian* gives the guidance for it, that *yi* relates to the carrying out of an action, and that *li* regulates its outward form. The four are interrelated. They are dependent upon each other in the perfecting of virtue.

Conclusion

In short, the main object of the New Life Movement is to substitute a rational life for the irrational, and to achieve this we must observe *li*, *yi*, *lian*, and *chi* in our daily life.

1. By the observance of these virtues, it is hoped that rudeness and vulgarity will be got rid of and that the life of our people will conform to the standard of art. By art we are not referring to the special enjoyment of the gentry. We mean the cultural standard of all the people, irrespective of sex, age, wealth, and class. It is the boundary line between civilized life and barbarism. It is the only way by which one can achieve the purpose of man, for only by artistically controlling oneself and dealing with others can one fulfill the duty of mutual assistance. . . . A lack of artistic training is the cause of suspicion, jealousy, hatred, and strife that are prevalent in our society today. . . . To investigate things so as to extend our knowledge, to distinguish between the fundamental and the secondary, to seek the invention of instruments, to excel in our techniques — these are the essentials of an artistic life, the practice of which will enable us to wipe out the defects of vulgarity, confusion, crudity, and baseness.

2. By the observance of these virtues, it is hoped that beggary and robbery will be eliminated and that the life of our people will be productive. The poverty of China is primarily caused by the fact that there are too many consumers and too few producers. Those who consume without producing usually live as parasites or as robbers. They behave thus because they are ignorant of the four virtues. To remedy this we must make them produce more and spend less. They must understand that luxury is improper and that living as a parasite is a shame.

3. By the observance of these virtues, it is hoped that social disorder and individual weakness will be remedied and that people will become more military-minded. If a country cannot defend itself, it has every chance of losing its existence. . . . Therefore our people must have military training. As a preliminary, we must acquire the habits of orderliness, cleanliness, simplicity, frugality, promptness, and exactness. We must preserve order, emphasize organization, responsibility, and discipline, and be ready to die for the country at any moment.

READING AND DISCUSSION QUESTIONS

1. What is the aim of the New Life Movement? What are its four components?

2. What criticisms does Jiang predict, and how does he answer them?

3. How does art figure into Jiang's vision of "New Life"? How is the promotion of art — or any other individual activity or attitude — supposed to have an impact on the nation?

4. Do you find Jiang's prescriptions for social improvement compelling? Why or why not?

KING VAJIRAVUDH

On the Siamese Nation

1914, 1917, 1920

Vajiravudh (1881–1925) was king of Siam from 1910 until his death in 1925 and — like his father before him — a major reformer in Siamese or Thai history. He took great pains to avoid the colonization of Siam and to guide Siamese involvement in the First World War through deft political alliances with powerful European and Asian nations. He also continued his father's policy of nourishing modern, Western-style reforms. Perhaps most important, Vajiravudh was instrumental in fostering Siamese nationalism, which would form the seeds of Thai nationalism after the 1933 coup d'état that created the nation of Thailand. Vajiravudh produced a range of speeches, essays, plays, poems, and even cartoons instructing the Siamese populace on the meaning and merits of Siamese nationalism. The first excerpt that follows is from a 1914 play; the second is from a 1917 poem written to commemorate the national flag that Vajiravudh himself designed; the third is the king's own cartoon depicting Siamese railroads pushing former German advisers out of the way.

FROM PHRA RUANG (1914)

I ask the Thai to join in love,
To join in fellowship,
So that when the enemy comes
We can fight him in full strength.
The Thai combining their power
Will be able to raise a staunch defense.
Even if a powerful foe comes,
He will be defeated.

Walter F. Vella, *Chaiyo! King Vajiravudh and the Development of Thai Nationalism* (Honolulu: University of Hawaii Press, 1978), 140, 211, 245.

I ask only that we Thai not destroy our nation.
Let us unite our state, unite our hearts, into a great whole.
Thai — do not harm or destroy Thai,
But combine your spirit and your strength to preserve the state
So that all foreign peoples
Will give us increasing respect.

Help one another to further our progress
So the name "Thai" will redound throughout the world.
Help one another to sustain
Both our nation and our faith
So they will last to the end of time.
Let us progress, Thai! Chaiyo![9]

POEM ON THE FLAG (1917)

Let me speak of the meaning
Behind the three colors.

White is for purity and betokens the three gems
And the law that guard the Thai heart.

Red is for our blood, which we willingly give up
To protect our nation and faith.

Blue is the beautiful hue of the people's leader,
And is liked because of him.[10]

Arranged in stripes, these three colors form the flag
That we Thai love.

Our soldiers carrying it forth to victory
Raise up the honor of Siam.

---

[9] **Chaiyo!**: A new exclamation designed and popularized by Vajiravudh, it roughly translates as "Olé!" or "Hurray!"

[10] **Blue is the beautiful hue . . . liked because of him**: According to Thai folk belief, each day of the week has a specific color; Vajiravudh claimed his birthday to be on a Friday, the color of which is blue.

CARTOON OF THE SIAMESE RAILROAD (1920)

Image © 1978 University of Hawaii Press. Reprinted with Permission.

READING AND DISCUSSION QUESTIONS

1. What themes does Vajiravudh use in the three excerpts to illustrate the virtues and importance of nationalism? What does Siamese/Thai nationalism mean to the king?

2. The three colors of the Thai flag (still in use today) are found in the flags of several prominent Western nations. How might these color choices have resonated on the international stage? What does the choice of these colors suggest about Vajiravudh's understanding of modern nationalism?

3. What is the message contained in the king's cartoon? How do you interpret the relative sizes of the figures?

4. The idea of a head of state producing poetry, plays, and cartoons may seem foreign to twenty-first-century readers. What is your reaction to Vajiravudh's personal involvement with defining Siamese/Thai nationalism? What might his contributions suggest about early twentieth-century nationalism in Asia, or nationalism in general?

DOCUMENT 29-6

CLAUDIE BEAUCARNOT

Vacation Diary

July 1943

Before the outbreak of the Second World War, Vietnam was part of the French colonial possessions in Southeast Asia known as Indochina, which also comprised contemporary Vietnam, as well as Cambodia and Laos. In 1940, despite the recent establishment of the Vichy French government in Europe, which supported the Axis powers in the war, the Japanese Army invaded Indochina and took control of the French colony, violating agreements with the French colonial rulers. During this conflict, a young French colonial woman, Claudie Beaucarnot, then nineteen, kept a vacation diary. Her 1943 account of her travels with her family and her interactions with Vietnamese and other Asians is an important record of the complex realities of imperialist policies.

WEDNESDAY, JULY 7th

At 9:00am we leave for Dalat[11] to make some purchases because we are lacking some necessities. Around here, all the houses are wooden: boards

---

Au Revoir Hanoï: The 1943 Vacation Diary of Claudie Beaucarnot, trans. David Del Testa (draft, 2002), 47–51.

[11] **Dalat**: The capital city of the Federation of Indochina from 1939 to 1945.

or logs. Wood is cut in the forest. After the forest are some small, completely cultivated valleys (tea).

Here's Entre-Rays. Its small wooden church resembles, from a distance, a construction game. We are dominating the mountains covered with pines, which look like cedars. It's kind of like the Libyan countryside. There are two different kinds of pines here: the large ones, which resemble the coastal pines, are the pitch pines. The others are smaller but provide more than those that one finds in Tonkin and Tam Dau.

Then it's the small Bosquet train station, in the middle of the pines with its tiny wooden houses bordering the road. We are passing through the middle of the Pasteur Institute's plantations.

Here's the Lang Bian Palace and the Parc Hotel Farm in Dalat. There are many vegetables. We are starting to see quite a few villas and we catch a glimpse of Dalat. Finally, here's Dalat.

While Mother is buying bread and Papa is looking for electrical wire, Nicole and I wait in the car. We had stopped in front of a Chinese boutique where some highlanders were providing fresh supplies. They put all their provisions into large varnished pots, which they carry on their backs with the aid of a support. There are men and women. They are all smoking pipes. When they aren't smoking, the women carry their pipes in their buns of hair. They have long embroidered skirts. Their tops are naked. And nevertheless it's cold out. I see an old highlander who has goose bumps. Another is wearing a vest made of coconut fibers. A third guy was continually taking his pipe out in order to spit. I watch him, fascinated, because he was flinging long jets of saliva without even parting his lips. A woman highlander is wrapped up in a blanket. They always have blankets, which they use as coats. The women have gaily-colored pearl necklaces. The men have belts made out of fabric around their backs and which goes between their legs. The belts are large in the front, leaving only a string in between the buttocks. It's their only article of clothing. They are almost all curly, but really filthy. The women have in their earlobes, circles of wood with a diameter of at least 5 centimeters. Those that have removed the pieces of wood have lobes, which dangle enormously. The men have smaller circles. Sometimes they have anklets made from circles of fabric. The women are carrying baskets. Because in these mountains everything is carried in baskets or in pots on the men's backs. They are all very tan and very muscular. What a beautiful race!

Bang, here a police officer . . . in a forage cap gives us a fine: it appears that we can't park here. Again, he must know! But that's how it is in Dalat. The safes of the municipality fill up quickly with games like this.

Now it's the return under the rain.

Thursday, July 8th

Housework, cooking. The servant and the cook were supposed to arrive on the train last night. They must have slept through the Arbre Broyé stop because they didn't get off and they should be in Dalat by now. We had to send the chauffeur to meet them.

Nicole and I made the beds. Mama swept the chalet, then went into the kitchen. The meal we had wasn't too bad. One of the chickens that we bought in Dalat was saved. We ran through the lemon trees, the coffee and tea plants, each one of us armed with a stick to catch it. It found refuge under the car in the garage, after making a tour of the garden. This is where the chauffeur caught it. He immediately wrung its neck. This way, he won't run and we'll eat it tomorrow. Mama wants to prepare it. We tease her, because one time in France, she made us eat a chicken that she forgot to eviscerate. We yell at the poisoner.

Nicole and I explored the Chinese of the area. There is a really small sordid boutique but we still find a nice selection of things. Papa bought a repetitive alarm clock there yesterday and we purchased some candy. This is the baker of the area. We buy bread from him and he even makes pastries, including occasionally somewhat sandy madeleines, but they're not bad! We asked him if he sells ice cream, because we are really craving a milkshake. He said no, that it wasn't worth it to turn the ice because the weather is sufficiently cold. He doesn't sell books either, which is too bad. But he wraps his merchandise in pieces of American newspapers, on which I found usually eccentric styles of dresses, but occasionally adorable. Like the other merchant in Arbre Broyé, there is a vegetable vendor. He's an old Tonkinese man who has been here for 45 years, he told us, and who has smoked opium for 30 years. His house is even dirtier than that of the Chinese, which is impossible. One can access it by three wooden steps. The interior is small and completely black. Behind a curtain, we make out a lamp for the opium, which is on a sideboard. It's underneath this where he spends the majority of his time. We give him our order for vegetables, and then we leave this hovel, completely happy to see the light and to breathe fresh air.

When we arrive at the chalet, Papa called me to go explore the forest. I am not very enthusiastic, but I'm wrong because we are going to see a really marvelous countryside.

We commit to the path, where little stones roll under our feet. It's weird: I feel very light/weak here, I run faster than on the plain, I walk easier and nevertheless I am breathing heavily and wheezing strongly. It appears that it takes five days to acclimatize. At the end of this lapse of time, the number of red corpuscles increases considerably and I breathe more fully. We continue to climb, me following Papa and from time to time running to catch up to him. I turn around and see down below the train station and the little huts of Arbre-Broyé. We are now walking over the pine needles. We are on a peak. It's the highest peak of the station, more than 600 meters. We walk a bit forward in the grass and now a splendid view meets our eyes: mountains everywhere, down below the Dran plain with an altitude of 1000 meters, this famous plain, which in reality is a plateau, is nothing but the Dan Nhim valley. Its length spans over 60 kilometers, to the toll bridge on the road that leads to Djring. The valley is covered with agriculture. From our viewpoint, the gardens resemble little compartments and the Dan Nhim snakes through the middle of them. On the left all at the far end and pretty far away that make one ask, how do you get there, we see the ocean? It's grandiose and even a little overwhelming. We feel miniscule and at the same time very large.

We are entirely out of breath. We regretfully leave our post, and then it's the descent. Papa wants to pass through the brush to prospect a little and return to our chalet in a straight line. I have some white leather sandals. They are not exactly the best for this type of walk, but these are the only ones that I brought with me. The closed-toe shoes will arrive with the servant and the cook. We slide the length of the slope over some ferns, dead leaves, roots, twigs, and dry branches. These crack under our feet. My feet are completely soaked and I am afraid of getting leeches.

It's much worse right now, because to keep a straight line, we entered into an inextricable jungle of sorts. Everywhere there are very tall and straight trees linked together by creepers, which hang, become entangled, and form a network in which it makes it difficult for us to circulate. Finally, a sort of clearing. We run to it. It's a small stream. Luckily, a natural bridge passes over it. It's a tree that is completely green because it is covered in green moss. I stop and catch myself with a thorn bush. Now, it's going quite well. From this side, we are in some coffee trees, some arabica coffee trees. The terrain is terraced and on each step grows a range of coffee trees. I have a bunch of thorns on my dress. Here we are, finally back to our place. I tell Nicole about our adventures, who caught me because I didn't wait for her before departing. I'm tired but it's a healthy tired. And wham, here's a visitor. It is necessary to serve aperitifs, to pass around little cookies, to laugh while pretending to listen. It's exhausting. It's 8:00pm. We are eating and then we'll try to sleep.

READING AND DISCUSSION QUESTIONS

1. What evidence do you find, if any, of the contrast between Beaucarnot's standard of living and those of the people she encounters? How does she comment on those differences, if at all?

2. How does Beaucarnot describe the Vietnamese, Chinese, and other Asian people she sees and meets? What kind of language does she use to talk about them, and what does this reveal about her sense of her own identity?

3. Are you more struck by Beaucarnot as a representative of French imperialist expansion in Asia or as a young woman on vacation with her family? Why? What might this imply for the nature of imperialism and colonialism?

4. How might Beaucarnot have spoken about Vietnamese (or Indochinese) nationalism? Do you think national identity was a concern for her?

5. In what sense could Beaucarnot be considered Asian? European?

COMPARATIVE QUESTIONS

1. Mary Graffam and Claudie Beaucarnot were American and British nationals, respectively, each abroad in an Asian country for very different purposes. What does the presence of women abroad in many capacities suggest about the international landscape during and after the First World War?

2. In each of the documents in this chapter, the question of national identity is addressed either implicitly or explicitly. How does each document take up the question of nationalism? What national identities are mentioned or described, and how?

3. How is nationalism presented as a positive or negative force in each document? Who is commenting on the value of nation and nationalism in each document, and what relationship can you identify between the author's identity and his or her views on nationalism?

4. How is nationalism connected to modernity in each document? How is nationalism linked to Western identity or Western ideas?

5. In Documents 29-4 and 29-5, we see Asian political and intellectual leaders attempting to define national identity for their countries. Compare and contrast the writings of Jiang Jieshi and King Vajiravudh. How do the authors' identities, the themes used to define and promote nationalism, or the use of foreign or Western ideas converge or differ in each text?

6. Lord Balfour and Sarojini Naidu represent the United Kingdom and its colony India, respectively. How do their writings reflect their position as imperial power or colony? Does any commonality of theme or purpose link them? On what do they agree, if anything?

CHAPTER 30

The Great Depression and World War II

1929–1945

The Great Depression may have had its origins in the economy of the United States, but its effects were rapidly experienced throughout most of the world, and the hardships it generated added stress to the already fragile social and political situations that existed after the First World War. In the United States, the Depression exacerbated social tensions; in Europe and elsewhere, it helped radicalize the political landscape, as men and women sought to create and make sense of new visions of state and citizen. New expressions of nationalism emerged, including the chilling racism of Hitler's Nazi Germany, Stalin's totalitarian order in the communist Soviet Union, and Mussolini's fascist control of Italy. While the Soviet Union's planned economy was largely spared the effects of the Depression, citizens there also struggled to understand how their lives fit new forms of state and society. Universally, these social and political developments helped to fuel the Second World War, which claimed millions of lives, ushered in the age of nuclear conflict, and reshaped the geopolitical landscape for decades.

DOCUMENT 30-1

WOODY GUTHRIE

"Do Re Mi"

1937

Singer-songwriter and social activist Woodrow Wilson (Woody) Guthrie (1912–1967) was born in a small town in Oklahoma. In the grips of the Great Depression, Woody left for Pampa, Texas, where he experienced the great drought and dust storms of 1935. Farmers from the Great Plains and elsewhere suffered crop failure and foreclosure, and Woody traveled with thousands of other migrants to California to find work. Woody found a public voice on a Los Angeles radio station, where he sang songs depicting the experiences of migrants. Woody became famous for calling attention to the plight of the victims of the Dust Bowl and the Depression. His song Do Re Mi *captured the dashed hopes of "Okies" — as Californians derogatorily referred to migrants fleeing the Dust Bowl — upon their arrival in California.*

Lots of folks back east, they say, is leavin' home ev'ry day,
Beatin' the hot old dusty way to the California line.
'Cross the desert sands they roll, getting out of that old dust bowl,
They think they're going to a sugar bowl, but here's what they find.
Now the police at the port of entry say,
"You're number fourteen thousand for today."

Oh, if you ain't got the do re mi, folks, If you ain't got the do re mi,
Why, you better go back to beautiful Texas, Oklahoma, Kansas, Georgia,
    Tennessee.
California is a garden of Eden, a paradise to live in or see;
But believe it or not, you won't find it so hot,
If you ain't got the do re mi.

If you want to buy you a home or a farm, that can't do nobody harm,
Or take your vacation by the mountains or sea,
Don't swap your old cow for a car, you'd better stay right where you are,
You'd better take this little tip from me.
'Cause I look through the want ads every day,
But the headlines on the papers always say:

Oh, if you ain't got the do re mi, folks, if you ain't got the do re mi,
Why, you better go back to beautiful Texas, Oklahoma, Kansas, Georgia,
    Tennessee.
California is a garden of Eden, a paradise to live in or see;
But believe it or not, you won't find it so hot
If you ain't got the do re mi.

READING AND DISCUSSION QUESTIONS

1. How does Guthrie use religious imagery to communicate the dream of California? What is the effect of using that imagery, both in terms of describing the migrant workers' plight and the meaning of religious faith?

2. How does Guthrie contrast the hopes of the migrant workers and the realities that they face?

3. Guthrie sings that migrants need "do re mi" in order to be admitted to and succeed in California. What is the effect of using the phrase "do re mi" here? Is the meaning clear, and does it seem that migrants could actually acquire "do re mi" and settle in California? If not, how does that shape the message of the song?

4. How might the reception of Guthrie's message be different if it were included in a poem or a speech, instead of in a song?

DOCUMENT 30-2

GERTRUD SCHOLTZ-KLINK

Speech to the National Socialist Women's Association

1935

Adolf Hitler rose to power on the promise of economic recovery, but he also sought a social revolution. Along with his attacks on Jews, Communists, Gypsies, and homosexuals, Hitler took aim at feminists and proponents of women's equality. He believed a woman's place was in the home, subordinate to her husband, and not in the workforce, government, or Nazi politics. Toward that end, all women's organizations were consolidated under the National Socialist Women's Association. In 1935, Gertrud Scholtz-Klink, newly appointed by party and government officials as national women's

Susan Groag Bell and Karen M. Offen, eds., *Women, the Family, and Freedom: The Debate in Documents*, vol. 2, 1880–1950 (Stanford, Calif.: Board of Trustees of the Leland Stanford Junior University, 1983).

leader, delivered a speech to the organization on how she planned to help women combine work with motherhood and learn to embrace national socialism.

A year has passed since the day we met here for the first time as a unified group of German women, to demonstrate our willingness to cooperate in our Führer's [Hitler's] work of reconstruction.

This year has been inspired by the desire to mark our times with our best efforts so that our descendants will be able to forget our nation's fourteen years of weakness and sickness.[1] We women knew, quite as well as German men, that we had to teach a people, partially sunk in self-despair, attitudes requiring those very qualities that had been deliberately suppressed in our nation. In order to carry out our intentions to unite and to march shoulder to shoulder, we demanded honor and loyalty, strength and sincerity, humility and respect — such virtues appeal to the soul of a people. In matters of the soul, however, it is no longer the majority who decide, but the strength and inner freedom of upright individuals. Therefore, we could only fulfill our task if it enabled us to penetrate the soul of the individual. . . .

When we came to the point of recognizing that the human eye reflected a nation's soul, we had to reach the women of our nation, once and for all, through our labor on women's behalf. Because as mothers our women have carried the heavy burden of the past fourteen years — and the ruins of the war and post-war period — in their hearts; and as future mothers other women must presently develop an understanding of the demands of our times — to both of these groups we dedicated the first important path that we built to the hearts of German women: our Reichs-Maternity Service.

Urged on by the tired eyes of many over-burdened mothers and the responsibility for the coming generation of mothers, we joined together under the leadership of the National Socialist Women's Association . . . and appealed to the German women especially trained for this work. When I tell you today that, between the 1st of October 1934 and the 1st of April 1935, we enrolled more than 201,700 women in 7,653 maternity school courses in about 2,000 locations throughout the German Reich, it may not seem much at first glance. But we must not forget that we had no

---

[1] **fourteen years of weakness and sickness:** Likely a reference to Germany's economic hardship following World War I and the terms of the Treaty of Versailles.

funds and met with much opposition, and that we had no patronage since we were quite unknown. But we did have absolute and unshakable faith. None of our traveling teachers asked: How much will I earn? Or, What are my pension rights? We have done this work out of a sense of duty to our nation — and our nation has responded. On Mothers' Day this year we were presented with 3.5 million marks for this work of maternity training. Moreover, on this day of honor for the mothers of Germany, when we all collected money in the streets, we found that our humblest fellow-countrymen were the most generous. This was surely the most wonderful reward for all of us, but it also gave practical evidence of where our major efforts must be directed. And when, only one or two months from now, we open our Reichs-Maternity School in Wedding, formerly one of the most solidly "red" [communist] quarters of Berlin, we will be able to congratulate ourselves on having prepared a place, on behalf of our Party and our State, that will reveal to all of you how we are solving our problems.

In this place, mothers of all ages and classes discuss their problems and their needs. Here they will become acquainted with the aims of a National Socialist state and will receive inspiration to pass them on from woman to woman, and thus to recover our national faith in ourselves. If by means of the Reichs-Maternity Service we gradually succeed in brightening the eyes of our mothers and in bringing some joy into their often difficult lives, perhaps even a song to their lips, we may consider that we have accomplished our task, because happy mothers will raise happy children. But our Reichs-Maternity Service must also make a point of teaching our young and future mothers those things that a liberal era did not teach them — for the omission of which our nation has had to pay dearly — namely, that through marriage we consciously become mothers of the nation; that is, we understand and share every national requirement laid upon German men, and that, therefore, as wives we must unconditionally become the companions of our men — not merely in personal terms, but in all national requirements.

First we pursued our task by appealing to the mothers of the nation, and then to that generation closest to the mothers, the girls between eighteen and twenty-five years of age. We called upon them to join voluntarily in the chain of helping hands and to create a relationship of unbreakable trust among German women. And they came, our girls of the German Women's Labor Service.[2]

---

[2] **German Women's Labor Service**: A program in which women worked on various public works projects. Participation became mandatory in 1939.

You, my girls, who have now spent two years with me in the struggle for the autonomy of the German people, have learned to carry every responsibility and have become the inspiration of our mothers. No matter whether our girls are cheerfully helping German settlers on the moors in their difficult work of creating new homes; or whether they are working in Rhön, Spessart, or in eastern Bavaria, hand in hand with the National Socialist Welfare Organization in giving help to careworn adults and joyless children, in reawakening a taste for beauty and a belief in themselves; or whether they are helping German peasant women harvest from dawn to dusk — one thing unites them all, for they know: We are needed, we are of some use, and we are playing our parts in the rebirth of our nation. . . .

Since at present we cannot satisfy all these demands [for compulsory labor service], owing to financial and organizational difficulties, we have begun by making only those demands that professional and university women can take the lead in supporting. . . . At one time, it was considered the height of achievement in Germany to know everything and thereby to lose the simple-mindedness of childhood. We wish to impress on our women at the universities that, as university students, they must place the intellectual abilities entrusted to them at the disposal of their nation with the same humility as that with which women workers and mothers fulfill their duties. . . . This summer our women students began to live in this manner and thereby joined the chain of helping hands we have created among ourselves. They went to German factories and replaced working women and mothers, enabling them to have a real vacation in order to regain strength for their hard day-to-day existence. For it is these women, these mothers of families, who are hardest hit by the short working hours or unemployment of their husbands, because at home their children sap their strength. . . .

This brings us to the point where we must consider the millions of German women who perform heavy labor in factories day in and day out. If we consider the human eye as the measure of people's soul, it is here that we find the deepest imprints of that fourteen-year-long attempt to strangle our national soul. We know that a great deal of industrial work must always be done by women, but it is essential that the woman at the machine should feel that she, in her position, represents her nation, in common with all other women. That is to say, we awaken her consciousness so that she will say to herself: "This is my responsibility, my attitude determines the attitude of the nation." . . .

I must deal briefly with a question that is constantly brought to our attention, that is, how our present attitude toward life differs from that of the previous women's movement. First, in principle we permit only Germans to be leaders of German women and to concern themselves with matters of importance to Germans. Second, as a matter of principle we never have demanded, nor shall we ever demand, equal rights for women with the men of our nation. Instead we shall always make women's special interests dependent upon the needs of our entire nation. All further considerations will follow from this unconditional intertwining of the collective fate of the nation.

READING AND DISCUSSION QUESTIONS

1. In what ways does Scholtz-Klink believe women have played and will continue to play an important role in the nation?

2. What lessons must the Maternity Service teach future mothers that the liberal era did not?

3. What does the author have to say on the subject of women and paid employment?

4. How do the ideas that Scholtz-Klink outlines differ from those of past women's movements?

DOCUMENT 30-3

The Nuremberg Laws: The Centerpiece of Nazi Racial Legislation

1935

Adolf Hitler's beliefs about Germanic racial superiority, first articulated in his 1925 book Mein Kampf, *became the foundation for the Nuremberg Laws, enacted after Hitler (1889–1945) seized power as German chancellor in 1933. Designed to preserve the purity of the German race, the laws — which*

U.S. *Chief of Counsel for the Prosecution of Axis Criminality,* Nazi Conspiracy and Aggression (Washington, D.C.: U.S. Government Printing Office, 1946), vol. 4, doc. no. 1417-PS, 8–10; vol. 4, doc. no. 2000-PS, 636–638.

were a manifestation of Hitler's fierce anti-Semitism — deemed Jews inferior, defined who was a Jew, and prohibited intermarriage between Germans and non-Germans (especially Jews). In the end, Jews lost not only citizenship rights and jobs but also their freedom and lives; ultimately, six million perished in the Holocaust.

ARTICLE 5

1. A Jew is anyone who descended from at least three grandparents who were racially full Jews. Article 2, par. 2, second sentence will apply.

2. A Jew is also one who descended from two full Jewish parents, if: (a) he belonged to the Jewish religious community at the time this law was issued, or who joined the community later; (b) he was married to a Jewish person, at the time the law was issued, or married one subsequently; (c) he is the offspring from a marriage with a Jew, in the sense of Section 1, which was contracted after the Law for the Protection of German Blood and German Honor became effective . . . ; (d) he is the offspring of an extramarital relationship, with a Jew, according to Section 1, and will be born out of wedlock after July 31, 1936. . . .

LAW FOR THE PROTECTION OF GERMAN BLOOD AND GERMAN HONOR OF SEPTEMBER 15, 1935

Thoroughly convinced by the knowledge that the purity of German blood is essential for the further existence of the German people and animated by the inflexible will to safe-guard the German nation for the entire future, the Reichstag[3] has resolved upon the following law unanimously, which is promulgated herewith:

Section 1

1. Marriages between Jews and nationals of German or kindred blood are forbidden. Marriages concluded in defiance of this law are void, even if, for the purpose of evading this law, they are concluded abroad. . . .

Section 2

Relation[s] outside marriage between Jews and nationals of German or kindred blood are forbidden.

---

[3] **Reichstag:** The German legislative assembly.

Section 3

Jews will not be permitted to employ female nationals of German or kindred blood in their household.

Section 4

1. Jews are forbidden to hoist the Reich and national flag and to present the colors of the Reich. . . .

Section 5

1. A person who acts contrary to the prohibition of Section 1 will be punished with hard labor.
2. A person who acts contrary to the prohibition of Section 2 will be punished with imprisonment or with hard labor.
3. A person who acts contrary to the provisions of Sections 3 or 4 will be punished with imprisonment up to a year and with a fine or with one of these penalties. . . .

READING AND DISCUSSION QUESTIONS

1. What makes someone a Jew, according to the Nuremberg Laws?
2. Why do you think so much attention is paid to "relations" between Germans and Jews in these laws?
3. Within the laws, what restrictions render Jews different from and inferior to other Germans?
4. What punishments are promised to those who break these laws?

DOCUMENT 30-4

Letters to Izvestiya: On the Issue of Abortion
1936

As Joseph Stalin (1879–1953) rose to absolute power in the Soviet Union between 1922 and 1927, he launched an ambitious and strict campaign to solidify socialism by placing all economic development under government control and promoting new cultural values. Women, who had gained greater equality after the 1917 Bolshevik Revolution, became a key focus. As birthrates dropped by up to 50 percent from 1930 to 1935, Stalin's government released propaganda celebrating women's traditional roles as wives and mothers and enacted legislation outlawing abortion except to save the mother's life. The public's thoughts on this legal change ran in newspapers such as Pravda *and* Izvestiya.

LETTER FROM A STUDENT [K.B.]

I have read in the press the draft law on the prohibition of abortion, aid to expectant mothers, etc., and cannot remain silent on this matter.

There are thousands of women in the same position as myself. I am a student reading the first course of the second Moscow Medical Institute. My husband is also a student reading the same course at our Institute. Our scholarships amount jointly to 205 rubles. Neither he nor I have a room of our own. Next year we intend to apply for admission to a hostel, but I do not know whether our application will be granted. I love children and shall probably have some in four or five years' time. But can I have a child now? Having a child now would mean leaving the Institute, lagging behind my husband, forgetting everything I have learnt and probably leaving Moscow because there is nowhere to live.

There is another married couple in our Institute, Mitya and Galya, who live in a hostel. Yesterday Galya said to me: "If I become pregnant I shall have to leave the Institute; one cannot live in a hostel with children."

"Letters to Izvestiya on the Abortion Issues," May–June 1936, in Rudolf Schlesinger, ed., The Family in the U.S.S.R. (London: Routledge, 1947), 255–259, 263–265.

I consider that the projected law is premature because the housing problem in our towns is a painful one. Very often it is the lack of living quarters that is the reason behind an abortion. If the draft included an article assuring married couples, who are expecting a baby, of a room — that would be a different matter.

In five years' time when I am a doctor and have a job and a room I shall have children. But at present I do not want and cannot undertake such a responsibility. . . .

ANSWER TO THE STUDENT K.B.

Your paper recently published a letter from a student, K.B., in which she raised objections to the prohibition of abortions. I think the author of the letter . . . has not grasped the full significance of the projected law. The difficulties about which K.B. writes and which, according to her, justify abortion are, she thinks, the difficulties of to-day which will have disappeared to-morrow. The writer of that letter completely ignored the fact that the government, by widening the network of child-welfare institutions, is easing the mother's task in looking after the child. The main mistake K.B. makes is, in my view, that she approaches the problem of childbearing as though it were a private matter. This would explain why she writes: "I shall have them (children) in four or five years' time." She hopes by that time to have completed her studies, obtained a medical diploma and found both a job and a room. But one must be logical! If during these years, K.B. intends to have recourse to abortions, who can vouch that by the time when she desires to have children she will still be able to do so? And for a normal woman to be deprived of the possibility of having children is as great a misfortune as the loss of a dear one.

I used to study in a factory and received a very small allowance while bringing up my small son whom I had to bring up on my own. (His father was dead.) It was a hard time. I had to go and unload trains or look for similar work that would bring in some money . . . that was in 1923. Now my son is a good, rough Komsomol[4] and a Red Army[5] soldier in the Far East. How great are my joy and pride that I did not shun the difficulties and that I managed to bring up such a son.

---

[4] **Komsomol**: Member of the Communist Youth Organization.
[5] **Red Army**: The reconstituted Soviet army founded by Commissar of Military and Naval Affairs Leon Trotsky (1879–1940) after the 1917 Bolshevik Revolution.

Letter from an Engineer [E.T.]

I am non-party [not Communist], married, with a 5-year-old son. I work as an engineer and have been and still am in a responsible position. I regard myself as a good citizen of the U.S.S.R.

I cannot agree with the prohibition of abortions. And I am very glad that this law has not entered into force but has been submitted to the workers for discussion.

The prohibition of abortion means the compulsory birth of a child to a woman who does not want children. The birth of a child ties married people to each other. Not everyone will readily abandon a child, for alimony is not all that children need. Where the parents produce a child of their own free will, all is well. But where a child comes into the family against the will of the parents, a grim personal drama will be enacted which will undoubtedly lower the social value of the parents and leave its mark on the child.

A categorical prohibition of abortion will confront young people with a dilemma: either complete sexual abstinence or the risk of jeopardizing their studies and disrupting their life. To my mind any prohibition of abortion is bound to mutilate many a young life. Apart from this, the result of such a prohibition might be an increase in the death-rate from abortions because they will then be performed illegally.

Letter from Professor K. Bogorekov, Leningrad

Abortions are harmful. One cannot disagree with that. But situations in life do exist when this harmful remedy will allow a woman to preserve normal conditions of life.

If a single child already ties a woman down, two, three, or four children leave her no possibility at all of participating in social life and having a job. A man suffers less. He gives the family his salary irrespective of the number of children — and the whole burden falls upon the mother.

Sometimes abortion is an extreme but decisive means of averting the disruption of a young woman's life. It may become imperative, through the accident of an unlucky liaison for a young girl-student without means for whom a child would be a heavy penalty, or through bad heredity of the parents or a number of other contingencies which play an important part in life and can often lead to its mutilation. All this must be taken into account.

It must not be thought that the majority of abortions are the result of irresponsible behavior. Experience shows that a woman resorts to abortion as a last resource when other methods of safeguard against pregnancy have failed and the birth of a child threatens to make her life more difficult.

Simple statistics show that in spite of this the birth-rate of our country is increasing rapidly.[6] And what is needed is not pressure, but a stimulation of the birth-rate by means of financial assistance, improved housing conditions, legal action against those who fail to pay alimony, etc. . . .

Abortions will become obsolete by themselves when knowledge of human anatomy spreads, methods of birth-control are more widely used and — last but not least — when housing conditions are improved. . . .

LETTER FROM PROFESSOR M. MALINOVSKY

Performing an abortion is an operation undoubtedly involving great risks. There are few operations so dangerous as the cleaning out of the womb during pregnancy. Under the best of conditions and in the hands of the most experienced specialist this operation still has a "normal" percentage of fatal cases. It is true that the percentage is not very high. Our surgeons have brought the technique of performing abortions to perfection. The foreign doctors who have watched operations in our gynæcological hospitals have unanimously testified that their technique is irreproachable. And yet . . . here are still cases in which it is fatal. This is understandable. The operation is performed in the dark and with instruments which, so far as their effect on so tender an organ as the womb is concerned, remind one of a crowbar. And even the most gifted surgeons, virtuosi at their job, occasionally cause great and serious injuries for which the woman often pays with her life. . . .

The slave-like conditions of hired labor, together with unemployment and poverty, deprive women in capitalist countries of the impulse for childbearing. Their "will to motherhood" is paralyzed. In our country all the conditions for giving birth to and bringing up a healthy generation exist. The "fear of motherhood," the fear of the morrow, the anxiety over the child's future are gone.

The lighthearted attitude towards the family, the feeling of irresponsibility which is still quite strong in men and women, the disgusting disrespect for women and children — all these must come before our guns. Every baseness towards women and every form of profligacy [extravagance] must be considered as serious antisocial acts. . . .

---

[6] **Birth-rate . . . increasing rapidly**: From what is known, this is a false statement.

READING AND DISCUSSION QUESTIONS

1. Why does K.B. argue that abortion must remain legal? What solution for reducing the number of abortions does she propose? What generational differences do you notice between K.B.'s position and the woman who responded to her?

2. Why does E.T. oppose the ban on abortion?

3. Professor K. Bogorekov says that abortion will cease when what happens?

4. What comparison does Professor Malinovsky make between socialist and capitalist countries?

VIEWPOINTS
Atomic Warfare Realized

DOCUMENT 30-5

HARRY S. TRUMAN
White House Press Release on Hiroshima
August 6, 1945

After the death of U.S. President Franklin Delano Roosevelt in April 1945, his vice president, Harry S. Truman (1884–1972), became president and inherited command of the Second World War. The U.S. government had engaged in nuclear weapons research since 1939, when notable scientists (including Albert Einstein) had signed a letter to the president warning of the possible military applications of atomic energy. The following press release, although formally issued after the August 6 nuclear attack on Hiroshima, was written by the War Department and submitted to President Truman

"Statement by the President of the United States" [White House press release], August 6, 1945 (Harry S. Truman Library and Museum, Ayers Papers), www.truman library.org/whistlestop/study_collections/bomb/large/documents/index.php ?documentdate=1945-08-06&documentid=59&studycollectionid=abomb&page number=1.

on July 30, a full week earlier. In effect, Truman's approval of this press release was a final go-ahead for the first military nuclear strike in history. The release itself was the first official notice to the American people — and the world — of the age of atomic weapons.

Sixteen hours ago an American airplane dropped one bomb on [Hiroshima] and destroyed its usefulness to the enemy.[7] That bomb had more power than 20,000 tons of T.N.T. It had more than two thousand times the blast power of the British "Grand Slam" which is the largest bomb ever yet used in the history of warfare.

The Japanese began the war from the air at Pearl Harbor.[8] They have been repaid many fold. And the end is not yet. With this bomb we have now added a new and revolutionary increase in destruction to supplement the growing power of our armed forces. In their present form these bombs are now in production and even more powerful forms are in development.

It is an atomic bomb. It is a harnessing of the basic power of the universe. The force from which the sun draws its power has been loosed against those who brought war to the Far East.

Before 1939, it was the accepted belief of scientists that it was theoretically possible to release atomic energy. But no one knew any practical method of doing it. By 1942, however, we knew that the Germans were working feverishly to find a way to add atomic energy to the other engines of war with which they hoped to enslave the world. But they failed. We may be grateful to Providence that the Germans got the V-1's and V-2's[9] late and in limited quantities and even more grateful that they did not get the atomic bomb at all.

The battle of the laboratories held fateful risks for us as well as the battles of the air, land and sea, and we have now won the battle of the laboratories as we have won the other battles.

Beginning in 1940, before Pearl Harbor, scientific knowledge useful in war was pooled between the United States and Great Britain, and many priceless helps to our victories have come from that arrangement. Under

---

[7] **[Hiroshima] . . . enemy**: While Hiroshima was an important port and military center, it was also a thriving city. In the original release, the city's name is withheld.
[8] **Pearl Harbor**: The U.S. Navy base in Hawaii and site of the 1941 Japanese attack on U.S. forces.
[9] **V-1's and V-2's**: Guided missiles used by Germany against targets in Great Britain during the Second World War.

that general policy the research on the atomic bomb was begun. With American and British scientists working together we entered the race of discovery against the Germans.

The United States had available the large number of scientists of distinction in the many needed areas of knowledge. It had the tremendous industrial and financial resources necessary for the project and they could be devoted to it without undue impairment of other vital war work. In the United States the laboratory work and the production plants, on which a substantial start had already been made, would be out of reach of enemy bombing, while at that time Britain was exposed to constant air attack and was still threatened with the possibility of invasion. For these reasons Prime Minister Churchill and President Roosevelt agreed that it was wise to carry on the project here. We now have two great plants and many lesser works devoted to the production of atomic power. Employment during peak construction numbered 125,000 and over 65,000 individuals are even now engaged in operating the plants. Many have worked there for two and a half years. Few know what they have been producing. They see great quantities of material going in and they see nothing coming out of these plants, for the physical size of the explosive charge is exceedingly small. We have spent two billion dollars on the greatest scientific gamble in history — and won.

But the greatest marvel is not the size of the enterprise, its secrecy, nor its cost, but the achievement of scientific brains in putting together infinitely complex pieces of knowledge held by many men in different fields of science into a workable plan. And hardly less marvellous has been the capacity of industry to design, and of labor to operate, the machines and methods to do things never done before so that the brain child of many minds came forth in physical shape and performed as it was supposed to do. Both science and industry worked under the direction of the United States Army, which achieved a unique success in managing so diverse a problem in the advancement of knowledge in an amazingly short time. It is doubtful if such another combination could be got together in the world. What has been done is the greatest achievement of organized science in history. It was done under high pressure and without failure.

We are now prepared to obliterate more rapidly and completely every productive enterprise the Japanese have above ground in any city. We shall destroy their docks, their factories, and their communications. Let there be no mistake; we shall completely destroy Japan's power to make war.

It was to spare the Japanese people from utter destruction that the ultimatum of July 26 was issued at Potsdam.[10] Their leaders promptly rejected that ultimatum. If they do not now accept our terms they may expect a rain of ruin from the air, the like of which has never been seen on this earth. Behind this air attack will follow sea and land forces in such numbers and power as they have not yet seen and with the fighting skill of which they are already well aware.

The Secretary of War, who has kept in personal touch with all phases of this project, will immediately make public a statement giving further details.

His statement will give facts concerning the sites of Oak Ridge near Knoxville, Tennessee, and at Richland near Pasco, Washington, and an installation near Santa Fe, New Mexico. Although the workers at the sites have been making materials to be used in producing the greatest destructive force in history they have not themselves been in danger beyond that of many other occupations, for the utmost care has been taken of their safety.

The fact that we can release atomic energy ushers in a new era in man's understanding of nature's forces. Atomic energy may in the future supplement the power that now comes from coal, oil, and falling water, but at present it cannot be produced on a basis to compete with them commercially. Before that comes there must be a long period of intensive research.

It has never been the habit of the scientists of this country or the policy of this Government to withhold from the world scientific knowledge. Normally, therefore, everything about the work with atomic energy would be made public.

But under present circumstances it is not intended to divulge the technical processes of production or all the military applications, pending further examination of possible methods of protecting us and the rest of the world from the danger of sudden destruction. I shall recommend that the Congress of the United States consider promptly the establishment of an appropriate commission to control the production and use of atomic power within the United States. I shall give further consideration and make further recommendations to the Congress as to how atomic power can become a powerful and forceful influence towards the maintenance of world peace.

---

[10] **The ultimatum of July 26 . . . at Potsdam**: The Potsdam Declaration of July 26, 1945, called for the "unconditional surrender" of Japanese military forces, warning of "prompt and utter destruction" unless Japan complied.

READING AND DISCUSSION QUESTIONS

1. Significant controversy exists among historians as to the U.S. motivation for using atomic weapons. How does Truman characterize Hiroshima and Japan in order to defend the use of the atomic bomb?

2. What points about the nuclear strike on Hiroshima does Truman emphasize? What details does he leave out?

3. Despite early competition and mutual suspicion between the United States and Great Britain, Truman emphasizes the collaboration and cooperation of the two countries in the effort to develop nuclear weapons. Why? What is the effect of this emphasis?

4. How do you evaluate Truman's statement that he would consider how atomic power could influence world peace?

DOCUMENT 30-6

TOSHIKO SAEKI

Interview with a Survivor of Hiroshima

1986

On August 6, 1945, the U.S. military attacked the Japanese city of Hiroshima with a nuclear weapon. Casualty estimates range from slightly below to well over 100,000 deaths caused by the immediate attack, with many more deaths linked to radiation and other long-term injuries. Although the firebombing of Tokyo, Dresden, and other cities had produced similarly high death tolls, the shocking destructive power of the atomic weapon was unprecedented. The experiences of survivors — known by the Japanese term hibakusha — *have been chronicled in many media and for a variety of reasons, including U.S. government studies on the effects of nuclear weapons on human populations. Here, a 1986 interview with a survivor by*

From the "Voice of Hibakusha" eyewitness accounts aired as part of *Hiroshima Witness,* produced by the Hiroshima Peace Cultural Center and NHK, the public broadcasting company of Japan. Translated into English and posted as "Testimony of Toshiko Saeki," AtomicArchive.com, www.atomicarchive.com/Docs/Hibakusha/Toshiko.shtml.

*representatives of the Hiroshima Peace Cultural Center presents a firsthand
account of the attack.*

Ms. Toshiko Saeki was 26 at the time of the bombing. She was at her parents' home in Yasufuruichi with her children. Returning to Hiroshima on
the afternoon of August 6th, she searched for her other relatives for many
days, but wasn't able to find them. Ms. Saeki lost thirteen members of her
family in the A-bomb attack.

SAEKI: I remember an airplane appeared from behind the mountains on
my left. I thought it was strange to see an airplane flying that time
all by itself. I looked at it and it was a B-29. It seemed very strange
since there were no anti aircraft guns firing at it. I watched it for a
while, then it disappeared. As soon as it disappeared, another airplane
appeared from the same direction. It seemed very, very strange. I was
still wondering what would happen. Then, suddenly there came a
flash of light. I can't describe what it was like. And then, I felt some hot
mask attacking me all of a sudden. I felt hot. I lay flat on the ground,
trying to escape from the heat. I forgot all about my children for a
moment. Then, there came a big sound, sliding wooden doors and
windows were blown off into the air. I turned around to see what had
happened to the house, and at one part of the ceiling, it was hanging
in the air. At some parts, the ceiling was caved in, burying my sister's
child and my child as well. When I saw what the blast had done to my
house which was far away from Hiroshima, I thought that Hiroshima
too must have been hit very hard. I begged my sister to let me go
back to Hiroshima to rescue my family. But by that time, things and
flames were falling from the sky. I was scared because I thought that
the debris might start fires in the mountains. By the time I managed
to prepare lunch to take along, it had started to rain, but I was glad to
have some rain. I went out to the main road, about five or six people
were coming [from] the direction of Hiroshima. And they were in a
horrible condition. They looked much worse than the actual exhibits today at the Peace Memorial Museum.[11] They were helping each
other. But they were barely making their way. I cried, "Which part of

---

[11] **Peace Memorial Museum**: A museum in Hiroshima, Japan, established in 1955
to preserve artifacts and testimony from the U.S. nuclear attack, its aftermath, and
related issues.

Hiroshima [was] attacked?" Everyone of them was only muttering, "Hiroshima was attacked. Hiroshima was badly hit." I began to run towards Hiroshima at full speed. As I was running, I saw a mad naked man running from the opposite direction. This man held a piece of iron over his head as if to hide his face since he had nothing on his body, I felt embarrassed. And I turned my back to him. The man was passing by me, then, I don't know why, but I ran after him and I asked him to stop for a moment. I asked him, "Which part of Hiroshima was attacked?" Then the man put down the piece of iron and he stared at me. He said, "You're Toshiko, aren't you?" He said, "Toshiko!"

INTERVIEWER: Who was this man?

SAEKI: Oh, I couldn't tell who he was right away. His face was so swollen I couldn't even tell whether his eyes were open. He called me, he said, "It's me! It's me, Toshiko! You can't tell?" Then I recognized him. He was my second eldest brother. He was heavily wounded.

INTERVIEWER: His body was covered with burns?

SAEKI: Yes, and he looked awful. He told me he'd been engulfed by flames and barely made his way out. He said that mother had woken him up . . . that morning, and that he was washing up when it happened. He told me that mother was on the third floor, and might have been blown away with the blast. He told me he thought that she must have died. I finally reached Hiroshima, well, afternoon I supposed.

INTERVIEWER: What was it like then in Hiroshima?

SAEKI: The whole town of Hiroshima was just in a mess. People were trying to find shelter, shelter elementary school building, anywhere. When I reached the local elementary school, people were even jammed in the hallways. Everywhere was filled with [moans] and groans and sobs and cries. Those of us who could move around were not treating the injured, but we were carrying dead bodies out of the building. I couldn't identify people by their faces. Trying to find my family, I had to take a look at their clothing, the clothes of the people who were still in the building. I couldn't find any of my family, so I went out to the playground. There were four piles of bodies and I stood in front of them. I just didn't know what to do. How could I find the bodies of my beloved ones? When I was going through the classrooms, I could take a look at each person, but these were mounds. If I tried to find my beloved ones, I would have to remove the bodies one by one. It just wasn't possible. I really felt sad. There were all kinds of bodies in the mounds. Not only human bodies but bodies of birds, cats and dogs and even that of a cow. It looked horrible. I can't find words to describe it. They were burned, just like human bodies, and some of them were half burnt. There was even a swollen horse. Just everything was there, everything.

INTERVIEWER: Ms. Saeki, how long did you search for your kin?

SAEKI: I went to Hiroshima to search on the 6th and the 7th, but on the 8th, they told me that there would be a big air-raid, so I didn't go on the 8th. And I didn't go on the 15th, but I went out almost everyday. I searched for mother for a long time. But I couldn't find her. I just couldn't find her. And finally on September 6th, my elder brother told us together in a living room. He called all the family members there together. He put something wrapped in a cloth. And he put it on the table which we used to take meals. My brother said, "Toshiko, unwrap Mother yourself. You've been out there looking for her everyday." So, I did as he told me and undid the wrapping expecting to find pieces of her bones. But it was the half of the burnt head of my mother. No eyes, no teeth, only a small portion of flesh was left on the back with some hair. And there were also her glasses. The glasses are exhibited near the exit of the Peace Memorial Museum as if to tell something to the people now.

INTERVIEWER: Your older brother, he also passed away?

SAEKI: Yes, after seeing the half burned head of our mother, my brother started to say funny things. He told us to bandage him well to cover the pores of his skin with white cloths. I asked what for and he said he was going to try to do some experiment to extract the radioactivity built up in his body. He told us to bandage him well, except for his eyes and his mouth. So even his nose was covered. Before he started the experiment, he drank a lot of water. He drank more than he could actually take, so, water was dripping from his nose and from his mouth. Then he said he was ready. He told us just to leave him alone and not to enter the room unless he cried out for help. He told us to go away and to keep away from him. And after a while, I peeped in the room. My brother was completely naked. He had stripped all the bandage cloths away. He was just lying still in the corner. I didn't know what was wrong with him. I thought he was dead. I banged at the door and I cried, "Brother! Brother, don't die!" He woke up and sat on the floor. He told me that the experiment had failed. He cried that it was a pity. He looked all right, but he was going crazy. He said, "I've grown bigger. Make an opening in the ceiling. This room is too small and I can't even stand up." After the horrible bomb hit Hiroshima, my brother's mind was shattered into pieces. War does not only destroy things, killing people, but shatters the hearts of people as well. This is war. And during the course of my life, I learned this on many various occasions. I know this now.

INTERVIEWER: Ms. Saeki, have you experienced any trouble concerning your health?

SAEKI: Yes, I have. By the end of August, maybe around, oh, the 28th or so, my hair started to fall out, I vomited blood. My teeth were coming out. And I had a fever of about 40 degrees. Nuclear war has nothing good. Whether you win or lose, it leaves you feeling futile with only your rage and with fear about the aftereffects of . . . radioactivity. The survivors have to live with this fear. At times I have thought I should have died then, it would have been better. But I must live for the sake of the people, all the people who lost their lives then. So I relate my experiences hoping that my talk would discourage people from making war. Our experience must not [be] forgotten. What we believed in during the war turned out to be worth nothing. We don't know to whom we should turn our rage. I went through hell on earth. . . . Hiroshima should not be repeated again. That is why I keep telling the same old story over and over again. And I'll keep repeating it.

READING AND DISCUSSION QUESTIONS

1. Toshiko Saeki gives a disturbingly personal account of the nuclear attack on Hiroshima. What is the value of her testimony, if any, in evaluating the history of atomic warfare?

2. Conventional weapons killed millions of people in the Second World War. What aspect of Saeki's testimony, if any, makes the atomic attacks on Hiroshima and Nagasaki unique in the war's long history of carnage?

3. Saeki repeatedly refers to the Peace Memorial Museum. What is the effect of bringing up the museum in her narrative? How does she compare or contrast the preservation of history with her own experiences? What does this suggest for your understanding of Saeki's experience and of the event?

COMPARATIVE QUESTIONS

1. The documents in this chapter present varying perspectives on individual lives and government policies during the Great Depression and the Second World War. What comparisons or contrasts can you draw among the documents based on the perspective of each author? Which documents present an "official" version and which a more personal version, and how does the author's perspective affect your reading of the documents?

2. Woody Guthrie presented the plight of migrant workers in popular song. What difference does the medium of his message (song) make? How does the medium of the other documents shape their content?

3. Both the Nuremberg Laws and Truman's press release reflect the efforts of very different governments to explain themselves or to further their respective interests. Compare and contrast these two documents.

4. Both the Scholtz-Klink and *Izvestiya* documents present issues related to women and society. Compare and contrast the goals and interests of women presented in each document, and describe how each document presents the intersection of female identity and the state.

5. The press release on Hiroshima and the interview with Toshiko Saeki present two very different accounts of the nuclear strike on the city of Hiroshima. How is the atomic bomb described in each document? How are the descriptions different, and how are they similar? If President Truman and Toshiko Saeki had met, what might they have said to one another?

6. In what ways does each document in this chapter quantify human suffering? When they cite numbers, what effect do those numbers give? Are numbers more or less powerful than other forms of description? Cite examples.

CHAPTER 31

Global Recovery and Division Between Superpowers

1945 to the Present

Almost immediately following the end of the Second World War, the competing economic and social systems of the United States and its European allies, on the one hand, and the Soviet Union and its allies, on the other, spawned the Cold War. This period of heightened military tension and mutual suspicion lasted more than four decades, as each side struggled to expand its influence through economic, political, and occasionally military activity while limiting that of its rival. Despite these tensions, international efforts to rebuild a war-torn world and promote new freedoms among former colonies demonstrated a persistent hope for a better future. Domestically, nations faced new challenges as the relative prosperity and security of a postwar world allowed a profound self-assessment of social, economic, and political values. The documents in this chapter present collective and individual attempts to understand and control the changing postwar world.

DOCUMENT 31-1

UNITED NATIONS GENERAL ASSEMBLY

Declaration on the Granting of Independence to Colonial Countries and Peoples

December 14, 1960

After centuries of empire building and colonization, European countries began to move toward decolonization in the decades after World War II. Many former colonies obtained their freedom after 1945, driven in large

General Assembly of the United Nations, Resolution 1514 (XV), December 14, 1960.

part by the increasing quest for self-government in Africa and Asia. In 1960, the United Nations formalized the gradual process of granting indepen- dence to these once-colonized peoples, outlining basic assumptions about human rights and self-rule that would guide much of the decolonization process. Most UN member nations voted in favor of the declaration; the nine that abstained, however, were all imperialist nations, including the United States, Great Britain, France, Spain, and Portugal.

GENERAL ASSEMBLY RESOLUTION 1514 (XV) OF 14 DECEMBER 1960

The General Assembly,

Mindful of the determination proclaimed by the peoples of the world in the Charter of the United Nations to reaffirm faith in fundamental human rights, in the dignity and worth of the human person, in the equal rights of men and women and of nations large and small and to promote social progress and better standards of life in larger freedom,

Conscious of the need for the creation of conditions of stability and well-being and peaceful and friendly relations based on respect for the principles of equal rights and self-determination of all peoples, and of universal respect for, and observance of, human rights and funda- mental freedoms for all without distinction as to race, sex, language, or religion,

Recognizing the passionate yearning for freedom in all dependent peoples and the decisive role of such peoples in the attainment of their independence,

Aware of the increasing conflicts resulting from the denial of or imped- iments in the way of the freedom of such peoples, which constitute a serious threat to world peace,

Considering the important role of the United Nations in assisting the movement for independence in Trust and Non-Self-Governing Territories,

Recognizing that the peoples of the world ardently desire the end of colonialism in all its manifestations,

Convinced that the continued existence of colonialism prevents the development of international economic co-operation, impedes the social, cultural, and economic development of dependent peoples and militates against the United Nations ideal of universal peace,

Affirming that peoples may, for their own ends, freely dispose of their natural wealth and resources without prejudice to any obligations arising out of international economic co-operation, based upon the principle of mutual benefit, and international law,

Believing that the process of liberation is irresistible and irreversible and that, in order to avoid serious crises, an end must be put to colonialism and all practices of segregation and discrimination associated therewith,

Welcoming the emergence in recent years of a large number of dependent territories into freedom and independence, and recognizing the increasingly powerful trends towards freedom in such territories which have not yet attained independence,

Convinced that all peoples have an inalienable right to complete freedom, the exercise of their sovereignty, and the integrity of their national territory,

Solemnly proclaims the necessity of bringing to a speedy and unconditional end colonialism in all its forms and manifestations;

And to this end

Declares that:

1. The subjection of peoples to alien subjugation, domination, and exploitation constitutes a denial of fundamental human rights, is contrary to the Charter of the United Nations, and is an impediment to the promotion of world peace and co-operation.
2. All peoples have the right to self-determination; by virtue of that right they freely determine their political status and freely pursue their economic, social, and cultural development.
3. Inadequacy of political, economic, social or educational preparedness should never serve as a pretext for delaying independence.
4. All armed action or repressive measures of all kinds directed against dependent peoples shall cease in order to enable them to exercise peacefully and freely their right to complete independence, and the integrity of their national territory shall be respected.
5. Immediate steps shall be taken, in Trust and Non-Self-Governing Territories or all other territories which have not yet attained independence, to transfer all powers to the peoples of those territories, without any conditions or reservations, in accordance with their freely expressed will and desire, without any distinction as to race, creed, or color, in order to enable them to enjoy complete independence and freedom.

6. Any attempt aimed at the partial or total disruption of the national unity and the territorial integrity of a country is incompatible with the purposes and principles of the Charter of the United Nations.

7. All States shall observe faithfully and strictly the provisions of the Charter of the United Nations, the Universal Declaration of Human Rights and the present Declaration on the basis of equality, non-interference in the internal affairs of all States, and respect for the sovereign rights of all peoples and their territorial integrity.

READING AND DISCUSSION QUESTIONS

1. According to this declaration, what goals do the peoples of the world share?

2. What problems would continued colonialism pose?

3. According to the declaration, what constitutes basic human rights?

4. How does the General Assembly describe its role in decolonization?

VIEWPOINTS

Clashes and Reforms Between Cold War Superpowers

DOCUMENT 31-2

HARRY S. TRUMAN

The Truman Doctrine

March 12, 1947

Not long after World War II ended, tensions heated up between leaders of the United States and the Soviet Union. Each country feared the other's influence on smaller nations and world politics. Joseph Stalin, who ruled the Soviet Union from 1927 to 1953, renewed efforts to spread communism,

President Harry S. Truman, Address Before a Joint Session of Congress, March 12, 1947.

prompting U.S. fears that if one nation fell to communism, others would surely follow. As the Soviet Union intensified its efforts to spread communism to countries such as Greece, Turkey, and Iran, President Harry S. Truman (in office 1945–1953) urged congressional approval for financial and military assistance to those same countries and others that sought to maintain free and democratic forms of government. This policy of containing communism became known as the Truman Doctrine.

Mr. President, Mr. Speaker, Members of the Congress of the United States:

The gravity of the situation which confronts the world today necessitates my appearance before a joint session of the Congress. The foreign policy and the national security of this country are involved. . . .

The very existence of the Greek state is today threatened by the terrorist activities of several thousand armed men, led by Communists, who defy the government's authority at a number of points, particularly along the northern boundaries. A Commission appointed by the United Nations Security Council is at present investigating disturbed conditions in northern Greece and alleged border violations along the frontier between Greece on the one hand and Albania, Bulgaria, and Yugoslavia on the other.

Meanwhile, the Greek Government is unable to cope with the situation. The Greek army is small and poorly equipped. It needs supplies and equipment if it is to restore the authority of the government throughout Greek territory. Greece must have assistance if it is to become a self-supporting and self-respecting democracy.

The United States must supply that assistance. We have already extended to Greece certain types of relief and economic aid but these are inadequate.

There is no other country to which democratic Greece can turn.

No other nation is willing and able to provide the necessary support for a democratic Greek government. . . .

Greece's neighbor, Turkey, also deserves our attention.

The future of Turkey as an independent and economically sound state is clearly no less important to the freedom-loving peoples of the world than the future of Greece. The circumstances in which Turkey finds itself today are considerably different from those of Greece. Turkey has been spared the disasters that have beset Greece. And during the war, the United States and Great Britain furnished Turkey with material aid.

Nevertheless, Turkey now needs our support.

Since the war Turkey has sought financial assistance from Great Britain and the United States for the purpose of effecting that modernization necessary for the maintenance of its national integrity.

That integrity is essential to the preservation of order in the Middle East.

The British government has informed us that, owing to its own difficulties can no longer extend financial or economic aid to Turkey.

As in the case of Greece, if Turkey is to have the assistance it needs, the United States must supply it. We are the only country able to provide that help.

I am fully aware of the broad implications involved if the United States extends assistance to Greece and Turkey, and I shall discuss these implications with you at this time.

One of the primary objectives of the foreign policy of the United States is the creation of conditions in which we and other nations will be able to work out a way of life free from coercion. This was a fundamental issue in the war with Germany and Japan. Our victory was won over countries which sought to impose their will, and their way of life, upon other nations.

To ensure the peaceful development of nations, free from coercion, the United States has taken a leading part in establishing the United Nations. The United Nations is designed to make possible lasting freedom and independence for all its members. We shall not realize our objectives, however, unless we are willing to help free peoples to maintain their free institutions and their national integrity against aggressive movements that seek to impose upon them totalitarian regimes. This is no more than a frank recognition that totalitarian regimes imposed on free peoples, by direct or indirect aggression, undermine the foundations of international peace and hence the security of the United States.

The peoples of a number of countries of the world have recently had totalitarian regimes forced upon them against their will. The Government of the United States has made frequent protests against coercion and intimidation, in violation of the Yalta agreement,[1] in Poland, Rumania, and Bulgaria. I must also state that in a number of other countries there have been similar developments.

---

[1] **Yalta agreement**: The 1945 accord reached by U.S. president Franklin Roosevelt, British prime minister Winston Churchill, and Soviet premier Joseph Stalin containing agreements to divide the peacetime world into three zones of occupation, to require an unconditional surrender from Germany, and to force Germany to make reparations to the Soviet Union.

At the present moment in world history nearly every nation must choose between alternative ways of life. The choice is too often not a free one.

One way of life is based upon the will of the majority, and is distinguished by free institutions, representative government, free elections, guarantees of individual liberty, freedom of speech and religion, and freedom from political oppression.

The second way of life is based upon the will of a minority forcibly imposed upon the majority. It relies upon terror and oppression, a controlled press and radio, fixed elections, and the suppression of personal freedoms.

I believe that it must be the policy of the United States to support free peoples who are resisting attempted subjugation by armed minorities or by outside pressures.

I believe that we must assist free peoples to work out their own destinies in their own way.

I believe that our help should be primarily through economic and financial aid which is essential to economic stability and orderly political processes.

It is necessary only to glance at a map to realize that the survival and integrity of the Greek nation are of grave importance in a much wider situation. If Greece should fall under the control of an armed minority, the effect upon its neighbor, Turkey, would be immediate and serious. Confusion and disorder might well spread throughout the entire Middle East.

Moreover, the disappearance of Greece as an independent state would have a profound effect upon those countries in Europe whose peoples are struggling against great difficulties to maintain their freedoms and their independence while they repair the damages of war.

It would be an unspeakable tragedy if these countries, which have struggled so long against overwhelming odds, should lose that victory for which they sacrificed so much. Collapse of free institutions and loss of independence would be disastrous not only for them but for the world. Discouragement and possibly failure would quickly be the lot of neighboring peoples striving to maintain their freedom and independence.

Should we fail to aid Greece and Turkey in this fateful hour, the effect will be far reaching to the West as well as to the East.

We must take immediate and resolute action.

I therefore ask the Congress to provide authority for assistance to Greece and Turkey in the amount of $400,000,000 for the period ending June 30, 1948. In requesting these funds, I have taken into consideration the maximum amount of relief assistance which would be furnished to Greece out of the $350,000,000 which I recently requested that the Congress authorize for the prevention of starvation and suffering in countries devastated by the war.

In addition to funds, I ask the Congress to authorize the detail of American civilian and military personnel to Greece and Turkey, at the request of those countries, to assist in the tasks of reconstruction, and for the purpose of supervising the use of such financial and material assistance as may be furnished. . . .

This is a serious course upon which we embark.

I would not recommend it except that the alternative is much more serious. The United States contributed $341,000,000,000 toward winning World War II. This is an investment in world freedom and world peace.

The seeds of totalitarian regimes are nurtured by misery and want. They spread and grow in the evil soil of poverty and strife. They reach their full growth when the hope of a people for a better life has died. We must keep that hope alive.

The free peoples of the world look to us for support in maintaining their freedoms.

If we falter in our leadership, we may endanger the peace of the world — and we shall surely endanger the welfare of our own nation.

Great responsibilities have been placed upon us by the swift movement of events.

I am confident that the Congress will face these responsibilities squarely.

READING AND DISCUSSION QUESTIONS

1. What reasons does Truman give to convince Congress to provide aid to Greece and Turkey? What consequences does he fear will result from not helping them?

2. How does Truman reconcile his proposal to Turkey and Greece with U.S. foreign policy goals?

3. What forms of government does he say people around the world must now choose between?

4. What conditions does Truman believe make the world ripe for totalitarian regimes?

DOCUMENT 31-3

NIKITA KHRUSHCHEV

On the Personality Cult and Its Consequences

1956

Following the end of the Second World War, the Soviet Union under Joseph Stalin directed its efforts toward rebuilding its infrastructure and, through military and economic means, competing with capitalist-aligned nations for global influence during the Cold War. Stalin's death in 1953 signaled the end of an era and occasioned a flurry of political repositioning. Nikita Khrushchev (1894–1971) emerged as leader of the Communist Party and, later, premier of the Soviet Union's government. During the February 1956 Communist Party Congress, Khrushchev gave his famous "Secret Speech," a dramatic repudiation of Stalin and his "cult of personality." The speech, excerpted here, indicated not only a shift in domestic Soviet policy, but also a tacit break with communist countries like China that had followed the USSR's Stalinist example.

Comrades! In the Party Central Committee's report to the 20th Congress, in a number of speeches by delegates to the Congress, and earlier at plenary sessions of the Party Central Committee, quite a lot has been said about the cult of the individual leader and its harmful consequences.

After Stalin's death the Party Central Committee began to implement a policy of explaining concisely and consistently that it is impermissible and foreign to the spirit of Marxism-Leninism to elevate one person, to transform him into a superman possessing supernatural characteristics akin to those of a god. Such a man supposedly knows everything, sees everything, thinks for everyone, can do anything, is infallible in his behavior.

Such a belief about a man — specifically about Stalin — was cultivated among us for many years.

The objective of the present report is not a thorough evaluation of Stalin's life and work. Concerning Stalin's merits, an entirely sufficient number of books, pamphlets and studies had already been written in his

Khrushchev Speaks: Selected Speeches, Articles, and Press Conferences, 1949–1961 (Ann Arbor: University of Michigan Press, 1963), 207–265.

lifetime. Stalin's role in the preparation and execution of the socialist revolution, in the Civil War, and in the fight for the construction of socialism in our country is universally known. Everyone knows this well. At present we are concerned with a question which has immense importance for the Party now and in the future — [we are concerned] with how the Stalin cult gradually grew, the cult which became at a certain specific stage the source of a whole series of exceedingly serious and grave perversions of Party principles, of Party democracy, of revolutionary legality.

Because not all as yet realize fully the practical consequences resulting from the cult of the individual leader, the great harm caused by the violation of the principle of collective direction of the Party, and because immense and limitless power was gathered in the hands of one person, the Party Central Committee considers it absolutely necessary to make the material pertaining to this matter available to the 20th Congress of the Communist Party of the Soviet Union.

Allow me first of all to remind you how severely the founders of Marxism-Leninism denounced every manifestation of the cult of the individual leader. In a letter to the German political worker Wilhelm Bloss, Marx stated: "Because of my antipathy to any cult of the individual, I never made public during the existence of the International the numerous addresses from various countries which recognized my merits, and which annoyed me. I did not even reply to them, except sometimes to rebuke their authors. Engels and I first joined the secret society of Communists on the condition that everything making for superstitious worship of authority would be deleted from its statutes. [Ferdinand] Lassalle subsequently did quite the opposite."

Some time later Engels wrote: "Both Marx and I have always been against any public manifestation with regard to individuals, with the exception of cases when it had an important purpose; and we most strongly opposed such manifestations as during our lifetime concerned us personally." . . .

Stalin acted not through persuasion, explanation and patient cooperation with people, but by imposing his concepts and demanding absolute submission to his opinion. Whoever opposed this concept or tried to prove his viewpoint and the correctness of his position was doomed to removal from the leading collective and to subsequent moral and physical annihilation. This was especially true during the period following the 17th Party Congress, when many prominent Party leaders and rank-and-file Party workers, honest and dedicated to the cause of communism, fell victim to Stalin's despotism. . . .

Stalin originated the concept "enemy of the people." This term automatically rendered it unnecessary that the ideological errors of a man or men engaged in a controversy be proved; this term made possible the use of the most cruel repression, violating all norms of revolutionary legality, against anyone who in any way disagreed with Stalin, against those who were only suspected of hostile intent, against those who had bad reputations. This concept, "enemy of the people," actually eliminated the possibility of any kind of ideological fight or the making of one's views known on this or that issue, even issues of a practical nature. In the main, and in actuality, the only proof of guilt used, contrary to all norms of current law, was the "confession" of the accused himself; and, as subsequent investigation has proved, "confessions" were obtained through physical pressures against the accused.

This led to glaring violations of revolutionary legality, and to the fact that many entirely innocent persons, who in the past had defended the Party line, became victims.

We must assert that, in regard to those persons who in their time had opposed the Party line, there were often no sufficiently serious reasons for their physical annihilation. The formula "enemy of the people" was specifically introduced for the purpose of physically annihilating such individuals. . . .

Stalin . . . used extreme methods and mass repressions at a time when the revolution was already victorious, when the Soviet state was strengthened, when the exploiting classes were already liquidated and socialist relations were rooted solidly in all phases of national economy, when our party was politically consolidated and had strengthened itself both numerically and ideologically. It is clear that here Stalin showed in a whole series of cases his intolerance, his brutality and his abuse of power. Instead of proving his political correctness and mobilizing the masses, he often chose the path of repression and physical annihilation, not only against actual enemies, but also against individuals who had not committed any crimes against the Party and the Soviet government. . . .

[Khrushchev details the purging and execution of members of government in the 1930s and 1940s, using secret police archives to argue for Stalin's murderous misuse of power.]

All the more monstrous are the acts, initiated by Stalin, which are gross violations of the basic Leninist principles of the nationalities policy of the Soviet state. We refer to the mass deportations from their native territory of whole nations, including all [their] Communists and Young Communists, without any exception; this deportation action was not dictated by any military considerations.

Thus, already at the end of 1943, when there occurred a permanent breakthrough on the fronts of the great patriotic war benefiting the Soviet Union, a decision was taken and carried out concerning deportation of all the Karachai from the lands on which they lived. In the same period, at the end of December 1943, the same lot befell the whole population of the Kalmyk Autonomous Republic. In March 1944, all the Chechen and Ingush people were deported and the Chechen-Ingush Autonomous Republic was liquidated. In April 1944, all Balkars were deported to faraway places from the territory of the Kabardino-Balkar Autonomous Republic and the republic itself was renamed the Kabardian Autonomous Republic. The Ukrainians avoided this fate only because there were too many of them and there was no place to which to deport them. Otherwise, he would have deported them too. . . .

Not only no Marxist-Leninist, but also no man of common sense can grasp how it is possible to make whole nations responsible for inimical activity, including women, children, old people, Communists and Young Communists, to use mass repression against them and to expose them to misery and suffering for the hostile acts of individual persons or groups of persons. . . .

Comrades! The cult of the individual caused the employment of faulty principles in Party work and in economic activity; it brought about gross violation of inner-Party and Soviet democracy, sterile administration by fiat, deviations of all sorts, covering up of shortcomings, and varnishing of reality. Our country gave birth to many flatterers and specialists in false optimism and deceit. . . .

Stalin's reluctance to consider life's realities and the fact that he was not aware of the real state of affairs in the provinces can be illustrated by his direction of agriculture.

All those who interested themselves even a little in the national situation saw the difficult situation in agriculture, but Stalin never even noted it. Did we tell Stalin about this? Yes; we told him; but he did not support us. Why? Because Stalin never traveled anywhere, did not meet city and collective farm workers; he did not know the actual situation in the provinces.

He knew the countryside and agriculture only from films. And these films had dressed up and beautified the existing situation in agriculture.

Many films pictured collective farm life as if the tables bent under the weight of turkeys and geese. Evidently Stalin thought that it was actually so. . . .

Stalin cut himself off from the people and never went anywhere. This lasted tens of years. The last time he visited a village was in January 1928, when he visited Siberia in connection with grain deliveries. How then could he have known the situation in the provinces?

And when he was once told during a discussion that our situation on the land was a difficult one and that the livestock situation was especially bad, . . . Stalin proposed that the taxes paid by the collective farms and by the collective farmers should be raised by 40,000,000,000 rubles. According to him, the peasants were well-off and the collective farmer would need to sell only one more chicken to pay his tax in full.

Imagine what this would have meant. Certainly 40,000,000,000 rubles is a sum which the collective farmers did not realize for all the products which they sold to the government. In 1952, for instance, the collective farms and the collective farmers received 26,280,000,000 rubles for all their products delivered and sold to the government.

Did Stalin's position rest, then, on data of any sort whatever? Of course not.

In such cases facts and figures did not interest him. If Stalin said anything, it meant it was so — after all, he was a "genius," and a genius does not need to count, he only needs to look and can immediately tell how it should be. When he expresses his opinion, everyone has to echo it and to admire his wisdom. . . .

Comrades! If today we sharply criticize the cult of the individual leader which was so widespread during Stalin's lifetime and if we speak about the many negative phenomena generated by this cult which is so alien to the spirit of Marxism-Leninism, various persons may ask: How could it be? Stalin headed the Party and the country for 30 years, and many victories were gained during his lifetime. Can we deny this? In my opinion, the question can be asked in this manner only by those who are blinded and hopelessly hypnotized by the cult of the individual leader, only by those who do not understand the essence of the revolution and of the Soviet state, only by those who do not understand in a Leninist manner the role of the Party and of the people in the development of Soviet society.

The socialist revolution was accomplished by the working class and the poor peasantry, with the partial support of the middle peasants. It was accomplished by the people under the leadership of the Bolshevist party. Lenin's great service consisted in that he created a militant party of the working class; he was armed with Marxist understanding of the laws of social development and with the science of proletarian victory in the struggle with capitalism, and he steeled this party in the crucible of the revolutionary struggle of the masses of the people. During this struggle the Party consistently defended the interests of the people, became their experienced leader, and led the working masses to power, to the creation of the first socialist state.

You remember well Lenin's wise words that the Soviet state is strong because of the awareness of the masses, because history is created by the millions and tens of millions of people.

Our historic victories were attained thanks to the organizational work of the Party, to the many local organizations, and to the self-sacrificing work of our great people. These victories are the result of the great drive and activity of the people and Party as a whole; they are not at all the fruit of Stalin's leadership, as was pictured during the period of the cult of the individual leader.

If we are to consider this matter as Marxists and as Leninists, then we must state unequivocally that the leadership practice which came into being during the last years of Stalin's life became a serious obstacle in the path of the development of Soviet society.

Stalin often failed for months to take up exceedingly important problems — the solution of which could not be postponed — concerning the life of the Party and state. During Stalin's leadership our peaceful relations with other nations were often threatened because one-man decisions could and often did cause great complications. . . .

Comrades! We must resolutely abolish the cult of the individual leader once and for all; we must draw the proper conclusions concerning both ideological-theoretical and practical work.

It is necessary for this purpose:

First, in a Bolshevist manner to condemn and to eradicate the cult of the individual leader as alien to Marxism-Leninism and not consonant with the principles of Party leadership and the norms of Party life, and to fight inexorably all attempts at bringing back this practice in one form or another.

To return to and actually practice in all our ideological work the very important Marxist-Leninist theses about the people as the maker of history and the creator of all mankind's material and spiritual benefits, about the decisive role of the Marxist party in the revolutionary struggle to change society, about the victory of communism.

In this connection we shall be obliged to do much to examine critically from the Marxist-Leninist viewpoint and to correct the widespread, erroneous views connected with the cult of the individual leader in the spheres of history, philosophy, economics and other sciences, as well as in literature and the fine arts. It is especially necessary that in the immediate future we compile a serious textbook of the history of our party, edited in accordance with scientific Marxist objectivism, a textbook of the history of Soviet society, a book pertaining to the events of the Civil War and the great patriotic war.

Secondly, to continue systematically and consistently the work done by the Party Central Committee during the past years, work characterized by scrupulous observance — in all Party organizations, from bottom to top — of the Leninist principles of Party leadership; characterized above all by the main principle, collective leadership; characterized by observance of the norms of Party life described in the Statutes of our party; and, finally, characterized by wide practice of criticism and self-criticism.

Thirdly, to restore completely the Leninist principles of Soviet, socialist democracy, expressed in the Constitution of the Soviet Union; to fight willfulness of individuals abusing their power. The evil caused by acts violating revolutionary socialist legality which accumulated over a long period as a result of the negative influence of the cult of the individual leader must be completely corrected.

Comrades! The 20th Congress of the Communist Party of the Soviet Union has manifested with new strength the unshakable unity of our party, its cohesiveness around the Central Committee, its resolute will to accomplish the great task of building communism.

READING AND DISCUSSION QUESTIONS

1. How does Khrushchev's speech challenge or support Soviet communism?

2. How does Khrushchev support his critique of Stalin, the leader of the Soviet Union for three decades? Why do you suppose he used the justification that he did?

3. Although Khrushchev gave the "secret speech" in a closed session, it was quickly reproduced and transmitted throughout the USSR and eastern Europe and printed in Western media shortly thereafter. What do you imagine Khrushchev hoped to accomplish with his speech? How might it have been received by ordinary Russians? By readers in the West?

MIKHAIL GORBACHEV

From Perestroika: New Thinking for Our Country and the World

1986

When Mikhail Gorbachev (b. 1931) came to power in the Soviet Union in 1985, his country faced serious challenges. The economy was suffering under the weight of the arms race with the United States and due to worker absenteeism and declining productivity. An ardent Socialist, Gorbachev recognized that the system needed an overhaul if it were to succeed. He also believed that political changes — including negotiations with the West and a democratization of socialism — were crucial. In his 1987 book, Perestroika, *Gorbachev outlined his solutions for reforming the Soviet Union, which included* perestroika *(economic restructuring) and* glasnost *(greater openness and expanded freedom of expression and speech).*

Perestroika[2] is an urgent necessity arising from the profound processes of development in our socialist society. This society is ripe for change. It has long been yearning for it. Any delay in beginning perestroika could have led to an exacerbated internal situation in the near future, which, to put it bluntly, would have been fraught with serious social, economic, and political crises. . . .

In the latter half of the seventies — something happened that was at first sight inexplicable. The country began to lose momentum. Economic failures became more frequent. Difficulties began to accumulate and deteriorate, and unresolved problems to multiply. Elements of what we call stagnation and other phenomena alien to socialism began to appear in the life of society. A kind of "braking mechanism" affecting social and

Mikhail Gorbachev, *Perestroika: New Thinking for Our Country and the World* (New York: Harper and Row, 1987).

[2] **Perestroika:** Gorbachev's economic restructuring reform included an easing of government price controls on some goods, more independence for state enterprises, and the establishment of profit-seeking private cooperatives to provide personal services for consumers.

economic development formed. And all this happened at a time when scientific and technological revolution opened up new prospects for economic and social progress. . . .

An absurd situation was developing. The Soviet Union, the world's biggest producer of steel, raw materials, fuel and energy, has shortfalls in them due to wasteful or inefficient use. One of the biggest producers of grain for food, it nevertheless has to buy millions of tons of grain a year for fodder. We have the largest number of doctors and hospital beds per thousand of the population and, at the same time, there are glaring shortcomings in our health services. Our rockets can find Halley's comet and fly to Venus with amazing accuracy, but side by side with these scientific and technological triumphs is an obvious lack of efficiency in using scientific achievements for economic needs, and many Soviet household appliances are of poor quality.

This, unfortunately, is not all. A gradual erosion of the ideological and moral values of our people began.

It was obvious to everyone that the growth rates were sharply dropping and that the entire mechanism of quality control was not working properly; there was a lack of receptivity to the advances in science and technology; the improvement in living standards was slowing down and there were difficulties in the supply of foodstuffs, housing, consumer goods, and services.

On the ideological plane as well, the braking mechanism brought about ever greater resistance to the attempts to constructively scrutinize the problems that were emerging and to the new ideas. Propaganda of success — real or imagined — was gaining the upper hand. Eulogizing and servility were encouraged; the needs and opinions of ordinary working people, of the public at large, were ignored. . . .

The presentation of a "problem-free" reality backfired: a breach had formed between word and deed, which bred public passivity and disbelief in the slogans being proclaimed. It was only natural that this situation resulted in a credibility gap: everything that was proclaimed from the rostrums and printed in newspapers and textbooks was put in question. Decay began in public morals; the great feeling of solidarity with each other that was forged during the heroic times of the Revolution [1917], the first five-year plans,[3] the Great Patriotic War,[4] and postwar rehabilitation was weakening;

---

[3] **five-year plans**: Stalin's attempts to transform the rural, agrarian Soviet Union into an industrial state. The first plan began in 1928, the second in 1932 (a year early), and succeeded at tremendous human cost.

[4] **Great Patriotic War**: Soviet name for World War II, in which the Soviets lost at least 20 million people.

alcoholism, drug addiction, and crime were growing; and the penetration of the stereotypes of mass culture alien to us, which bred vulgarity and low tastes and brought about ideological barrenness increased. . . .

An unbiased and honest approach led us to the only logical conclusion that the country was verging on crisis. . . .

I would like to emphasize here that this analysis began a long time before the April Plenary Meeting[5] and that therefore its conclusions were well thought out. It was not something out of the blue, but a balanced judgment. It would be a mistake to think that a month after the Central Committee Plenary Meeting in March 1985, which elected me General Secretary, there suddenly appeared a group of people who understood everything and knew everything, and that these people gave clear-cut answers to all questions. Such miracles do not exist.

The need for change was brewing not only in the material sphere of life but also in public consciousness. People who had practical experience, a sense of justice and commitment to the ideals of Bolshevism[6] criticized the established practice of doing things and noted with anxiety the symptoms of moral degradation and erosion of revolutionary ideals and socialist values. . . .

Perestroika is closely connected with socialism as a system. That side of the matter is being widely discussed, especially abroad, and our talk about perestroika won't be entirely clear if we don't touch upon that aspect.

Does perestroika mean that we are giving up socialism or at least some of its foundations? Some ask this question with hope, others with misgiving.

There are people in the West who would like to tell us that socialism is in a deep crisis and has brought our society to a dead end. That's how they interpret our critical analysis of the situation at the end of the seventies and beginning of the eighties. We have only one way out, they say: to adopt capitalist methods of economic management and social patterns, to drift toward capitalism.

They tell us that nothing will come of perestroika within the framework of our system. They say we should change this system and borrow from the experience of another socio-political system. To this they add that, if the Soviet Union takes this path and gives up its socialist choice, close links with the West will supposedly become possible. They go so far

---

[5] **April Plenary Meeting**: Regular meeting of the Communist Party's officials.
[6] **Bolshevism**: Lenin's program of Soviet communism was enacted in Russia after the October Revolution of 1917 (see Document 28-3).

as to claim that the October 1917 Revolution was a mistake which almost completely cut off our country from world social progress.

To put an end to all the rumors and speculations that abound in the West about this, I would like to point out once again that we are conducting all our reforms in accordance with the socialist choice. We are looking within socialism, rather than outside it, for the answers to all the questions that arise. We assess our successes and errors alike by socialist standards. Those who hope that we shall move away from the socialist path will be greatly disappointed. Every part of our program of perestroika — and the program as a whole, for that matter — is fully based on the principle of more socialism and more democracy. . . .

We will proceed toward better socialism rather than away from it. We are saying this honestly, without trying to fool our own people or the world. Any hopes that we will begin to build a different, nonsocialist society and go over to the other camp are unrealistic and futile. Those in the West who expect us to give up socialism will be disappointed. It is high time they understood this, and, even more importantly, proceeded from that understanding in practical relations with the Soviet Union. . . .

We want more socialism and, therefore, more democracy.

READING AND DISCUSSION QUESTIONS

1. What does Gorbachev believe caused the Soviet Union's difficulties?
2. Why is the "credibility gap" such a key factor?
3. What do critics outside the Soviet Union have to say about perestroika?
4. Is perestroika meant to move the Soviet Union away from socialism? What is Gorbachev's vision of perestroika as a solution to his country's woes?

DOCUMENT 31-5

GEORGE C. WALLACE
School House Door Speech
June 11, 1963

George C. Wallace (1919–1998) was an American politician and defender of the segregation of whites and African Americans. Despite more nuanced stances on race and equality earlier in his career, Wallace fought vigorously as governor of Alabama against the federal government's efforts to enforce the 1954 Supreme Court decision that outlawed separate public schools for white and African American citizens. His multiple presidential campaigns, while unsuccessful, revealed significant national support for his inflammatory rhetoric of anti-elite, racist populism. This speech, delivered while Wallace physically blocked two African American students from entering the University of Alabama in 1963, both exhibited his segregationist rhetoric and vaulted him to national prominence. More immediately, however, Wallace was made to step aside when President John F. Kennedy federalized the Alabama National Guard and sent them to the campus.

As Governor and Chief Magistrate of the State of Alabama I deem it to be my solemn obligation and duty to stand before you representing the rights and sovereignty of this State and its peoples.

The unwelcomed, unwanted, unwarranted and force-induced intrusion upon the campus of the University of Alabama today of the might of the Central Government[7] offers frightful example of the oppression of the rights, privileges and sovereignty of this State by officers of the Federal Government. This intrusion results solely from force, or threat of force, undignified by any reasonable application of the principle of law, reason and justice. It is important that the people of this State and nation understand that this action is in violation of rights reserved to the State by the

---

"Governor George C. Wallace's School House Door Speech," Alabama Department of Archives and History, www.archives.state.al.us/govs_list/schooldoor.html.

[7] **intrusion upon the campus . . . of the might of the Central Government**: Wallace refers here both to the policies of the federal government and to the presence of federal marshals, the deputy attorney general of the United States, and members of the Alabama National Guard on the University of Alabama's campus.

Constitution of the United States and the Constitution of the State of Alabama. While some few may applaud these acts, millions of Americans will gaze in sorrow upon the situation existing at this great institution of learning.

Only the Congress makes the law of the United States. To this date no statutory authority can be cited to the people of this Country which authorizes the Central Government to ignore the sovereignty of this State in an attempt to subordinate the rights of Alabama and millions of Americans. There has been no legislative action by Congress justifying this intrusion.

When the Constitution of the United States was enacted, a government was formed upon the premise that people, as individuals are endowed with the rights of life, liberty, and property, and with the right of self-government. The people and their local self-governments formed a Central Government and conferred upon it certain stated and limited powers. All other powers were reserved to the states and to the people.

Strong local government is the foundation of our system and must be continually guarded and maintained. The Tenth Amendment to the Constitution of the United States reads as follows:

> "The powers not delegated to the United States by the Constitution, nor prohibited by it to the States, are reserved to the states respectively, or to the people."

This amendment sustains the right of self-government and grants the State of Alabama the right to enforce its laws and regulate its internal affairs.

This nation was never meant to be a unit of one . . . but a united [sic] of the many. . . . This is the exact reason our freedom loving forefathers established the states, so as to divide the rights and powers among the states, insuring that no central power could gain master government control.

There can be no submission to the theory that the Central Government is anything but a servant of the people. We are a God-fearing people — not government-fearing people. We practice today the free heritage bequeathed to us by the Founding Fathers.

I stand here today, as Governor of this sovereign State, and refuse to willingly submit to illegal usurpation of power by the Central Government. I claim today for all the people of the State of Alabama those rights reserved to them under the Constitution of the United States. Among those powers so reserved and claimed is the right of state authority in the operation of the public schools, colleges and Universities. My action does not constitute disobedience to legislative and constitutional provisions. It is not defiance — for defiance sake, but for the purpose of raising basic and fundamental constitutional questions. My action is raising a call for strict adherence to the Constitution of the United States as it was written — for a cessation of usurpation and abuses. My action seeks to avoid having state sovereignty sacrificed on the altar of political expediency.

Further, as the Governor of the State of Alabama, I hold the supreme executive power of this State, and it is my duty to see that the laws are faithfully executed. The illegal and unwarranted actions of the Central Government on this day, contrary to the laws, customs and traditions of this State is calculated to disturb the peace.

I stand before you here today in place of thousands of other Alabamians whose presence would have confronted you had I been derelict and neglected to fulfill the responsibilities of my office. It is the right of every citizen, however humble he may be, through his chosen officials of representative government to stand courageously against whatever he believes to be the exercise of power beyond the Constitutional rights conferred upon our Federal Government. It is this right which I assert for the people of Alabama by my presence here today.

Again I state — this is the exercise of the heritage of the freedom and liberty under the law — coupled with responsible government.

Now, therefore, in consideration of the premises, and in my official capacity as Governor of the State of Alabama, I do hereby make the following solemn proclamation:

WHEREAS, the Constitution of Alabama vests the supreme executive powers of the State in the Governor as the Chief Magistrate, and said Constitution requires of the Governor that he take care that the laws be faithfully executed; and,

WHEREAS, the Constitution of the United States, Amendment 10, reserves to the States respectively or to the people, those powers not delegated to the United States; and,

WHEREAS, the operation of the public school system is a power reserved to the State of Alabama under the Constitution of the United States and Amendment 10 thereof; and,

WHEREAS, it is the duty of the Governor of the State of Alabama to preserve the peace under the circumstances now existing, which power is one reserved to the State of Alabama and the people thereof under the Constitution of the United States and Amendment 10 thereof.

NOW, THEREFORE, I, George C. Wallace, as Governor of the State of Alabama, have by my action raised issues between the Central Government and the Sovereign State of Alabama, which said issues should be adjudicated in the manner prescribed by the Constitution of the United

States; and now being mindful of my duties and responsibilities under the Constitution of the United States, the Constitution of the State of Alabama, and seeking to preserve and maintain the peace and dignity of this State, and the individual freedoms of the citizens thereof, do hereby denounce and forbid this illegal and unwarranted action by the Central Government.

READING AND DISCUSSION QUESTIONS

1. What issue does Wallace cite in this document as his principal concern? What is the legal and moral basis for his actions?

2. Where, if anywhere, does Wallace mention racial integration in his speech? How might this speech have appealed to Americans in other states?

3. Imagine that the U.S. federal government and Wallace had taken opposite positions: that the U.S. government had mandated segregation and Wallace had protested it. If Wallace had delivered this exact speech to denounce the federal government's right to segregate public schools, would your response to the speech be different? If so, how? If not, why not?

> DOCUMENT 31-6

MALE JAPANESE CITIZENS
"Ikigai"
2003

Following Japan's cataclysmic defeat in the Second World War, the American-led occupation forces worked closely with Japanese political and industrial leaders to rebuild the war-torn country and, during the Cold War, to make

---

Excerpted from Gordon Mathews, "Can a Real Man Live for His Family? *Ikigai* and Masculinity in Today's Japan," in James Roberson and Nobue Suzuki, eds., Men and Masculinities in Contemporary Japan (New York: RoutledgeCurzon, 2003), 109–225.

Japan a bulwark against communism in East Asia. Close relationships between industry and government, a hallmark of the prewar economy, continued to drive Japan's postwar economic recovery, though in slightly different forms. Within the corporate world, a highly gendered Japanese workforce also depended on long-term relationships, and lifetime employment at a single company became the norm for Japanese men. After the collapse of the economic "bubble" in the early 1990s, however, Japanese men began to question their relationship with Japan's economy and society. The selections here present a range of contemporary Japanese male voices on the changing definition of ikigai — *that which makes life worth living.*

Corporate Executive

For the past thirty years, my *ikigai* has been the companies I've worked for; they've been more important to me than my family. I don't expect much from my family; they don't expect me to be at home on weekends anymore. Yes, I can't say that I'm a family man. I have more human communication with the young girls . . . in my office than I do with my own daughters. . . .

There are fewer and fewer company men like me these days; there are many more "my home" types — these kind of people aren't at all happy if I tell them to come to the office on Sunday! I've never said no to any of my job assignments — I was always there when they needed me. I like men who do that: manly men . . . , like Western cowboys! Men living for their companies are better than those who live for their families; that's why Japan's developed! I get upset when I see a young man with dyed hair driving around in a fancy car with a pretty girl. Fifty years ago, people his age all died in the war; they didn't have the chance to enjoy their youth! I want to drag that young man out of his car and put a judo hold on him, teach him a lesson!

High School Teacher

Maybe Americans can separate business and private life, but I can't, and most Japanese can't. If you don't have business, you can't have any private life. . . . In my house, my wife was like a widow; I was busy, even on Sundays, with my school clubs. So now, if I'm not home, everyone feels more relaxed! . . .

Young people today overwhelmingly value being with their families. They calmly say, "My child's sick. I'll take the day off." Nobody ever did that when I was young! Today's young people don't have any fighting spirit! They relax with their families before they think about work!

Sarariman (White-Collar Worker) 1

The problem was that we worked too hard, generated too much money, that had to be ploughed back into the system, into stocks and land, creating "the bubble economy." . . . If only Japanese hadn't worked so hard, maybe the economic downturn would never have happened.

Sarariman 2

If you ask my coworkers whether they find *ikigai* in work for this company, they might say they do. But they'd be lying. . . . But, then, maybe they really do find *ikigai* here. If you don't have time to do anything but work, then isn't that your *ikigai*?

Retired Railroad Worker

You know how work is. The husband has to be subservient to his boss, and so when he comes home, he wants to boss around his wife and children: "Turn off the TV! Put the kids to bed!" And communication between husband and wife, father and children, goes bad.

Self-Employed Repairman

I believe that the husband's the boss of the family. A wife should know what her husband is thinking by looking at his face. She should properly send him off to work in the morning; and when he comes home at night, there should be a drink and some good food waiting for him. A husband should educate his wife to do that. . . . When I got married, my wife fell in love with me; I didn't care whether I married her or not. She works part-time at the supermarket as a cashier — she's a little overbearing now, since she's got her own money.

Sarariman 3

Early in our marriage, my wife was always angry because I came home late from work, and because I wasn't *yasashii* (affectionate); I didn't take her anywhere on weekends, I didn't convey to her that I loved her. We came very close to divorce several times. Once my wife left with the kids and didn't come home for three days; I still don't know where they went. I wasn't thinking much about my family then; that's why my wife got so upset. I realized that I'd have to change. My wife made me promise that, unless I was out of town on business, I'd have breakfast with the family no matter how late I came home the previous night. I also spend every Sunday — at least half the day — with my family. Saturdays I use for myself: I go fishing. . . . I feel exhausted because of the stress on my job — that's why I need Saturdays for myself. When I'm with my family, I just can't get rid of stress.

BANK WORKER

I don't like my work — I really hate it — but I wouldn't want to stay at home either, taking care of my children. Maybe that's my pride — maybe I don't want to deviate from the ideal image of a man. A man is supposed to work outside the home. In Japan, if a man says his child rather than his work is his *ikigai*, he'll be considered a sissy. . . . I could never say that. . . . In Japan women are discriminated against in the workplace, but at the same time they have less obligation; they have more time to follow their own pursuits. Do I wish I could be a woman instead of a man? Well . . . I could never say that; but it's possible that it's true.

JUNIOR HIGH SCHOOL TEACHER

I want to be with my wife when she gives birth; I'll need to take three days off from school for that. When I told that to the mothers in the PTA, they said, "That's great — go ahead!" I thought they were going to say, "What? Why so long a vacation!" But they didn't. They really appreciate me! . . . I usually get home by 7:30 or 8:00; sometimes not until 9:00 or 10:00. All I can do after I come home so late is bathe, eat and sleep; that's tough on my wife. I'm really tired. Sometimes it's just too much trouble to listen to her, to be honest. I'd really like more free time. . . . My family — my wife and child to be — is more important than my work. I'd quit my work, if I had to, for my family. My family is my *ikigai*. I just wish I had more time to be with my family.

CONSTRUCTION WORKER AND FORMER ROCK MUSICIAN

I like myself now because I'm working hard for my family, but I hate myself because I gave up music. I'm not a bad father — I'm supporting my family — but maybe it'd be better for my two kids if I showed them a father who's pursuing his dream. Life isn't only a matter of making money; that's why I half regret my life now. I want to quit my job and play music again. But it'd be hard. The older you get, the less courage you've got. Compared to five years ago, I'm much more of a coward than I used to be. Maybe I've become a better husband and father to the extent that I've grown chicken-hearted! . . . I live for my dream of music, but I also live for my wife: she too is my *ikigai*. But yeah, I guess that my real *ikigai* is music. I don't play the guitar much these days, but I have that desire — I'll have that for the rest of my life.

READING AND DISCUSSION QUESTIONS

1. How do these accounts of *ikigai* present Japan's economic success in the postwar era?

2. Some of these accounts deal explicitly with Japanese history, including the Second World War. How does history inform each of these accounts? Why might history play a larger role in some accounts than in others?

3. How does each of these accounts talk about gender? What women's roles are described here? Based on these accounts, what can you say about gender roles in contemporary Japan?

COMPARATIVE QUESTIONS

1. Each of the documents in this chapter expresses a socioeconomic change of some sort. What change does the author of each document confront, and how? Does the author celebrate or resist the change?

2. Truman, Khrushchev, and Gorbachev deal explicitly with Cold War tensions between the capitalist and communist blocs — the so-called First and Second Worlds. How does each document present these tensions? Are there any common themes that unite the capitalist and communist documents? If so, what are they?

3. Several of these documents deal with the question of freedom. How do Truman, Wallace, and the Japanese men present the twin ideas of freedom and authority? What authority or structure is presented in each case, and how is that authority evaluated? What limits, if any, should be placed on freedom?

4. The range of opinions in the document on *ikigai* can be compared both with earlier Japanese attitudes, such as the unwavering nationalism of

Saigō Takamori's writings in Meiji Japan (Document 26-3), and with the plight of workers expressed in Woody Guthrie's ballad (Document 30-1). How can you read the ideas of *ikigai* as connected to Japanese history through Saigō, and how can you connect them to the uncertain realities of capitalist life expressed by Guthrie? With which do they have more in common, and why?

5. Wallace and Khrushchev were both strong speakers who garnered many supporters. How might Khrushchev have replied to Wallace's argument for the state's power?

CHAPTER 32

Independence, Progress, and Conflict in Asia and the Middle East

1945 to the Present

For centuries, Western authors have represented the vast and diverse territory of Asia as "the Orient," lumping together cultures as diverse as Arab Muslims, Han Chinese, Indian Hindus, and Vietnamese Buddhists. The colonial presence of Europeans and Americans in regions from North Africa to Vietnam helped to reinforce the image of a mysterious and backward Orient that was defined only through its subordinate relationship to the West. However, the end of the Second World War, the advent of the Cold War, and independence movements in former colonies occasioned a dramatic reshaping of political and economic relationships. In some cases, former Asian and Middle Eastern colonies gained not only independence, but also global economic and military influence; at the same time, nationalist and ethnic struggles (often inadvertently or deliberately fueled by colonial rule) claimed thousands if not millions of lives and spread beyond their regions to become global conflicts. In all cases, the actions and rhetoric of Asian and Middle Eastern peoples worked both within and beyond the context of Cold War tensions to reshape global economic and political relationships into the twenty-first century.

DOCUMENT 32-1

HO CHI MINH
Declaration of Independence of the Democratic Republic of Vietnam
September 1945

In September 1945, closely following the surrender of Japan and the end of the Second World War, longtime independence fighter and Communist revolutionary Ho Chi Minh (born Nguyen That Thanh, 1890–1969) delivered the following speech to declare the independence of the country of Vietnam. Vietnam had been maintained as a French colony since 1885, and during the Second World War, it was controlled by the Japanese. The Vietminh (or Viet Minh), an independence movement launched by Ho Chi Minh in 1940, fought against both French and Japanese occupiers throughout the war. Following Japan's surrender, Ho Chi Minh and the Vietminh seized the opportunity to proclaim the country's independence. France's refusal to cede the colony led to prolonged warfare in which the United States was ultimately embroiled.

"All men are created equal. They are endowed by their Creator with certain inalienable rights, among these are Life, Liberty, and the pursuit of Happiness."

This immortal statement was made in the Declaration of Independence of the United States of America in 1776. In a broader sense, this means: All the peoples on the earth are equal from birth, all the peoples have a right to live, to be happy and free.

The Declaration of the French Revolution made in 1791 on the Rights of Man and the Citizen also states: "All men are born free and with equal rights, and must always remain free and have equal rights." Those are undeniable truths.

Nevertheless, for more than eighty years, the French imperialists, abusing the standard of Liberty, Equality, and Fraternity, have violated our Fatherland and oppressed our fellow-citizens. They have acted contrary

Ho Chi Minh, "Declaration of Independence," Embassy of the Socialist Republic of Vietnam in the United States of America, www.vietnamembassy-usa.org/learn _about_vietnam/politics/dec_of_independence.

to the ideals of humanity and justice. In the field of politics, they have deprived our people of every democratic liberty.

They have enforced inhuman laws; they have set up three distinct political regimes in the North, the Center and the South of Vietnam in order to wreck our national unity and prevent our people from being united.

They have built more prisons than schools. They have mercilessly slain our patriots — they have drowned our uprisings in rivers of blood. They have fettered public opinion; they have practiced obscurantism [deliberately obscuring the facts] against our people. To weaken our race they have forced us to use opium and alcohol.[1]

In the fields of economics, they have fleeced us to the backbone, impoverished our people, and devastated our land.

They have robbed us of our rice fields, our mines, our forests, and our raw materials. They have monopolised the issuing of bank-notes and the export trade.

They have invented numerous unjustifiable taxes and reduced our people, especially our peasantry, to a state of extreme poverty.

They have hampered the prospering of our national bourgeoisie; they have mercilessly exploited our workers.

In the autumn of 1940, when the Japanese Fascists violated Indochina's territory to establish new bases in their fight against the Allies, the French imperialists went down on their bended knees and handed over our country to them.

Thus, from that date, our people were subjected to the double yoke of the French and the Japanese. Their sufferings and miseries increased. The result was that from the end of last year to the beginning of this year, from Quang Tri province to the North of Vietnam, more than two million of our fellow-citizens died from starvation. On March 9 [1945], the French troops were disarmed by the Japanese. The French colonialists either fled or surrendered, showing that not only were they incapable of "protecting" us, but that, in the span of five years, they had twice sold our country to the Japanese.

---

[1] **they have forced us to use opium and alcohol**: The French colonial government assumed total control over the production and sale of opium and alcohol in Vietnam in order to foster colonial revenue, and in some cases the French government forced Vietnamese to purchase and consume their products.

On several occasions before March 9, the Vietminh League urged the French to ally themselves with it against the Japanese. Instead of agreeing to this proposal, the French colonialists so intensified their terrorist activities against the Vietminh members that before fleeing they massacred a great number of our political prisoners detained at Yen Bai and Cao Bang.[2]

Not withstanding all this, our fellow-citizens have always manifested toward the French a tolerant and humane attitude. Even after the Japanese putsch [coup] of March 1945, the Vietminh League helped many Frenchmen to cross the frontier, rescued some of them from Japanese jails, and protected French lives and property.

From the autumn of 1940, our country had in fact ceased to be a French colony and had become a Japanese possession.

After the Japanese had surrendered to the Allies, our whole people rose to regain our national sovereignty and to found the Democratic Republic of Vietnam.

The truth is that we have wrested our independence from the Japanese and not from the French.

The French have fled, the Japanese have capitulated, Emperor Bao Dai has abdicated.[3] Our people have broken the chains which for nearly a century have fettered them and have won independence for the Fatherland. Our people at the same time have overthrown the monarchic regime that has reigned supreme for dozens of centuries. In its place has been established the present Democratic Republic.

For these reasons, we, members of the Provisional Government, representing the whole Vietnamese people, declare that from now on we break off all relations of a colonial character with France; we repeal all the international obligation that France has so far subscribed to on behalf of Vietnam and we abolish all the special rights the French have unlawfully acquired in our Fatherland.

---

[2] **Yen Bai and Cao Bang**: Provinces in the north of present-day Vietnam.

[3] **Emperor Bao Dai has abdicated**: Bao Dai (1913–1997) was ruler of the state of Annam, one of the three component states that became present-day Vietnam. He ruled under French and then Japanese control until abdicating in 1945 at Japan's surrender. Bao Dai was reinstated from 1949 to 1955 and is widely regarded as having been complicit with French occupation.

The whole Vietnamese people, animated by a common purpose, are determined to fight to the bitter end against any attempt by the French colonialists to reconquer their country.

We are convinced that the Allied nations which at Tehran and San Francisco[4] have acknowledged the principles of self-determination and equality of nations, will not refuse to acknowledge the independence of Vietnam.

A people who have courageously opposed French domination for more than eighty years, a people who have fought side by side with the Allies against the Fascists during these last years, such a people must be free and independent.

For these reasons, we, members of the Provisional Government of the Democratic Republic of Vietnam, solemnly declare to the world that Vietnam has the right to be a free and independent country and in fact it is so already. The entire Vietnamese people are determined to mobilise all their physical and mental strength, to sacrifice their lives and property in order to safeguard their independence and liberty.

READING AND DISCUSSION QUESTIONS

1. Why do you suppose Ho Chi Minh quoted directly from the U.S. Declaration of Independence and the French Declaration of the Rights of Man and Citizen? What are the effects of incorporating those quotes in this document?

2. What justification does Ho Chi Minh provide for Vietnam's independence? How does he use other countries to make his point?

---

[4] **Tehran and San Francisco**: At the 1943 conference at Tehran, Allied powers discussed postwar arrangements for former Japanese territories. The 1945 convention of Allied powers and other states in San Francisco produced the charter for the United Nations.

DOCUMENT 32-2

JAWAHARLAL NEHRU

The Partitioning of the Punjab

1947

On June 3, 1947, the British Governor-General of India, Lord Mount-batten — in effect, the ruler of British-controlled India — announced the Indian Independence Act, granting India independence from Great Britain. Years of Hindu-Muslim antagonism fueled by deliberate British colonial policies of "divide and rule" culminated in the partitioning of India into separate Hindu and Muslim states. Although designed by the British, the partitioning was accomplished after the declaration of independence, and was therefore the legal responsibility of the new Indian and Pakistani governments. Millions of Hindus, Muslims, and Sikhs were subjected to relocation based on the new religion-defined territories, and the ensuing deprivation and violence claimed up to a million lives. In these documents, Jawaharlal Nehru (1889–1964) — then a prominent figure in the Indian National Congress, and later the first Prime Minister of India — writes to Indonesian Prime Minister Sultan Shahrir and to Lord Mountbatten, describing the worsening violence in the Punjab region of what is now India and Pakistan.

To Sultan Shahrir

New Delhi
17th June 1947

My dear Shahrir,
I have received your letter of May 29th from Jakarta.

As you know, we have been intensely occupied here ever since Mountbatten came. As a result of numerous talks we have agreed to a division of India, that is to say to allow certain provinces and parts of provinces to vote themselves out of India if they so choose. Probably this process of voting, etc. will be completed within a month from now. The other process of a division of assets is a much more complicated one and will take longer.

Selected Works of Jawaharlal Nehru, ed. S. Gopal. Published by the Jawaharlal Nehru Memorial Fund. 40+ vols. (New Delhi: Indraprastha Press, 1985), 3:156–158, 179–182.

But the main picture should be clear enough by the end of July. You will appreciate that the division of the Army offers a formidable difficulty.

We have agreed to this division after much searching of heart and painful thought. For generations past we have dreamt of a free and united India, and for any part of it to go out is most painful to contemplate. Nevertheless we thought that the passions that have been aroused can only be dealt with by as great a measure of forbearance as possible. Countries and peoples sometimes develop psychological attitudes and pathological phases which cannot be dealt with by purely political and logical means. One has to apply to some extent the method of psychoanalysis to them as to individuals. On my part I feel sure that after the present passions have cooled down and a sense of freedom has come to all of us, we shall be able to consider our mutual relations in a better atmosphere and context. Then I think it will be inevitable for close relations to grow up between India and the parts that secede from India.

The effect of this division will be that roughly 20% of the population and area of India will secede and form a new State presumably called Pakistan. There is much talk of Pakistan and Hindustan. Now Hindustan is our normal word in Hindustani for India. But this talk of Hindustan and Pakistan is likely to lead to a misapprehension of the real situation. Legally and constitutionally the position is this. India has an international personality and the Government of India continues as before. Our connection with the U.N.O. [United Nations Organization] and with various countries continues without change. Out of India, however, a certain part secedes and is formed into a new State which can cultivate such relations as it likes with other countries. Thus we have the continuing entity of India and a new State of Pakistan. All the treaties and arrangements which India has with other countries remain unchanged.

About the 15th August there will be a major change in our constitutional position. The British Parliament is passing legislation to confer both upon India and the seceding part of it, Dominion Status.[5] How does this Dominion Status fit in with our ideal of an independent Republic? As a matter of fact we adhere as before to our ideal of an independent Republic and our Constituent Assembly has already declared that in a Resolution of Objectives. When our new constitution is ready and we can give effect

---

[5] **Dominion Status**: A legal term originally denoting a self-governing colony of the British Empire and, after 1948, a fully independent nation that shares Britain's monarch.

to it, I have no doubt that we shall declare India to be a sovereign independent Republic. Even Dominion Status gives that right to complete independence and severance of any connection with Britain. We want to have close relations with Britain in many ways, but we do not want to give up the idea of the Republic. Indeed we could not do so because of the very strong public sentiment in regard to it.

Dominion Status is thus a temporary phase for an interim period to give place to other arrangements later. We have accepted this not in place of the other arrangements but only for the interim period.

Conditions in India have been very peculiar of late. In effect there is no real stable and final authority, although in law there is such an authority. The British Government which is still legally supreme cannot function satisfactorily and the administrative structure is breaking down. On the other hand no new authority can function. Thus there is deterioration and conflict in many places. It has become essential to get over this intervening period by the establishment of full authority in Indian hands. Every day's delay adds to the confusion. Dominion Status, which will give us full authority by August next, will help us to meet these present conditions and to prepare the ground for a final changeover. What exactly our relations will be with the British Commonwealth I cannot just say now. But whatever they may be, I am sure that India will function as an independent Republic. . . .

I have given you above some brief and rough idea of conditions in India at present so that you may be able to follow events here. We are going to have a difficult time during the next few months, but we are determined to face every difficulty and to overcome it. . . .

1. To Lord Mountbatten

New Delhi
22 June 1947

Dear Lord Mountbatten,
You have not returned from Kashmir[6] yet and are due back tomorrow. I am, however, writing this to you rather late at night because I am distressed and the sending of this letter will perhaps give some relief to my mind.

---

[6] **Kashmir**: Territory straddling what is now the border of India, Pakistan, and China. Here, Kashmir may refer to the Kashmir Valley, the larger territory of Kashmir, or the former state of Jammu and Kashmir.

2.   I am writing about what is happening in Lehore and to some extent in Amritsar.[7] Yesterday I went with Gandhiji to Hardwar[8] and visited the numerous refugee camps there. There were, till yesterday, about 32,000 refugees there from the Frontier Province[9] and the Punjab. Most of them were from the Frontier Province. Daily some 200 or so fresh arrivals came there. Apart from these refugee camps in Hardwar, there are similar large camps at half a dozen other places, some in the U.P.[10] and some in the Indian States like Patiala, Alwar, etc. The condition of many of these people is pitiable although many relief societies and local governments are trying to help them.

3.   But this letter is mainly about the city of Lahore where fires are raging and consuming hundreds of houses. It is reported that 100 houses were burnt down last night and this morning. During the previous two days about 250 houses were set fire to and burnt. At this rate the city of Lahore will be just a heap of ashes in a few days' time. The human aspect of this is appalling to contemplate.

4.   Amritsar is already a city of ruins, and Lahore is likely to be in a much worse state very soon. Lahore is, of course, a much larger city than Amritsar.

5.   If you will forgive a personal touch, I should like to tell you that my mother came from Lahore and part of my childhood was spent there. The fate of Lahore, therefore, affects me perhaps more intimately than it might many other people who are not connected with that city.

6.   Human beings have an amazing capacity to endure misfortune. They can bear calamity after calamity; but it is very difficult to have to bear something which can apparently be avoided. I do not know if it can be said that what is happening in Lahore is beyond human control. It is certainly beyond the control of those who ought to control it. I do not know who is

---

[7] **Lahore . . . Amritsar**: Cities in the Punjab region of India; Lahore became part of Pakistan after the partition of India on August 15, 1947.

[8] **Ghandiji to Hardwar**: Ghandiji is an honorific term for Mohandas Gandhi (1869–1948). Nehru traveled with Gandhi to a city in the state of Uttarakhand, east of Punjab.

[9] **Frontier Province**: A province near Punjab in contemporary Pakistan.

[10] **U.P.**: Uttar Pradesh, an Indian state southeast of Punjab.

to blame and I do not want to blame anybody for it. But the fact remains that horror succeeds horror and we cannot put a stop to it. Meanwhile vast numbers of human beings, men, women and children, live in the midst of this horror, often in streets and pavements, or run away in search of some peace and shelter elsewhere. It is curious that when tragedy affects an individual we feel the full force of it, but when that individual is multiplied a thousand-fold, our senses are dulled and we become insensitive.

7.   Apart from newspaper reports, people have come from Lahore to see me today and they have given descriptions of what is happening there. Whether their accounts are correct or not, I cannot say. They tell me that repeatedly, when houses were set fire to, the residents of those houses rushed out into the streets and lanes and these people were fired at by the police for breach of the curfew order. Most of these fires occurred at the time of the curfew. I am told that the District Magistrate has ordered that people should keep open the doors of their houses and lanes so as to allow refugees from burning houses to enter other houses, because if they remain in the streets during curfew hours, they will be fired at by the police.

8.   This is a very strange state of affairs and few persons would like to be residents of Lahore at present. Surely something effective has to be done to stop this tragedy, if existing methods have failed and the police are incapable of controlling the situation. As I told you once, the insistent demand is either for the military to take charge, or for the withdrawal of the police and the military so that the people can look after themselves. You were surprised at this last demand and it is surprising enough. But it is passionately repeated. All manner of charges are made against the police of committing arson and of preventing people from putting out fires and firing at them when they try to do so. It is not possible for me to know the truth of these charges; but the fact remains that there is this strongly-felt feeling about the police and further that the situation continues to deteriorate. Are we to be passive spectators while a great city ceases to exist and hundreds of thousands of its inhabitants are reduced to becoming homeless wanderers, or else to die in their narrow lanes?

9.   You gave an assurance before June 3rd and subsequently that any kind of disorder will be put down with vigour. I am afraid we are not honouring that assurance in some places at least, notably in Lahore and Amritsar.

Gurgaon[11] also is still more or less a battlefield, although similar and adjoining areas on the U.P. side are fully under control.

10.   From all accounts that I have received, the statement of June 3rd has had a sobering and calming effect in most places. Whether people like the decisions or not, they accept them and have a general feeling that a settlement has been arrived at. The old tension is gone or is much less. There is no more talk, as there used to be, of civil war and the like.

11.   But this does not apply to Lahore, Amritsar and Gurgaon. Gurgaon is a wide area and already several hundred villages have been burnt down. The damage bas been done and, I suppose, sooner or later the trouble there will end, though it is still continuing to some extent. Lahore is an even more serious matter, not only because it affects a very large number of persons and valuable property, but also because it is the nerve-centre of the Punjab. There appears to be a deliberate policy being pursued there of smoking out people. It is an astonishingly foolish policy from any point of view and can do no good to anybody. Nevertheless it has succeeded in a large measure, and if it is continued on this scale for another ten days or so, there will be little left in the city of Lahore to save. If anything has got to be done, it must be done immediately.

12.   There is one other matter I should like to refer to. This relates to numerous refugees in various places. I think there should be an organised and scientific approach to their problem. So far nothing of this kind has been done and they have been left largely to their own resources or to the charity of various institutions. It may be said that the Central Government is not directly concerned because most of these refugees are in the U.P. or in some State. I think, however, that it is only the Central Government that can view the problem as a whole and help in laying down uniform policies. It is not so much a question of money but of proper direction. The Central Government may have to find some money too. What I would like to suggest, however, is for us to appoint a competent relief officer with a few able assistants to collect full particulars about these refugees and to report how their problems can be tackled. He would naturally consult local authorities who are dealing with the problem now. Some kind of

---

[11] **Gurgaon**: A city in the Indian state of Haryana, close to Punjab.

effort should be made to engage the refugees in productive work as far as possible. Their trades and professions should be noted down. This will at least give us the data for the formulation of any policy. Personally I feel that most of them should go back to their own homes. But where the homes have ceased to exist, something will have to be done for them even there. Many may not be able to go back because of changed political conditions. Perhaps the final decision in this matter will have to await some time. Meanwhile all this data can be collected and relief organised on a proper basis. Discarded military camps might be used for their residence.

13.   Please forgive me for this long letter which you will get on your return from Kashmir. I tried to stop myself writing it, but the thought of Lahore burning away obsessed me and I could not restrain myself.

Yours sincerely,
Jawaharlal Nehru

READING AND DISCUSSION QUESTIONS

1.   What difficulties regarding partition does Nehru outline in his letter to Shahrir?

2.   How does Nehru foresee India moving forward in its relationship with Britain?

3.   How does Nehru's letter to Mountbatten contrast with his letter to Shahrir?

4.   How does Nehru appeal to Mountbatten?

VIEWPOINTS

Transitions in Modern China

DOCUMENT 32-3

FORMER RED GUARD

Away from Madness

1996

After the disastrous excesses of the Great Leap Forward (1958–1961), Mao Zedong (1893–1976) found himself discredited and marginalized in the Communist Party and the Chinese government. In 1966, Mao seized the opportunity provided by a controversial play to encourage student protesters and their critique of supposedly "counter-revolutionary" elements in schools and universities. Mao encouraged the "red guard" students to campaign against the "four olds" of customs, culture, habits, and thought. The Red Guards' campaign quickly descended into violent anarchy. Once his political opponents were purged and his status as leader of the Red Guard movement secure, Mao suppressed the Red Guards through brutal military force and enforced relocation to rural areas. The following excerpt from a former Red Guard gives an intimate account of the confusion and motivations of the movement. In 1966, he was sixteen and a junior student in middle school.

The first thing I'd like to tell you is: I am a non-participant! I didn't join in any faction or organization during the Cultural Revolution. All I did was follow the crowd, raising my hand at mass meetings, humming songs about Chairman Mao's quotations, and playing poker. I didn't beat up anybody and I was not beaten up by others. Never did I gain any personal power, nor was I the target of attack. In one word, my body was in the movement but my mind was not. As a non-participant, I was as happy as I could be! . . .

On August 18, 1966, when Chairman Mao received the Red Guards for the first time, I walked hundreds of *li* to Beijing in order to be at

Feng Jicai, *Ten Years of Madness: Oral Histories of China's Cultural Revolution* (San Francisco: China Books and Periodicals, 1996), 5–14.

Tiananmen Square at that time. . . . Well, have I caught your attention now? Good! I'll start from the very beginning.

I decided to be a non-participant soon after the Cultural Revolution began. With articles criticizing the Peking Opera *The Ghost Concubine Takes Revenge* and the writing group named "Three-Family Village," the *People's Daily* had kindled the flames of the Cultural Revolution, which swept my school like wild fire.

One day when I arrived at school, a huge poster caught my eye. It was hanging from the third floor of the main building all the way down to the ground. Four Chinese characters, each as large as one story, were written on the poster: Revolutionary Tempest. Students waving red flags were standing everywhere: outside and inside the main gate, and on top of the main building. All of a sudden, my heart was jumping so violently I could feel the Cultural Revolution was taking place right in front of my eyes.

Then all classes stopped to make way for revolution: putting up big-character posters and struggling against the teachers. Those teachers who were considered "problematic" were dragged onto a stage to be criticized. Their heads were splashed with glue and donned with tall paper hats so that they would be humiliated. Many people were excited about what was happening. Some honestly felt justified in participating in this violent action of "one class overthrowing another." At first, I was also a little carried away. However, the attack on a fellow student, a boy named Zhao, completely changed my attitude.

Looking back, it is clear that people were totally out of their minds at the time, doing everything possible to search for class enemies. The students cast their eyes not only on their teachers, but also on their own schoolmates.

Zhao and I were in the same grade, but not the same class, so I don't even know his first name. He was nicknamed "Little Thumb" because of his small build. His shoulders were only half as broad as mine. He was a skinny and pale little boy with a pair of quite small feet. But it was said that he was a genius in mathematics. When he was still a second-year student at middle school, he was able to solve mathematical questions for high school seniors. Somehow the word came that he was the son of Xia Meng, a famous Hong Kong movie star. In those days, people with relatives overseas were all suspected of being "foreign spies." Someone suggested that he be hung over a tree branch with his ten fingers tightly fastened by flaxen threads. This they did, and I saw with my own eyes that his fingers lengthened, bit by bit, until they were doubly long. His screams were so horrible that I can remember them even today. Although I didn't take part in this cruel torture, being only a bystander, I felt guilty, as if it were I who had done such ghastly things to him.

But don't think I became a non-participant because of this incident alone. The Cultural Revolution was in many ways enchantingly attractive. On August 18, 1966, when I saw Chairman Mao at Tiananmen Square, I was once again attracted to the movement.

At noon the previous day, one of my classmates, Little Kong, came to me with a secret: Chairman Mao was going to review the Red Guards in Tiananmen Square! On hearing this, I felt as if the world was alight, as if I was on top of a mountain watching the sunrise. Little Kong warned me and another friend, Big-Eyed Chang, that we must keep this secret from others, including our parents. He didn't mention the source of the news, but we decided to set off for Beijing that very day at three o'clock in the afternoon. We started off on foot, and our hearts were filled with happiness. We had to cover the distance of several hundred *li* in order to arrive in Beijing early next morning. We thought that the review would most likely take place in the morning.

We walked and hitch-hiked until we finally made it to Tiananmen at 8:30 the next morning. Then we were told that the review would not take place until early in the afternoon. We stationed ourselves at a place near the ornamental column at the west side in front of Tiananmen Gate in order to have the best view of the reviewing stand where Chairman Mao would appear. We hadn't eaten or drunk anything since the previous afternoon, but we didn't feel thirsty or hungry at all. We were in high spirits, as if we had been bewitched.

In the early afternoon, groups of Red Guards and students began to swarm into the square carrying flags. I paid no attention to them and just fixed my eyes to the reviewing stand on top of the gate for fear I might miss some precious moment. As soon as Chairman Mao appeared, the shouting and greetings from the square were deafening. Because I was over excited, I could not distinguish the people on the reviewing stand. When I finally made out the figure of Chairman Mao, I jumped and shouted, throwing away my straw hat. Several times I almost lost my glasses. If I had, I would have never been able to find them again because I was sandwiched by a sea of people. I shouted at the top of my voice, but I couldn't hear myself.

When the ceremony ended and people dispersed, I could see that the ground was covered with hats, buttons and girls' shoe buckles. People were jubilant, their eyes shining and their faces burning. When I looked at my friends, Kong and Chang, their faces were as red as flames. We intended to tell each other how happy we were, but we had lost our voices. We held each other's hands and jumped around.

We were the first Red Guards reviewed by Chairman Mao! The next day, when we went back to our school, our schoolmates envied us more than people envy today's movie stars. We plunged ourselves into the movement right away as if injected with a new energy for the revolution.

After the "August 18th Review," the Red Guard movement was alive with added energy. The movement called "Destroying the Four Olds" swept across the whole country. The Red Guards started to ransack people's homes and confiscate their property.

One day we heard that the Red Guards from No. 21 Middle School were attacking the old Xikai Church. We hurried to the spot, but were too late — everything in the church had already been smashed to pieces. Only the big cross on top of the church was still intact. Without fear, we climbed a ladder to reach the cross, 50 meters above the ground. We sawed it up, and when I tried to push it down to the ground, I almost fell. Luckily, Little Kong grabbed my belt to keep me from falling. Otherwise I wouldn't be sitting here today. However, I felt no fear at all. I stood high above the ground with my hands on my hips, looking at the people in the streets who were looking up at me. I felt like a real hero!

After destroying Xikai Church, I led my friends to another church, the one with a pinnacle not far from my own house. The iron fence was locked. I was the first one to climb over it. The main gate was locked, too. With an ax installed there in case of fire, I smashed the door open. . . .

The greatest discovery in that church was its books. The two big rooms on both sides of the church were filled with books. Later we were told that church also served as the city library for reference materials about religion. At that time, however, we couldn't care less about "reference materials" — they were all reactionary propaganda to us. We piled the books in the courtyard and used two drums of gasoline to burn them. There were thousands of books to be burned, and their hard covers made the job difficult. We had to tear some of the covers off before we could set fire to them. There were more than twenty of us, and we spent the whole night and the next morning burning those books. When we finished, the trees across the street were scorched and our faces were smeared with dirt and ashes.

After that, we didn't go home but went on to ransack people's houses. If you had met me at that time, you would never have believed that I would become a "non-participant." In fact, that was the only time I took part in a house raid, which was also the reason why I became a non-participant.

In one house we ransacked there lived a childless old couple. I heard that the man had once studied abroad and was one of the share-holders of a cement plant, which made him a capitalist who exploited the workers. The two-story building was tastefully furnished. This only made us more determined to tear it apart. Based on the logic at that time, the better a house was furnished, the more its owner had exploited the working class, and the more reactionary he must be.

When we searched the second floor, we found two boxes of Western glassware. As we were about to smash them, the man cried out, "Those are precious furnishings from the French Palace. I spent a fortune on them in France. Please don't smash them!" But his words only angered us more. We were the ones who would decide what to do. How dared he tell us not to smash the glassware. Little Kong jumped on the man and hit him with a club. He hit him in the mouth, but the sound was such that it was like hitting a piece of porcelain. When I looked at the man, I was appalled by the sight. With a mouthful of blood, the man spit out many teeth! It was as horrible as the sight of the lengthened fingers of Zhao, my schoolmate. I was completely stunned and just stood there until the other students reminded me that we were there to smash the glassware.

We threw the glassware, piece by piece, out of the window until every piece was broken. The man and his wife were on their knees behind us, crying their hearts out, as if we were throwing their children out of the window. When we finished and were ready to leave, I looked at the man. His toothless mouth was open, a gaping blood hole on his face. His stare was blank, yet he was concentrating as if he was trying to memorize every detail about me. I avoided his eyes. With a guilty feeling, I ran away from the house as quickly as I could.

When we had dinner that night, Grandmother suddenly asked me, "You didn't beat up people, did you?"

I was scared. Although I didn't beat up anyone, I felt as if I had. I learned that earlier that day Grandma had gone out to the vegetable market and saw a group of Red Guards parading some capitalists through the streets. One of the students thrashed the capitalists with the brass buckle on his belt. A man's eyeball popped out as a result of this treatment. Grandma was so frightened that she immediately came back home without buying anything.

Honestly speaking, I didn't think too much about the situation. But deep in my heart I knew I could not continue to do this kind of thing. Perhaps I was born with a soft heart. I couldn't stand seeing other people suffer, bleed, or weep. I found it hard to face those defenseless "targets of revolution." Without knowing it, I was drifting away from the "golden road of revolution" and becoming a "non-participant."

Towards the end of August 1966, the Red Guards began to travel around the country with free passage to "exchange revolutionary ideas" and to "fan up revolutionary flames." I took advantage of the situation and traveled extensively from the summer of 1966 to the end of 1967. I went to Heilongjiang in the Northeast, Urumqi in Xinjiang in the Northwest, and to Xiamen, Guangzhou, Guilin, and Nanning in the South. I learned a great deal during these trips. At first I was welcomed everywhere I went as a Red Guard from a big city. Moreover, I had been among the Red Guards reviewed by Chairman Mao on August 18th, which made me feel as if I was sent down directly by the central authorities.

. . . Everywhere the Red Guards were smashing things, ransacking houses, and beating up innocent people. The seeds of doubt once again were planted deep in my heart.

Once I was caught in the middle of an armed fight in Baoding, Hebei Province, late at night. In the small hostel where I was staying, bullets were flying through the air and windows were broken. I found myself hidden under the bed without knowing how I got there. At dawn the city was deathly quiet. Peeping out of the window, I saw the whole street littered with trucks that couldn't move because of their flat tires. There were dead bodies hanging in the trees. I thought this must be what was called "exposing corpses," a form of punishment in ancient times. The image of the Cultural Revolution was no longer gloriously radiant to me, but had become confusingly blurred in my mind. . . .

Once in November, when the weather was getting cold, a friend of mine told me that Chairman Mao was to review the Red Guards again, and he dragged me along. Altogether Chairman Mao reviewed the Red Guards eight times. Only the first time was there spontaneous participation from the bottom up. The other times were strictly organized from the top down. Take this time for example. Chairman Mao was in an open jeep, riding from west to east in front of the Tiananmen Gate. The students had been waiting on the square for a long time, while soldiers forced them to sit still. They were not allowed to stand. When the jeep passed by, many students were on their knees in order to have a better look of the Chairman. I had found a place in the front row. Chairman Mao was only two meters away from me when the jeep passed. We were separated only by a soldier who was standing on guard in front of us.

Chairman Mao was stalwart, vigorously waving his arm. When his jeep passed in front of me, he suddenly turned towards my side, waving with his other arm. I saw his face clearly, even his cigarette-stained teeth. The other students, especially those from other cities, were shouting slogans and showing extreme enthusiasm and excitement. When the ceremony ended and people dispersed, the square was littered with even more hats, buttons, shoe-buckles, pens, and glasses than it was the first time I saw Chairman Mao. I picked up a small diary book left behind by some Red Guard from Shandong Province. He had taken detailed notes, by the hours and days, of how he came to Beijing on foot to be reviewed by Chairman Mao. The notes ended right before the appearance of Chairman Mao, when he wrote, "The magnificent tune of 'The East Is Red' is now being broadcast in the Square. . . ." Strangely such enthusiastic words no longer moved me. For several months I had gone through excitement, sacred feelings, zeal, fighting . . . but everything had by now passed. . . .

Whenever people's enthusiasm reached its peak, the images of lengthened fingers, blood stained teeth, and dead bodies hanging in trees came back to me. They were like ghosts haunting me, cooling me down whenever I was about to get excited again.

After traveling around to "exchange revolutionary ideas," I came back home. By then, armed fighting had started between the two factions of the Red Guards, but I found myself completely removed from the movement. I would not even be a bystander. You remember my friend Little Kong? After becoming the leader of a faction, one of his legs was maimed and he could never ride a bike again. . . .

Have I made it clear why I became a non-participant? To sum it up, it was all because I am soft-hearted, afraid to see people hurt and kill each other, afraid of the sight of blood and tears. It would be dishonest if I claimed that I thought more profoundly than others. Nobody could think independently in those days. Those were times full of attractions and temptations. Therefore I attribute my actions to my natural instinct. In other words, most of the non-participants in the Cultural Revolution were kind-hearted people. I believe they are the ones who have lived peacefully and free of guilt. What do you think?

READING AND DISCUSSION QUESTIONS

1. The author refers to himself as a nonparticipant, yet gives a clear account of his participation. What does his claim of nonparticipation mean?

2. To what extent was the author's participation in the Red Guards connected to Mao Zedong? What else motivated his participation?

DOCUMENT 32-4

DENG XIAOPING

Build Socialism with Chinese Characteristics

June 30, 1984

Following the death of Mao Zedong in 1976, the longtime Chinese Communist Party leader Deng Xiaoping (1904–1997) gained control of the party and of the Chinese government. Espousing the Four Modernizations of agriculture, industry, military, and science and technology, Deng sought to move China away from the upheaval of Mao's radical leadership and toward a reconciliation with Western modernity. This transition laid the foundation for China's rapid economic growth, while retaining its distinctly authoritarian political structures. Deng Xiaoping delivered the following speech to a group of Japanese delegates in 1984, using classical Marxist theory to explain the necessity of a capitalist economy for the ultimate realization of Communist values.

People may ask, If China had taken the capitalist instead of the socialist road, could the Chinese people have liberated themselves and could China have finally stood up? The Nationalists took that road for more than twenty years and proved that it does not work. By contrast, the Chinese Communists, by adhering to Marxism and integrating Marxism with actual conditions in China in accordance with Mao Zedong Thought, took their own road and succeeded in the revolution by encircling the cities from the countryside. Conversely, if we had not been Marxists, or if we had not integrated Marxism with Chinese conditions and followed our own road, China would have remained fragmented, with neither independence nor unity. China simply had to adhere to Marxism. If we had not fully believed in Marxism, the Chinese revolution would never have succeeded. That belief was the motive force. After the founding of the People's Republic, if we had taken the capitalist rather than the socialist road, we would not have ended the chaos in the country or changed its conditions — inflation, unstable prices, poverty, and backwardness. We started from a backward past. There was virtually no industry for us to inherit from old China, and

Sources of Chinese Tradition, ed. Wm. Theodore de Bary and Richard Lufrano, 2 vols. (New York: Columbia University Press, 2000), 2:507–510.

we did not have enough grain for food. Some people ask why we chose socialism. We answer that we had to, because capitalism would get China nowhere. We must solve the problems of feeding and employing the population and of reunifying China. That is why we have repeatedly declared that we shall adhere to Marxism and keep to the socialist road. But by Marxism we mean Marxism that is integrated with Chinese conditions, and by socialism we mean socialism that is tailored to Chinese conditions and has Chinese characteristics.

What is socialism and what is Marxism? We were not quite clear about this before. Marxism attaches utmost importance to developing the productive forces. We advocate communism. But what does that mean? It means the principle of from each according to his ability, to each according to his needs, which calls for highly developed productive forces and overwhelming material wealth. Therefore, the fundamental task for the socialist stage is to develop the productive forces. The superiority of the socialist system is demonstrated by faster and greater development of the productive forces than under the capitalist system. One of our shortcomings since the founding of the People's Republic was that we neglected the development of the productive forces. Socialism means eliminating poverty. Pauperism is not socialism, still less communism. The superiority of the socialist system lies above all in its ability to increasingly develop the productive forces and to improve the people's material and cultural life. The problem facing us now is how China, which is still backward, is to develop the productive forces and improve the people's living standard. This brings us back to the point of whether to continue on the socialist road or to stop and turn onto the capitalist road. The capitalist road can only enrich less than 10 percent of the Chinese population; it can never enrich the 90 percent. That is why we must adhere to socialism. The socialist principle of distribution to each according to his work will not create an excessive gap in wealth. Consequently, no polarization will occur as our productive forces become developed over the next twenty to thirty years.

The minimum target of our Four Modernizations is to achieve a comparatively comfortable standard of living by the end of the century. . . . By a "comfortable standard" we mean that per capita GNP [gross national product] will reach U.S. $800. That is a low level for you, but it is really ambitious for us. China has a population of 1 billion now and it will reach 1.2 billion by then. If, when the GNP reached $1,000 billion, we applied the capitalist principle of distribution, it would not amount to much and could not help to eliminate poverty and backwardness. Less than 10 percent of the population would enjoy a better life, while more than 90 percent remained in poverty. But the socialist principle of distribution can enable all the people to become relatively comfortable. This is why we want to uphold socialism. Without socialism, China can never achieve that goal.

However, only talking about this is not enough. The present world is an open one. China's past backwardness was due to its closed-door policy. After the founding of the People's Republic, we were blockaded by others, and so the country remained closed to some extent, which created difficulties for us. Some "left" policies and the Cultural Revolution in particular were disastrous for us. In short, the experience of the past thirty years or more proves that a closed-door policy would hinder construction and inhibit development. . . . Our political line focuses on the four modernizations, on continuing to develop the productive forces. Nothing short of world war would make us release our grip on this essential point. Even should world war break out, we would engage in reconstruction after the war. A closed-door policy would not help construction. There are two kinds of exclusion: one is directed against other countries; the other is directed against China itself, with one region or department closing its doors to the others. We are suggesting that we should develop a little faster — just a little, because it would be unrealistic to go too fast. To do this, we have to invigorate the domestic economy and open up to the outside. We must first of all solve the problem of the countryside, which contains 80 percent of the population. China's stability depends on the stability of the countryside with this 80 percent — this is the reality of China from which we should proceed. No matter how successful our work in the cities is, it will not mean much without the stable base of the countryside. Therefore, we must first of all solve the problem of the countryside by invigorating the economy and adopting an open policy so as to bring the initiative of 80 percent of the population into full play. We adopted this policy at the end of 1978, and after several years in operation it has produced the desired results. . . .

As for our relations with foreign countries, we shall pursue the policy of opening up still wider to the outside world. We have opened fourteen medium and large coastal cities. We welcome foreign investment and advanced techniques. Management is also a kind of technique. Will they undermine our socialism? Not likely, because the socialist economy is our mainstay. Our socialist economic base is so huge that it can absorb tens and hundreds of billions of dollars' worth of foreign funds without shaking the socialist foundation. Besides, we adhere to the socialist principle of distribution and do not tolerate economic polarization. Thus, foreign investment will doubtless serve as a major supplement to the building of socialism in our country. And as things stand now, this supplement is indispensable. Naturally, some problems will arise in the wake of foreign investment. But the negative aspects are far less significant than the positive use we can make of it to accelerate our development. It may entail a slight risk, but not much.

Well, those are our plans. We shall accumulate experience and try new solutions as new problems arise. In general, we believe the road we have chosen — building socialism with Chinese characteristics — is the right one and will work. We have followed this road for five and a half years and have achieved satisfactory results. We want to quadruple China's GNP by the end of the century. The pace of development so far exceeded our projections. And so I can tell our friends that we are even more confident now.

READING AND DISCUSSION QUESTIONS

1. How does Deng justify market capitalism as a part of socialism?

2. How are international affairs connected to Deng's plan? How does Deng plan to change China's stance toward the world?

3. What aspect of Deng's argument convinces you? What leaves you skeptical that his plan could succeed?

DOCUMENT 32-5

GAMAL ABDEL NASSER

Suez Canal Nationalization Speech

September 15, 1956

Gamal Abdel Nasser (1918–1970) became president of Egypt in 1956 after taking part in the 1952 revolution that toppled the Egyptian monarchy. His efforts to unite the Arab world around anti-imperialism took an important

The Suez Canal Problem, 26 July–22 September 1956, U.S. Department of State Publication No. 6392 (Washington, D.C.: Government Printing Office, 1956), 345–351.

turn when the United States, in retribution for Egypt's recognition of Communist China, refused Egypt funds to construct the new Aswan High Dam. Nasser, a major figure in the Non-aligned Movement, which eschewed allegiance to both the United States and the Soviet Union, responded by nationalizing the Suez Canal. British, French, and Israeli troops attacked Egypt to regain control of the canal, inspiring the fledgling United Nations to intervene. The final result was a political triumph for Nasser, who was viewed throughout the Arab world as a force against Western imperialism and for Arab independence. His 1956 speech announcing the nationalization of the Canal captures both the sense of crisis and the political skill with which Nasser mobilized Egyptian and Arab resistance to the West.

In these decisive days in the history of mankind, these days in which truth struggles to have itself recognized in international chaos where powers of evil domination and imperialism have prevailed, Egypt stands firmly to preserve her sovereignty. Your country stands solidly and staunchly to preserve her dignity against imperialistic schemes of a number of nations who have uncovered their desires for domination and supremacy.

In these days and in such circumstances Egypt has resolved to show the world that when small nations decide to preserve their sovereignty, they will do that all right and that when these small nations are fully determined to defend their rights and maintain their dignity, they will undoubtedly succeed in achieving their ends. . . .

I am speaking in the name of every Egyptian Arab and in the name of all free countries and of all those who believe in liberty and are ready to defend it. I am speaking in the name of principles proclaimed by these countries in the Atlantic Charter.[12] But they are now violating these principles and it has become our lot to shoulder the responsibility of reaffirming and establishing them anew. . . .

We have tried by all possible means to cooperate with those countries which claim to assist smaller nations and which promised to collaborate with us but they demanded their fees in advance. This we refused so they started to fight with us. They said they will pay toward building the High Dam and then they withdrew their offer and cast doubts on the Egyptian economy. Are we to [disclaim] our sovereign right? Egypt insists her

---

[12] **Atlantic Charter**: The 1941 policy signed by the Allied nations in World War II that defined the goals of war, including preventing territorial changes made against the will of the people.

sovereignty must remain intact and refuses to give up any part of that sovereignty for the sake of money.

Egypt nationalized the Egyptian Suez Canal company. When Egypt granted the concession to de Lesseps[13] it was stated in the concession between the Egyptian Government and the Egyptian company that the company of the Suez Canal is an Egyptian company subject to Egyptian authority. Egypt nationalized this Egyptian company and declared freedom of navigation will be preserved.

But the imperialists became angry. Britain and France said Egypt grabbed the Suez Canal as if it were part of France or Britain. The British Foreign Secretary forgot that only two years ago he signed an agreement stating the Suez Canal is an integral part of Egypt.

Egypt declared she was ready to negotiate. But as soon as negotiations began threats and intimidations started. . . .

Eden[14] stated in the House of Commons there shall be no discrimination between states using the canal. We on our part reaffirm that and declare there is no discrimination between canal users. He also said Egypt shall not be allowed to succeed because that would spell success for Arab nationalism and would be against their policy, which aims at the protection of Israel.

Today they are speaking of a new association whose main objective would be to rob Egypt of the canal and deprive her of rightful canal dues. Suggestions made by Eden in the House of Commons which have been backed by France and the United States are a clear violation of the 1888 convention,[15] since it is impossible to have two bodies organizing navigation in the canal. . . .

Those who attack Egypt will never leave Egypt alive. We shall fight a regular war, a total war, a guerrilla war. Those who attack Egypt will soon realize they brought disaster upon themselves. He who attacks Egypt attacks the whole Arab world. They say in their papers the whole thing will be over in forty-eight hours. They do not know how strong we really are.

We believe in international law. But we will never submit. We shall show the world how a small country can stand in the face of great powers threatening with armed might. Egypt might be a small power but she is

---

[13] **de Lesseps**: Ferdinand de Lesseps (1805–1894) was the French diplomat and developer who conceived and developed the Suez Canal.

[14] **Eden**: Robert Eden (1897–1977) was prime minister of Great Britain from 1955–1957.

[15] **1888 convention**: The Convention of Constantinople in 1888 declared the Suez Canal a neutral zone, but allowed for Egyptian military action to defend that nation.

great inasmuch as she has faith in her power and convictions. I feel quite certain every Egyptian shares the same convictions as I do and believes in everything I am stressing now.

We shall defend our freedom and independence to the last drop of our blood. This is the staunch feeling of every Egyptian. The whole Arab nation will stand by us in our common fight against aggression and domination. Free peoples, too, people who are really free will stand by us and support us against the forces of tyranny. . . .

READING AND DISCUSSION QUESTIONS

1. How does Nasser use "sovereignty" as a concept in his speech?

2. What are the "powers of evil domination" to which Nasser refers?

3. How does Nasser balance Egyptian and Arab identity? What is the value of embracing either, or both?

DOCUMENT 32-6

UNYA SHAVIT

Arab and Israeli Soccer Players Discuss Ethnic Relations in Israel

November 3, 2000

Since the creation of the state of Israel in 1948, tensions between Arabs and Jews in the region have continued to generate conflict and inspire fierce loyalty within each group. Jews consider the region their rightful homeland, while Arabs see it as part of their home of Palestine. In September 2000, following failed negotiations between Yasir Arafat, the leader of the Palestine Liberation Organization (PLO), and Israeli prime minister Ehud Barak, violence surged in Israel, the West Bank, and the Gaza Strip. Writing for the Hebrew daily paper Ha'aretz, *journalist Unya Shavit explored the complex issues of nationalism and discrimination among Arab and Jewish soccer teammates.*

Unya Shavit, "Playing for Keeps," *Ha'aretz*, November 3, 2000.

Two weeks ago, having suffered three losses and four ties, Maccabi Ahi Nazareth found itself last in the National League. The team's lackluster performance did little to improve the atmosphere in Nazareth,[17] its mood already dampened by the recent rioting and its harsh economic consequences. In an effort to keep from sinking to a lower league, the team's management fired coach Samir Issa and appointed Eli Mahpoud in his place. Surprisingly, the replacement of an Arab coach with a Jewish one, even in these tense times, was accepted in Nazareth without protest. The Ahi Nazareth fans, it seems, just want their team to stay in the National League, the second of the six divisions in Israeli soccer, under the Premier League. If nothing else, at least that. This is Mahpoud's second stint in Nazareth. Last season, when Maccabi Ahi Nazareth found itself in similar straits, Mahpoud came on as its coach and succeeded in keeping it in the National League. When the season ended, he accepted the better contract offered by Maccabi Kiryat Gat. But the relationship with Kiryat Gat proved short-lived, and Mahpoud found himself out of a job — a common enough occurrence in the dizzying game of musical chairs that is Israeli soccer. When the offer from Nazareth came, Mahpoud agreed almost immediately.

The recent outbreak of violence, he says, had little influence on his deliberations on whether or not to accept the job. "I was worried only that the roads might be closed, and I would not be able to make it to practice. Those around me were more concerned than I was. I did not give much thought to what happened in Nazareth. I like to think positive. There are radical minorities everywhere. I don't know the city, but I do know the team and its fans, and they're wonderful people. They welcomed me warmly when I signed back on." . . . .

Driving to practice from his home in Petah Tikva last week, Mahpoud was unwilling to talk politics. His radio was tuned to the all-music station Galgalatz throughout the two-hour trip to Nazareth and to local sports news on the 90-minute drive back. The fact that he coaches an Arab team is mere coincidence, as far as he is concerned. People who work in sports, he believes, should worry only about sports.

Mahpoud claims that the team's four Jewish players — Sagi Strauss, Shlomi Ben-Hamu, Arik Hangali, and Emil Castiel — were similarly unaffected by the current crisis. "The rioting in Nazareth had no effect on anyone in the team, Jewish or Arab," he says. "None of the Jewish players came and said they wanted to leave. Soccer players are soccer players: they want to play." . . .

---

[17] **Nazareth**: A city in northern Israel.

Issam Issami, the team's striker, is a Druze[18] who served in the Israeli army. He spent last season playing for Maccabi Netanya and had hoped to move to Betar Jerusalem for the current season. "I was at the Betar tryouts this summer. By the end of the first week, I felt I was not welcome there. Fans yelled curses at me during the first practice. The players didn't say anything to my face, but I knew that behind my back they were asking, 'Why did they have to bring the Arab player?' I knew what would happen if I made a mistake during the first game, that the crowd would call me a dirty Arab. Jerusalem has Jews and goys [non-Jews]. I'm a goy to them. I spent three years in the army, and I'm a goy to them."

Is it possible that you simply weren't good enough for Betar?

"Of course that's what they'd say. But that's not what I feel. Look, it's my country. I feel that it's my country. But you won't give me the space to feel that. You act like it's not my country, not in soccer, and not in other areas."

LIFE AS AN ARAB PLAYER

Mahpoud, once a star player in Hapoel Petah Tikva, was first recommended for the job by his friend Azmi Nassar, who two years ago led the Palestinian national team to third place in the Pan Arab Games. Nassar says he thought Mahpoud would work well with an Arab team. "He's an honest person, understands a lot about soccer. He has this restaurant in Petah Tikva where he works with Arab employees, and he gets along with them. I was sure he would not be patronizing or dismissive toward the Arab players."

Nassar is now coach of Bnei Sakhnin, the National League's other Arab team. Bnei Sakhnin now faces a double challenge. It is struggling not only to remain in the league, but also to maintain its status as "Israel's leading Arab team." Maccabi Ahi Nazareth is its arch-enemy. Last week the two teams played each other; Bnei Sakhnin won 2–1.

In the days preceding this much-awaited match, Mahpoud and Nassar's friendship helped take some of the sting out of the fierce rivalry. There was, however, another reason why passions did not quite rise to their expected frenzy: up until the last minute, it was not clear whether the game would even take place.

---

[27] **Druze:** A member of a religious community in parts of Israel and the Middle East that incorporates some Islamic symbolism with a belief that al-Hakim, a tenth-century Islamic leader and successor to Muhammad, represented God's earthly form. The Druze are considered a legal nationality in Israel.

The police refused to allow the match to be held in Nazareth. When Kiryat Eliezer was suggested as an alternative site, the insurance company demanded an exorbitant security deposit. "It's hard to prepare a team for a match this way," Mahpoud said last Tuesday, during the break between morning and afternoon practice. "You have to divide up the practice load, follow a plan, and you can't do that under these conditions. The Arab teams are harmed through no fault of their own."

Do you support the Arab players' claims that they suffer from discrimination?

"People in Ahi Nazareth say that the referees are prejudiced against them. In some games I feel that it's true. I think it's mostly because we're a small team, even for the second league. But it's also true that the life of an Arab player is much harder.

"They tell me that players on rival teams curse them, calling them 'dirty Arab' and names like that. That infuriates me. I always tell them that you can't allow yourself to be affected by these provocations. This is their job, their livelihood, and they have to keep it. I also get sworn at by the fans of rival teams. When I was coaching a Jewish team, the curses were much softer. Here people yell, 'You son of a bitch, why are you coaching Arabs?'"

What about your friend Azmi Nassar?

"Azmi did not get a single offer from a Jewish team, despite his many successes. I don't know why that is. He's an excellent coach. Speaking in purely professional terms, he has what it takes to coach a Premier League team. Maybe it's because soccer is such an emotional business. If his team failed, well, you know the kind of position the administration would then be in, having hired an Arab coach." . . .

Carpools and Music

Having finished their lunch, four of the Ahi Nazareth players [Shomi Ben Hamu, Arik Hangali, Ashraf Suliman, and Abed Titi] sit around a table in a downtown restaurant and talk. . . .

The four are friends, and not only on the soccer field. Titi, Ben Hamu and Hangali carpool to practice, meeting each day at the Netanya junction. Whoever is driving gets to choose the music, so that Ben Hamu and Hangali are constantly exposed to the latest Arab hits.

SULIMAN: We in Nazareth want good players. We don't care if they're Jewish, Arab or foreign, as long as they play well.

HANGALI: I never thought I'd end up playing for an Arab team, but from the moment I got here, I felt at home. I was treated very warmly, and I knew I was staying. You have to know how to keep sports and politics apart. We're in sports, we all have the same goal. I feel that I represent the city of Nazareth. I have no problem with that. But I also represent myself — if I don't play well, I'll disgrace myself, too. We're not repressing reality. Titi and Suliman are really our friends. If a few extremists raised some hell, is that any reason to be mad at them?

TITI: We only want peace and quiet. What does anyone, Jewish or Arab, have to gain from people being killed? Why can't we all have fun together?

SULIMAN: Iad Lawabneh, the first casualty from Nazareth, was a big fan of ours. He was killed 15 minutes before our game against Kiryat Gat began. Our management asked to have the game postponed, but it wasn't. We lost.

BEN HAMU: I had no problem playing when the riots started. I never thought of leaving the team. All in all, I know both the people here and the administration. People in my family were worried about me, said I should look into other options. But eventually, when things calmed down, those fears disappeared, too.

HANGALI: When we came to practice on the days of the rioting, we found fans waiting. They said they'd look out for us. Today, when people in Tel Aviv ask me whether I'm afraid to go to Nazareth, I laugh. What's there to be afraid of?

BEN HAMU: Joining Nazareth changed something for me. I didn't know any Arabs before, had no Arab friends. I knew nothing about their mentality. Today I get together with friends from the Arab team even after practice. We go out to eat or go bowling. Today all I want is for there to be peace. . . .

READING AND DISCUSSION QUESTIONS

1. How does the author explain the apparent lack of protest when Maccabi Ahi Nazareth replaced its Arab coach with a Jewish one despite the tense political climate and strained Arab-Jewish relations?

2. Do Arab or Jewish players seem to face more discrimination? Why might this be the case?

3. What are some of the obstacles the coaches and players face in order to play within their league? Where do those obstacles come from?

4. What reasons, if any, might the interviewed players have to downplay ethnic differences and the experiences of playing in sometimes hostile and violent environments?

COMPARATIVE QUESTIONS

1. How does each document in this chapter fit in an international context — drawing comparisons with, seeking independence from, or resolving conflicts between multiple countries? In each case, how is the author's own country situated among other countries, and why?

2. How do capitalism and religion work together — or against one another — in the Punjab and Shavit documents? How does the intersection of capitalism and religion affect the tone and content of each document?

3. What is the connection between nationalism and socialism evident in the Vietnamese declaration of independence and in Nasser's speech on the Suez Canal? How does nationalism work with or against socialism in each case?

4. What do the documents on China during and after Mao Zedong's rule — "Away from Madness" and "Building Socialism with Chinese Characteristics" — indicate about developments in modern Chinese history? How do you explain those developments?

5. Which of these documents seem most concerned with individual lives, and which with grand-scale geopolitics? Do any combine the two? Does each author seem to be more or less in control of his or her environment and self? How does this personal/political balance affect your reading of each document?

6. Each of the documents focuses on a particular aspect or aspects of modern identity. What are they in each case? What similarities and differences in the definition of citizen or human being do you detect across the documents?

CHAPTER 33

The Global South: Latin America and Africa

1945 to the Present

F ollowing the global depression and the Second World War, a variety of Latin America movements and Africa nations sought to end Western colonial rule and regain control of their social, political, and economic futures. Some movements embraced new nationalist identities, while others focused on regional or even global alliances. In either case, Latin Americans and Africans fought for freedom from the colonial oppression of governments and multinational corporations who had long exploited their vast natural resources. Despite their inherently anticolonial nature, these movements were often embroiled in the global logic of the Cold War, as former colonies struggled to create independent identities between the poles of communist and capitalist influence. And while colonial governments have begun to accept the realities of decolonization, the legacy of dependence and conflict sown by Western imperialism continues to trouble Latin American and African nations today.

DOCUMENT 33-1

PABLO NERUDA

From Canto General: *"Standard Oil Co."*
and "United Fruit Co."

1950

The Chilean poet, politician, and Nobel laureate Pablo Neruda (1904–1973) was a champion of left-wing political and social causes. He became politically active during the Spanish Civil War (1936–1939) and worked on

Pablo Neruda, *Canto General*, trans. Jack Schmitt (Berkeley: University of California Press, 1991), 176–179.

behalf of the Chilean government to assist Spanish émigrés to Chile fleeing fascism in their native country. His membership in the Chilean Communist Party and his support for Soviet leader Joseph Stalin (which he later recanted) won him as many enemies as supporters. Similarly, his support for the 1970 election of Marxist Salvador Allende as president of Chile earned him political persecution when Allende died in a coup d'état supported by the U.S. government and corporate interests. The two poems here, taken from his epic collection Canto General, *present his attack on the multinational corporations that, along with U.S. government policy, played a major role in modern Latin American history.*

STANDARD OIL CO.[1]

When the drill bored down
toward the stony fissures
and plunged its implacable intestine
into the subterranean estates,
and dead years, eyes
of the ages, imprisoned
plants' roots
and scaly systems
became strata of water,
fire shot up through the tubes
transformed into cold liquid,
in the customs house of the heights,
issuing from its world
of sinister depth,
it encountered a pale engineer
and a title deed.

However entangled the petroleum's
arteries may be, however the layers
may change their silent site
and move their sovereignty
amid the earth's bowels,
when the fountain gushes
its paraffin foliage,
Standard Oil arrived beforehand

---

[1] **Standard Oil Co.**: A major U.S. oil and energy company at the end of the nineteenth century, considered a prime example of monopoly capitalism.

with its checks and its guns,
with its governments and its prisoners.

Their obese emperors
from New York are suave
smiling assassins
who buy silk, nylon, cigars,
petty tyrants and dictators.

They buy countries, people, seas,
police, county councils,
distant regions where
the poor hoard their corn
like misers their gold:
Standard Oil awakens them,
clothes them in uniforms, designates
which brother is the enemy.
The Paraguayan fights its war,
and the Bolivian wastes away[2]
in the jungle with its machine gun.

A President assassinated
for a drop of petroleum,
a million-acre
mortgage, a swift
execution on a morning
mortal with light, petrified,
a new prison camp for
subversives, in Patagonia,
a betrayal, scattered shots
beneath a petroliferous moon,
a subtle change of ministers
in the capital, a whisper
like an oil tide,
and zap, you'll see
how Standard Oil's letters
shine above the clouds,
above the seas, in your home,
illuminating their dominions.

---

[2] **Paraguayan fights . . . Bolivian wastes away**: Neruda refers to the Chaco War
(1932–1935) between Paraguay and Bolivia and the role oil exploration and oil companies played therein.

United Fruit Co.[3]

When the trumpet blared everything
on earth was prepared
and Jehovah [God] distributed the world
to Coca-Cola Inc., Anaconda,
Ford Motors and other entities:
United Fruit Inc.
reserved for itself the juiciest,
the central seaboard of my land,
America's sweet waist.
It rebaptized its lands
the "Banana Republics,"[4]
and upon the slumbering corpses,
upon the restless heroes
who conquered renown,
freedom and flags,
it established the comic opera:
it alienated self-destiny,
regaled Caesar's crowns,
unsheathed envy, drew
the dictatorship of flies:
Trujillo flies, Tacho flies,
Carías flies, Martínez flies,
Ubico flies,[5] flies soaked
in humble blood and jam,
drunk flies that drone

---

[3] **United Fruit Co.**: An American producer of bananas, founded in 1899, that became a massive commercial and political presence in Central and South America. The company's influence on host governments — sometimes in cooperation with the U.S. government — inspired American author H. L. Mencken to coin the term "banana republic."

[4] **"Banana Republics"**: Countries that are heavily dependent on foreign capital and the production of one or a few exports. They are usually characterized by a corrupt government and exploitative labor practices.

[5] **Trujillo . . . Ubico**: Rafael Trujillo (1891–1961), Anastasio ("Tacho") Somoza Garcia (1896–1956), Tiburcio Carías Andino (1876–1969), Maximiliano Hernandez Martínez (1882–1966), and Jorge Ubico (1878–1946) were all mid-twentieth-century Central American dictators who symbolized corruption, collusion with foreign business interests, brutal suppression of dissent, and often mass killings of citizens perceived to be a threat to their political interests.

over the common graves,
circus flies, clever flies
versed in tyranny.

Among the bloodthirsty flies
the Fruit Co. disembarks,
ravaging coffee and fruits
for its ships that spirit away
our submerged lands' treasures
like serving trays.

Meanwhile, in the seaports'
sugary abysses,
Indians collapsed, buried
in the morning mist:
a body rolls down, a nameless
thing, a fallen number,
a bunch of lifeless fruit
dumped in the rubbish heap.

READING AND DISCUSSION QUESTIONS

1. How does Neruda portray the representatives of the two companies?
    How does he portray the companies themselves?

2. How does the poet present citizens of Latin American countries? What
    about Latin American leaders?

3. How might Neruda's political affiliations color his presentation of for-
    eign investment in Latin American economies? Does he seem to be
    writing from a political or a regional point of view — as a Communist,
    as a Latin American citizen, or both?

DOCUMENT 33-2

FIDEL CASTRO

Interview with Dan Rather

September 30, 1979

In October 1979, President Jimmy Carter informed the American public of his administration's "serious concern" over the presence of Soviet troops in Cuba. He outlined several measures that the United States would take, including increased military presence in the Caribbean and increased sur- veillance of Cuba. The resulting international and domestic uproar cost Carter support for a recent arms treaty with the Soviet Union. Anticipating the president's announcement, U.S. journalist Dan Rather had traveled to Cuba in late September to interview Cuban president Fidel Castro. The following text from the interview, which aired on 60 Minutes, presents Cas- tro's vision of the roles of Cuba and the United States in Latin American affairs.

RATHER: . . . President Carter's official spokesman said . . . that this is not an artificial crisis. They say it's a real problem. That there's something new in Cuba. A Soviet combat brigade.

CASTRO: That is precisely where the falsehood lies. Do you under- stand? . . .

We are a sovereign country. The United States has no rights, privilege, or jurisdiction over Cuba. Cuba is not the property of the United States; Latin America is not the property of the United States. We consider ourselves to be a free country, and we have the right to think like a free country. If I were to stoop to giving an explanation about the nature of these military installations, I would be calling into question Cuba's right to adopt the defensive measures it deems neces- sary. Besides, we are no less than Japan, England, the FRG [Federal Republic of Germany], no less than Spain or any other country which has felt it even has the right to station troops of another country on its soil for its defense. So I do not accept questioning Cuba's right to do likewise and I'm not going to give any explanations on that score.

Michael Taber, ed., *Fidel Castro Speeches* (New York: Pathfinder Press, 1981), 319–330.

That's not the problem, it really isn't. Why has the crisis been created? I have the following to say: That Soviet military personnel, which the U.S. government calls a brigade and we call Training Center Number 12, is a military installation which has been in Cuba for seventeen years — seventeen years! Their number and nature are similar to what they were seventeen years ago. This installation was set up after the October Crisis,[6] in keeping with the spirit of the solution of the October Crisis and in line with the status quo created during the October Crisis. That is, it isn't anything new. . . .

RATHER: Has there been any change in the nature of the Soviet troops in this country since that time?

CASTRO: There has been no change in the nature nor in the functions of the Soviet personnel in Cuba in the last seventeen years. That is the key to the matter.

Kennedy, Johnson, Nixon, and Ford were perfectly aware of the existence of this installation, and Carter had to know about it. It's impossible for them to have been unaware of it given that it's an installation which has existed for seventeen years in a country over which they have carried out hundreds of flights, where they have sent hundreds of espionage agents, a country in which the United States has used all its electronic means to discover what's going on. Who do they think is going to believe that they were unaware of the existence of this installation for seventeen years? Who do they expect to believe this? That's why I challenge Carter to explain the truth to the people of the United States and to world opinion and to say since when this alleged brigade has been here. Since when? He should say if it was set up under his own administration, during the Ford administration in 1976, during the Nixon administration in 1970, during the Johnson administration in 1965, or whether it has been here since October 1962. I think this is the key to the matter, and this is where the falsehood lies; in trying to make world opinion and U.S. opinion believe that the Soviet Union and Cuba have taken steps of a military nature to create a problem and create a crisis. That is the key to the issue.

RATHER: I agree that that's the key, and I can assure you that I believe President Carter tomorrow night is going to say to the American people

---

[6] **October Crisis**: Also known as the Cuban Missile Crisis. In October 1962, the U.S. government became aware of the presence of Soviet nuclear weapons in Cuba. After a U.S. naval blockade and the negotiated secret reduction in U.S. missiles elsewhere, the crisis ended and the missiles in Cuba were removed.

that the nature of the Soviet presence in Cuba has changed. That for the first time in his knowledge there is a Soviet combat brigade in Cuba — not a training brigade, but a combat brigade.

CASTRO: Well, if President Carter says tomorrow that there has been a change in the number, nature, or functions of the Soviet military personnel in Cuba since 1962, he will be telling a big lie to U.S. public opinion and to world opinion. Because I assert that there has been no change in their number, nature, or functions in the last seventeen years.

RATHER: . . . There are reports circulating in Washington tonight about possible American military movements, strengthening U.S. forces in Key West, Puerto Rico, even sending a contingent of U.S. marines to Guantánamo, and the possibility of sending a U.S. aircraft carrier to the Caribbean Sea. This may be what President Carter will announce tomorrow night. Now, do you have any intelligence information indicating this is true?

CASTRO: My information is what has appeared in newspapers, in dispatches. We haven't detected military movements with our means for some time.

RATHER: What is your reaction to that kind of attitude?

CASTRO: First of all, I think that what the United States should do, what Carter should do, is not create a crisis with no legal basis — with no legal basis! — and with no moral basis. I think the only thing the U.S. government should do is refrain from doing that, refrain from doing it because it means heading for conflicts and crises.

I think it would be much more constructive for Carter to announce the contrary: the willingness of the U.S. government to respect Cuba's sovereign rights; to end the economic blockade, which includes medicine, that it has maintained for twenty years;[7] and to express its willingness to dismantle the Guantánamo base and withdraw its ships and troops from our waters and territory.

Now, what's our reaction? We aren't frightened by any of this, we aren't intimidated. We've been subjected to this hostility on the

---

[7] **economic blockade . . . for twenty years**: The U.S. economic embargo of Cuba was established in response to Cuba's nationalization of private property, including some property owned by U.S. citizens. The embargo was strengthened in 1962 and remains in effect as of 2011.

United States's part for twenty years. They're going to send soldiers to Puerto Rico? I don't think Puerto Ricans will like that. They're going to send soldiers to Key West? The tourists won't like that. They're going to send soldiers to Guantánamo? That will cost U.S. taxpayers more money. None of that will affect us; we won't let ourselves be intimidated and we aren't going to get nervous about the situation. . . .

RATHER: Mr. President, I want to make very clear: you have flatly denied that there is a Soviet combat brigade in Cuba?

CASTRO: I'm not denying that there is Soviet military personnel in our country. What I'm saying is that it is exactly the same personnel, organized in the same way, as seventeen years ago. That is what I'm stating clearly and categorically. You call that Soviet personnel, or part of that Soviet personnel, a brigade and we call it a training center.

RATHER: Mr. President, how is the situation right now different from the October Crisis of 1962, if it is different?

CASTRO: It's different in every sense.

First, during the 1962 crisis there was a real and objective danger of nuclear conflict: and that's not the case now.

The October Crisis was a real crisis; this is a fabricated crisis. The October Crisis could have been a tragedy; this is a comedy.

Now then, during the October Crisis there were dozens of nuclear missiles here; there were more than forty thousand Soviet soldiers in Cuba, there were squadrons of IL-28 bombers. That's not the case now.

When a settlement of the October Crisis was reached, an agreement between the USSR and the United States — an agreement in which we did not participate and therefore to which we do not feel committed — when that agreement was reached, by virtue of which the Soviet Union decided to withdraw all those weapons in exchange for a guarantee that Cuba would not be invaded, the situation was different from what it is now. None of these problems exist now.

When Kennedy reached those agreements with Khrushchev, he was satisfied with the withdrawal of those weapons. It isn't that he was right or that he had any right! Those are two different things. We didn't agree then, but it was a different problem: there was a real threat to peace at that time. Kennedy was satisfied, Kennedy wasn't concerned about the 2,000 or 3,000 Soviet military personnel left behind. Do you understand? He didn't attach any importance to that.

I ask myself why Carter has revived the issue, why he has created a crisis. Why has Carter staged this comedy over 2,000 or 3,000

Soviet military personnel in Cuba? I want him to explain why, if Kennedy didn't do so, nor Johnson, nor Nixon, nor Ford, why has Carter done so? How can he explain this? What's the reason? What's the justification?

He won't get the people of the United States to believe that no U.S. president was aware of this. That's like saying that the CIA doesn't exist, that the government of the United States is absolutely misinformed about all problems.

There are two factors that explain this. First, the attempt to sabotage . . . the Sixth Summit.[8] Second, the effort to improve Carter's image and overcome the problems he is facing to be reelected. That, in my opinion, is the only explanation of why Carter has created this problem. . . .

RATHER: Thank you. Mr. President, if you ask the Soviet troops to leave Cuba — all the troops — would they leave?

CASTRO: You talk of troops, I speak of Soviet military personnel. You speak of brigades and I of a training center, of a military installation.

Now that I've made this point what is your question'?

RATHER: If you asked all the Russians on this island to leave — whatever you want to call them, military trainers — if you asked them to leave, would they leave?

CASTRO: Of course, there's no doubt about it.

RATHER: You see, so many people in the United States question that.

CASTRO: But why?

RATHER: For one thing, President Carter has said that it isn't true, that you're a Soviet puppet, a satellite.

CASTRO: And in order to prove we're not we have to ask the Soviet personnel to leave?

I think this is absurd. That statement is completely absurd. We have no intention of asking the Soviet personnel to leave Cuba, but it would be absurd to think that if we were to ask them to leave, they would want to stay.

That's absurd. That's inconceivable. . . . What I am sure of though, is that we have told the U.S. forces to leave Guantánamo and they haven't. They are the only ones who are capable of staying in the territory of another country against the will of the people. . . .

---

[8] **Sixth Summit**: The Sixth Conference of Heads of State of Nonaligned Countries, held September 3–9, 1979, in Havana, Cuba.

RATHER: Another question. This is a quote from a newspaper. I quote: "The Soviets have assumed that the presence of their troops in Cuba will discourage the United States from stopping any of Fidel Castro's military adventures in this hemisphere."

CASTRO: And what are Fidel Castro's adventures in Latin America?

RATHER: Nicaragua.[9]

CASTRO: What is it that makes Nicaragua Castro's adventure? It was an adventure of the United States. It was the United States that intervened in Nicaragua, that set up the National Guard and installed Somoza in power and kept him there for over forty years. It was the United States's big adventure, not Cuba's.

It wasn't Cuba nor was it Cuban soldiers that overthrew the government of Nicaragua, that is, the Somoza dictatorship. It was the Sandinistas, the people of Nicaragua. And the United States itself recognizes this: President Carter recently met with representatives of the Nicaraguan government.

RATHER: Were you the principal arms supplier for the Nicaraguan rebels?

CASTRO: There is absolutely no proof of that. But I have no intention of answering that question.

RATHER: You asked what are Fidel Castro's adventures in the Western Hemisphere referred to here. El Salvador?

CASTRO: I ask myself what they are referring to. What's happening in El Salvador? There is a corrupt, tyrannical, genocidal government, and the people are no longer willing to tolerate the regime. Why must we be blamed for that?

RATHER: Because you were training the people, you are supplying the arms, the money. . . .

CASTRO: I think that the United States is the one that has trained all those armies — the one in Chile that murders the people, the one in Uruguay that has killed thousands of Uruguayans, Somoza's army, and that of El Salvador — the United States has trained and equipped all the genocidal governments in this hemisphere, not Cuba.

---

[9] **Nicaragua**: In July 1979, then-president of Nicaragua, Anastasio Somoza, was overthrown by the Sandinista Socialist Party. The Somoza family, which exercised repressive power and was criticized for brutal human rights abuses and corruption, had ruled Nicaragua since the 1930s with the strong backing of the U.S. government, although Carter withdrew some support for Somoza during his term in office.

If we were to help the revolutionaries we would have the right to do so, but I'm not going to say here that we are doing so.

That is our affair and not a matter to be discussed on television.

RATHER: But you don't deny it?

CASTRO: I neither confirm it nor deny it, I proclaim it as a right; furthermore, as a duty.

RATHER: So many Americans — set aside the government — not President Carter, not Mr. Brzezinski,[10] but American people, rank-and-file people, believe, many of them believe, that Cuba is a nuclear pistol pointed at their heads.

CASTRO: A nuclear pistol?

RATHER: Pointed at their heads.

CASTRO: I think the people of the United States are too intelligent to believe such a thing. Who could have convinced the people to believe such a thing?

We have no nuclear weapons. I said that on Friday. It's not that we don't have the right to; we don't relinquish that right. We'll relinquish that right when all countries of the world renounce nuclear weapons.

But the only country that could supply us with nuclear weapons is the Soviet Union, and on this issue the Soviet Union worked out an agreement with the United States. As a result, we have no possibility of having nuclear weapons.

READING AND DISCUSSION QUESTIONS

1. What is Castro's response to the charge that there was a Soviet combat brigade in Cuba?

2. How does Castro respond to the allegation that Cuba interferes in the foreign affairs of other countries?

3. What relationship does Castro claim regarding Cuba and the Soviet Union? How does he defend that claim?

4. What is the proper U.S. role in Cuba's affairs, according to Castro?

---

[10] **Mr. Brzezinski**: Zbigniew Kazimierz Brzezinski (b. 1928) was Jimmy Carter's National Security Advisor from 1977 to 1981.

DOCUMENT 33-3

CHARLES DE GAULLE
Comments on Algeria
April 11, 1961

The lengthy Algerian War (1954–1962) was actually a series of conflicts rooted in the movement for Algerian independence from France. A Muslim West African country, Algeria provided colonial France with access to Saharan oil reserves as well as a base for commerce and industry. In return, France offered Algeria ongoing economic aid. However, years of violent Algerian resistance to colonial rule had drained France's resources. Pulled in both directions, French president Charles de Gaulle (in office 1958–1969) devised the controversial strategy of issuing a referendum to the Algerian people. If they chose independence — as they ultimately did — he would end France's hold on the country. At a 1961 press conference, de Gaulle explained his willingness to accept Algerian independence.

I should like it to be well understood that in France's policy toward Algeria, the following essential idea must be faced squarely: in the world of today and in the times in which we live, France has no interest whatsoever in maintaining under her jurisdiction and under her dependence an Algeria which would choose another destiny, and it would not be in France's interest to be responsible for the population of an Algeria which would have become master of its own fate and would have nothing to offer in exchange for what it would ask. The fact is that, to say the least, Algeria costs us much more than it is worth to us. Whether in the matter of administrative expenses, economic investments, social welfare, cultural development, or the many obligations with regard to the maintenance of law and order — what we furnished to it in effort, money, and human ability has no counterpart that anywhere nearly approaches it.

"Fourth Press Conference Held by General Charles de Gaulle as President of the French Republic in Paris and the Elysee Palace on April 11, 1961," in *Major Addresses, Statements, and Press Conferences of General Charles de Gaulle, May 19, 1958–January 31, 1964* (New York: French Embassy Press and Information Division, 1964), 113–118.

It must in the same way be realized that France's present responsibilities in Algeria constitute heavy military and diplomatic burdens for her. And that is why France would consider today with the greatest calm a solution whereby Algeria would cease to be a part of France — a solution which in former times might have seemed disastrous for us but which, I say it again, we consider with a perfectly calm mind. . . .

There are people who will say: "But it is the rebellion which leads you to think in this way." . . . It is not this that makes me speak as I do; I do not deny that the events which have occurred, which are occurring in Algeria have confirmed what I have thought and demonstrated for more than twenty years, without any joy of course — and you can well understand why — but with the certainty of serving France well.

Since Brazzaville,[10] I have not ceased to affirm that the populations dependent on us should have the right to self-determination. In 1941, I granted independence to the mandated States of Syria and Lebanon. In 1945, I gave all Africans, including Algerian Moslems, the right to vote. In 1947, I approved the Statute of Algeria which, if it had been applied, would probably have led to the progressive institution of an Algerian State Associated with France.[11] . . . I agreed that the protectorate treaties concerning Tunisia and Morocco should be approved. . . . In 1958, having resumed leadership,[12] I, along with my Government, created the Community[13] and later recognized and aided the independence of the young States in Black Africa and Madagascar. Not having returned to power in time to prevent the Algerian insurrection, immediately upon my return I proposed to its leader to conclude the peace of the brave and to open political talks . . . and I and my government have not ceased to act in order

---

[10] **Brazzaville**: De Gaulle and some forty colonial administrators attended the Brazzaville Conference in French West Africa in 1944. No Africans participated, and independence was not discussed. The conference proposed a number of reforms in the French African colonies.

[11] **Statute of Algeria . . . France**: Algerians were given the right to vote for members of the three assemblies that met in 1946 to determine the constitutional framework of postwar Algeria. However, voting was weighted in such a way as to guarantee French dominance of the assemblies.

[12] **having resumed leadership**: In June 1958, French president René Coty asked de Gaulle to handle the Algerian situation.

[13] **the Community**: The French Community was a plan proposed by de Gaulle in 1958, according to which French colonies, primarily in Africa, would continue to receive French economic and technical aid and would gain control of their internal affairs.

to promote a Moslem leadership in Algeria and to put the Moslems in a position to take local affairs into their own hands, until such time as they are able to take over on the government level. . . .

In conclusion, what does this add up to: to decolonization. But if I have undertaken and pursued this task for a long time, it is not only because we could foresee and later because we witnessed the vast movement toward freedom which the world war and its aftermath unleashed in every corner of the globe, and which the rival bids of the Soviet Union and America did not fail to emphasize. I have done it also, and especially, because it seemed to me contrary to France's present interests and new ambition to remain bound by obligations and burdens which are no longer in keeping with the requirements of her strength and influence. . . .

Moreover, this is true for others as well. It must be recognized that in the great transformation which is taking place from one end of the universe to the other, the itching for independence of erstwhile dominated peoples and also the incitements thrown out by all the demagogues of the world are not the only motivating forces. There is another which is not always very clearly perceived. . . . We French built our empire at a time when our internal activities had reached a sort of ceiling — an industry which was not breaking any new ground, an agriculture which was not making any changes, trade channels which were fixed, salaries and wages unchanged, practically stereotyped budgets, gold currency, interest rates at 3%, etc. On the other hand, our old ambitions of European hegemony and natural frontiers were countered by the treaties of 1815 and, after 1870,[14] by the unity and strength of a threatening Germany. Then we sought in distant extensions a new role for the surplus of our enterprising abilities, a complement to our prestige and soldiers for our defense.

France does not have to be at all sorry for what she has achieved overseas in this capacity and in this form. I have said it often and I repeat: it constitutes a great human accomplishment which — notwithstanding certain abuses and errors and despite all the endless spouting of all sorts of worthless demagogues — will forever be a credit to France. But how many things have changed today.

Now our great national ambition is our own national progress, constituting a real source of power and influence. Now the modern era permits

---

[14] **treaties of 1815 . . . 1870**: A treaty approved at the Congress of Vienna (1815) essentially returned France to its prerevolutionary borders. The Treaty of Paris (1870), which followed the French defeat by the Germans in the Franco-Prussian War, resulted in the French loss of the border region of Alsace and most of Lorraine.

us, compels us, to undertake a vast development. Now for this development to succeed we must first of all employ the means and resources at our disposal on our own behalf, in our own country. All the more so as we need these means and resources to ensure our own defense and that of our neighbors against the greatest imperialism that the world has ever known — the imperialism of the Soviet Union. We also need these means to win out in the tremendous economic, technical, and social struggle now under way between the forces of humanity and the forces of slavery [i.e., the Cold War].

It is a fact: our interest, and consequently our policy, lies in decolonization. Why should we continue to cling to costly, bloody, and fruitless domination when our country has to undergo complete renovation, when all the underdeveloped countries, beginning with those which yesterday were our dependencies and which today are our favorite friends, ask for our aid and our assistance? But this aid and this assistance — why should we extend them if it is not worthwhile, if there is no cooperation, if what we give finds no return? Yes, it is a matter of exchange, because of what is due us, but also because of the dignity of those with whom we are dealing. . . .

Some people say, "What would happen to these territories if France withdrew? They would straightaway fall into misery and chaos, until Communism took over." That is, no doubt, what would happen to them; but then we would no longer have any duty toward them other than to pity them.

Some people say also, "Either the Soviet Union or the United States — or both at once — would try to take France's place in the territories from which she withdrew." My answer is: I wish both of them a lot of fun.

But it is also possible that the Algerian populations — through self-determination, while deciding on the institution of a sovereign State — will express their desire to see the new Algeria associated with the new France. In such an event, it would have to be known on both sides what this actually meant. That is why a solution should be submitted to the vote of the Algerian people — pending ratification by the French people — a solution agreed upon beforehand by the Government and the different political elements in Algeria, the rebels in particular. France would undoubtedly be willing to lend her economic, administrative, financial, cultural, military, and technical aid to the young Mediterranean State, provided the organic cooperation between the Algerian communities, preferential conditions for economic and cultural exchange, and finally the bases and facilities necessary for our defense, are assured and guaranteed. . . .

Naturally we are anxious that, once peace has been re-established and civil liberties restored, the populations may sincerely choose their destiny. After which, if it is not in vain, France will undoubtedly be led, by her heart and her reason, to give her aid and friendship.

That is what I wanted to say about Algeria.

READING AND DISCUSSION QUESTIONS

1. What reasons does de Gaulle present to support his statement that it is not in France's interest to hold on to Algeria?

2. How does de Gaulle counter charges that his decision to support independence was prompted by Algerian insurrections?

3. What role does de Gaulle say World War II played in decolonization?

4. According to de Gaulle, what are the differences between France's goals in building its overseas empire and the country's goals in 1961?

DOCUMENT 33-4

KWAME NKRUMAH

Speech on the Tenth Anniversary of the Convention People's Party

1960

Kwame Nkrumah (1909–1972) was the first president of the Republic of Ghana. While an important voice for Ghanaian nationalism, he stressed the larger ideal of pan-Africanism and was a founding member of the Organization of African Unity. In 1949, Nkrumah founded the Convention People's Party to mobilize for the independence of Ghana, then called the Gold Coast. Nkrumah practiced increasingly autocratic rule; he imprisoned political enemies and declared himself president for life in 1964. He lost his position in a coup d'état in 1966. Despite this, he continues to be upheld as

Selected Speeches of Kwame Nkrumah, ed. Samuel Obeng, 5 vols. (Accra, Ghana: Afram, 1997), 1:4–12.

a powerful voice for African unity and development. The speech excerpted here, which was delivered to his Convention People's Party, reflects his sense of the challenges and opportunities facing the African continent in the post-colonial era.

Coming to the international scene, I must emphasise that our Party's foreign policy continues to be based upon positive neutralism and non-alignment. We are convinced that by our policy of non-alignment we are able to speak our minds frankly and without fear and favour on issues as they arise. Our policy is not a negative one. Positive neutralism and non-alignment does not mean keeping aloof of burning international issues. On the contrary, it means a positive stand based on our own convictions completely uninfluenced by any of the power blocs. We believe that we could help to bridge the unfortunate and undesirable gap between the so-called East and West blocs by not aligning ourselves to either side. We hold the view that as to the issues between them, neither bloc can claim to be permanently right or permanently wrong. As such, it will not be in the interest of international understanding and unity for us and the other independent states of Africa to involve ourselves in the disputes of the power blocs by taking sides. We should be free to take our stand without previously committing ourselves to any bloc on any matters which affect the peace, progress and, indeed, the destiny of Africa. We believe that it would be suicidal to involve ourselves in the disputes of the great powers by taking sides. We will continue to cultivate and maintain friendly relations with all countries, and to be enemy to none.

Concerning Africa, the Convention People's Party has shown the light and the people will surely find the way. We are proud of our achievements in this regard, and we make no apologies whatsoever to anyone for the role the Party has played, and continues to play, in pursuing the cause of independence and unity of Africa. We shall continue to give encouragement, comfort and support to the nationalist movements for independence, which are now developing in many parts of the African continent.

One of the cardinal tenets of our policy is to see all Africa free from foreign rule, for we believe that freedom for Africans on their native continent of Africa is essential for world peace. The great wave of nationalism at present sweeping Africa is a fact which should be recognised; it is a force that no one can hold in check.

To meet the challenge of nationalism and to prepare colonial territories on a planned basis for independence based on the principle of "one man one vote," it is important that target dates acceptable to the countries concerned should be agreed upon as soon as possible. Ghana believes that the peoples of the territories will measure up to the responsibilities demanded by the prospects of self-rule and that they themselves will propose a realistic timetable.

Whether the protagonists of colonialism like it or not, and whatever will be their machinations, African nationalism will not budge an inch until the whole of Africa is free from foreign domination. Africa is in rebellion against oppression and discrimination and is now a continent to be reckoned with. It will be even more so in the next decade before us. . . .

All over the continent of Africa, the Africans are beginning to assert their right to govern themselves, and everywhere in Africa today there is a determined demand for complete independence and unity.

The colonial powers have now been compelled to recognise the force of African nationalism and they have now realised that it is absolutely impossible and, in fact, unrealistic on their part to resist the rising tide of nationalism in Africa.

The imperialists faced with this new situation in Africa are now talking about the granting of independence to "our overseas territories." But we must be sure that the independence which they now promise is the real one — for any independence which makes the territory still economically dependent on the colonial power is not real.

We must be vigilant, for colonialism and imperialism may come to Africa in different guises. We must therefore alert ourselves to be able to recognise this whenever and wherever it rears its head, and prepare ourselves to fight against it, for it is only with the complete interment of imperialism and colonialism that Africa will be free from menace and able to live and breathe in full liberty where not only men of colour everywhere but also men of all races shall walk with their heads high in human dignity.

As I have said, the colonial powers and their imperialist allies are beginning to advance a new subtle theory — and a disguised one, at that — to safeguard their position in Africa and to beguile and bamboozle the Africans. They are prepared to grant political independence but, at the same time, they are also planning to continue to dominate the African territories in the economic field by establishing control over the economic life of the newly independent African countries. There is no difference between political imperialism and economic imperialism.

By these methods, the enemies of African freedom hope to be able to use the new African States as puppets to continue to dominate Africa, while, at the same time, making the Africans to believe that they are, in fact, free and independent.

This new type or concept of independence has been described as "international independence" and it is now the new slogan which is being preached in many colonial territories in Africa.

Under certain conditions, the colonial powers are prepared even now to grant independence to many of their territories. As independent states, these territories are supposed to acquire international personality and establish diplomatic relations with other states and also have representation in the various international organisations, including the United Nations.

Once this stage has been reached, the devil of colonialism will put all its energies into establishing control over the foreign relations and policies of the new African States, and thus make it difficult or even impossible for the African people to work together to establish a Union of African States.

The new policy or concept of "conditional independence," which the colonial powers are now planning to adopt, is a policy which is intended to create several weak independent states in Africa. These States are designed to be so weak and unstable in the organisation of their national economies and administrations that they will be compelled by internal as well as external pressures to continue to depend upon the colonial powers who have ruled them for several years. The weaker and the less stable an African State is, the easier it is for the colonial power concerned to continue to dominate the affairs and fortunes of the new State, even though it is supposed to have gained independence.

This policy of creating several unstable and weak, but none-the-less independent states in Africa, was the same policy adopted by the Great Powers at the Congress of Vienna which balkanised Eastern Europe. It is now an indisputable historical fact that the creation of the small independent States in Europe provided the fertile soil out of which developed the national jealousies, dissentions and disputes which culminated in the First and Second World Wars. . . .

We believe that considerations of mutual security and prosperity of our people demand that all the independent States in Africa should work together to create a Union of African States. We are aware of the various plans of the colonial powers and the enemies of African freedom to check the movement for independence and unity of Africa. We are determined not to fall victims to these plans.

We ask all African nationalists, wherever they are throughout the continent, to be vigilant and to watch out for the new forces of colonial domination, which are now being released to stem the tide of African nationalism and to destroy the efforts of the African movements for independence and unity. . . .

The imperialists know that a union of independen[t] states of Africa will be a force to be reckoned with in world politics. They are aware of the tremendous impact a free and united Africa can have on all aspects of world affairs.

They would prefer an Africa balkanised into small states which will dissipate their energies and efforts in fruitless rivalries among themselves. For they know that independence without unity can still give them room in our continent to perpetuate economic imperialism and racial discrimination. It is therefore plain common sense and in Africa's own interest that the attainment of national independence by new African nations should be accompanied by the evolvement of an African personality within an African community. . . .

In this connection I appeal to you, the people of Ghana — especially to the youth — to play our dutiful part in this crusade to liberate and unite Africa. We must learn to love and serve Ghana and Africa. We must be imbued with a deep sense of patriotism for our country and inspired by an equally deep sense of mission to work for Africa's emancipation.

What must in the long run unite Africa is not only the ultimate but certain victory over the common foreign domination of our continent. What should unite Africa is the deep love for our continent and our determination to serve it loyally. What must unite the continent of Africa is an ideology — our common Africanism.

READING AND DISCUSSION QUESTIONS

1. How does Nkrumah link Ghanaian policies with world affairs?
2. What threats from the international community does Nkrumah identify?
3. How might political independence be a negative thing for African nations?

VIEWPOINTS

Race and Power in South Africa

DOCUMENT 33-5

NATIONAL PARTY OF SOUTH AFRICA

The National Party's Colour Policy

March 29, 1948

When the Union of South Africa was established as a quasi-autonomous dominion of the British Empire in 1910, its legal and political system embraced the policies of segregation and disenfranchisement of non-whites that had flourished in colonial times. Not until the 1948 South African parliamentary election, however, did the formal system of "apartheid," or separation, become official state policy. Inhabitants of South Africa were strictly defined according to government racial criteria that determined where they could live, whom they could marry or have sexual relationships with, what they could study, and whether they were in fact citizens. The resulting system of white supremacy emphasized the threat of decolonization and the need for unity among the white minority. Several points in the government's policy are laid out here in this 1948 government proclamation, as catalogued by the United Nations.

There are two sections of thought in South Africa in regard to the policy affecting the non-European community.[15] On the one hand there is the policy of equality, which advocates equal rights within the same political structure for all civilized and educated persons, irrespective of race or

From U.N. General Assembly, Eighth Session. Supplement No. 16. *Report of the United Nations Commission on the Racial Situation in the Union of South Africa,* 1953. (A/2505 and A/2505/ADD.1). Official Record.

[15] **non-European community**: As used in this report, *European* loosely means "white," and *non-European* is approximately the same as "Coloured" or "Native." South Asians in Africa are also nonwhite, but not native.

colour, and the gradual granting of the franchise to non-Europeans as they become qualified to make use of democratic rights.

On the other hand there is the policy of separation (*apartheid*) which has grown from the experience of established European population of the country, and which is based on the Christian principles of Justice and reasonableness.

Its aim is the maintenance and protection of the European population of the country as a pure White race, the maintenance and protection of the indigenous racial groups as separate communities, with prospects of developing into self-supporting communities within their own areas, and the stimulation of national pride, self-respect, and mutual respect among the various races of the country.

We can act in only one of two directions. Either we must follow the course of equality, which must eventually mean national suicide for the White race, or we must take the course of separation (*apartheid*) through which the character and the future of every race will be protected and safeguarded with full opportunities for development and self-maintenance in their own ideas, without the interests of one clashing with the interests of the other, and without one regarding the development of the other as undermining or a threat to himself.

The party therefore undertakes to protect the White race properly and effectively against any policy, doctrine or attack which might undermine or threaten its continued existence. At the same time the party rejects any policy of oppression and exploitation of the non-Europeans by the Europeans as being in conflict with the Christian basis of our national life and irreconcilable with our policy.

The party believes that a definite policy of separation (*apartheid*) between the White races and the non-White racial groups, and the application of the policy of separation also in the case of the non-White racial groups, is the only basis on which the character and future of each race can be protected and safeguarded and on which each race can be guided so as to develop his own national character, aptitude and calling.

All marriages between Europeans and non-Europeans will be prohibited.

In their areas the non-European racial groups will have full opportunities for development in every sphere and will be able to develop their own institutions and social services whereby the forces of the progressive non-Europeans can be harnessed for their own national development (*volkeepbou*). The policy of the country must be so planned that it will eventually promote the ideal of complete separation (*algehele apartheid*) in a national way.

A permanent advisory body of experts on non-European affairs will be established.

The State will exercise complete supervision over the moulding of the youth. The party will not tolerate interference from without or destructive propaganda from the outside world in regard to the racial problems of South Africa.

The party wishes all non-Europeans to be strongly encouraged to make the Christian religion the basis of their lives and will assist churches in this task in every possible way. Churches and societies which undermine the policy of *apartheid* and propagate doctrines foreign to the nation will be checked.

The Coloured community takes a middle position between the European and the Natives. A policy of separation (*apartheid*) between the Europeans and Coloureds and between Natives and Coloureds will be applied in the social, residential, industrial and political spheres. No marriage between Europeans and Coloureds will be permitted. The Coloureds will be protected against unfair competition from the Natives in so far as where they are already established.

The Coloured community will be represented in the Senate by a European representative to be appointed by the Government by reason of his knowledge of Coloured affairs.

The present unhealthy system which allows Coloureds in the Cape to be registered on the same voters' roll as Europeans and to vote for the same candidate as Europeans will be abolished and the Coloureds will be represented in the House of Assembly by three European representatives.

These Coloured representatives will be elected by a Coloured representative council. They will not vote on:

(1)   Votes on confidence in the Government.
(2)   A declaration of war, and
(3)   A change in the political rights of non-Europeans.

A State Department of Coloured Affairs will be established.

The Coloured community will be represented in the Cape Provincial Council by three Europeans elected by the Coloured representative council.

A Coloured representative council will be established in the Cape Province consisting of representatives elected by the Coloured community, divided into constituencies with the present franchise qualifications, the head of the Department of Coloured Affairs and representatives nominated by the Government. In their own areas the Coloured community will have their own councils with their own public services which will be managed by themselves within the framework of the existing councils with higher authority.

Attention will be given to the provision of social, medical and welfare services in which the efforts of the Coloured themselves can be harnessed, and in which they will be taught as far as possible to be self-supporting.

READING AND DISCUSSION QUESTIONS

1. What is the rationale presented by the national government for the institution of apartheid?

2. How is religion used in this document, and to what end? What limitations, if any, are placed on religion?

3. What rights are given to "Coloured" people, and what rights are denied them? What can you imagine to be the probable outcomes of such restrictions?

4. Does this document represent the voice of Europeans or Africans? Who wrote this document?

DOCUMENT 33-6

NELSON MANDELA

The Rivonia Trial Speech to the Court

April 20, 1964

The white Afrikaner government that came to power in South Africa following World War II enacted extreme forms of legal segregation (apartheid) that relegated blacks to the lowest-paid jobs and the poorest regions of the

Nelson Mandela, *No Easy Walk to Freedom*, ed. Ruth First (New York: Basic Books, 1965), 163–168.

country. In the 1950s and 1960s, the African National Congress (ANC), led by young attorney Nelson Mandela (b. 1918), protested these racist policies first peacefully and later violently. The organization was outlawed in 1961, but Mandela continued to run the ANC while in hiding for seventeen months before he was arrested, tried, and found guilty of treason. He was imprisoned until 1990. Mandela first presented this defense following the 1963 arrest of ANC leaders at Liliesleaf Farm, Rivonia, and later included it in reports he released after becoming the first democratically elected president of South Africa in 1994.

In my youth . . . I listened to the elders of my tribe telling stories of the old days. Amongst the tales they related to me were those of wars fought by our ancestors in defense of the father-land. . . . I hoped then that life might offer me the opportunity to serve my people and make my own humble contribution to their freedom struggle. This is what has motivated me in all that I have done in relation to the charges made against me in this case. . . .

I have already mentioned that I was one of the persons who helped to form Umkonto.[16] I, and the others who started the organization, did so for two reasons. Firstly, we believed that as a result of Government policy, violence by the African people had become inevitable, and that unless responsible leadership was given to canalize and control the feelings of our people, there would be outbreaks of terrorism which would produce an intensity of bitterness and hostility between the various races of this country which is not produced even by war. Secondly, we felt that without violence there would be no way open to the African people to succeed in their struggle against the principle of White supremacy. All lawful modes of expressing opposition to this principle had been closed by legislation, and we were placed in a position in which we had either to accept a permanent state of inferiority, or to defy the Government. . . .

But the violence which we chose to adopt was not terrorism. We who formed Umkonto were all members of the African National Congress, and had behind us the ANC tradition of non-violence and negotiation as a means of solving political disputes. We believed that South Africa belonged to all the people who lived in it, and not to one group, be it Black

---

[16] **Umkonto:** Short for "Umkonto we Sizwe," or Spear of the Nation, a militant subgroup of the African National Congress that Mandela founded while in hiding in 1961.

or White. We did not want an interracial war, and tried to avoid it to the last minute. . . .

The African National Congress was formed in 1912 to defend the rights of the African people. . . . For thirty-seven years — that is until 1949 — it adhered strictly to a constitutional struggle. It put forward demands and resolutions; it sent delegations to the Government in the belief that African grievances could be settled through peaceful discussion and that Africans could advance gradually to full political rights. But White Governments remained unmoved, and the rights of Africans became less instead of becoming greater. . . .

Even after 1949, the ANC remained determined to avoid violence. At this time, however, there was a change from the strictly constitutional means of protest which had been employed in the past. The change was embodied in a decision which was taken to protest against apartheid legislation by peaceful, but unlawful, demonstrations against certain laws. Pursuant to this policy the ANC launched the Defiance Campaign, in which I was placed in charge of volunteers. This campaign was based on the principles of passive resistance.[17] More than 8,500 people defied apartheid laws and went to jail. Yet there was not a single instance of violence in the course of this campaign on the part of any defier. . . .

In 1960 there was the shooting at Sharpeville,[18] which resulted in the proclamation of a state of emergency and the declaration of the ANC as an unlawful organization. My colleagues and I, after careful consideration, decided that we would not obey this decree. The African people were not part of the Government and did not make the laws by which they were governed. We believed in the words of the Universal Declaration of Human Rights,[19] that "the will of the people shall be the basis of authority of the Government," and for us to accept the banning was equivalent to accepting the silencing of the Africans for all time. The ANC refused to dissolve, but instead went underground. . . .

Each disturbance pointed clearly to the inevitable growth among Africans of the belief that violence was the only way out — it showed that a

---

[17] **passive resistance**: A form of nonviolent political protest used and popularized by Indian leader Mohandas Gandhi (1869–1948).

[18] **shooting at Sharpeville**: The Sharpeville Massacre of 1960, in which police killed 69 and wounded 178 anti-apartheid demonstrators.

[19] **Universal Declaration of Human Rights**: A declaration of the rights entitled to every human being, adopted by the United Nations on December 10, 1948.

Government which uses force to maintain its rule teaches the oppressed to use force to oppose it. . . .

The avoidance of civil war had dominated our thinking for many years, but when we decided to adopt violence as part of our policy, we realized that we might one day have to face the prospect of such a war. . . . We did not want to be committed to civil war, but we wanted to be ready if it became inevitable.

Four forms of violence were possible. There is sabotage, there is guerrilla warfare, there is terrorism, and there is open revolution. We chose to adopt the first method and to exhaust it before taking any other decision.

In the light of our political background the choice was a logical one. Sabotage did not involve loss of life, and it offered the best hope for future race relations. Bitterness would be kept to a minimum and, if the policy bore fruit, democratic government could become a reality. . . .

Attacks on the economic lifelines of the country were to be linked with sabotage on Government buildings and other symbols of apartheid. These attacks would serve as a source of inspiration to our people. In addition, they would provide an outlet for those people who were urging the adoption of violent methods and would enable us to give concrete proof to our followers that we had adopted a stronger line and were fighting back against Government violence. . . .

Another of the allegations made by the State is that the aims and objects of the ANC and the Communist Party are the same. . . .

It is true that there has often been close cooperation between the ANC and the Communist Party. But cooperation is merely proof of a common goal — in this case the removal of White supremacy — and is not proof of a complete community of interests. . . .

It is perhaps difficult for White South Africans, with an ingrained prejudice against communism, to understand why experienced African politicians so readily accept communists as their friends. But to us the reason is obvious. Theoretical differences amongst those fighting against oppression is a luxury we cannot afford at this stage. What is more, for many decades communists were the only political group in South Africa who were prepared to treat Africans as human beings and their equals; who were prepared to eat with us, talk with us, live with us, and work with us. They were the only political group which was prepared to work with the Africans for the attainment of political rights and a stake in society. Because of this, there are many Africans who, today, tend to equate freedom with communism. . . .

Our fight is against real, and not imaginary, hardships or, to use the language of the State prosecutor, "so-called hardships." Basically, we fight against two features which are the hallmarks of African life in South Africa and which are entrenched by legislation which we seek to have repealed. These features are poverty and lack of human dignity. . . .

South Africa is the richest country in Africa, and could be one of the richest countries in the world. But it is a land of extremes and remarkable contrasts. The Whites enjoy what may well be the highest standard of living in the world, whilst Africans live in poverty and misery. Forty percent of the Africans live in hopelessly overcrowded and, in some cases, drought-stricken Reserves, where soil erosion and the overworking of the soil make it impossible for them to live properly off the land. Thirty percent are laborers, labor tenants, and squatters on White farms and work and live under conditions similar to those of the serfs of the Middle Ages. The other 30 percent live in towns where they have developed economic and social habits which bring them closer in many respects to White standards. Yet most Africans, even in this group, are impoverished by low incomes and [the] high cost of living. . . .

The lack of human dignity experienced by Africans is the direct result of the policy of White supremacy. White supremacy implies Black inferiority. Legislation designed to preserve White supremacy entrenches this notion. Menial tasks in South Africa are invariably performed by Africans. When anything has to be carried or cleaned the White man will look around for an African to do it for him, whether the African is employed by him or not. Because of this sort of attitude, Whites tend to regard Africans as a separate breed. They do not look upon them as people with families of their own; they do not realize that they have emotions — that they fall in love like White people do; that they want to be with their wives and children like White people want to be with theirs; that they want to earn enough money to support their families properly, to feed and clothe them and send them to school. And what "house-boy" or "garden-boy" or laborer can ever hope to do this? . . .

Poverty and the breakdown of family life have secondary effects. Children wander about the streets of the townships because they have no schools to go to, or no money to enable them to go to school, or no parents at home to see that they go to school, because both parents (if there be two) have to work to keep the family alive. This leads to a breakdown in moral standards, to an alarming rise in illegitimacy, and to growing violence which erupts, not only politically, but everywhere. Life in the townships is dangerous. There is not a day that goes by without somebody being stabbed or assaulted. And violence is carried out of the townships in the White living areas. People are afraid to walk alone in the streets after dark. Housebreakings and robberies are increasing, despite the fact that the death sentence can now be imposed for such offenses. Death sentences cannot cure the festering sore. . . .

During my lifetime I have dedicated myself to this struggle of the African people. I have fought against White domination, and I have fought against Black domination. I have cherished the ideal of a democratic and free society in which all persons live together in harmony and with equal opportunities. It is an ideal which I hope to live for and to achieve. But if needs be, it is an ideal for which I am prepared to die.

READING AND DISCUSSION QUESTIONS

1. What reason does Mandela give for the ANC's decision to defy the government decree that outlawed the group?

2. What form of violence did the formerly nonviolent ANC adopt, and how does Mandela justify this decision?

3. How does Mandela describe the experience of blacks under apartheid?

4. Why does Mandela believe that the fundamental theories of communism hold a certain appeal to black South African politicians, while white South Africans reject it?

COMPARATIVE QUESTIONS

1. Compare and contrast the issues and concerns facing Latin America in the documents in this chapter with those facing Africa. Can you identify common goals or concerns? What differences are apparent, and why?

2. Of these authors, only Charles de Gaulle represents the voice of colonizers. How do his calls for decolonization resonate with the voices of Pablo Neruda, Fidel Castro, Kwame Nkrumah, and Nelson Mandela? How is his message different from theirs, and why?

3. The proclamation of the National Party of South Africa is a stark contrast not only to the writings of Nelson Mandela, but to every other document in this chapter. To what extent do the voices of the National Party and Nelson Mandela represent domestic South African issues, and to what extent do they concern broader colonial/imperial issues? Explain.

4. Nkrumah's proclamation warns against the possible dangers of political independence. How might he have commented specifically on the other documents presented in this chapter?

5. What offenses has the United States inflicted upon Latin America according to Neruda and Castro? How do you weigh those claims against the reasons the United States might give for taking action in Latin American or African countries?

6. Compare the sentiments of the proclamation of the National Party of South Africa to the writings of Cecil Rhodes (Document 25-3). What are the similarities and/or differences between the writings of Rhodes, an English imperialist, and those of South African white supremacists?

CHAPTER 34

A New Era
in World History

The 1990s marked the beginning of a new era in world history. The Cold War was over, new human rights initiatives were springing up in long-repressed countries, and the so-called age of globalization was under way. By the early twenty-first century, the political and economic systems of all countries were more intricately linked and interdependent than ever before. Booms and busts, environmental issues, terrorism, war, and the spread of multinational corporations had become concerns for all nation-states. The United Nations emerged as an important voice in the global political arena. Western corporations reached into developing nations promising economic improvement on the one hand, and seeking new and cheaper sources of labor on the other. For some, the global economy has led to growth, technological development, and the promise of social and political reform. For others, the greater worldwide interconnectedness has exposed vast differences in values and wealth. One international constant remains — the struggle of people to be responsible global citizens.

VIEWPOINTS

Defining Arabic and Islamic Identities

DOCUMENT 34-1

GEORGE TARABISHI

*A Roundtable Discussion of Globalization
and Its Impact on Arab Culture*

October 26, 2000

*Many leaders and thinkers, particularly those in the East and in smaller
countries, worry about globalization's long-term impact. They debate
whether globalization will decimate local culture and replace it with that
of the West, and whether globalization will make the rich richer and the
poor — the vast majority of the world's people — poorer. To address these
concerns, Bahrain's Ministry of Culture convened a roundtable of Arab
intellectuals. Panel member George Tarabishi, who writes about the world
for the French and Arab press, shared highlights of the event and his own
views in the article excerpted below.*

When Muslim theological scholars used to determine that an issue is
conflictual, they meant that it is permissible to disagree about it, that
ijtihad [the application of reason] is necessary, and that this conflict and
this *ijtihad* cannot be considered heretical. It is within this specific context
that I declare that globalization is a conflictual matter. . . .

GLOBALIZING THE WORLD

There is no doubt that the ability to read globalization as a conflictual
matter derives from its seriousness as a phenomenon, from the looseness of

George Tarabishi, "Globalization and Its Impact on Arab Culture: Globalization as
a Matter of Conflict," *al-Bahrain al-Thaqafia* 26 (October 26, 2000). Translated by
Akram Khater.

its meaning, and from its capacity to be loaded with conflicting meanings and values. In addition, the vastness of this phenomenon and its multiple facets allows it to take as its basis an existential duality and thus a Manichaean[1] reading that depends on feelings and value judgments more than on knowledge. Thus, these approaches to globalization deal with it on the level of the singularities of good and evil, or love and hate, or right and left. Therefore, anyone who speaks of globalization must define first what he means. For me, globalization . . . means nothing more than the world becoming one. Before economy, before media, and before cultural production, the world itself is becoming globalized. We must not forget that the world, in its largest meaning, is a modern concept. Before overcoming the law of distances with modern means of transportation and communication, the world was made of worlds. The borders within these worlds were not merely geographical but also linguistic, religious, and ethnic. It was rare to imagine that each of these partial worlds was the world in its totality.

However, this world, which is being united by globalization — and herein lies the problem — cannot be unified except on the basis of its division into two dualities of a developed world and an underdeveloped world, a world of the rich and a world of the poor, a world that produces information and knowledge and a world where there is not even the means to consume these. According to a famous United Nations description [of the world], 20 percent of the world's population owns 80 percent of its riches, and 80 percent of its people own less than 20 percent of its resources. This places four-fifths of humanity on one side and one-fifth on the other side. According to another report, 20 percent of the world's rich own 85 percent of the global production, while 20 percent of the world's poor own no more than 1.1 percent.

Contrary to a strongly held belief, the globalization of the world — on the basis of this problematic dual division — is not limited to the economic sector alone. . . . In addition to economic globalization — which is without doubt the most obvious and most predisposed to quantification — there is technological globalization, environmental globalization, food globalization, legal globalization, media globalization, and finally cultural globalization.

---

[1] **Manichaean**: A philosophical understanding of the world in terms of good versus evil or dark versus light.

GLOBALIZING THE ARAB WORLD

If the Arab countries do not have sufficient cultural capacity to absorb globalization, then the concept of counter-globalization, as it is being propounded in the Arab cultural arena today, appears as if it is being activated under an attractive theoretical name — what we have called the mechanism of hegemony [dominance] . . . by a sizable number of intellectuals. It is true that the person who shaped this concept — the Tunisian linguist 'Abd al-Salam al-Masdi, has himself warned against dealing in a utopian fashion with the concept. . . . He clearly stated: "The concept of globalization that we have constructed in our cultural discussion in the book *Globalization and Counter-Globalization* does not mean that we deny the phenomenon of globalization. Nor do we object fundamentally to its existence. Nor are we in any way calling to completely oppose it. Had we done or claimed any of these, then we would be utopian in the absolute sense of the word. What we are calling for is the introduction of a new idea where counter-globalization would be a mentality that eschews negative criticism and embraces positive criticism."

Despite this [warning], it appears that this concept [counter-globalization] . . . has escaped like the genie from the bottle and has acquired an ideological independence that is not related to the rational purpose that produced it. It has imposed itself with incredible speed in the Arab world as a slogan for opposition and resistance, and as an alternative or contrary globalization, which some have defined as "the true globalization as opposed to the fake globalization," others as "the humane versus the monstrous globalization," or, as [Egyptian writer] Mahmud Amin al-'Alam has said, "the globalization of truth not falsehood, the globalization of liberty not enslavement and hegemony, the globalization of science, knowledge and creativity not ignorance, alienation, underdevelopment and dependency."

To draw ourselves away from the intellectually crippling gravitational pull between *globalization* and *counter-globalization*, I believe that we must be armed with both a realistic and critical awareness. This is not meant to confront and counter but to improve our chances of benefiting from its [globalization's] advantages and avoiding its negative aspects. In the large global village that the world is on the verge of becoming, the Arab world — which is more divided than ever — is in need of becoming first a regional singular village. This, I believe, is the shortest path to enter the village of globalization — or its jungle, as its opponents claim — safely.

Since one of the possible definitions of globalization is the erasure of borders, and we are dealing specifically here with cultural globalization, let us then add quickly that the borders that we think we ought to remove in the Arab world are cultural borders. We are realistic enough to realize that the political borders in the Arab world — despite our previous ideological illusions about these borders being artificial — are currently and for the foreseeable future not subject to removal. However, the Arab world is capable, despite the consecration of its divisions and its regional and national characteristics with borders, of representing a singular cultural group. If it was not for this ability, then the Arab world would not have been able to distinguish itself — and be distinguished by others — as an Arab world.

So as not to float in the ethereal world of abstraction, let us say right away that it is new communication technologies that allow for the relatively safe and effective circumvention of Arab cultural borders. The first indication of this penetration is embodied in the Arab satellite television channels, which — regardless of what has been said about their performance or funding and purpose — have succeeded, however partially, in shrinking the Arab world despite its vastness and the invincibility of its political topography.

Another example is presented to us by the capability — which has become a reality in some cases — provided by new communication technologies to publish multiple editions of the same Arabic newspaper or magazine in various Arab capitals and at the same time. If, in the near future, we can develop the spread of the Internet in the Arab world, then another aspect of internal Arab borders — and we mean regional censorship of thought and the means of exchanging it through books, journals, and newspapers — will fall or at least be circumvented. On the Internet the scissors of the censor cannot intrude.

We do not need to view the circumventing or the removal of the cultural borders as solely negative. We can envision a type of positive Arab globalization in which the Arab League — after revising its purpose toward elevating its cultural role — can play an effective role. We can envision, within this context, the establishment of an Arab network that links Arab scientific and university institutions to limit the chaos of Arab research, to lessen duplication and the waste of effort and money, and to allow for a real possibility for coordination of university research and for disseminating that research so that it benefits the Arab world and does not remain locked away collecting dust. Within this context also, we can envision a network to link Arab museums and another network to "revive" Arabic manuscripts in Arab and foreign universities and libraries and thus allow all researchers access without having to travel and waste money and time.

Proponents of the theory of Arab cultural security may object that circumvention of the borders will not be accomplished solely by Arabs but by necessity will be carried out also by "foreign" forces. . . . As is sometimes said in the world of strategy, the best defense is offense. Therefore, we say that the best way to confront globalization is to be present, not absent. In any case, globalization is already here, whether we like it or not. So let us learn how to participate in it. . . . Just as globalization has made possible the emergence of a new economic pole in the world, the Asian pole, and just as it has made possible the crystallization of a European media pole (Euro News in opposition to CNN, for example), there is nothing to keep us from anticipating the emergence of an Arab cultural pole one day. Although light-years separate us from the realization of this dream — whose accomplishment is linked to a chain of democratic, modernizing, and radical changes in the Arab world — we see no reason not to look forward to it. . . . We believe that the world is heading toward becoming for the first time in history a single civilization with multiple cultures. Globalization may be the tool for this dialogue between world civilization and national cultures. But this dialogue should take place on the condition — which some may say is utopian — that globalization ceases to be a tool for *hegemony* and instead becomes a tool for *participation*.

To avoid appearing as if I am simply making a play on words, allow me to say that adjusting the equation of globalization from hegemony to participation does not presume absolute equality in the shares of the partners. Globalization is closer to an incorporated company, and our position within the corporation is decided by the size of our stock portfolio. According to our demographic size, our share cannot exceed 3.4 percent; otherwise, we would become hegemonic like others. But even this level is higher than what we can arrive at in the foreseeable future. [This is so] first, because the Arab world does not enter into the company of globalization as a singular stockholder. Its portfolio is distributed among many partners, who in many instances are fighting among themselves. Moreover, the Arab world, most of which belongs to the Third World — some parts even belong to the Fourth World[2] — is not equal to the other stockholders in the globalization company in terms of its capacity for material and intellectual production. This disparity is particularly evident vis-à-vis the large partners who — despite being numerically small — own 80 percent of humanity's material production and 95 percent of its intellectual production. We will

---

[2] **Fourth World**: The countries of the Third World, primarily in Africa and Asia, that have the lowest rates of development.

be realistic if we dream of increasing our share, in stages, from 0.001 to 1 percent within a time frame that is no less than a quarter of a century. This 1 percent is the minimum requirement for "takeoff," as the experiences of East and Southeast Asian nations indicate. If we, some or all of us, fail to "take off" in the next quarter of a century, we must not attribute our failure in adjusting the equation of globalization to a failure of globalization itself. The formula for globalization is open and multifaceted and ever changing in its values, and if there is an unknown that is difficult to determine, it is the Arab unknown, because we are living in a period of high tension between those who support and those who oppose modernity. . . .

From a cultural point of view, globalization is not a neutral phenomenon, for it occurs within a particular culture. At a time when Arab culture, like the other cultures of the world, has no option but to engage with it [globalization], then it would appear that this engagement, in the Arab case, will be conflictual rather than cooperative. This is so because the cultural values contained within globalization appear, to a large extent, at odds with predominant Arab values.

We can describe the culture of globalization as being of this world — we do not say secular — while Arab culture is still counted within the religious segment [of cultures] and is still preoccupied with matters of the spiritual world. The culture of globalization, because it is the culture of wealthy society, has a hedonistic tendency to squeeze all pleasure from the present moment and to engage in hyper-consumption. In contrast, Arab culture . . . is dominated by the logic of contentment, abstention, and thrift, and spiritual saving for future dark days.

The culture of globalization — by definition a visual culture — depends on the presence of the human body and does not hesitate to uncover and denude it, particularly the female body. Arab culture, in contrast, is a culture of modesty — manifested by covering the body, particularly the female body. The two cultures also diverge greatly on the issue of sexual abstinence and permissiveness. The culture of globalism goes to extremes in allowing for sexual love, while Arab culture goes to extremes in limiting it.

These differences, among others, make the intersection of Arab culture and the culture of globalism a point of painful ruptures. But a certain measure of rupture and pain may be necessary to provide the impetus for what we will call . . . cultural mobility. . . .

Nobody can predict what will happen to the Arab world in the next twenty-five years, and how the struggle over the mother of conflicts — which is globalization in our time — will be resolved. However, the study of reality, which does not allow for miraculous transformations . . . forces us to be more pessimistic about the start of this new era, without being overly pessimistic about its end.

READING AND DISCUSSION QUESTIONS

1. How does Tarabishi define globalization? What was the world like before globalization?

2. In Tarabishi's view, what makes globalization "conflictual" for the Arab world?

3. What does Tarabishi believe the Arab world needs to do if it is to benefit from globalization?

DOCUMENT 34-2

OSAMA (USAMA) BIN LADEN
A Call on Muslims to Take Up Arms Against America
1998

Years before Osama bin Laden (1957–2011) was linked to the 2001 terrorist attacks on the World Trade Center and the Pentagon, he began building a movement to create an Islamic state and oust secular governments in Islamic countries. He shrewdly capitalized on dissatisfaction among Islamic fundamentalists with U.S. foreign policy, which they saw as anti-Arab. Bin Laden's anti-Western and frequently anti-U.S. rhetoric, like that used in this 1998 al-Qaeda call to arms, helped him amass a huge following in the 1990s. In the interview with his followers excerpted below, bin Laden shared his philosophy and foreshadowed his use of terrorism in 2001. After years in hiding, bin Laden was found and killed in a U.S. military strike in Pakistan in 2011.

"Interview with Usama Bin Laden by His Followers," *Nida'ul Islam* 15 (October–November 1998). Translated by Akram Khater.

INTERVIEW WITH USAMA BIN LADEN BY HIS FOLLOWERS, 1998

Q. What is the meaning of your call for Muslims to take up arms against America in particular, and what is the message that you wish to send to the West in general?

The call to wage war against America was made because America has spearheaded the crusade against the Islamic nation, sending tens of thousands of its troops to the land of the two Holy Mosques, over and above its meddling in its affairs and its politics and its support of the oppressive, corrupt, and tyrannical regime that is in control. These are the reasons behind the singling out of America as a target. And not exempt from responsibility are those Western regimes whose presence in the region offers support to the American troops there. We know at least one reason behind the symbolic participation of the Western forces and that is to support the Jewish and Zionist plans for expansion of what is called the Great Israel. Surely, their presence is not out of concern over their interests in the region. . . . Their presence has no meaning save one and that is to offer support to the Jews in Palestine who are in need of their Christian brothers to achieve full control over the Arab Peninsula, which they intend to make an important part of the so called Greater Israel. . . .

Q. Many of the Arabic as well as the Western mass media accuse you of terrorism and of supporting terrorism. What do you have to say to that?

There is an Arabic proverb that says, "She accused me of having her malady, then snuck away." Besides, terrorism can be commendable and it can be reprehensible. Terrifying an innocent person and terrorizing him is objectionable and unjust, also unjustly terrorizing people is not right.

Whereas, terrorizing oppressors and criminals and thieves and robbers is necessary for the safety of people and for the protection of their property. There is no doubt in this. Every state and every civilization and culture has to resort to terrorism under certain circumstances for the purpose of abolishing tyranny and corruption. Every country in the world has its own security system and its own security forces, its own police, and its own army. They are all designed to terrorize whoever even contemplates an attack on that country or its citizens. The terrorism we practice is of the commendable kind, for it is directed at the tyrants and the aggressors and the enemies of Allah, the tyrants, the traitors who commit acts of treason against their own countries and their own faith and their own prophet and their own nation. Terrorizing those and punishing them are necessary measures to straighten things and to make them right. Tyrants and oppressors who subject the Arab nation to aggression ought to be punished. The wrongs and the crimes committed against the Muslim nation are far greater than can be covered by this interview. America heads the list of aggressors against Muslims. The recurrence of aggression against Muslims everywhere is proof enough. For over half a century, Muslims in Palestine have been slaughtered and assaulted and robbed of their honor and of their property. Their houses have been blasted, their crops destroyed. And the strange thing is that any act by them to avenge themselves or to lift the injustice befalling them causes great agitation in the United Nations, which hastens to call for an emergency meeting only to convict the victim and to censure the wronged and the tyrannized whose children have been killed and whose crops have been destroyed and whose farms have been pulverized. . . .

In today's wars, there are no morals, and it is clear that mankind has descended to the lowest degrees of decadence and oppression. They rip us of our wealth and of our resources and of our oil. Our religion is under attack. They kill and murder our brothers. They compromise our honor and our dignity and if we dare to utter a single word of protest against the injustice, we are called terrorists. This is compounded injustice. And the United Nations' insistence to convict the victims and support the aggressors constitutes a serious precedent that shows the extent of injustice that has been allowed to take root in this land. . . .

Q. What is your relationship with the Islamic movements in various regions of the world, such as Chechnya and Kashmir and other Arab countries?

Cooperation for the sake of truth and righteousness is demanded from Muslims. A Muslim should do his utmost to cooperate with his fellow Muslims. But Allah says of cooperation that it is not absolute, for there is cooperation to do good, and there is cooperation to commit aggression and act unjustly. A Muslim is supposed to give his fellow Muslim guidance and support. He [Allah] said, "Stand by your brother be he oppressor or oppressed." When asked how were they to stand by him if he were the oppressor, he answered them, saying, "by giving him guidance and counsel." It all goes to say that Muslims should cooperate with one another and should be supportive of one another, and they should promote righteousness and mercy. They should all unite in the fight against polytheism, and they should pool all their resources and their energy to fight the Americans and the Zionists and those with them. They should, however, avoid side issues and rise over the small problems, for these are less detrimental. Their fight should be directed against unbelief and unbelievers. . . .

Q. We heard your message to the American government and later your message to the European governments who participated in the occupation of the Gulf. Is it possible for you to address the people of these countries?

As we have already said, our call is the call of Islam that was revealed to Muhammad. It is a call to all mankind. We have been entrusted with good cause to follow in the footsteps of the Messenger and to communicate his message to all nations. It is an invitation that we extend to all the nations to embrace Islam, the religion that calls for justice, mercy, and fraternity among all nations, not differentiating between black and white or between red and yellow except with respect to their devotedness. All people who worship Allah, not each other, are equal before him. We are entrusted to spread this message and to extend that call to all the people. We nonetheless fight against their governments and all those who approve of the injustice they practice against us. We fight the governments that are bent on attacking our religion and on stealing our wealth and on hurting our feelings. And as I have mentioned before, we fight them, and those who are part of their rule are judged in the same manner. . . .

Q. In your last statement, there was a strong message to the American government in particular. What message do you have for the European governments and the West in general?

Praise be to Allah and prayers and peace upon Muhammad. With respect to the Western governments that participated in the attack on the land of the two Holy Mosques regarding it as ownerless, and in the siege against the Muslim people of Iraq,[3] we have nothing new to add to the previous message. What prompted us to address the American government in particular is the fact that it is on the head of the Western and the crusading forces in their fight against Islam and against Muslims. The two explosions that took place in Riyadh and in Khobar recently were but a clear and powerful signal to the governments of the countries that willingly participated in the aggression against our countries and our lives and our sacrosanct symbols. It might be beneficial to mention that some of those countries have

---

[3] **siege against the Muslim people of Iraq:** Bin Laden is referring to the U.S. bombing of Iraq during the Gulf War in 1991.

begun to move toward independence from the American government with respect to the enmity that it continues to show toward the Muslim people. We only hope that they will continue to move in that direction, away from the oppressive forces that are fighting against our countries. We, however, differentiate between the Western government and the people of the West. If the people have elected those governments in the latest elections, it is because they have fallen prey to the Western media, which portray things contrary to what they really are. And while the slogans raised by those regimes call for humanity, justice, and peace, the behavior of their governments is completely the opposite. It is not enough for their people to show pain when they see our children being killed in Israeli raids launched by American planes, nor does this serve the purpose. What they ought to do is change their governments that attack our countries. The hostility that America continues to express against the Muslim people has given rise to feelings of animosity on the part of Muslims against America and against the West in general. Those feelings of animosity have produced a change in the behavior of some crushed and subdued groups, who, instead of fighting the Americans inside the Muslim countries, went on to fight them inside the United States of America itself.

The Western regimes and the government of the United States of America bear the blame for what might happen. If their people do not wish to be harmed inside their very own countries, they should seek to elect governments that are truly representative of them and that can protect their interests. . . .

The enmity between us and the Jews goes far back in time and is deep-rooted. There is no question that war between the two of us is inevitable. For this reason it is not in the interest of Western governments to expose the interests of their people to all kinds of retaliation for almost nothing. It is hoped that people of those countries will initiate a positive move and force their governments not to act on behalf of other states and other sects. This is what we have to say, and we pray to Allah to preserve the nation of Islam and to help them drive their enemies out of their land.

Q. American politicians have painted a distorted picture of Islam, of Muslims, and of Islamic fighters. We would like you to give us the true picture that clarifies your viewpoint. . . .

The leaders in America and in other countries as well have fallen victim to Jewish Zionist blackmail. They have mobilized their people against Islam and against Muslims. These are portrayed in such a manner as to drive people to rally against them. The truth is that the whole Muslim world is the victim of international terrorism, engineered by America at the United Nations. We are a nation whose sacred symbols have been looted and whose wealth and resources have been plundered. It is normal for us to react against the forces that invade our land and occupy it. . . .

Q. Quite a number of Muslim countries have seen the rise of militant movements whose purpose is to stand up in the face of the pressure exerted on the people by their own governments and other governments. Such is the case in Egypt and Libya and North Africa and Algiers, and such was the case in Syria and in Yemen. There are also other militant groups currently engaged in the fight against the unbelievers and the crusaders, as is the case in Kashmir and Chechnya and Bosnia and the African horn. Is there any message you wish to convey to our brothers who are fighting in various parts of the Islamic World?

Tell the Muslims everywhere that the vanguards of the warriors who are fighting the enemies of Islam belong to them and the young fighters are their sons. Tell them that the nation is bent on fighting the enemies of Islam. Once again, I have to stress the necessity of focusing on the Americans and the Jews, for they represent the spearhead with which the members of our religion have been slaughtered. Any effort directed against America and the Jews yields positive and direct results, Allah willing. It is far better for anyone to kill a single American soldier than to squander his efforts on other activities.

JIHAD[4] AGAINST JEWS AND CRUSADERS: WORLD ISLAMIC FRONT STATEMENT, 23 FEBRUARY 1998

Shaykh Usamah Bin-Muhammad Bin-Ladin
Ayman al-Zawahiri, amir [commander] of the Jihad Group in Egypt
Abu-Yasir Rifa'i Ahmad Taha, Egyptian Islamic Group
Shaykh Mir Hamzah, secretary of the Jamiat-ul-Ulema-e-Pakistan
Fazlur Rahman, amir of the Jihad Movement in Bangladesh

Praise be to God, who revealed the Book [Qur'an], controls the clouds, defeats factionalism, and says in His Book: "But when the forbidden months are past, then fight and slay the pagans wherever ye find them, seize them, beleaguer them, and lie in wait for them in every stratagem (of

---

[2] **Jihad**: Muslim holy war or crusade against infidels (nonbelievers).

war)"; and peace be upon our Prophet, Muhammad Bin-'Abdallah, who said: I have been sent with the sword between my hands to ensure that no one but God is worshiped, God who put my livelihood under the shadow of my spear and who inflicts humiliation and scorn on those who disobey my orders.

The Arabian Peninsula has never — since God made it flat, created its desert, and encircled it with seas — been stormed by any forces like the crusader armies spreading in it like locusts, eating its riches, and wiping out its plantations. All this is happening at a time in which nations are attacking Muslims like people fighting over a plate of food. In the light of the grave situation and the lack of support, we and you are obliged to discuss current events, and we should all agree on how to settle the matter.

No one argues today about three facts that are known to everyone; we will list them, in order to remind everyone:

First, for over seven years the United States has been occupying the lands of Islam in the holiest of places, the Arabian Peninsula, plundering its riches, dictating to its rulers, humiliating its people, terrorizing its neighbors, and turning its bases in the peninsula into a spearhead through which to fight the neighboring Muslim peoples.

If some people have in the past argued about the fact of the occupation, all the people of the peninsula have now acknowledged it. The best proof of this is the Americans' continuing aggression against the Iraqi people using the peninsula as a staging post, even though all its rulers are against their territories being used to that end, but they are helpless.

Second, despite the great devastation inflicted on the Iraqi people by the crusader-Zionist alliance, and despite the huge number of those killed, which has exceeded 1 million. . . . Despite all this, the Americans are once again trying to repeat the horrific massacres, as though they are not content with the protracted blockade imposed after the ferocious war or the fragmentation and devastation.

So here they come to annihilate what is left of this people and to humiliate their Muslim neighbors.

Third, if the Americans' aims behind these wars are religious and economic, the aim is also to serve the Jews' petty state and divert attention from its occupation of Jerusalem and murder of Muslims there. The best proof of this is their eagerness to destroy Iraq, the strongest neighboring Arab state, and their endeavor to fragment all the states of the region — such as Iraq, Saudi Arabia, Egypt, and Sudan — into paper statelets and through their disunion and weakness to guarantee Israel's survival and the continuation of the brutal crusade occupation of the peninsula.

All these crimes and sins committed by the Americans are a clear declaration of war on God, his messenger, and Muslims. And "ulama" [Muslim scholars] have throughout Islamic history unanimously agreed that the jihad is an individual duty if the enemy destroys the Muslim countries. . . .

On that basis, and in compliance with God's order, we issue the following fatwa [legal decree] to all Muslims:

The ruling to kill the Americans and their allies — civilians and military — is an individual duty for every Muslim who can do it in any country in which it is possible to do it, in order to liberate the al-Aqsa Mosque and the holy mosque [Mecca] from their grip, and in order for their armies to move out of all the lands of Islam, defeated and unable to threaten any Muslim. This is in accordance with the words of Almighty God, "and fight the pagans all together as they fight you all together," and "fight them until there is no more tumult or oppression, and there prevail justice and faith in God."

This is in addition to the words of Almighty God: "And why should ye not fight in the cause of God and of those who, being weak, are ill treated (and oppressed)? — women and children, whose cry is: 'Our Lord, rescue us from this town, whose people are oppressors; and raise for us from thee one who will help!'"

We — with God's help — call on every Muslim who believes in God and wishes to be rewarded to comply with God's order to kill the Americans and plunder their money wherever and whenever they find it. We also call on Muslim "ulama," leaders, youths, and soldiers to launch the raid on Satan's U.S. troops and the devil's supporters allying with them, and to displace those who are behind them so that they may learn a lesson.

Almighty God said: "O ye who believe, give your response to God and His Apostle, when He calleth you to that which will give you life. And know that God cometh between a man and his heart, and that it is He to whom ye shall all be gathered."

Almighty God also says: "O ye who believe, what is the matter with you, that when ye are asked to go forth in the cause of God, ye cling so heavily to the earth! Do ye prefer the life of this world to the hereafter? But little is the comfort of this life, as compared with the hereafter. Unless ye go forth, He will punish you with a grievous penalty, and put others in your place; but Him ye would not harm in the least. For God hath power over all things."

Almighty God also says: "So lose no heart, nor fall into despair. For ye must gain mastery if ye are true in faith."

READING AND DISCUSSION QUESTIONS

1. What does bin Laden say is the real motivation for the presence of Western troops in the Middle East?

2. What reasons does he give to justify his version of terrorism?

3. What distinction does bin Laden make between Western people and Western governments? How does he explain the election of Western leaders?

4. What three facts about Americans does he say are indisputable?

DOCUMENT 34-3

JOHN YOO

Memoranda Regarding U.S. Military Interrogations

2002, 2003

Following the attacks of September 11, 2001, the United States' most visible responses were military action against and invasion of Afghanistan (2001) and Iraq (2003). Domestically, President George W. Bush's administration moved to clarify the legal and political grounds for what was termed the war on terrorism, an effort that involved the detention and interrogation of both U.S. citizens and aliens. Deputy Assistant Attorney General of the United States John Yoo was asked by then-Counsel to the President Alberto R. Gonzalez, and later by General Counsel of the Department of Defense William J. Haynes II, to provide a legal opinion on the power of the president to interrogate prisoners and whether such interrogation was prosecutable as torture. His responses, excerpted here from 50- and 80-page letters, respectively, were widely understood to condone interrogation techniques such as

---

John Yoo, Deputy Assistant Attorney General of the United States, to Alberto R. Gonzales, Counsel to the President, August 1, 2002, Office of Legal Counsel, U.S. Department of Justice, Washington, D.C. John Yoo, Deputy Assistant Attorney General of the United States, to William J. Haynes II, General Counsel of the Department of Defense, March 14, 2003, Office of Legal Counsel, U.S. Department of Justice, Washington, D.C.

"waterboarding," adding to the controversy surrounding the U.S. response to the attacks of September 11.

Memorandum for Alberto R. Gonzales, Counsel to the President

August 1, 2002

Re: Standards of Conduct for Interrogation
Under 18 U.S.C. 2340–2340A

You have asked for our Office's views regarding the standards of conduct under the Convention Against Torture and Other Cruel, Inhuman and Degrading Treatment or Punishment as implemented by Sections 2340–2340A of title 18 of the United States Code.[5] As we understand it, this question has arisen in the context of the conduct of interrogations outside of the United States. We conclude . . . that Section 2340A proscribes acts inflicting, and that are specifically intended to inflict, severe pain or suffering, whether mental or physical. Those acts must be of an extreme nature to rise to the level of torture within the meaning of Section 2340A and the Convention. We further conclude that certain acts may be cruel, inhuman, or degrading, but still not produce pain and suffering of the requisite intensity to fall within Section 2340A's proscription against torture. . . .

We conclude that for an act to constitute torture as defined in Section 2340, it must inflict pain that is difficult to endure. Physical pain amounting to torture must be equivalent in intensity to the pain accompanying serious physical injury, such as organ failure, impairment of bodily function, or even death. For purely mental pain or suffering to amount to torture under Section 2340, it must result in significant psychological harm of significant duration, e.g., lasting for months or even years. We conclude that the mental harm also must result from one of the predicate acts listed in the statute, namely: threats of imminent death; threats of infliction of the kind of pain that would amount to physical torture; infliction of such physical pain as a means of psychological torture; use of drugs or other procedures designed to deeply disrupt the senses, or fundamentally alter an individual's personality; or threatening to do any of these things to a third party. The legislative history simply reveals that Congress intended

---

[5] **Sections 2340–2340A . . . United States Code**: United States Code Title 18, Part I, Chapter 113C, Sections 2340 and 2340A define torture and make it illegal both within and beyond the United States.

for the statute's definition to track the Convention's definition of torture and the reservations, understandings, and declarations that the United States submitted with its ratification. We conclude that the statute, taken as a whole, makes plain that it prohibits only extreme acts. . . .

We conclude that the treaty's text prohibits only the most extreme acts by reserving criminal penalties solely for torture and declining to require such penalties for "cruel, inhuman, or degrading treatment or punishment." This confirms our view that the criminal statute penalizes only the most egregious conduct. . . .

We examine international decisions regarding the use of sensory deprivation techniques. These cases make clear that while many of these techniques may amount to cruel, inhuman or degrading treatment, they do not produce pain or suffering of the necessary intensity to meet the definition of torture. From these decisions, we conclude that there is a wide range of such techniques that will not rise to the level of torture.

. . . We discuss whether Section 2340A may be unconstitutional if applied to interrogations undertaken of enemy combatants pursuant to the President's Commander-in-Chief powers. We find that in the circumstances of the current war against al Qaeda and its allies, prosecution under Section 2340A may be barred because enforcement of the statute would represent an unconstitutional infringement of the President's authority to conduct war.

MEMORANDUM FOR WILLIAM J. HAYNES II, GENERAL COUNSEL OF THE DEPARTMENT OF DEFENSE

March 14, 2003

Re: Military Interrogation of Alien Unlawful Combatants Held Outside the United States

You have asked our Office to examine the legal standards governing military interrogations of alien unlawful combatants held outside the United States. . . .

We conclude that the Fifth and Eighth Amendments,[6] as interpreted by the Supreme Court, do not extend to alien enemy combatants held abroad. . . . Federal criminal laws of general applicability do not apply to properly-authorized interrogations of enemy combatants, undertaken by

---

[6] **Fifth and Eighth Amendments**: U.S. constitutional amendments guaranteeing citizens protection against government abuse in legal procedures and prohibiting the federal government from imposing cruel and unusual punishments, respectively.

military personnel in the course of an armed conflict. Such criminal statutes, if they were misconstrued to apply to the interrogation of enemy
combatants, would conflict with the Constitution's grant of the Commander in Chief power solely to the President. . . .

Given the ongoing threat of al Qaeda attacks, the capture and interrogation of al Qaeda operatives is imperative to our national security and
defense. Because of the asymmetric nature of terrorist operations, information is perhaps the most critical weapon for defeating al Qaeda. Al Qaeda is
not a nation-state, and has no single country or geographic area as its base
of operations. It has no fixed, large-scale military or civilian infrastructure.
It deploys personnel, material, and finances covertly and attacks without
warning using unconventional weapons and methods. As the September
11, 2001 attacks and subsequent events demonstrate, it seeks to launch
terror attacks against purely civilian targets within the United States, and
seeks to acquire weapons of mass destruction for such attacks. Because of
the secret nature of al Qaeda's operations, obtaining advance information
about the identity of al Qaeda operatives and their plans may prove to be
the only way to prevent direct attacks on the United States. Interrogation
of captured al Qaeda operatives could provide that information; indeed, in
many cases interrogation may be the only method to obtain it. Given the
massive destruction and loss of life caused by the September 11 attacks, it
is reasonable to believe that information gained from al Qaeda personnel
could prevent attacks of a similar (if not greater) magnitude from occurring in the United States. . . .

One of the core functions of the Commander in Chief is that of capturing, detaining, and interrogating members of the enemy. . . . It is well
settled that the President may seize and detain enemy combatants, at least
for the duration of the conflict, and the laws of war make clear that prisoners
may be interrogated for information concerning the enemy, its strength, and
its plans. Numerous Presidents have ordered the capture, detention, and
questioning of enemy combatants during virtually every major conflict in
the Nation's history, including recent conflicts such as the Gulf, Vietnam,
and Korean wars. Recognizing this authority, Congress has never attempted
to restrict or interfere with the President's authority on this score. . . .

We conclude below that the Fifth Amendment Due Process Clause
is inapplicable to the conduct of interrogations of alien enemy combatants held outside the United States for two independent reasons. First, the
Fifth Amendment Due Process Clause does not apply to the President's
conduct of a war. Second, even if the Fifth Amendment applied to the

conduct of war, the Fifth Amendment does not apply extraterritorially to aliens who have no connection to the United States. We address each of these reasons in turn. . . .

Under traditional practice as expressed in the customary laws of war, the treatment of unlawful belligerents is left to the sovereign's discretion. . . . Under our Constitution, the sovereign right of the United States on the treatment of enemy combatants is reserved to the President as Commander-in-Chief. In light of the long history of discretion given to each nation to determine its treatment of unlawful combatants, to construe these statutes to regulate the conduct of the United States toward such combatants would interfere with a well-established prerogative of the sovereign. While the Geneva Convention (III) Relative to the Treatment of Prisoners of War, Aug. 12, 1949, . . . imposes restrictions on the interrogations of prisoners of war, it does not provide prisoner of war status to those who are unlawful combatants. . . . Those restrictions therefore would not apply to the interrogations of unlawful belligerents such as al Qaeda or Taliban members.

The second exception recognized by the Supreme Court arises where the application of general laws to a government official would create absurd results, such as effectively preventing the official from carrying out his duties. In *Nardone*, the Supreme Court pointed to "the application of a speed law to a policeman pursuing a criminal or the driver of a fire engine responding to an alarm" as examples of such absurd results. . . . For the reasons we explain above, the application of these general laws to the conduct of the military during the course of a war would create untenable results. . . .

In the context of interrogations, we believe that interrogation methods that do not involve physical contact will not support a charge of assault resulting in substantial injury or assault resulting in serious bodily injury or substantial bodily injury. Moreover, even minimal physical contact, such as poking, slapping, or shoving the detainee, is unlikely to produce the injury necessary to establish either one of these types of assault. . . .

[On Maiming]

Another criminal statute applicable in the special maritime and territorial jurisdiction is 18 U.S.C. § 114. Section 114 makes it a crime for an individual (1) "with the intent to torture (as defined in section 2340), maim, or disfigure" to (2) "cut, bite, or slit the nose, ear, or lip, or cut out or disable the tongue, or put out or destroy an eye, or cut off or disable a limb or any member of another person." . . . It further prohibits individuals from "throw[ing] or pour[ing] upon another person any scalding water, corrosive acid, or caustic substance" with like intent. . . .

The offense requires the specific intent to torture, maim or disfigure. . . . Moreover, the defendant's method of maiming must be one of the types the statute specifies — i.e., cutting, biting, slitting, cutting out, disabling, or putting out — and the injury must be to a body part the statute specifies — i.e., the nose, ear, lip, tongue, eye, or limb. . . . Similarly, the second set of acts applies to a very narrow band of conduct. It applies only to the throwing or pouring of some sort of scalding, corrosive, or caustic substance. . . .

Here, so long as the interrogation methods under contemplation do not involve the acts enumerated in section 114, the conduct of those interrogations will not fall within the purview of this statute. Because the statute requires specific intent, i.e., the intent to maim, disfigure or torture, the absence of such intent is a complete defense to a charge of maiming. . . .

[On Criminal Prohibitions Applicable to Conduct Occurring Outside the Jurisdiction of the United States]

There are two criminal prohibitions that apply to the conduct of U.S. persons outside the United States: the War Crimes Act, 18 U.S.C. § 2441, and the prohibition against torture, 18 U.S.C. §§ 2340–2340A. We conclude that the War Crimes Act does not apply to the interrogation of al Qaeda and Taliban detainees because, as illegal belligerents, they do not qualify for the legal protections under the Geneva or Hague Conventions that section 2441 enforces. In regard to section 2340, we conclude that the statute, by its terms, does not apply to interrogations conducted within the territorial United States or on permanent military bases outside the territory of the United States. Nonetheless, we identify the relevant substantive standards regarding the prohibition on torture should interrogations occur outside that jurisdictional limit. . . .

Section 2340A of Title 18 makes it a criminal offense for any person "outside the United States [to] commit or attempt to commit torture." The statute defines "the United States" as "all areas under the jurisdiction of the United States including any of the places described in" 18 U.S.C. § 5, and 18 U.S.C.A. § 7. 18 U.S.C. § 2340(3). Therefore, to the extent that interrogations take place within the special maritime and territorial jurisdiction, such as at a U.S. military base in a foreign state, the interrogations are not subject to sections 2340–2340A. If, however, the interrogations take place outside the special maritime and territorial jurisdiction and are otherwise outside the United States, the torture statute applies. Thus, for example, interrogations conducted at GTMO[7] would not be subject to this prohibition, but interrogations conducted at a non-U.S. base in Afghanistan would be subject to section 2340A. . . .

Thus, to establish the offense of torture, the prosecution must show that: (1) the torture occurred outside the United States; (2) the defendant acted under the color of law; (3) the victim was within the defendant's custody or physical control; (4) the defendant specifically intended to cause severe physical or mental pain or suffering; and (5) that the act inflicted severe physical or mental pain or suffering. . . .

To violate section 2340A, the statute requires that severe pain and suffering be inflicted with specific intent. . . . For a defendant to act with specific intent, he must expressly intend to achieve the forbidden act. . . .

Here, because section 2340 requires that a defendant act with the specific intent to inflict severe pain, the infliction of such pain must be the defendant's precise objective. . . .

[In Summary]

Section 2340's definition of torture must be read as a sum of these component parts. . . . Each component of the definition emphasizes that torture is not the mere infliction of pain or suffering on another, but is instead a step well removed. The victim must experience intense pain or suffering of the kind that is equivalent to the pain that would be associated with serious physical injury so severe that death, organ failure, or permanent damage resulting in a loss of significant body function will likely result. If that pain or suffering is psychological, that suffering must result from one of the acts set forth in the statute. In addition, these acts must cause long-term mental harm. Indeed, this view of the criminal act of torture is consistent with the term's common meaning. Torture is generally understood to involve "intense pain" or "excruciating pain," or put another way, "extreme anguish of body or mind." . . . In short, reading the definition of torture as a whole, it is plain that the term encompasses only extreme acts. . . .

As we have made clear in other opinions involving the war against al Qaeda, the Nation's right to self-defense has been triggered by the events

---

[7] **GTMO**: The military abbreviation for the prison maintained by the U.S. government at Guantánamo Bay, Cuba.

of September 11. If a government defendant were to harm an enemy combatant during an interrogation in a manner that might arguably violate a criminal prohibition, he would be doing so in order to prevent further attacks on the United States by the al Qaeda terrorist network. In that case, we believe that he could argue that the executive branch's constitutional authority to protect the nation from attack justified his actions. This national and international version of the right to self-defense could supplement and bolster the government defendant's individual right.

Conclusion

For the foregoing reasons, we conclude that the Fifth and Eighth Amendments do not extend to alien enemy combatants held abroad. Moreover, we conclude that different canons of construction indicate that generally applicable criminal laws do not apply to the military interrogation of alien unlawful combatants held abroad. Were it otherwise, the application of these statutes to the interrogation of enemy combatants undertaken by military personnel would conflict with the President's Commander-in-Chief power.

We further conclude that CAT[8] defines U.S. international law obligations with respect to torture and other cruel, inhuman, or degrading treatment or punishment. The standard of conduct regarding torture is the same as that which is found in the torture statute, 18 U.S.C. §§ 2340–2340A. Moreover, the scope of U.S. obligations under CAT regarding cruel, inhuman, or degrading treatment or punishment is limited to conduct prohibited by the Eighth, Fifth and Fourteenth Amendments. Customary international law does not supply any additional standards.

Finally, even if the criminal prohibitions outlined above applied, and an interrogation method might violate those prohibitions, necessity or self-defense could provide justifications for any criminal liability.

Please let us know if we can be of further assistance.

John C. Yoo
Deputy Assistant Attorney General

---

[8] **CAT**: The UN Convention Against Torture and Other Cruel, Inhumane, or Degrading Punishment, to which the United States is a signatory.

READING AND DISCUSSION QUESTIONS

1. How do these memos define *torture*?

2. What arguments does Yoo put forward concerning the power of the presidency?

3. These memos provide a legal framework for interrogations conducted by representatives of the U.S. government according to U.S. law. How does Yoo address international law? Judging by these memos, how does the United States balance international and domestic concerns?

DOCUMENT 34-4

CAROLINA SIC

An Interview with Women United for Worker Justice

2005

The increasing influence of multinational corporations in developing countries has been a major component of the rise of a global economy in the late twentieth and early twenty-first centuries. The impact of the multinationals has been hotly debated. Though they bring jobs and technology to poorer countries, they often ally with governments to hold down labor costs and prevent unions from forming. They have also come under scrutiny for worker abuse and substandard working conditions. In late 2003, a group of workers at Korean-based Nobland International, an export apparel manufacturer (maquila) in Guatemala, successfully unionized under the leadership of Carolina Sic, who was only twenty-two when she was interviewed.

Pushing Back: Women Workers Speak Out on Free Trade (Washington, D.C.: Stitch: Women United for Worker Justice, 2005), 24–30.

I would like to know a little about your background, to get an idea —
what was your childhood like? How many siblings do you have?

I was born here in Guatemala, in the capital, and my childhood was difficult. I have two brothers, one older and one younger. The older one isn't
doing so well in life, and the other, the same thing. I'm 22 years old, I have
a partner and two babies.

My mother is single because my father left us. My brothers and I used
to live in the Children's House, for street kids, until I was seven, when our
relatives took us out. Afterwards, I went to a school in zone five. Since my
mom was working in a maquila, we would stay with my grandmother. I
only got to fifth grade, because my mom didn't have enough money to
keep us in school. So then I spent my time helping my grandmother, who
made tortillas. By the time I was twelve I was going with my mom to a
workshop that had machines. She taught me a lot about the maquila. . . .

When I was 18, I became pregnant and decided to go live with my
husband because my mother and I didn't get along. When I went with
him, we went through some difficult things. No one in his family was
working when I came. My mother-in-law had been fired, and since she
had been the only one supporting the family, we didn't know what to do.
I sold all my things. These are hard things — you can get so crazy with it.
We would look for wood to make fires. My mother-in-law started making
tortillas. Pregnant, I would take in washing, or sell things. My husband
finally got a job, but when they found out he was underage, they fired him.
By then I was about to have the baby, but I didn't have anything to give
the child — since I didn't have a job, I didn't have social security (public
healthcare), nothing. So I had the baby. It was a horrible moment, but
the baby kept on growing and I decided to go work in this maquila, NB
(Nobland), because once again no one in the family was working.

How did you feel when you started in the maquila?

I was nursing at the time. I was worried about my baby, but also excited
about having a job and being able to take care of my family. The first two
weeks I worked, they paid me the minimum wage, even though I had
reached the production goal several days.

So from there I kept working, and as the months went along, I got
to know the compañeros and compañeras [male and female coworkers]
better. Since a lot of us lived in the same neighborhood, we had a lot
of contact and still do. It's really a group of friends that we've had since
we were little. Some of us, we met when I was in the streets. We'd get to

talking — "What do you think of this?" or, "Why are they treating so-and-so like that?" But since we didn't know what to do, we just kept quiet. There were just five of us.

What were the conditions and treatment like inside the maquila?

It was really hot. The atmosphere was really tense also, because you couldn't leave. They would say, "Hurry up! We've got to make the goal!" They'd scold you. They'd use offensive words. They'd say they weren't going to give you your salary. We would want to leave, but they would make us stay later and then not pay us overtime — instead they'd just pay like it was regular hours. I wasn't used to being treated like that, because I'd only worked in workshops before, with my mom, and they hadn't treated us like that. In this factory though, the pressure was extreme, but since all of us there needed the job, we dealt with it.

I had been working in the maquila for 10 months when we had finally had enough. By that time, I had one of my friends on each line, and we started talking. So that's how we started the first strike. We formed a group and went to the office and told them what was going on. The company fired us. There were a lot of us — 46. As a result, the majority of us were able to get our jobs back because the company didn't want to pay severance for all of us. They lowered our pay for 15 days for having gone on strike. But we were convinced that what we were doing was right, because we were defending our rights.

We started working again. There were something like five strikes that year. We decided on something, everyone would stop work, and we'd go up to the office. We saw what we were missing — the incentives, the overtime pay. But the management never paid attention to us, never said "Look, let's resolve this problem."

How did you get started with these actions? How did you come to agreement? Were there meetings?

During work hours, we would talk and discuss the things that were going badly, and then one person would take responsibility for telling everyone to stop work, and then we would go to the office to talk. There was a period where they wanted to hit us — they'd say we were like animals. But they couldn't fire us, because if they fired one of us, they'd have to fire everyone. There were over 40 of us, and they didn't want to pay severances, so they decided instead to split us up into two lines, so we couldn't communicate with each other.

We held another strike where we went to the office because the Korean manager had hit a compañera, and we said if they were going to hit one of us, they'd have to hit all of us. They fired all of us that day. I was a month and a half pregnant then, but I didn't know it — I thought I'd been feeling bad because of all the pressure. So I went to the hospital, and they told me that I was pregnant. I saw that as my only opportunity to get my job back, because when you're pregnant, they can't fire you. So I went back to work, but the whole length of the pregnancy was awful: they cut my pay, they cut my overtime, and they took away a bunch of things. They would look at someone who was talking with me and say, "Don't talk with her because she's a troublemaker." They wanted me to quit, but I wasn't going to quit something I had a right to.

When I was eight months pregnant, it was close to the holidays and things got ugly. They made me work at night, but the extra hours didn't show up on my paycheck. They suspended me for a lot of days out of every pay period, and that lowered my salary even more. And since Christmas was coming, I didn't know how I was going to be able to buy anything for my son. I was really confused — I didn't know what to do. On the one hand, I was dealing with so much pressure, and I couldn't take any more. On the other hand, I needed the job and I couldn't lose it. They treated me in such a nasty way, said such nasty things to me — that since I was pregnant, I was useless. They made me cry, but inside I knew that I wasn't the person they were saying I was. They also cut my social security benefits: on my social security certificate they said I earned only 20 quetzales (about US$2.50) a day when really I was earning 70 (about US$8.75). So social security gave me only 1,100 quetzales (about US$136) for my maternity benefit, when my friends had received up to 3,000 (about US$375) for the same three months.

So now I was nine months along, and one Saturday we were working when I felt some pains and knew I was going to have the baby. When I asked for permission to leave, since I might be going into labor, they wouldn't give it to me. They said overtime was obligatory until 4:30 pm. I felt so awful at that point. So I worked that day until 4:30 pm, with labor pains that had started at 1:00 pm. I gave birth early Sunday morning.

Did you know at that time about labor unions?

We didn't know what a union was. Once I saw an ad about a union on TV, and I asked my mom what a union was, and she explained to me that it's something that fights for your rights. But I didn't analyze the issue to the point of joining a union. Also, I had heard that having a union was dangerous because they could even kill you for it.

One time, after being fired after a strike, all of us went to the Labor Ministry. There were about 30 of us, and we said, "Well, either they do right by us or we'll see what happens." For all we'd done at that point, we really didn't know anything about what the laws were or what we could really do. We spoke with a labor inspector. He just talked about reinstatement. He didn't give us any idea to say okay, this, this, and this is going to happen or we're going to strike. We'd hold work stoppages but we didn't get what we wanted. All we got out of it was that they treated us badly and took away everything. We were tired. And while I was suspended for having organized a strike earlier, there was another strike and they fired about 30 workers.

So when these 30 people went to file a complaint because they wouldn't let them return to work, I was already back in the factory. They told me that they had met a girl at the Labor Ministry that worked forming unions. She asked them what the problem was and started talking to them about what a union was. Everyone said to me, "Fine, if you're in a union they kill you and run you out and turn on you, and I don't know — they disappear you." That scared me. But my compañeras said, "Let's do it. Maybe it will work and they'll treat us better." I thought about it and decided to participate. So, several of us started to form the union.

Since I sell things outside the maquila like pants and blouses, everyone comes up to me and I have a lot of people who know me. I know how to interact with them. I know my people, I know how they truly are. Of course when we're with the Koreans, we're not the same people. When we started to have a lot of folks, then we'd meet in my house or in another compañera's house. Every Saturday we would meet with that same organizer to make decisions.

What things changed once the union was formed?

When we got organized, we saw a lot of changes. When we got the injunction and announced that we had a union, we were so proud. We knew that we were going to stand up to defend our compañeras, and we did. When we stood up for a compañera who was being yelled at, the Korean manager didn't believe that we were actually defending her, that we had the right to defend her. That supervisor left. Another supervisor decided to leave too. We got rid of these two supervisors who were really the ones that treated the workers badly. It was such a sense of pride, to be able to say, "I'm going to defend my compañera here and no one can stop me from doing it."

Now, the treatment from the supervisors isn't like it was before. Things are calmer. We had a meeting with the company directly where we were able to say that we weren't going to tolerate mistreatment anymore. And that they couldn't force us to work overtime. And that if we did do one hour of overtime, we would be keeping track, and they would have to pay us. The production goals before, they didn't pay us for reaching them. Now they do. In other words, the whole environment has changed.

How did your family feel about the impact of your union participation on your family life?

Well, with my mom, I didn't have any problems because she was in the same situation in her time. She also worked in a maquila and did the same thing. So she told me it was fine, to stick with it. I did have some trouble with my partner; he didn't accept it. He didn't understand the abuse that took place in the maquila. So he would say that being in a union I could get killed. We had a lot of problems because of it.

They say that with what they call "free trade," the companies will have an easier time leaving any country whenever they want. How does this impact workers?

Oh, like saying "Let's go to Nicaragua" or "Let's go to El Salvador" — it could become a big competition, if in El Salvador they do the same work for less pay. So they'd leave us here without work. I also think that the Labor Ministry takes part, the way that the Labor Ministers say, "Fine, so here the law doesn't apply" so that the maquilas stay put. The businessmen say, "In Guatemala the laws are stricter than in El Salvador, so let's go to El Salvador." I feel the laws are good here. The Labor Ministry should take the role of defending them. If we are on the side of the law, it defends us. If we're not on the side of the law, it can't.

Before we had the union and we'd go to the Labor Ministry, they'd send a labor inspector and when we got to the factory, the legal declaration [formal report] was already signed. We had no idea what it meant to sign a declaration, what it meant to file a complaint. We'd sign the papers, and we didn't even read them. We thought the inspectors had been bought off, because you'd fight, fight, fight, and they wouldn't do anything. If from my very first complaint they had said, "Look, your help will come through this organization," I would have been in the union for three years by now. But they don't give you any information.

And how has it affected the lives of the workers and of their union when the company says it's going to move to another country?

Psychologically, it affects the people because they're afraid of being left without a job. When you form a union, the company starts to say that because of the union they're going to leave. That's when the people start to speak against us, because we're playing a role in fighting for the workers, and then the company takes the line, "Fine, have your union but we're leaving and you'll be out of a job."

What do most people in your community do to try to improve things in their lives?

They work. That, and then a lot of people from my neighborhood have gone to the United States, because they say they pay well there. Even my husband has said that if things don't look up here that we should go to the U.S. because his brother is there. If the work situation here doesn't improve, what road can you take?

What we would agree with, for the workers of Guatemala, would be to have more work, but not just maquila jobs. Instead, I think there could be other kinds of work, something that gives Guatemalan workers opportunities. The maquila only pays enough for beans and tortillas. You lose your whole day being exploited, the pay is so low. . . .

READING AND DISCUSSION QUESTIONS

1. What examples of employer abuse does Carolina Sic describe?

2. What convinced Sic and her compañeras to unionize?

3. According to Sic, how did the companies in Guatemala typically respond to strikes and other forms of labor organizing? What happened in her union's case?

4. How did Sic's coworkers, family, and friends react to her involvement in organizing against unfair labor practices?

DOCUMENT 34-5

AL GORE

On Solving the Climate Crisis

September 18, 2006

Former U.S. vice president Al Gore has become almost synonymous with the movement to end global warming. Awarded the Nobel Peace Prize in 2007 for his efforts — which included the Oscar-winning documentary An Inconvenient Truth *— Gore has tirelessly campaigned worldwide to end practices that hasten the dangerous degradation of the earth's natural cooling systems. In a 2006 speech at New York University, he denied claims made by business and political leaders that the problem of global warming is insurmountable and offered a viable strategy to counter it. He also alluded to — and countered — the less popular argument that global warming is a fabrication or part of a natural ecological process.*

A few days ago, scientists announced alarming new evidence of the rapid melting of the perennial ice of the north polar cap, continuing a trend of the past several years that now confronts us with the prospect that human activities, if unchecked in the next decade, could destroy one of the earth's principal mechanisms for cooling itself. Another group of scientists presented evidence that human activities are responsible for the dramatic warming of sea surface temperatures in the areas of the ocean where hurricanes form. A few weeks earlier, new information from yet another team showed dramatic increases in the burning of forests throughout the American West, a trend that has increased decade by decade, as warmer temperatures have dried out soils and vegetation. All these findings come at the end of a summer with record-breaking temperatures and the hottest twelve-month period ever measured in the U.S., with persistent drought in vast areas of our country. *Scientific American* introduces the lead article in its special issue this month with the following sentence: "The debate on global warming is over."

Many scientists are now warning that we are moving closer to several "tipping points" that could — within as little as 10 years — make it impos-

Al Gore, Speech at New York University School of Law, September 18, 2006.

sible for us to avoid irretrievable damage to the planet's habitability for human civilization. In this regard, just a few weeks ago, another group of scientists reported on the unexpectedly rapid increases in the release of carbon and methane emissions from frozen tundra in Siberia, now beginning to thaw because of human-caused increases in global temperature. The scientists tell us that the tundra in danger of thawing contains an amount of additional global warming pollution that is equal to the total amount that is already in the earth's atmosphere. Similarly, earlier this year, yet another team of scientists reported that the previous twelve months saw 32 glacial earthquakes on Greenland between 4.6 and 5.1 on the Richter scale — a disturbing sign that a massive destabilization may now be underway deep within the second largest accumulation of ice on the planet, enough ice to raise sea level 20 feet worldwide if it broke up and slipped into the sea. Each passing day brings yet more evidence that we are now facing a planetary emergency — a climate crisis that demands immediate action to sharply reduce carbon dioxide emissions worldwide in order to turn down the earth's thermostat and avert catastrophe.

The serious debate over the climate crisis has now moved on to the question of how we can craft emergency solutions in order to avoid this catastrophic damage.

This debate over solutions has been slow to start in earnest not only because some of our leaders still find it more convenient to deny the reality of the crisis, but also because the hard truth for the rest of us is that the maximum that seems politically feasible still falls far short of the minimum that would be effective in solving the crisis. This no-man's land — or no-politician zone — falling between the farthest reaches of political feasibility and the first beginnings of truly effective change is the area that I would like to explore in my speech today. . . .

My purpose is not to present a comprehensive and detailed blueprint — for that is a task for our democracy as a whole — but rather to try to shine some light on a pathway through this terra incognita [unknown land] that lies between where we are and where we need to go. Because, if we acknowledge candidly that what we need to do is beyond the limits of our current political capacities, that really is just another way of saying that we have to urgently expand the limits of what is politically possible.

I have no doubt that we can do precisely that, because having served almost three decades in elected office, I believe I know one thing about America's political system that some of the pessimists do not: it shares something in common with the climate system; it can appear to move only at a slow pace, but it can also cross a tipping point beyond which it can move with lightning speed. Just as a single tumbling rock can trigger a massive landslide, America has sometimes experienced sudden avalanches of political change that had their beginnings with what first seemed like small changes.

Two weeks ago, Democrats and Republicans joined together in our largest state, California, to pass legally binding sharp reductions in CO_2 emissions. Two hundred ninety-five American cities have now independently "ratified" and embraced CO_2 reductions called for in the Kyoto Treaty.[9] Eighty-five conservative evangelical ministers publicly broke with the Bush-Cheney administration to call for bold action to solve the climate crisis. Business leaders in both political parties have taken significant steps to position their companies as leaders in this struggle and have adopted a policy that not only reduces CO_2 but makes their companies zero carbon companies. Many of them have discovered a way to increase profits and productivity by eliminating their contributions to global warming pollution.

Many Americans are now seeing a bright light shining from the far side of this no-man's land that illuminates not sacrifice and danger, but instead a vision of a bright future that is better for our country in every way — a future with better jobs, a cleaner environment, a more secure nation, and a safer world.

After all, many Americans are tired of borrowing huge amounts of money from China to buy huge amounts of oil from the Persian Gulf to make huge amounts of pollution that destroys the planet's climate. Increasingly, Americans believe that we have to change every part of that pattern.

When I visit port cities like Seattle, New Orleans, or Baltimore, I find massive ships, running low in the water, heavily burdened with foreign cargo or foreign oil arriving by the thousands. These same cargo ships and tankers depart riding high with only ballast water to keep them from rolling over. One-way trade is destructive to our economic future. We send money, electronically, in the opposite direction. But, we can change this by inventing and manufacturing new solutions to stop global warming

---

[9] **Kyoto Treaty**: A 1995 agreement produced by the UN Conference on Climate Change in Kyoto, Japan, under which signatory countries vowed to reduce their emissions of greenhouse gases between 2008 and 2012 and agreed to instruments to measure compliance. The treaty was ratified by 141 nations and took effect in 2005; however, President George W. Bush pulled the United States from the agreement in 2001.

right here in America. I still believe in good old-fashioned American ingenuity. We need to fill those ships with new products and technologies that we create to turn down the global thermostat. Working together, we can create jobs and stop global warming. But we must begin by winning the first key battle — against inertia and the fear of change. . . .

So, what would a responsible approach to the climate crisis look like if we had one in America?

Well, first of all, we should start by immediately freezing CO_2 emissions and then beginning sharp reductions. Merely engaging in high-minded debates about theoretical future reductions while continuing to steadily increase emissions represents a self-delusional and reckless approach. In some ways, that approach is worse than doing nothing at all, because it lulls the gullible into thinking that something is actually being done when in fact it is not.

An immediate freeze has the virtue of being clear, simple, and easy to understand. It can attract support across partisan lines as a logical starting point for the more difficult work that lies ahead. . . .

A responsible approach to solving this crisis would also involve joining the rest of the global economy in playing by the rules of the world treaty that reduces global warming pollution by authorizing the trading of emissions within a global cap.

At present, the global system for carbon emissions trading is embodied in the Kyoto Treaty. It drives reductions in CO_2 and helps many countries that are a part of the treaty to find the most efficient ways to meet their targets for reductions. . . .

The absence of the United States from the treaty means that 25 percent of the world economy is now missing. It is like filling a bucket with a large hole in the bottom. When the United States eventually joins the rest of the world community in making this system operate well, the global market for carbon emissions will become a highly efficient closed system and every corporate board of directors on earth will have a fiduciary duty to manage and reduce CO_2 emissions in order to protect shareholder value.

Many American businesses that operate in other countries already have to abide by the Kyoto Treaty anyway, and unsurprisingly, they are the companies that have been most eager to adopt these new principles here at home as well. The United States and Australia are the only two countries in the developed world that have not yet ratified the Kyoto Treaty. Since the Treaty has been so demonized in America's internal debate, it is difficult to imagine the current Senate finding a way to ratify it. But the United States should immediately join the discussion that is now under way on the new tougher treaty that will soon be completed. We should plan to accelerate its adoption and phase it in more quickly than is presently planned.

Third, a responsible approach to solutions would avoid the mistake of trying to find a single magic "silver bullet" and recognize that the answer will involve what Bill McKibben has called "silver-buckshot" — numerous important solutions, all of which are hard, but no one of which is by itself the full answer for our problem. . . .

First, dramatic improvements in the efficiency with which we generate, transport, and use energy will almost certainly prove to be the single biggest source of sharp reductions in global warming pollution. Because pollution has been systematically ignored in the old rules of America's marketplace, there are lots of relatively easy ways to use new and more efficient options to cheaply eliminate it. Since pollution is, after all, waste, business and industry usually become more productive and efficient when they systematically go about reducing pollution. After all, many of the technologies on which we depend are actually so old that they are inherently far less efficient than newer technologies that we haven't started using. . . .

We worry today that terrorists might try to inflict great damage on America's energy infrastructure by attacking a single vulnerable part of the oil distribution or electricity distribution network. So . . . we should develop a distributed electricity and liquid fuels distribution network that is less dependent on large coal-fired generating plants and vulnerable oil ports and refineries.

Small windmills and photovoltaic solar cells distributed widely throughout the electricity grid would sharply reduce CO_2 emissions and at the same time increase our energy security. Likewise, widely dispersed ethanol and biodiesel production facilities would shift our transportation fuel stocks to renewable forms of energy while making us less dependent on and vulnerable to disruptions in the supply of expensive crude oil from the Persian Gulf, Venezuela, and Nigeria, all of which are extremely unreliable sources upon which to base our future economic vitality. It would also make us less vulnerable to the impact of a category 5 hurricane hitting coastal refineries or to a terrorist attack on ports or key parts of our current energy infrastructure. . . .

A second group of building blocks to solve the climate crisis involves America's transportation infrastructure. We could further increase the value and efficiency of a distributed energy network by retooling our failing auto giants — GM and Ford — to require and assist them in switching to the manufacture of flex-fuel, plug-in, hybrid vehicles. The owners of such vehicles would have the ability to use electricity as a principal source of power and to supplement it by switching from gasoline to ethanol or biodiesel. . . .

Our current ridiculous dependence on oil endangers not only our national security, but also our economic security. Anyone who believes that the international market for oil is a "free market" is seriously deluded. It has many characteristics of a free market, but it is also subject to periodic manipulation by the small group of nations controlling the largest recoverable reserves, sometimes in concert with companies that have great influence over the global production, refining, and distribution network. . . .

Several important building blocks for America's role in solving the climate crisis can be found in new approaches to agriculture. As pointed out by the "25 by 25" movement (aimed at securing 25 percent of America's power and transportation fuels from agricultural sources by the year 2025) we can revitalize the farm economy by shifting its mission from a focus on food, feed, and fiber to a focus on food, feed, fiber, fuel, and ecosystem services. We can restore the health of depleted soils by encouraging and rewarding the growing of fuel source crops like switchgrass and sawgrass, using no-till cultivation, and scientific crop rotation. We should also reward farmers for planting more trees and sequestering more carbon. . . .

Similarly, we should take bold steps to stop deforestation and extend the harvest cycle on timber to optimize the carbon sequestration that is most powerful and most efficient with older trees. On a worldwide basis, 2 and 1/2 trillion tons of the 10 trillion tons of CO_2 emitted each year come from burning forests. So, better management of forests is one of the single most important strategies for solving the climate crisis.

Biomass — whether in the form of trees, switchgrass, or other sources — is one of the most important forms of renewable energy. And renewable sources make up one of the most promising building blocks for reducing carbon pollution.

Wind energy is already fully competitive as a mainstream source of electricity and will continue to grow in prominence and profitability. . . .

The most important set of problems . . . that must be solved in charting solutions for the climate crisis have to do with coal, one of the dirtiest sources of energy that produces far more CO_2 for each unit of energy output than oil or gas. Yet, coal is found in abundance in the United States, China, and many other places. Because the pollution from the burning of coal is currently excluded from the market calculations of what it costs, coal is presently the cheapest source of abundant energy. And its relative role is growing rapidly day by day.

Fortunately, there may be a way to capture the CO_2 produced as coal is burned and sequester it safely to prevent it from adding to the climate crisis. It is not easy. This technique, known as carbon capture and sequestration (CCS), is expensive and most users of coal have resisted the investments necessary to use it. However, when the cost of *not* using it is calculated, it becomes obvious that CCS will play a significant and growing role as one of the major building blocks of a solution to the climate crisis. . . .

Global warming pollution, indeed all pollution, is now described by economists as an "externality." This absurd label means, in essence: we don't [need] to keep track of this stuff so let's pretend it doesn't exist.

And sure enough, when it's not recognized in the marketplace, it does make it much easier for government, business, and all the rest of us to pretend that it doesn't exist. But what we're pretending doesn't exist is the stuff that is destroying the habitability of the planet. We put 70 million tons of it into the atmosphere every 24 hours and the amount is increasing day by day. . . .

Many of our leading businesses are already making dramatic changes to reduce their global warming pollution. General Electric, Dupont, Cinergy, Caterpillar, and Wal-Mart are among the many who are providing leadership for the business community in helping us devise a solution for this crisis.

Leaders among unions — particularly the steel workers — have also added momentum to this growing movement.

Hunters and fishermen are also now adding their voices to the call for a solution to the crisis. In a recent poll, 86 percent of licensed hunters and anglers said that we have a moral obligation to stop global warming to protect our children's future.

And, young people — as they did during the Civil Rights Revolution — are confronting their elders with insistent questions about the morality of not moving swiftly to make these needed changes.

Moreover, the American religious community — including a group of 85 conservative evangelicals and especially the U.S. Conference of Catholic Bishops — has made an extraordinary contribution to this entire enterprise. . . . Individual faith groups have offered their own distinctive views. And yet — uniquely in religious life at this moment and even historically — they have established common ground and resolve across tenacious differences. . . .

Individual Americans of all ages are becoming a part of a movement, asking what they can do as individuals and what they can do as consumers and as citizens and voters. Many individuals and businesses have decided to take an approach known as "Zero Carbon." They are reducing their CO_2 as much as possible and then offsetting the rest with reductions elsewhere, including by the planting of trees. . . . This is not a political issue. This is a moral issue. It affects the survival of human civilization. It is not a question of left vs. right; it is a question of right vs. wrong. Put simply, it is wrong to destroy the habitability of our planet and ruin the prospects of every generation that follows ours. . . . By rising to meet the climate crisis, we will find the vision and moral authority to see them not as political problems but as moral imperatives. . . .

READING AND DISCUSSION QUESTIONS

1. According to Al Gore, why have solutions to the global environmental crisis been lacking?

2. What steps does Gore outline for ending the climate crisis?

3. How does Gore link oil dependence and U.S. national security?

4. What different groups have united behind this single cause, and how have they come together?

DOCUMENT 34-6

JONAS BENDIKSEN

"New Settlement": A Slum in Caracas, Venezuela

ca. 2007

In 2011, more than one billion people on earth lived in areas defined as slums. These often massive clusters of makeshift housing sprung up around major urban centers in various world regions to accommodate migrants, refugees, foreign workers, and others who are unable to afford safer and more stable accommodations. While slums have been a feature of urban environments throughout the modern era, contemporary slums are both much larger and much less permanent than their historical counterparts. Slums in the twenty-first century operate outside or on the margins of regular urban infra-structures; sanitation, health care, crime prevention, and other services are usually absent, and slum populations are often only informally connected to the networks of commerce and government that structure other urban areas and populations. The photograph here shows a makeshift slum structure in Caracas, Venezuela.

Jonas Bendiksen, Magnum Photos.

READING AND DISCUSSION QUESTIONS

1. What buildings are featured in this photograph? What is the effect of presenting these buildings together?

2. What does the lack of walls and the visibility of furniture and other possessions imply about the lives of the people living in this dwelling?

3. The figures in the foreground appear to be playing or dancing. Are their actions or attitudes surprising, given the context? Explain.

COMPARATIVE QUESTIONS

1. Compare George Tarabishi's and Osama bin Laden's reactions to the impact of globalization on the Arab world. Which points, if any, do they agree on?

2. In what ways does Carolina Sic's experience of globalization resonate or conflict with Tarabishi's theories?

3. Both Al Gore and John Yoo present visions of how the United States can and should interact with the international community. What assumptions does each make about the rights and responsibilities of the United States, both domestically and internationally?

4. Many of these documents address the question of globalization or global issues. How would each author define globalization? Is it a positive or negative force in each case? How does each author juxtapose globalization and his or her national or personal identity?

5. Does the photograph of a Caracas slum present global as well as personal issues? If so, what issues? How might the authors of the other documents — particularly Tarabishi, Sic, and Gore — analyze the photograph of the slum, and why?

Acknowledgments (*continued from p. ii*)

INTRODUCTION
From *Maya Conquistador* by Matthew Restall, copyright © 1998 by Matthew Restall. Reproduced with permission of Beacon Press, Boston.

CHAPTER 16
16-1. Zheng He, "Stele Inscription." From *China and Africa in the Middle Ages*, by Teobaldo Filesi, trans. by David Morison. Copyright © 1972. Reprinted by permission of Taylor & Francis Books UK.

16-2. Christopher Columbus, "Letter from the Third Voyage" from *Select Documents Illustrating the Four Voyages of Columbus*, vol. 2, ed. and trans. by Cecil Jane. Published by Hakluyt Society, 1967. Reprinted by permission of David Higham Associates Ltd.

16-3. King Dom Manuel of Portugal, "Grant of Rights of Trade" from *Europeans in West Africa*, ed. and trans. by John William Blake (1941) is reprinted by permission of David Higham on behalf of the Hakluyt Society.

16-4. Bartolomé de las Casas, "Brief Account of the Devastation of the Indies" from *The Devastation of the Indies: A Brief Account*, trans. by Herma Briffault (Continuum 1974). Reprinted by permission of the publisher.

16-7. From *China in the Sixteenth Century* by Matthew Ricci, trans. by Louis J. Gallagher S.J. Copyright 1942, 1953, and renewed 1970 by Louis J. Gallagher, S.J. Used by permission of Random House, Inc. For online information about other Random House, Inc. books and authors see the Internet website at http://www.random house.com.

CHAPTER 17
17-5. Catherine the Great, "Two Decrees" from *A Sourcebook for Russian History from Early Times to 1917*, vol. 2. Copyright © 1972 Yale University. Reprinted by permission of Yale University Press.

17-6. Emilian Ivanovich Pugachev, "A Decree and a Manifesto" from *A Sourcebook for Russian History from Early Times to 1917*, vol. 2. Copyright © 1972 Yale University. Reprinted by permission of Yale University Press.

CHAPTER 18
18-1a. Galileo Galilei, "Letter to the Grand Duchess Christina" from *Discoveries and Opinions of Galileo*, trans. by Stillman Drake, copyright © 1957 by Stillman Drake. Used by permission of Doubleday, a division of Random House, Inc.

18-1b. Galileo Galilei, "To The Discerning Reader" from *Dialogue Concerning the Two Chief World Systems*, trans. by Stillman Drake. Copyright © 1953, 1962, and 1967 by the Regents of the University of California. Renewed 1981 by Stillman Drake. Reprinted by permission of the University of California Press via the Copyright Clearance Center. Electronic rights administered by the Estate of Stillman Drake.

18-3a. Peter the Great, "Decree on the Acceptance of Gottfried Leibniz into Russian Service" from *A Sourcebook for Russian History from Early Times to 1917*, vol. 2. Copyright © 1972 Yale University. Reprinted by permission of Yale University Press.

18-3b. Peter the Great, "Draft of Leibniz's Memorandum on the Improvement of Arts and Sciences in Russia" from *A Sourcebook for Russian History from Early Times to 1917*, vol. 2. Copyright © 1972 Yale University. Reprinted by permission of Yale University Press.

18-3c. Peter the Great, excerpt from "A Decree on Monsters" quoted and trans. by Anthony Anemone, "The Monsters of Peter the Great," *Slavic and East European Journal*, vol. 44, no. 4. Winter 2000, 583–602, from T. V. Staniukovich, Kunstkamera Peterburgskoi Akademii Nauk, Moscow/Leningrad, 1953. Reprinted by permission of the publisher AATSEEL of the US, Inc.

18-5. Immanuel Kant, "What Is Enlightenment?" trans. by Peter Gay from *Introduction to Contemporary Civilization: A Source Book*, copyright © 1954 Columbia University Press. Reprinted with permission of the publisher and the Contemporary Civilizations Department of Columbia College.

CHAPTER 19

19-1. Nzinga Mbemba, excerpts from letters to Alfonso I of Portugal from *The African Past*, trans. by Basil Davidson. Copyright © 1964 by Basil Davidson. Reprinted by permission of Curtis Brown, Ltd.

19-2. Leo Africanus, "A Description of Timbuktu" from "The Description of Africa" (1526), trans. by Paul Brians, from Paul Brians et al., *Reading About the World*, vol. 2, Third Edition (Harcourt Brace College Custom Books). Copyright © by Paul Brians. Reprinted with the permission of Paul Brians, www.wsu.edu/~wldciv/world_civ _reader/world_civ_reader_2/leo_africanus.html.

19-3. Osei Bonsu, "An Asante King Questions British Motives in Ending the Slave Trade" from *Sources of the African Past: Case Studies of Five Nineteenth-Century African Societies* by David Robinson and Douglas Smith (Africana, 1979). Reprinted with permission of the publisher, Holmes & Meier.

19-4. Anna Maria Falconbridge, from *Narrative of Two Voyages to the River Sierra Leone*, ed. by Christopher Fyfe (Liverpool: Liverpool University Press, 2000), 89–94, reprinted with permission of the publisher.

CHAPTER 20

20-1. Sultan Selim I, "Letter to Shah Ismail of Persia." Reprinted with the permission of Simon & Schuster, Inc. from *The Muslim World on the Eve of Europe's Expansion*, ed. and trans. by John J. Saunders. Copyright © 1966 by Prentice-Hall, Inc. All rights reserved.

20-6. "Correspondences on Persian Trade" from Willem Floor and Mohammad H. Faghfoory, *The First Dutch-Persian Commercial Conflict* (Costa Mesa, CA: Mazda Publishers, 2004), 221–222 and 232–233. Reprinted with permission of the publisher.

CHAPTER 21

21-1. Toyotomi Hideyoshi, "Letter to His Wife" from *101 Letters of Hideyoshi*, trans. and ed. by Adriana Boscaro (Tokyo: Sophia University, 1975). Reprinted by permission of the publisher and translator.

21-2. Huang Zongxi, "On the Prince" and "On Ministership" from *Sources of Chinese Tradition*, vol. 2, comp. by Wm. Theodore de Bary. Copyright © 2000 by Columbia University Press. Reprinted with permission of the publisher.

21-3. Engelbert Kaempfer, "From *History of Japan*," from *Kaempfer's Japan: Tokugawa Culture Observed*, ed. and trans. by Beatrice M. Bodart-Bailey (Honolulu: University of Hawaii Press, 1999). Reprinted by permission of the publisher.

21-4. Kaibara Ekiken and Kaibara Token, "Common Sense Teaching for Japanese Children" and "Greater Learning for Women" from *Japan: A Documentary History*, ed. David J. Lu (Armonk, N.Y.: M. E. Sharpe, 1997), 258–261. English translation copyright © 1997 by David J. Lu. Reprinted with permission of M. E. Sharpe, Inc. All Rights Reserved. Not for Reproduction.

21-6. Li Ruzhen, from *Flowers in the Mirror*, trans. and ed. by Lin Tai-yi. (Berkeley: University of California Press, 1965). Reprinted with permission of Peter Owen Publishers.

CHAPTER 22
22-3. Olympe de Gouges, "The Declaration of the Rights of Woman," from *Women in Revolutionary Paris, 1789–1795: Selected Documents Translated with Notes and Commentary*, trans. with notes and commentary by Darline Gay Levy, Harriet Branson Applewhite, and Mary Durham Johnson. Copyright © 1979 by the Board of Trustees of the University of Illinois. Used with permission of the editors and the University of Illinois Press.

22-6. "The Haitian Declaration of Independence" from Thomas Madiou, *Histoire d'Haiti* (Port-au-Prince, 1847–1848), 3: 146–150, as excerpted in *Slave Revolution in the Caribbean, 1789–1804: A Brief History with Documents*, ed. and trans. by Laurent Dubois and John D. Garrigus (Boston: Bedford/St. Martin's, 2006). Reprinted by permission of the publisher.

CHAPTER 24
24-6. Beatrice Webb, "Why I Became a Socialist," is reprinted from *My Apprenticeship* by Beatrice Webb with the permission of Cambridge University Press. Copyright © 1980 by Cambridge University Press.

CHAPTER 25
25-2. Excerpt from "Ottoman government decree issued to the Amir of Shamr, His Excellency Firhan Pasha," June 19, 1870, from Ottoman archives of Directorate General of State Archives at the Prime Ministry. Mosul: Tapu Tahrir, 1869–1872. Trans. by Akram Khater. Reprinted with permission of the translator.

25-4. Ndansi Kumalo, "On the British Incursion in Zimbabwe," from *Ten Africans*, ed. by Margery Perham. Originally published by Faber & Faber Ltd. in 1936. Used by permission of the Trustees of the Will of the Late Dame Margery Perham.

25-5. Roger Casement and David Engohahe, "Victims of Belgian Congo Atrocities," from "The Congo Rubber Atrocities: A Case Study" in *African Historical Studies*, vol. 4, no. 1 (1971). Copyright © 1971 by the Trustees of Boston University. Reprinted by permission of the African Studies Center, Boston University.

CHAPTER 26
26-3. Saigō Takamori, "Letter on the Korean Question," from *Sources of Japanese Tradition*, vol. II, Part Two *(1868–2000)*, comp. by Wm. Theodore de Bary. Copyright © 2005 by Columbia University Press. Reprinted with permission of the publisher.

26-5. Sun Yatsen, "The Three People's Principles and the Future of the Chinese People" from *Prescriptions for Saving China: Selected Writings of Sun Yat-sen*, edited by Julie Lee Wei, Ramon H. Myers, and Donald G. Gillin. Translation copyright © 1994 by the Board of Trustees of the Leland Stanford Junior University. Reprinted with permission of the publisher, Hoover Institution Press.

CHAPTER 28
28-2. Extracts of correspondence from *An Echo in My Heart: The Letters of Elnora Evelyn (Kelly) Albright and Frederick Stanley Albright*, compiled and edited by Lorna Brooke, http://sites.google.com/site/echoinmyheartsite/home. Letters and material pertaining to the Albright collection are housed in The Archives and Research Collections Centre in the D. B. Weldon Library at the University of Western Ontario, London, Canada.

28-6. Konoe Fumimaro, "Against a Pacifism Centered on England and America" from *Sources of Japanese Tradition*, vol. 2, comp. by Wm. Theodore de Bary. Copyright © 2005 by Columbia University Press. Reprinted with permission of the publisher.

CHAPTER 29
29-4. Jiang Jiesh, "The New Life Movement" from *Sources of Chinese Tradition*, vol. 2, comp. by Wm. Theodore de Bary. Copyright © 2000 by Columbia University Press. Reprinted with permission of the publisher.

29-5. King Vajiravudh, "On the Siamese Nation" from Walter F. Vella, *Chaiyo! King Vajiravudh and the Development of Thai Nationalism*. Copyright © 1978 University of Hawaii Press. Reprinted with permission.

CHAPTER 30
30-1. Woody Guthrie, lyrics to "Do Re Mi." Words and music by Woody Guthrie. WGP/TRO-© Copyright 1961 (Renewed) 1963 (Renewed) Woody Guthrie Publications, Inc. & Ludlow Music, Inc., New York, NY. Administered by Ludlow Music, Inc. International copyright secured. Made in U.S.A. All rights reserved including public performance for profit. Used by permission.

30-2. Gertrude Scholtz-Klink, "Speech to the National Socialist Women's Association, September 1935" from *Women, the Family, and Freedom: The Debate in Documents*, vol. 2, 1880–1950, by Susan Groag Bell and Karen M. Offen, eds. Copyright © 1983 by the Board of Trustees of the Leland Stanford Junior University. All rights reserved. Used with permission of Stanford University Press, www.sup.org.

30-4. "Letters to Izvestia on the Abortion Issue, May–June 1936" from *The Family in the U.S.S.R.*, ed. by Rudolf Schlesinger. Copyright 1949. Reprinted with the permission of Taylor & Francis Books UK.

30-6. Toshiko Saeki, "Interview with a Survivor of Hiroshima" from the "Voice of Hibakusha" eyewitness accounts aired as part of "Hiroshima Witness," produced by the Hiroshima Peace Cultural Center and NHK, the public broadcasting company of Japan. Translated into English and posted as "Testimony of Toshiko Saeki," Atomic Archive.com. Published in a limited edition by Andrew Mossberg. Reprinted by permission of Andrew Mossberg.

CHAPTER 31

31-4. Mikhail Gorbachev, excerpt from *Perestroika: New Thinking for Our Country and the World*. Copyright © 1987 by Mikhail Gorbachev. Reprinted by permission of HarperCollins Publishers. Electronic rights administered by the Gorbachev Foundation.

31-6. "Ikigai" from "Can a Real Man Live for His Family? *Ikigai* and Masculinity in Today's Japan" by Gordon Mathews in James Roberson and Nobue Suzuki, eds., *Men and Masculinities in Contemporary Japan* (New York: Routledge, 2003) is reprinted by permission of Gordon Mathews.

CHAPTER 32

32-1. Ho Chi Minh, "Declaration of Independence." Embassy of the Socialist Republic of Vietnam in the United States of America. http://www.vietnamembassy-usa.org/learn_about_vietnam/politics/dec_of_independence/. Reprinted by permission of The Embassy of Vietnam.

32-2. Letters from *Selected Works of Jawaharlal Nehru*, second series, vol. 3, published by Jawaharlal Nehru Memorial Fund. Copyright © 1985. All rights reserved.

32-3. "Away from Madness" from *Ten Years of Madness: Oral Histories of China's Cultural Revolution*, by Feng Jicai (San Francisco: China Books & Periodicals, Inc., 1996) is reprinted by permission of the publisher.

32-4 Deng Xiaoping, "Build Socialism with Chinese Characteristics" from *Sources of Chinese Tradition*, vol. 2, comp. by Wm. Theodore de Bary. Copyright © 2000 by Columbia University Press. Reprinted with permission of the publisher.

32-6. Unya Shavit, "Arab and Israeli Soccer Players Discuss Ethnic Relations in Israel," excerpted from "Playing for Keeps" from *Ha'aretz*, Nov. 3, 2000. Copyright © 2000 by Ha'aretz Daily Newspaper, Ltd. Reprinted by permission of the publisher.

CHAPTER 33

33-1. "Standard Oil Co." and "United Fruit Co." from *Canto General*, by Pablo Neruda, trans. by Jack Schmitt (Berkeley: University of California Press, 1991). Copyright © 1991 by the Regents of the University of California. Reprinted by permission of the University of California Press via the Copyright Clearance Center. Electronic rights by permission of Agencia Literaria Carmen Balcells, S. A. Copyright © Fundación Pablo Neruda, 2011.

33-2. Fidel Castro, "Interview with Dan Rather." Excerpts reprinted from *60 Minutes*: "Castro," Sept. 30, 1979, by permission of CBS News Archives.

33-3. Charles de Gaulle, "Comments on Algeria." Excerpt from "Fourth Press Conference Held by General Charles de Gaulle as President of the French Republic in Paris and the Élysée Palace on April 11, 1961," from *Major Addresses, Statements, and Press Conferences of General Charles de Gaulle*, May 19, 1958–January 31, 1964 (New York: French Embassy Press and Information Division, 1964).

33-4. Kwame Nkrumah, "Speech on the Tenth Anniversary of the Convention People's Party" from *Selected Speeches of Kwame Nkrumah*, ed. Samuel Obeng, vol. 1 (Accra: Afram Publications [Ghana] Ltd., 1997) is reprinted by permission of the publisher.

33-6. Excerpts from "The Rivonia Trial Speech to the Court" from *In His Own Words* by Nelson Mandela with a foreword by President Bill Clinton. Copyright © 2003 by

Nelson Mandela Foundation (Speeches). Copyright © 2003 by The Editors (Compilation). Used by permission of Little, Brown and Company. Electronic rights by permission of the Nelson Mandela Foundation.

CHAPTER 34

34-1. George Tarabishi, excerpts from "Globalization and Its Impact on Arab Culture: Globalization as a Matter of Conflict" from *al-Bahrain al-Thaqafia,* no. 26 (October 26, 2000). Translated by Akram Khater. Reprinted with permission of the translator.

34-2. "Interview with Usama Bin Laden by His Followers" from *Nida'ul Islam* 15 (October–November 1998). Translated by Akram Khater. Reprinted with permission of the translator.

34-4. Caroline Sic, "An Interview with Women United for Worker Justice" in *Pushing Back: Women Workers Speak Out on Free Trade* (Washington, D.C.: STITCH, 2005). Reprinted with permission of the publisher.

34-5. Al Gore, "On Solving the Climate Crisis." From speech at New York University School of Law, September 18, 2006. Copyright © 2006 by Al Gore. Reprinted with permission of The Wylie Agency LLC.